りんね

RIN-NE

**Story and Art by
Rumiko Takahashi**

RIN-NE

Contents

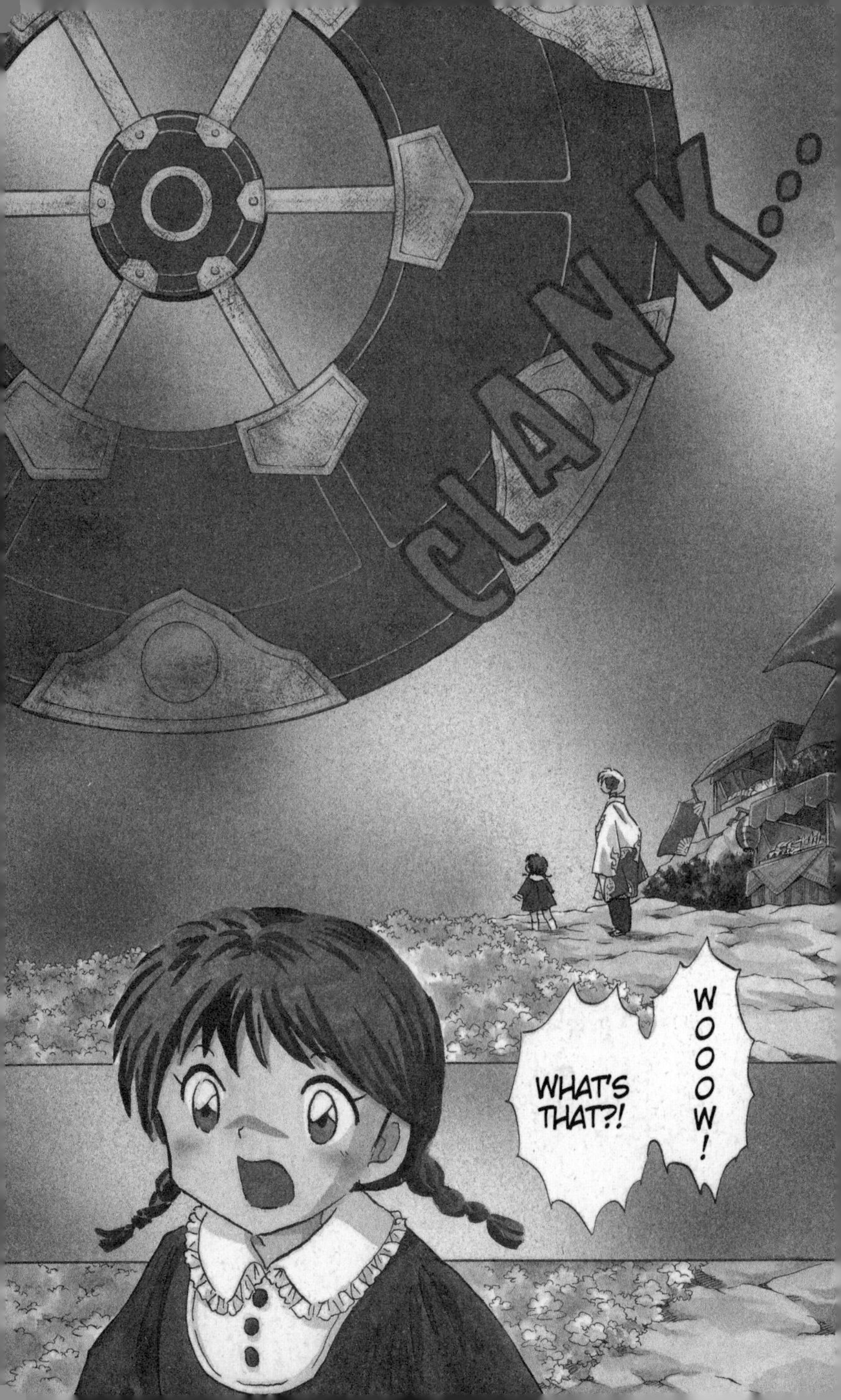
CLANK K...
WOOOOW!
WHAT'S THAT?!

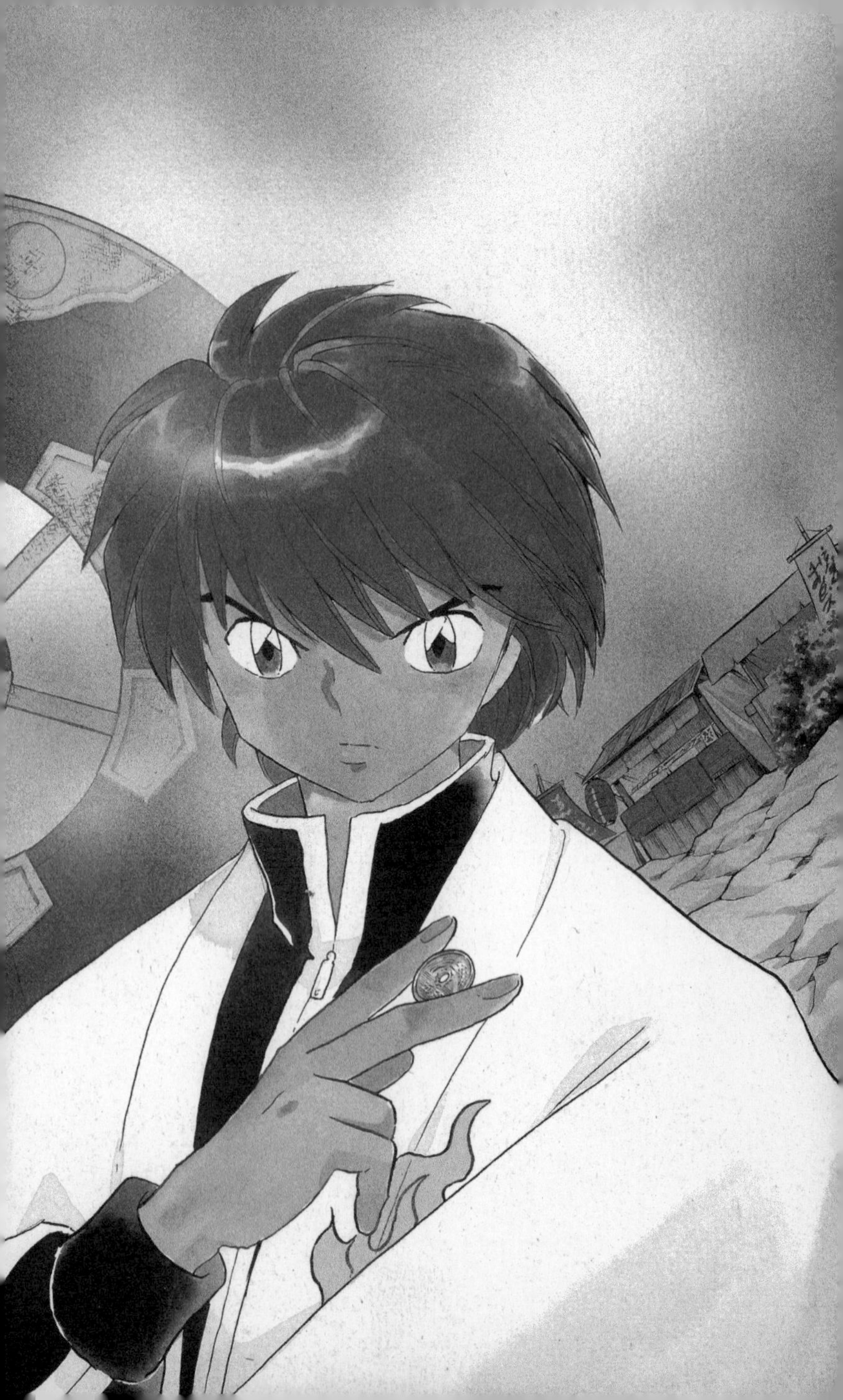

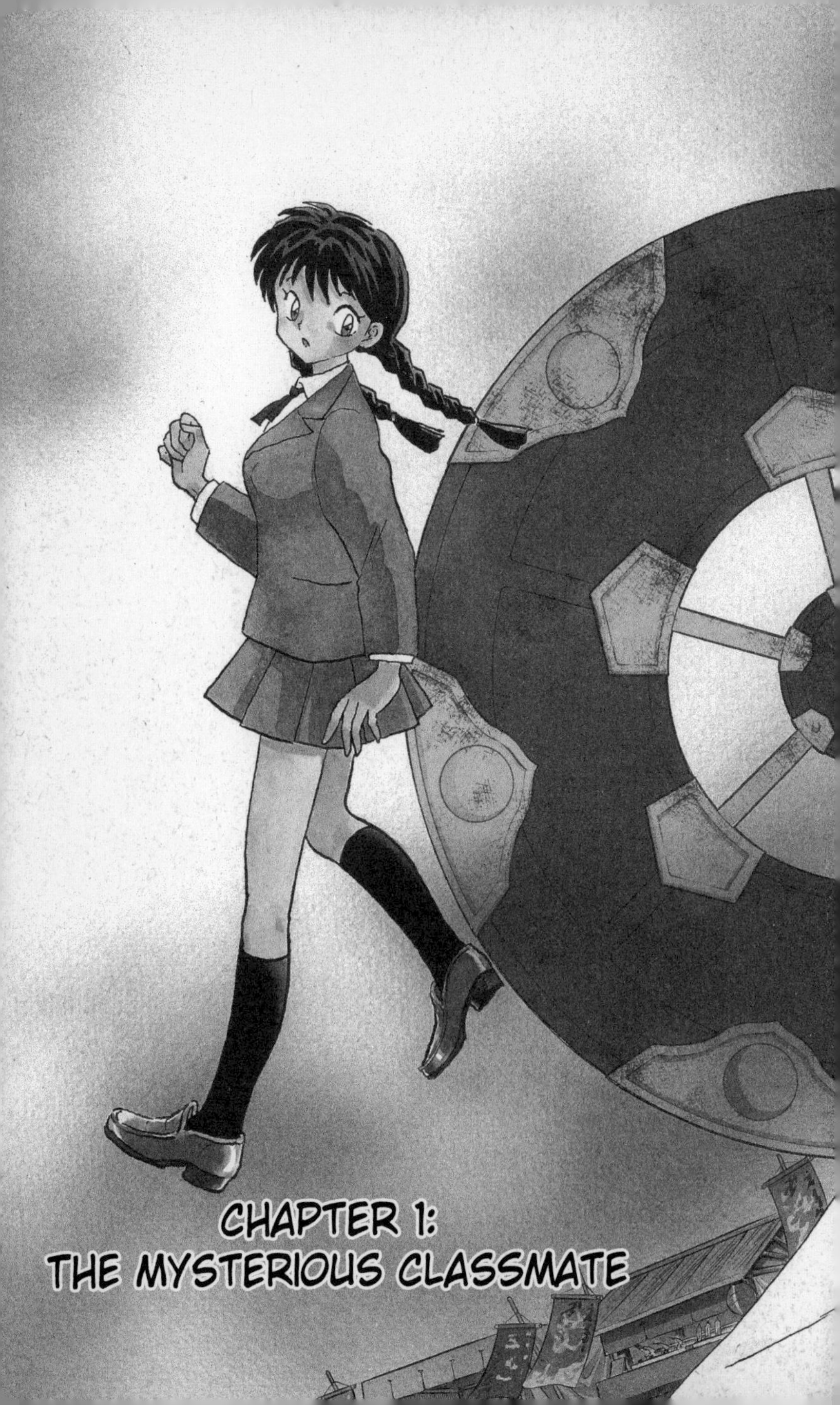

CHAPTER 1: THE MYSTERIOUS CLASSMATE

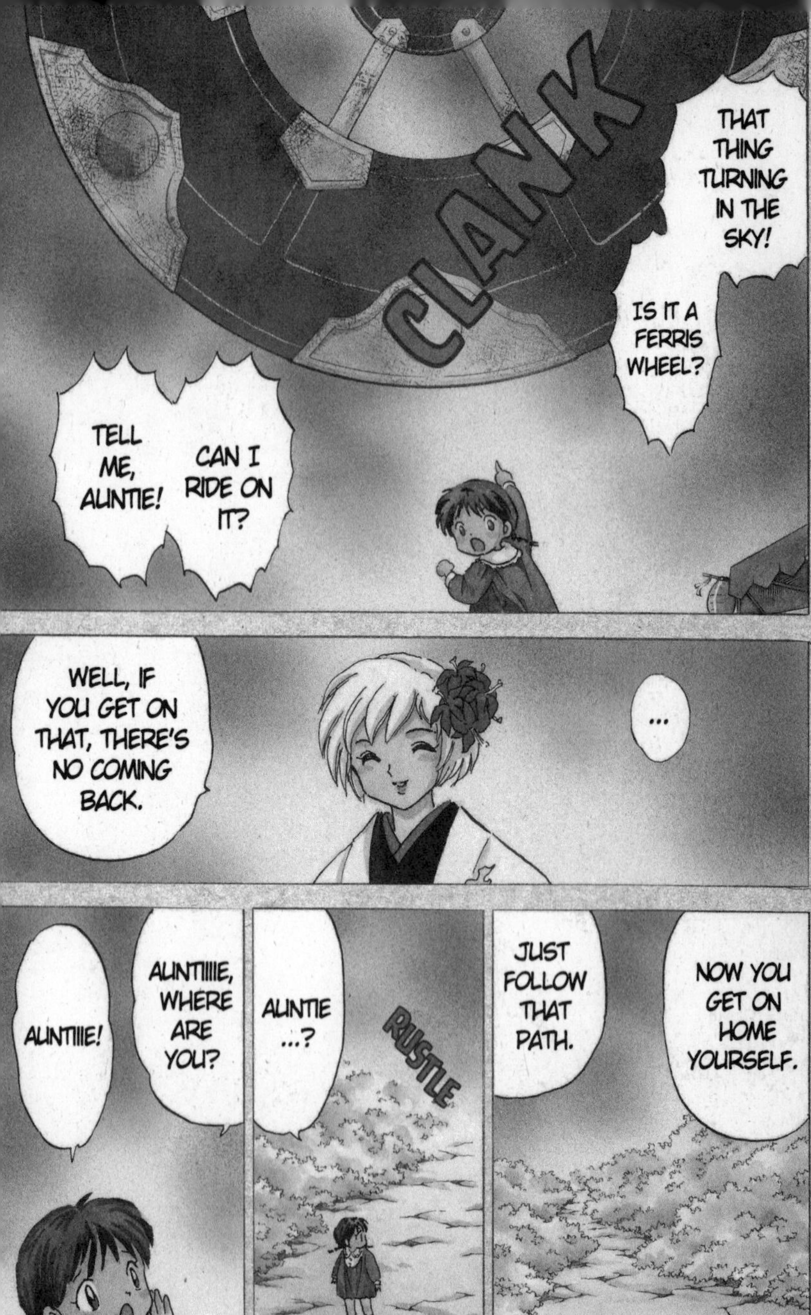
THAT THING TURNING IN THE SKY!
CLANK
IS IT A FERRIS WHEEL?
CAN I RIDE ON IT?
TELL ME, AUNTIE!
...
WELL, IF YOU GET ON THAT, THERE'S NO COMING BACK.
NOW YOU GET ON HOME YOURSELF.
JUST FOLLOW THAT PATH.
RUSTLE
AUNTIE ...?
AUNTIIIE, WHERE ARE YOU?
AUNTIIIE!

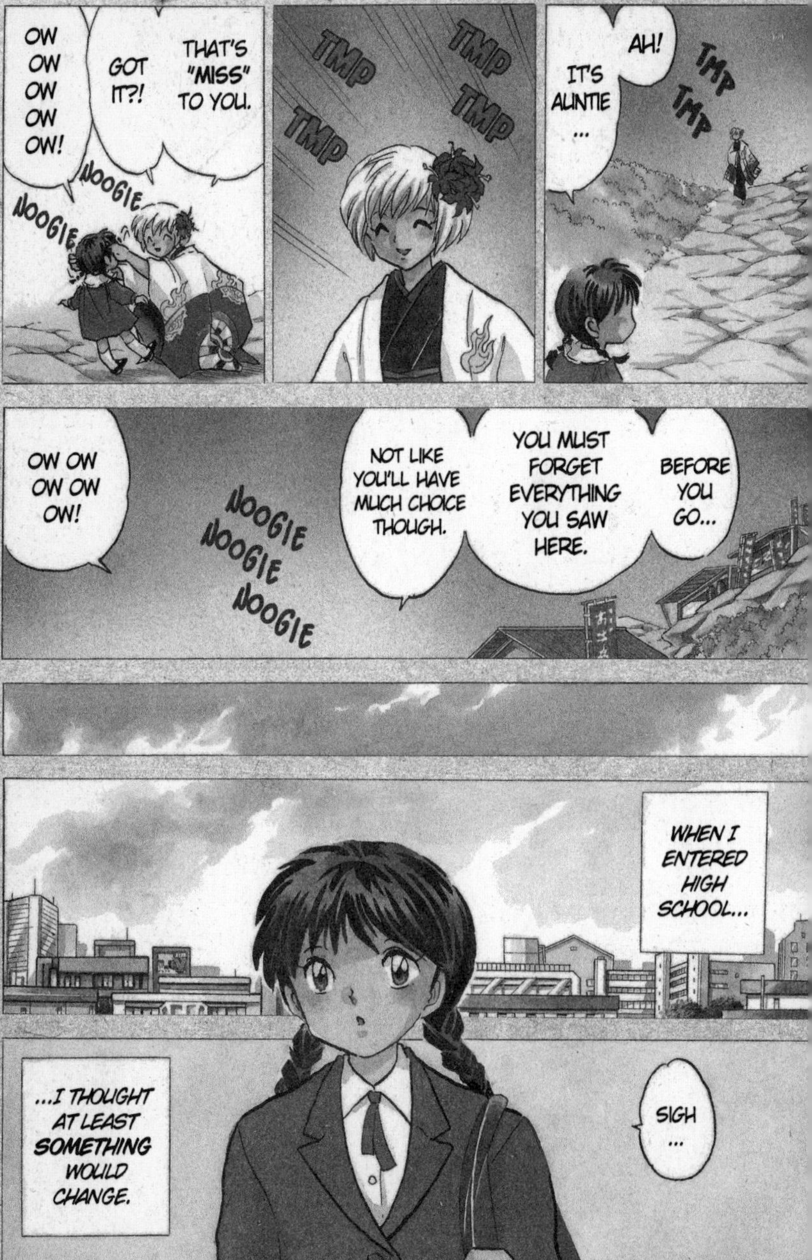
AH!
IT'S AUNTIE ...
TMP TMP
TMP TMP TMP TMP
THAT'S "MISS" TO YOU.
GOT IT?!
OW OW OW OW OW!
NOOGIE
NOOGIE
BEFORE YOU GO...
YOU MUST FORGET EVERYTHING YOU SAW HERE.
NOT LIKE YOU'LL HAVE MUCH CHOICE THOUGH.
NOOGIE NOOGIE NOOGIE
OW OW OW OW OW!
WHEN I ENTERED HIGH SCHOOL...
SIGH ...
...I THOUGHT AT LEAST SOMETHING WOULD CHANGE.

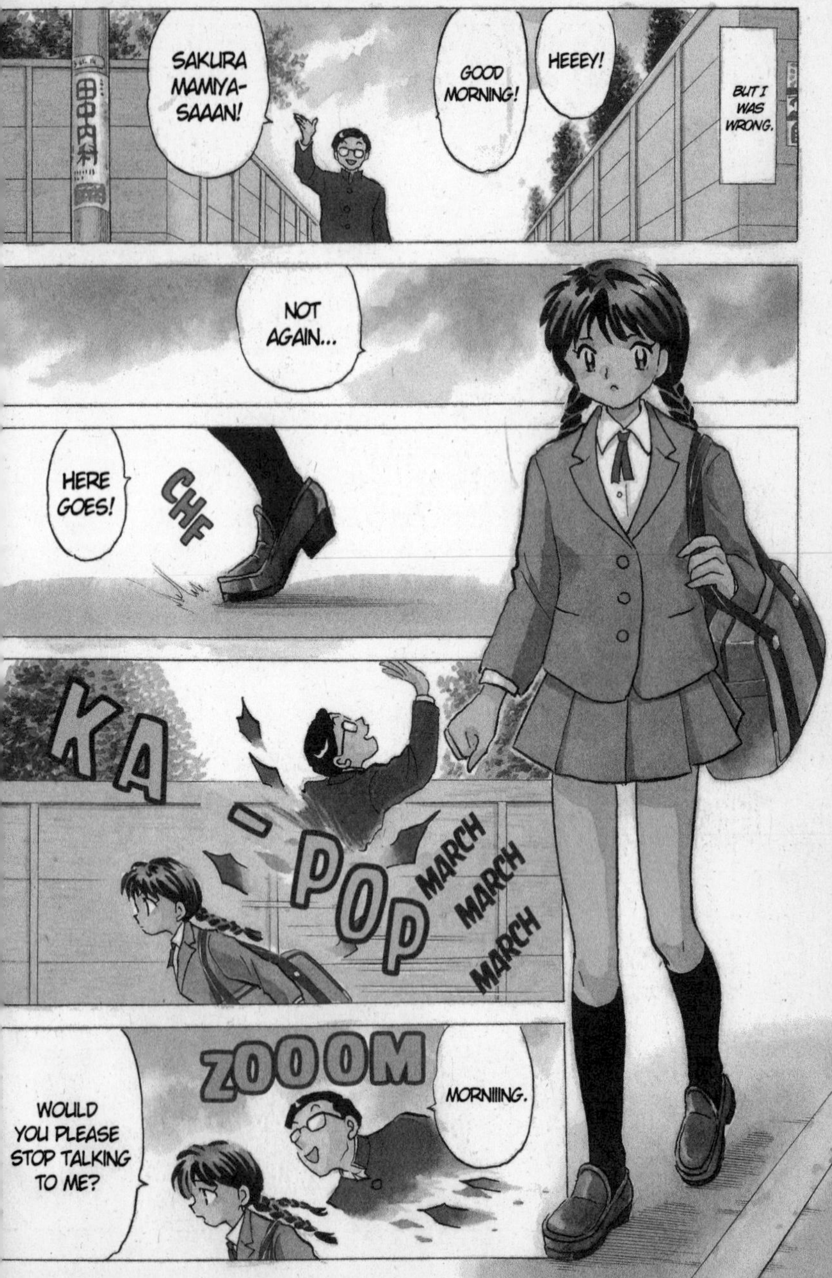
BUT I WAS WRONG.
HEEEY!
GOOD MORNING!
SAKURA MAMIYA-SAAAN!
NOT AGAIN...
HERE GOES!
CHF
KA-POP
MARCH MARCH MARCH
ZOOOM
MORNIIING.
WOULD YOU PLEASE STOP TALKING TO ME?

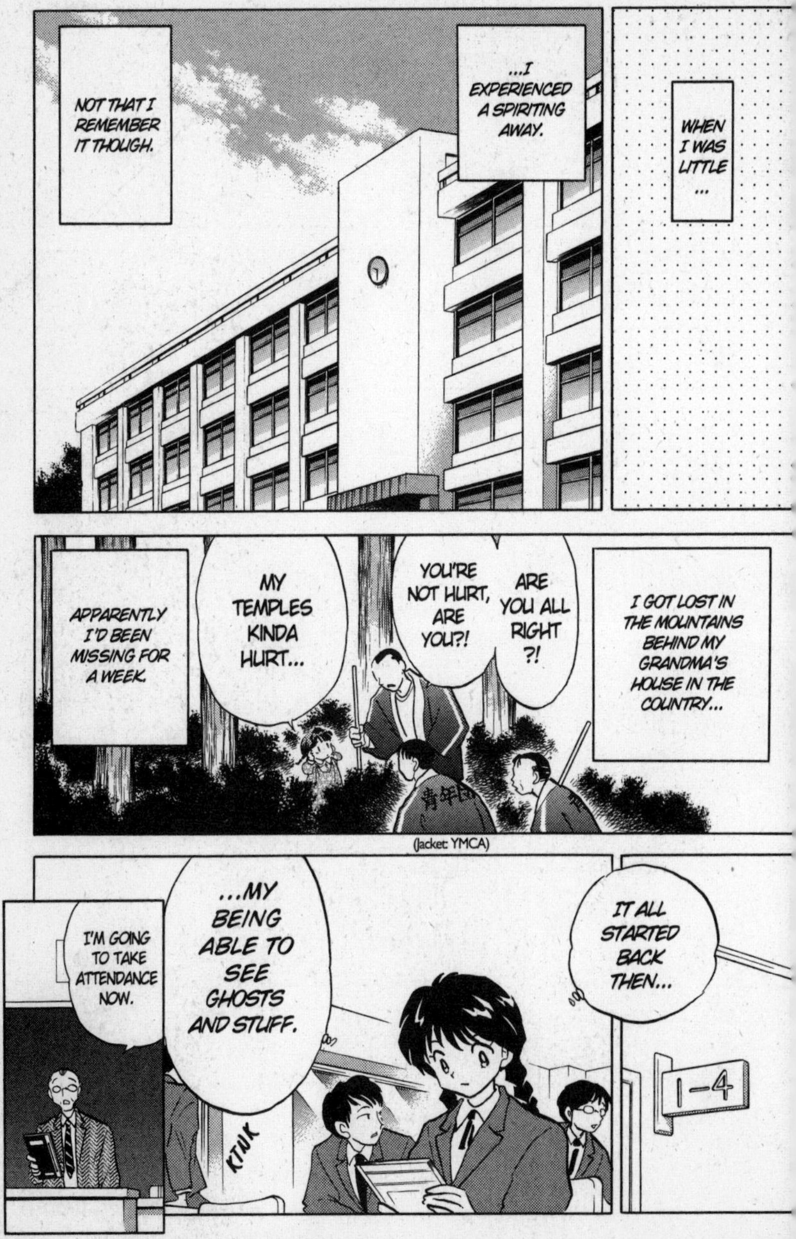
WHEN I WAS LITTLE...
...I EXPERIENCED A SPIRITING AWAY.
NOT THAT I REMEMBER IT THOUGH.
I GOT LOST IN THE MOUNTAINS BEHIND MY GRANDMA'S HOUSE IN THE COUNTRY...
ARE YOU ALL RIGHT?!
YOU'RE NOT HURT, ARE YOU?!
MY TEMPLES KINDA HURT...
APPARENTLY I'D BEEN MISSING FOR A WEEK.
(Jacket: YMCA)
IT ALL STARTED BACK THEN...
1-4
...MY BEING ABLE TO SEE GHOSTS AND STUFF.
KTUK
I'M GOING TO TAKE ATTENDANCE NOW.

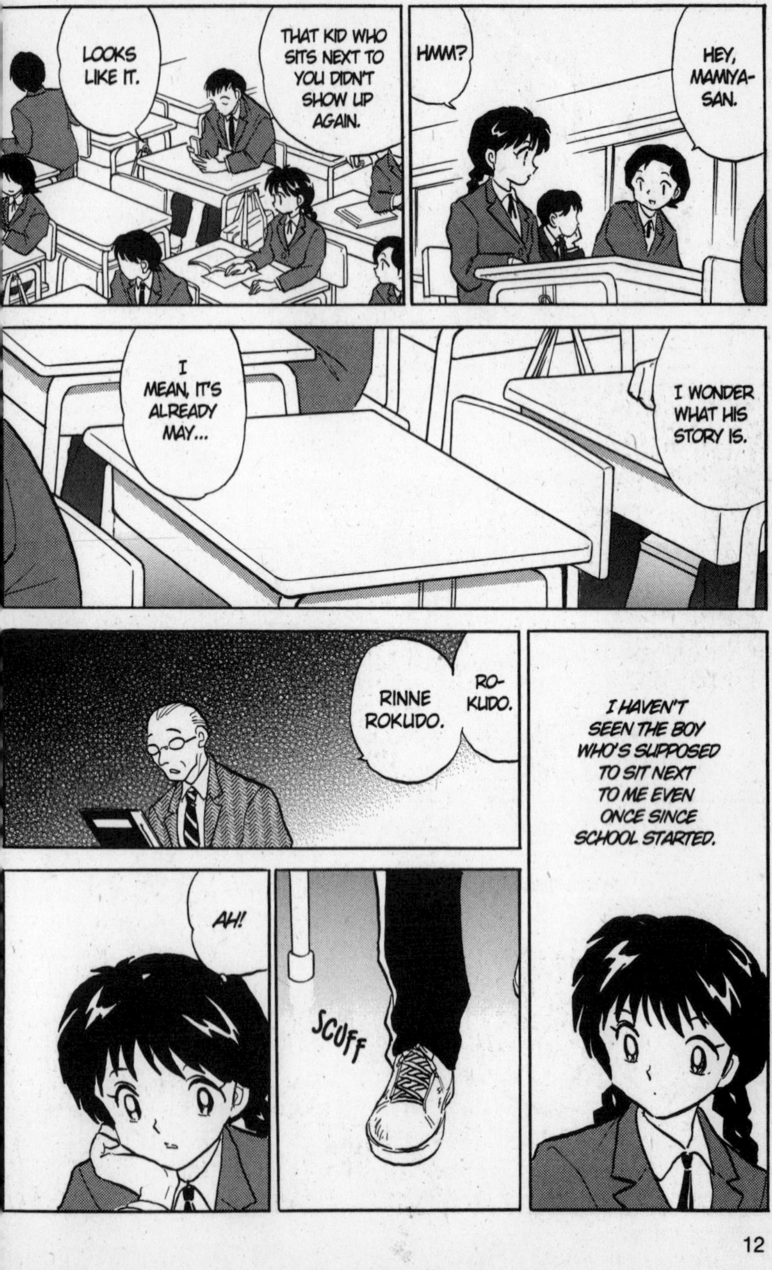
HEY, MAMIYA-SAN.
HMM?
THAT KID WHO SITS NEXT TO YOU DIDN'T SHOW UP AGAIN.
LOOKS LIKE IT.
I WONDER WHAT HIS STORY IS.
I MEAN, IT'S ALREADY MAY...
I HAVEN'T SEEN THE BOY WHO'S SUPPOSED TO SIT NEXT TO ME EVEN ONCE SINCE SCHOOL STARTED.
RO-KUDO.
RINNE ROKUDO.
SCUFF
AH!

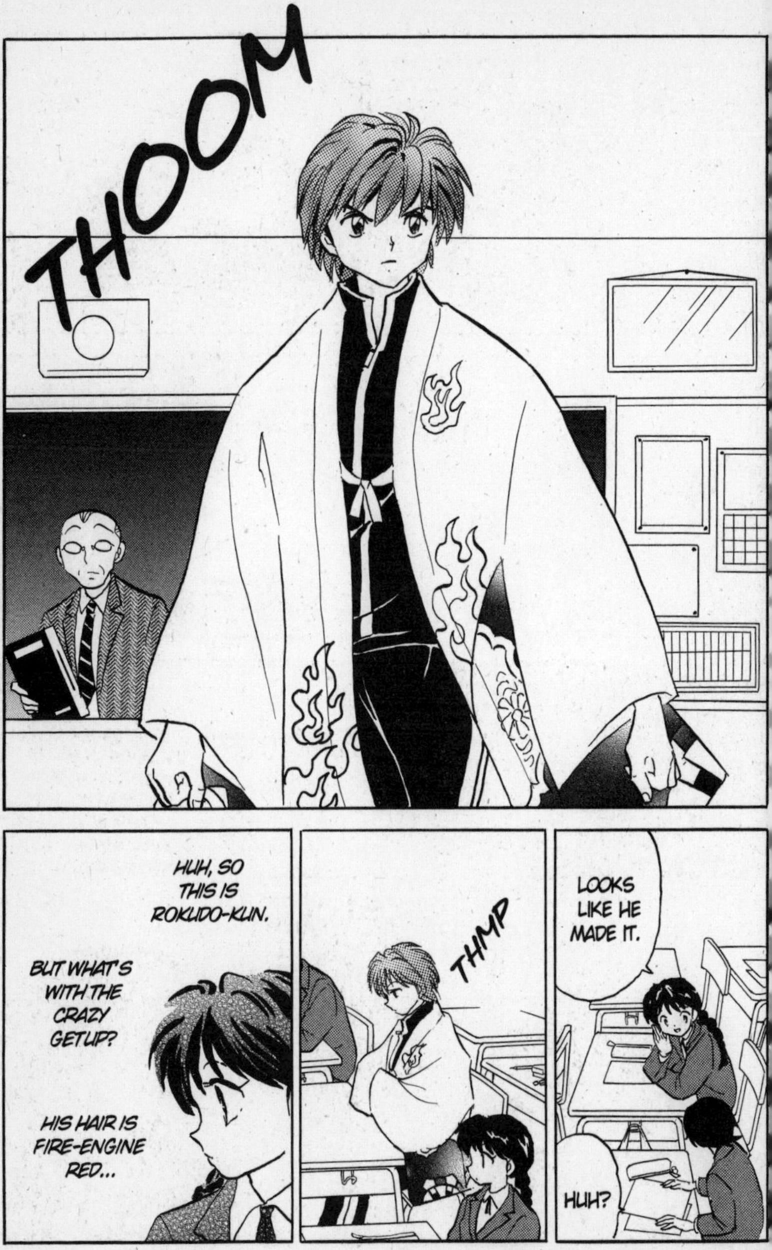
THOOM
LOOKS LIKE HE MADE IT.
HUH?
THMP
HUH, SO THIS IS ROKUDO-KUN.
BUT WHAT'S WITH THE CRAZY GETUP?
HIS HAIR IS FIRE-ENGINE RED...

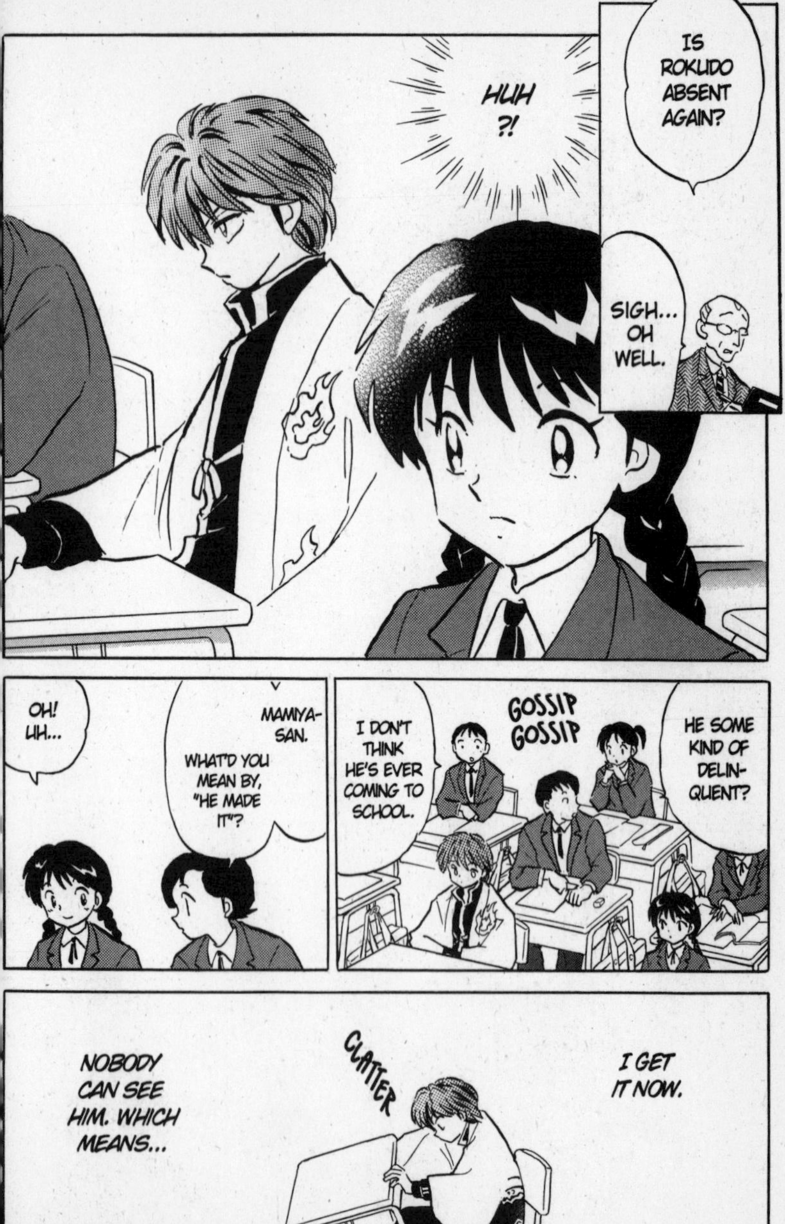
IS ROKUDO ABSENT AGAIN?
SIGH... OH WELL.
HUH ?!
HE SOME KIND OF DELIN-QUENT?
GOSSIP GOSSIP
I DON'T THINK HE'S EVER COMING TO SCHOOL.
MAMIYA-SAN.
WHAT'D YOU MEAN BY, "HE MADE IT"?
OH! UH...
I GET IT NOW.
CLATTER
NOBODY CAN SEE HIM. WHICH MEANS...

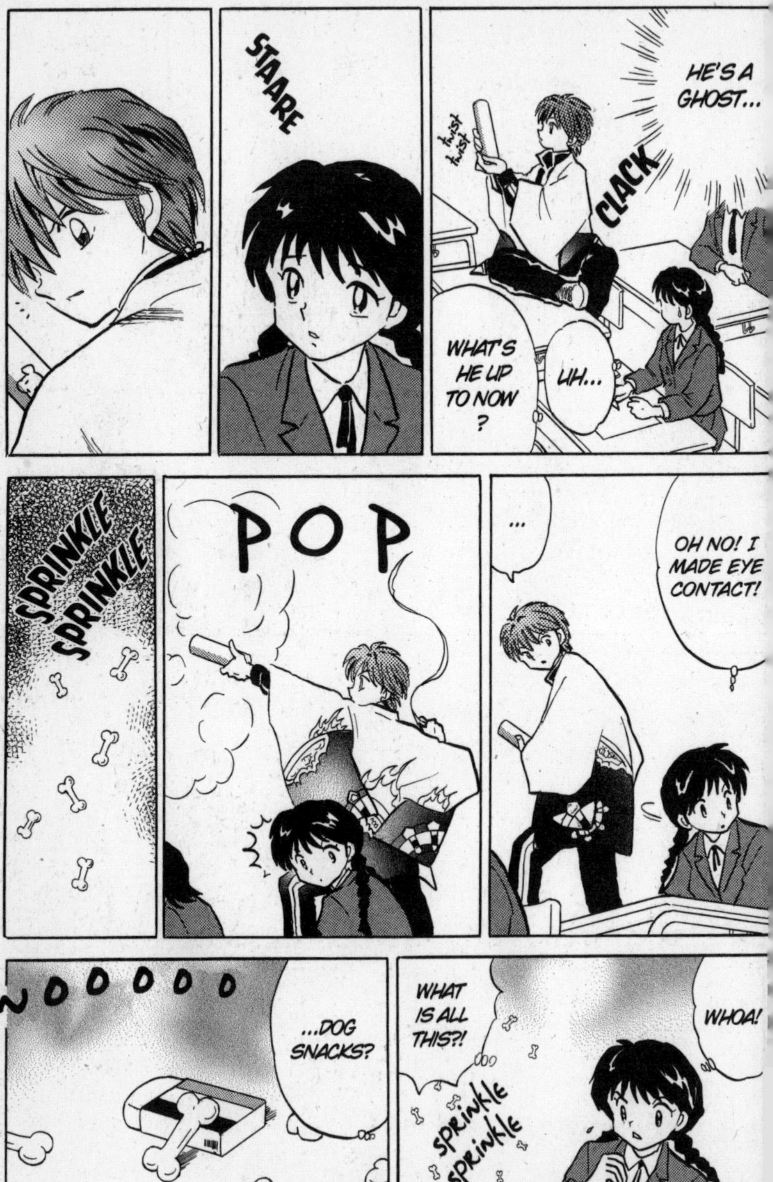
HE'S A GHOST...
CLACK
twist twist
UH...
WHAT'S HE UP TO NOW ?
STAARE
OH NO! I MADE EYE CONTACT!
...
POP
SPRINKLE SPRINKLE
WHOA!
WHAT IS ALL THIS?!
sprinkle sprinkle
WOOOOO
...DOG SNACKS?

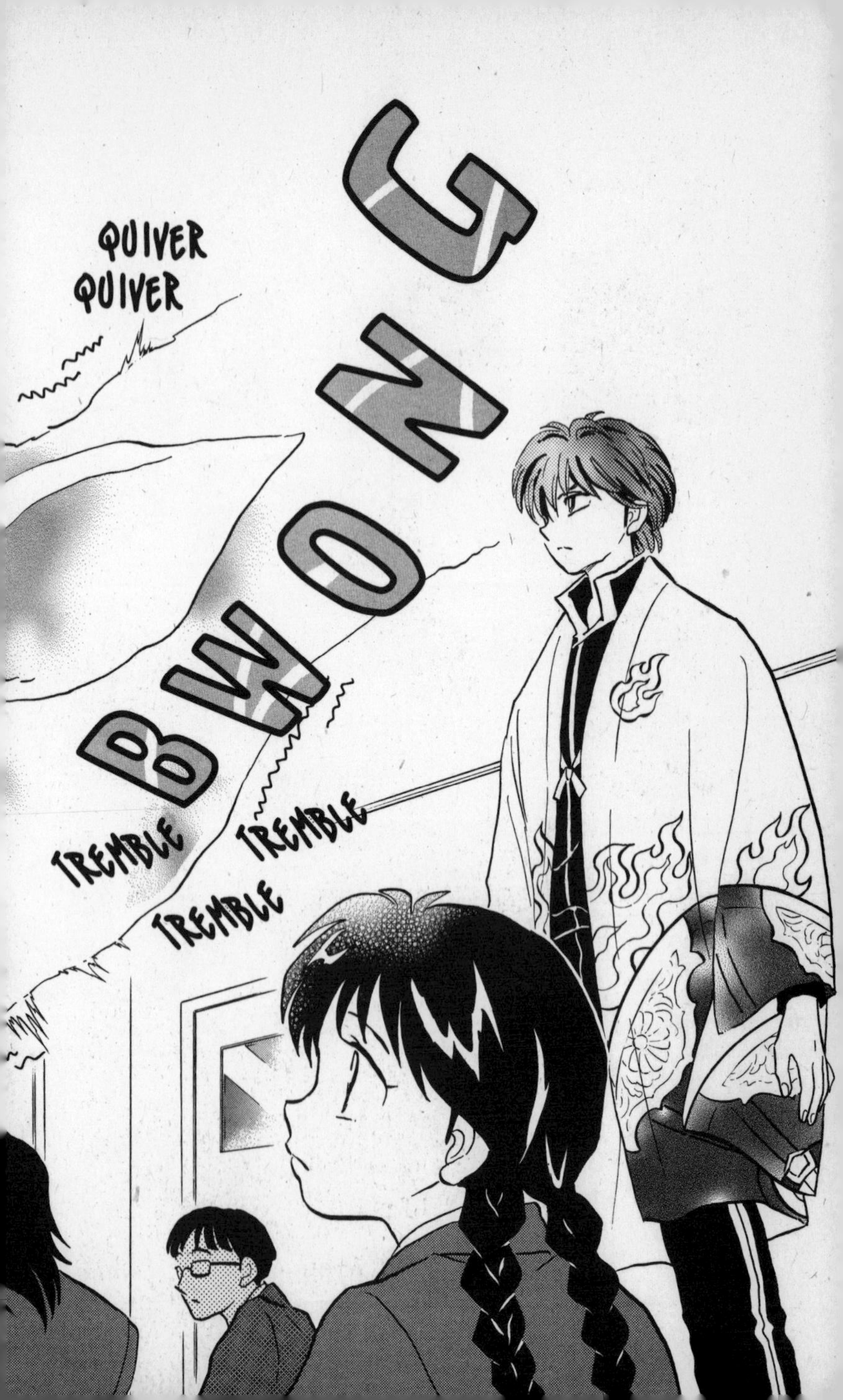
BWONG
QUIVER
QUIVER
TREMBLE
TREMBLE
TREMBLE

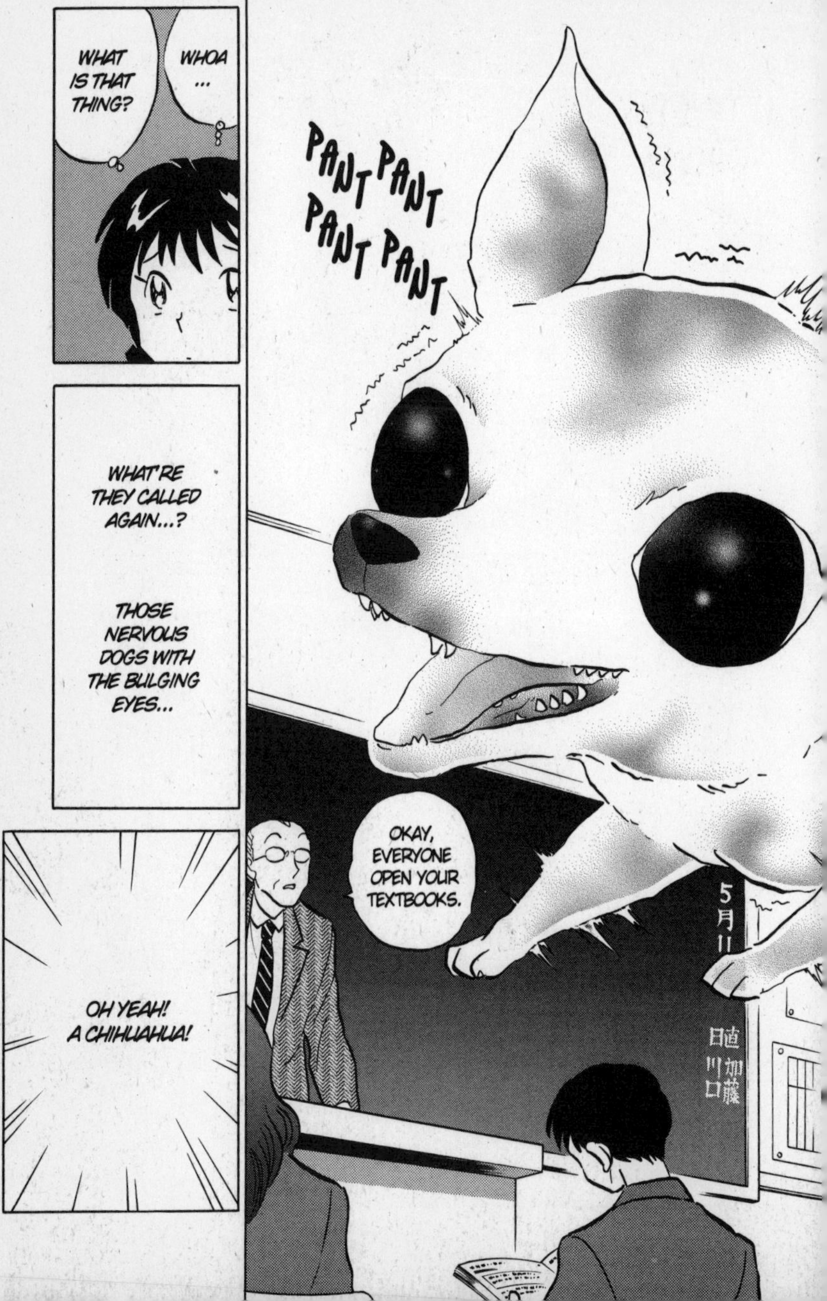
PANT PANT PANT PANT
OKAY, EVERYONE OPEN YOUR TEXTBOOKS.
5月11
WHOA ...
WHAT IS THAT THING?
WHAT'RE THEY CALLED AGAIN...?
THOSE NERVOUS DOGS WITH THE BULGING EYES...
OH YEAH! A CHIHUAHUA!

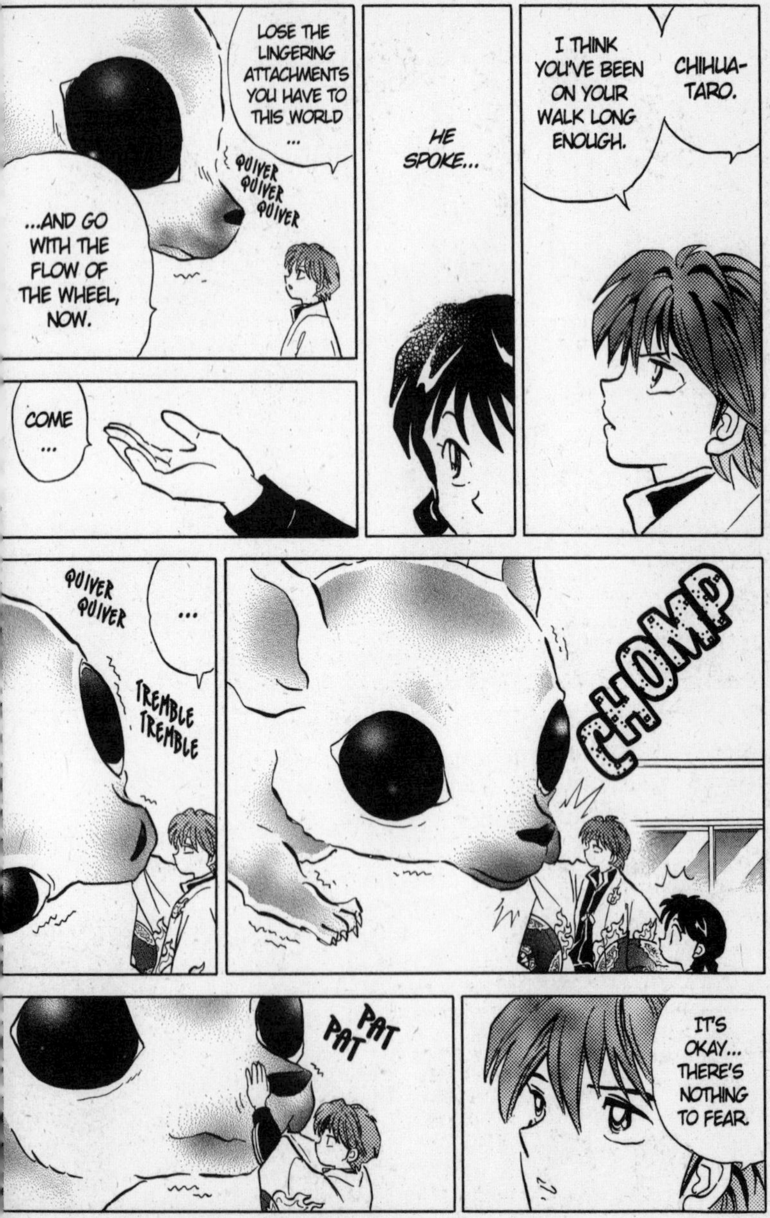
CHIHUA-TARO.
I THINK YOU'VE BEEN ON YOUR WALK LONG ENOUGH.
HE SPOKE...
LOSE THE LINGERING ATTACHMENTS YOU HAVE TO THIS WORLD ...
QUIVER QUIVER QUIVER
...AND GO WITH THE FLOW OF THE WHEEL, NOW.
COME ...
CHOMP
...
QUIVER QUIVER
TREMBLE TREMBLE
IT'S OKAY... THERE'S NOTHING TO FEAR.
PAT PAT

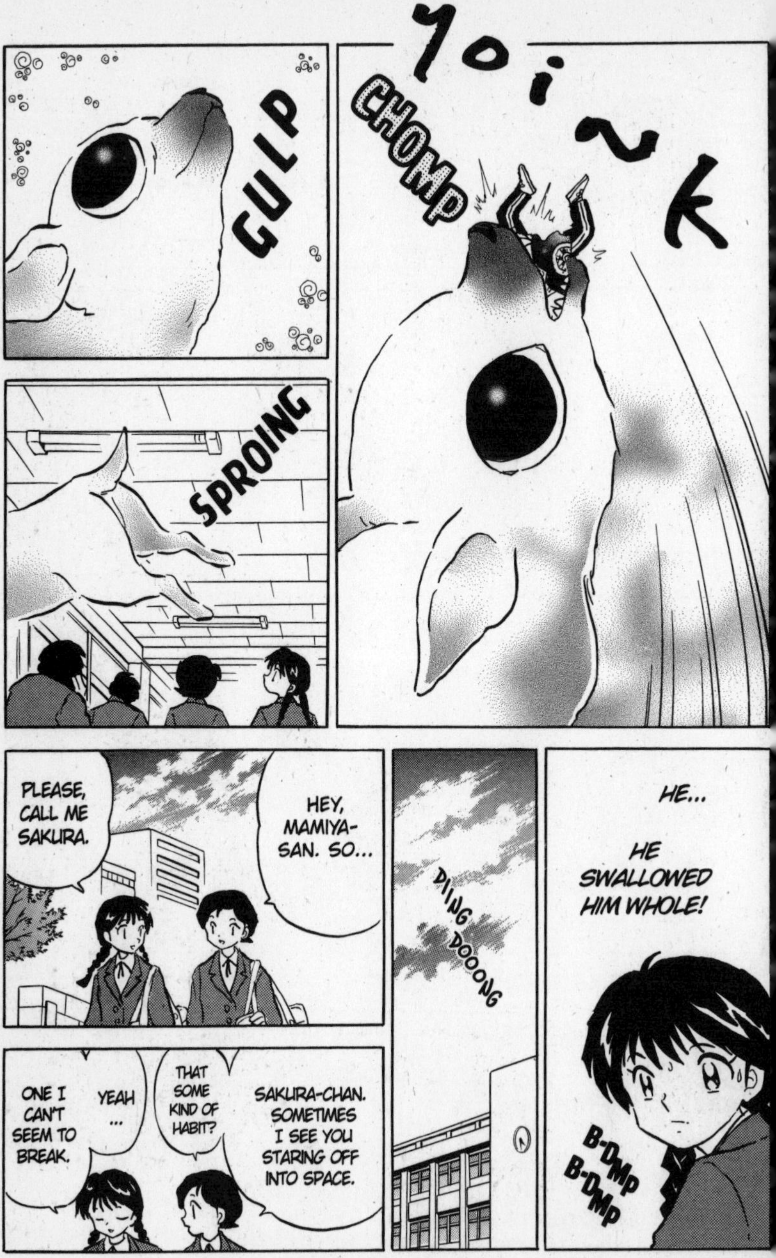

yoink
CHOMP
GULP
SPROING
HE...
HE SWALLOWED HIM WHOLE!
B-DMP B-DMP
DING DOOONG
HEY, MAMIYA-SAN. SO...
PLEASE, CALL ME SAKURA.
SAKURA-CHAN. SOMETIMES I SEE YOU STARING OFF INTO SPACE.
THAT SOME KIND OF HABIT?
YEAH ...
ONE I CAN'T SEEM TO BREAK.

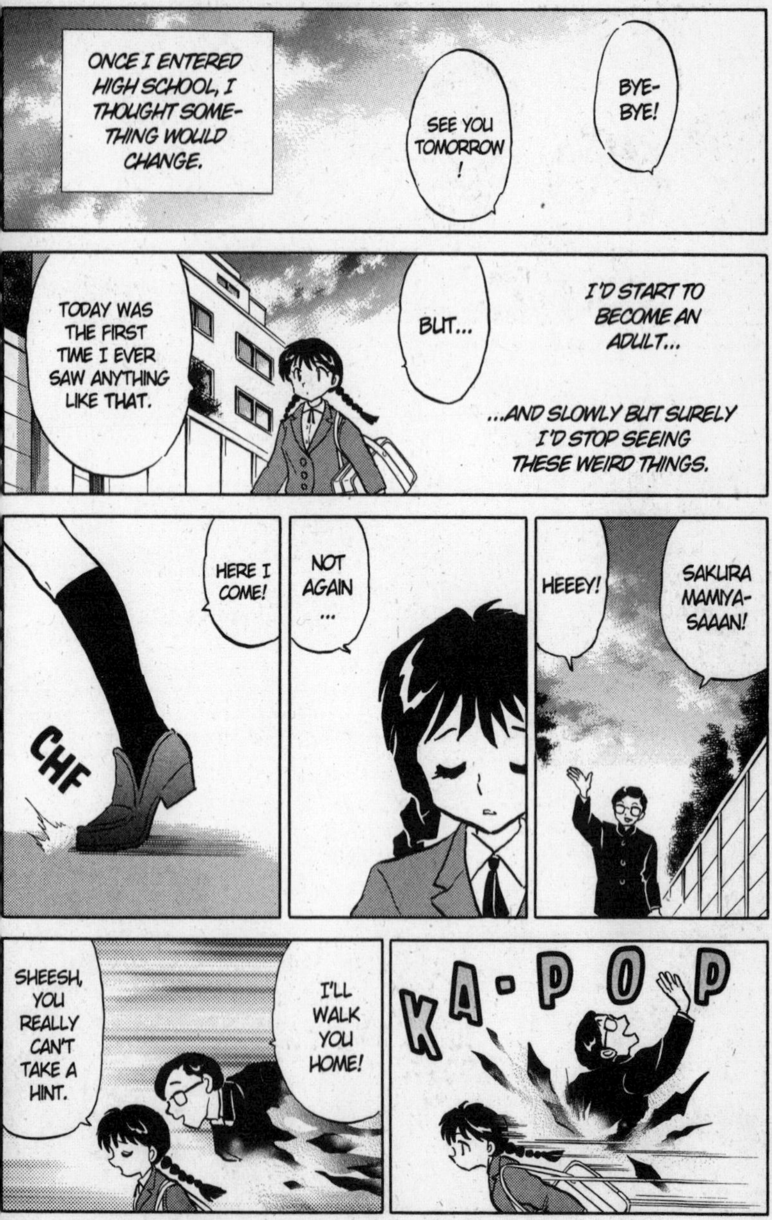
BYE-BYE!
SEE YOU TOMORROW!
ONCE I ENTERED HIGH SCHOOL, I THOUGHT SOME-THING WOULD CHANGE.
I'D START TO BECOME AN ADULT...
...AND SLOWLY BUT SURELY I'D STOP SEEING THESE WEIRD THINGS.
BUT...
TODAY WAS THE FIRST TIME I EVER SAW ANYTHING LIKE THAT.
SAKURA MAMIYA-SAAAN!
HEEEY!
NOT AGAIN...
HERE I COME!
CHF
KA-POP
I'LL WALK YOU HOME!
SHEESH, YOU REALLY CAN'T TAKE A HINT.

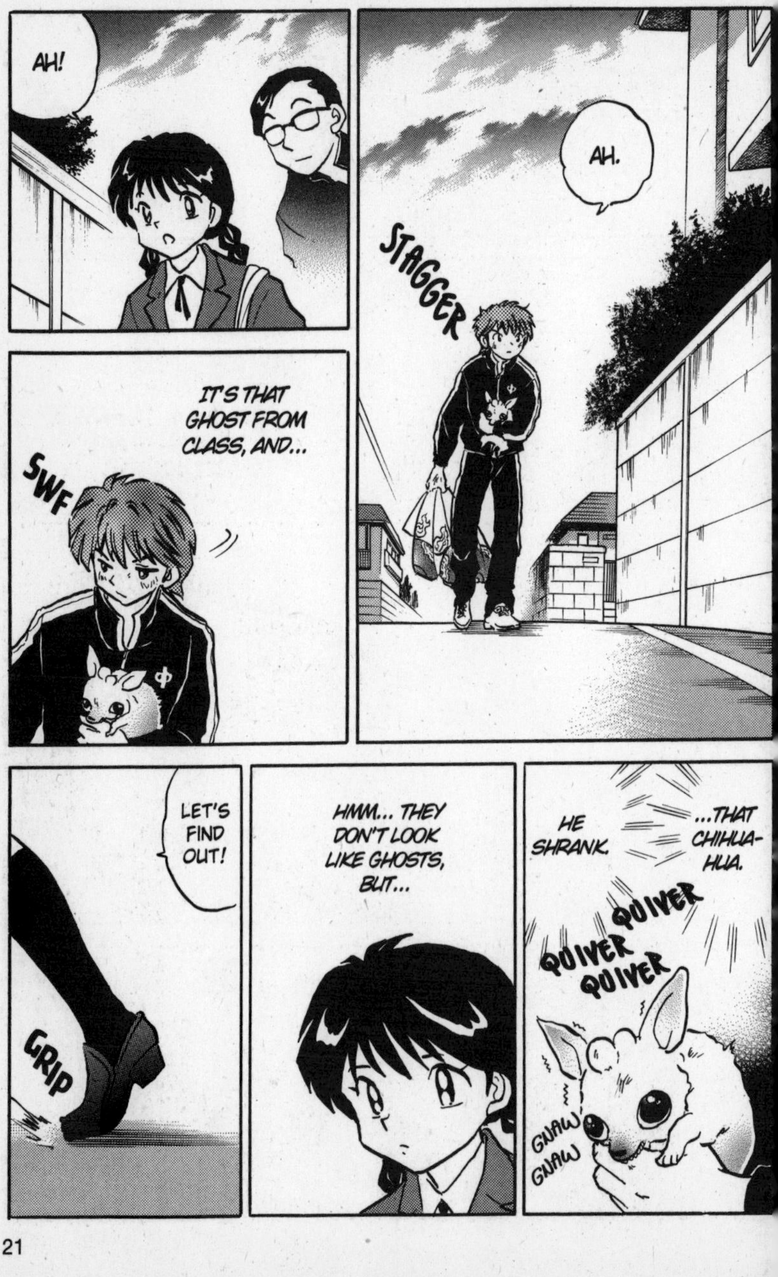
AH.
STAGGER
AH!
IT'S THAT GHOST FROM CLASS, AND...
SWF
...THAT CHIHUAHUA.
HE SHRANK.
QUIVER
QUIVER
QUIVER
GNAW
GNAW
HMM... THEY DON'T LOOK LIKE GHOSTS, BUT...
LET'S FIND OUT!
GRIP

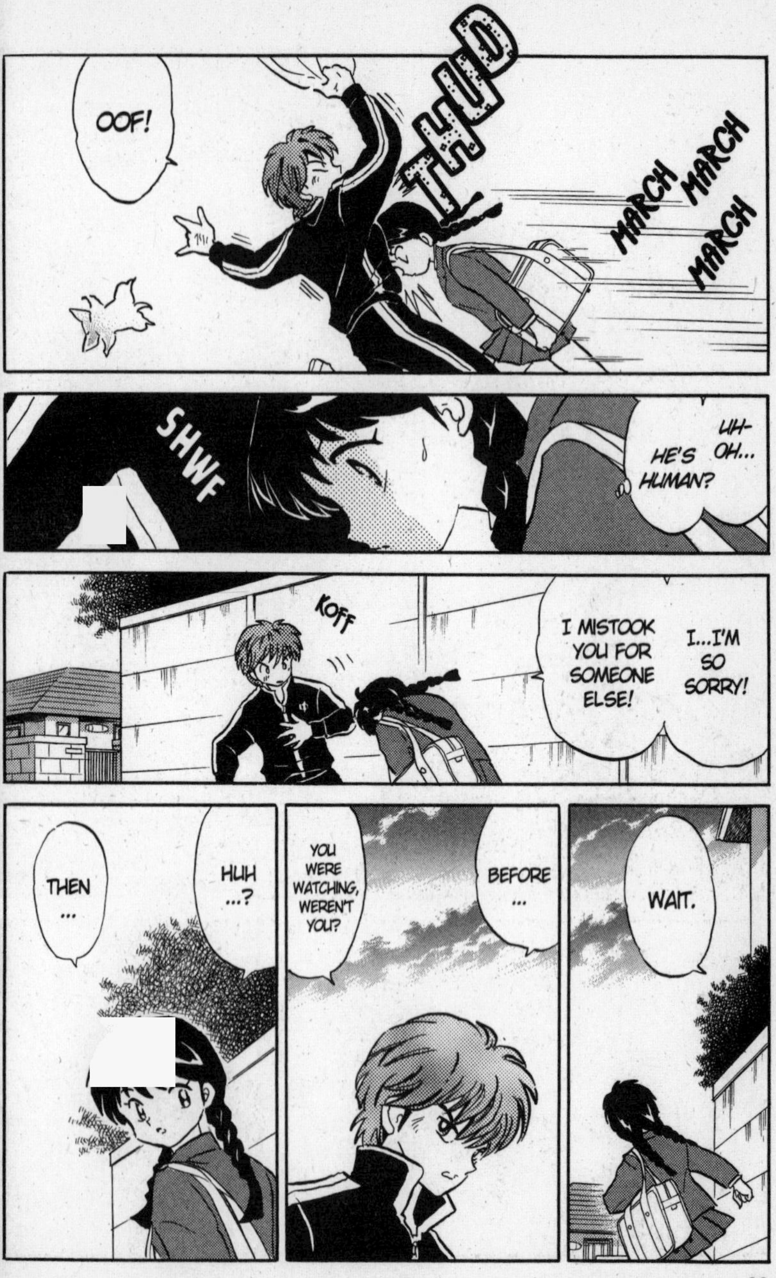
MARCH MARCH MARCH
THUD
OOF!
UH-OH...
HE'S HUMAN?
SHWF
I...I'M SO SORRY!
I MISTOOK YOU FOR SOMEONE ELSE!
KOFF
WAIT.
BEFORE...
YOU WERE WATCHING, WEREN'T YOU?
HUH...?
THEN...

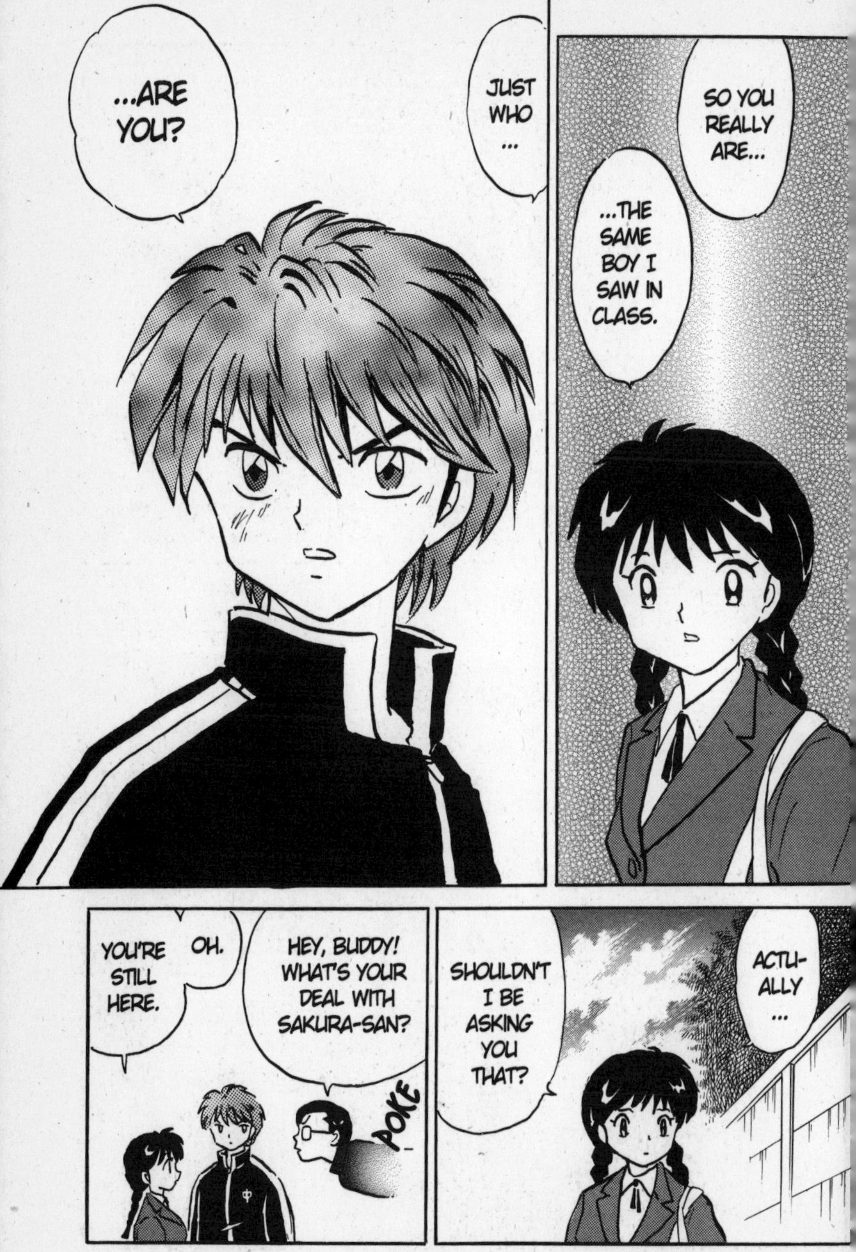
SO YOU REALLY ARE...
...THE SAME BOY I SAW IN CLASS.
JUST WHO ...
...ARE YOU?
ACTU-ALLY ...
SHOULDN'T I BE ASKING YOU THAT?
HEY, BUDDY! WHAT'S YOUR DEAL WITH SAKURA-SAN?
POKE
OH.
YOU'RE STILL HERE.

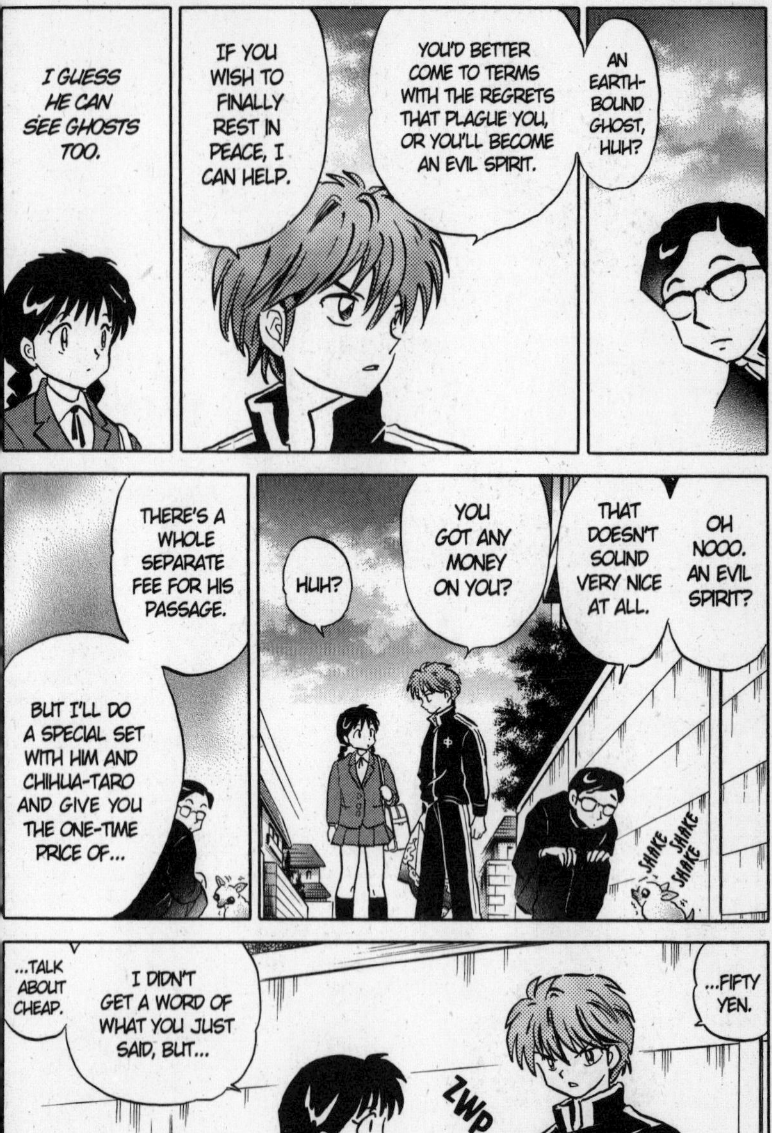
AN EARTH-BOUND GHOST, HUH?
YOU'D BETTER COME TO TERMS WITH THE REGRETS THAT PLAGUE YOU, OR YOU'LL BECOME AN EVIL SPIRIT.
IF YOU WISH TO FINALLY REST IN PEACE, I CAN HELP.
I GUESS HE CAN SEE GHOSTS TOO.
OH NOOO. AN EVIL SPIRIT?
THAT DOESN'T SOUND VERY NICE AT ALL.
SHAKE SHAKE SHAKE
YOU GOT ANY MONEY ON YOU?
HUH?
THERE'S A WHOLE SEPARATE FEE FOR HIS PASSAGE.
BUT I'LL DO A SPECIAL SET WITH HIM AND CHIHUA-TARO AND GIVE YOU THE ONE-TIME PRICE OF...
...FIFTY YEN.
ZWP
I DIDN'T GET A WORD OF WHAT YOU JUST SAID, BUT...
...TALK ABOUT CHEAP.

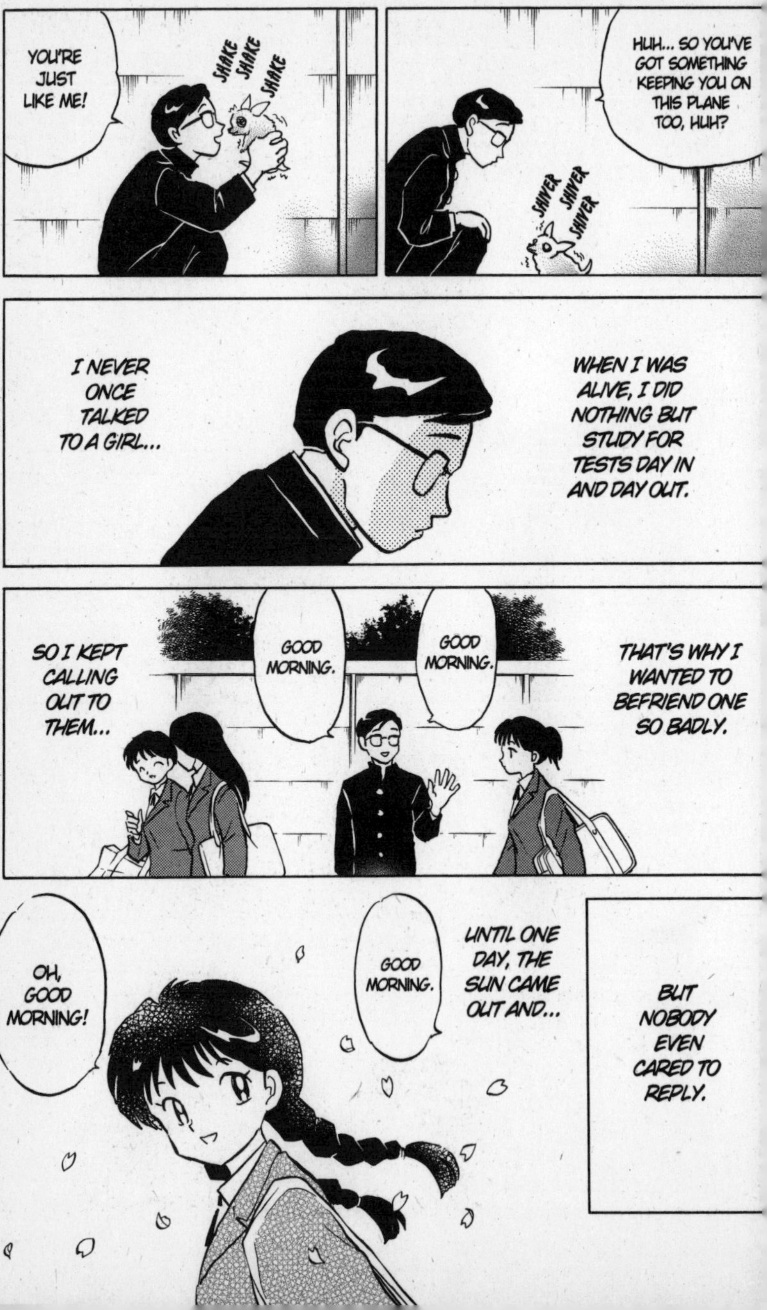
HUH... SO YOU'VE GOT SOMETHING KEEPING YOU ON THIS PLANE TOO, HUH?
SHIVER SHIVER SHIVER
YOU'RE JUST LIKE ME!
SHAKE SHAKE SHAKE
WHEN I WAS ALIVE, I DID NOTHING BUT STUDY FOR TESTS DAY IN AND DAY OUT.
I NEVER ONCE TALKED TO A GIRL...
THAT'S WHY I WANTED TO BEFRIEND ONE SO BADLY.
GOOD MORNING.
GOOD MORNING.
SO I KEPT CALLING OUT TO THEM...
BUT NOBODY EVEN CARED TO REPLY.
UNTIL ONE DAY, THE SUN CAME OUT AND...
GOOD MORNING.
OH, GOOD MORNING!

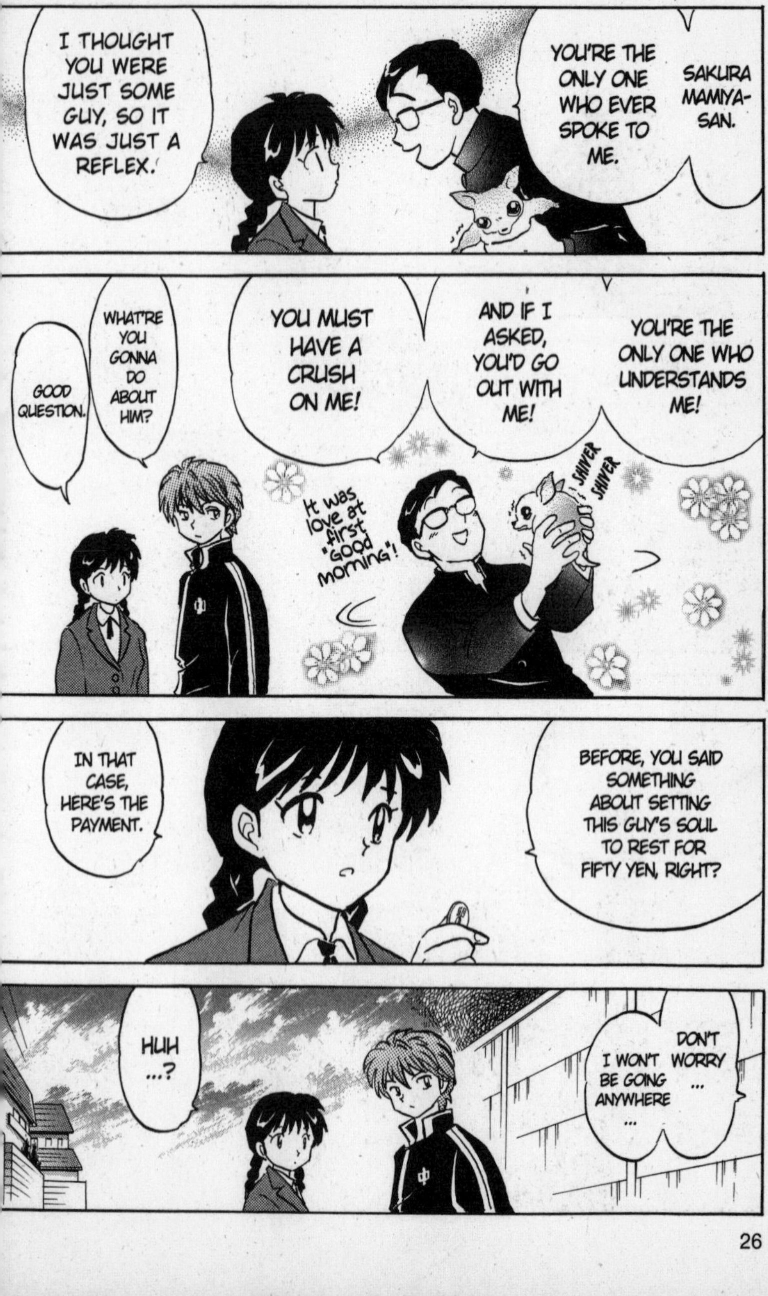
SAKURA MAMIYA-SAN.
YOU'RE THE ONLY ONE WHO EVER SPOKE TO ME.
I THOUGHT YOU WERE JUST SOME GUY, SO IT WAS JUST A REFLEX.
YOU'RE THE ONLY ONE WHO UNDERSTANDS ME!
AND IF I ASKED, YOU'D GO OUT WITH ME!
YOU MUST HAVE A CRUSH ON ME!
SHIVER SHIVER
It was love at first "Good morning"!
WHAT'RE YOU GONNA DO ABOUT HIM?
GOOD QUESTION.
BEFORE, YOU SAID SOMETHING ABOUT SETTING THIS GUY'S SOUL TO REST FOR FIFTY YEN, RIGHT?
IN THAT CASE, HERE'S THE PAYMENT.
DON'T WORRY ...
I WON'T BE GOING ANYWHERE ...
HUH ...?

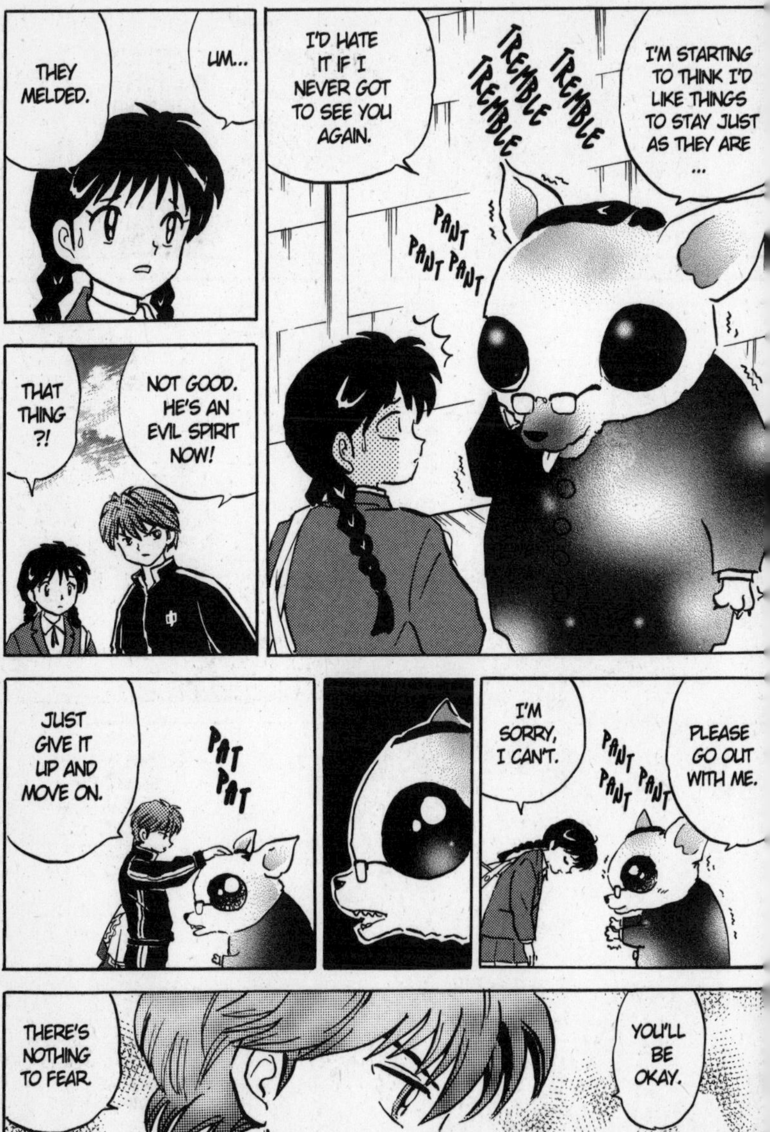
I'M STARTING TO THINK I'D LIKE THINGS TO STAY JUST AS THEY ARE ...
TREMBLE
TREMBLE
TREMBLE
I'D HATE IT IF I NEVER GOT TO SEE YOU AGAIN.
PANT PANT PANT
UM...
THEY MELDED.
NOT GOOD. HE'S AN EVIL SPIRIT NOW!
THAT THING ?!
PLEASE GO OUT WITH ME.
PANT PANT PANT
I'M SORRY, I CAN'T.
PAT PAT
JUST GIVE IT UP AND MOVE ON.
YOU'LL BE OKAY.
THERE'S NOTHING TO FEAR.

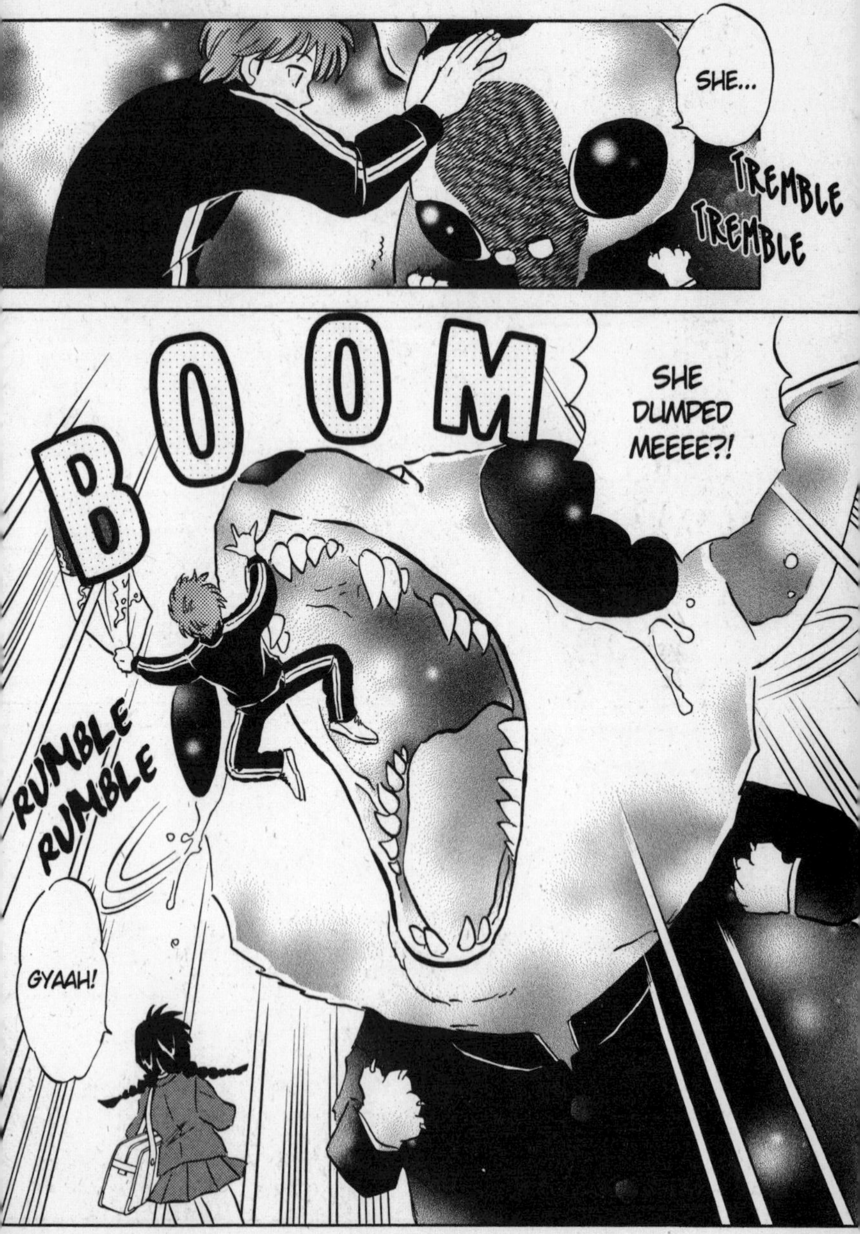
SHE...
TREMBLE TREMBLE
SHE DUMPED MEEEE?!
BOOM
RUMBLE RUMBLE
GYAAH!

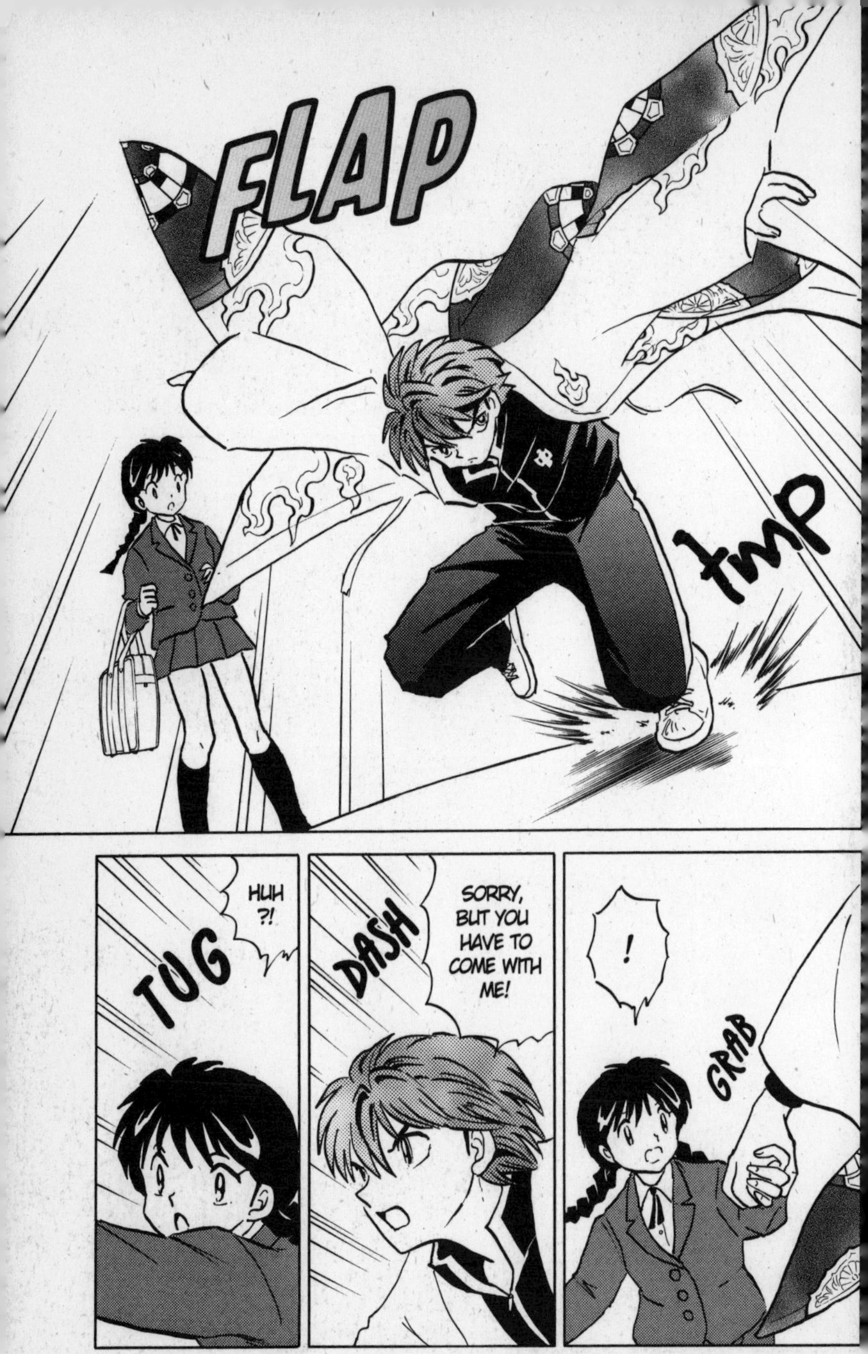
FLAP
TMP
GRAB
!
DASH
SORRY, BUT YOU HAVE TO COME WITH ME!
TUG
HUH ?!

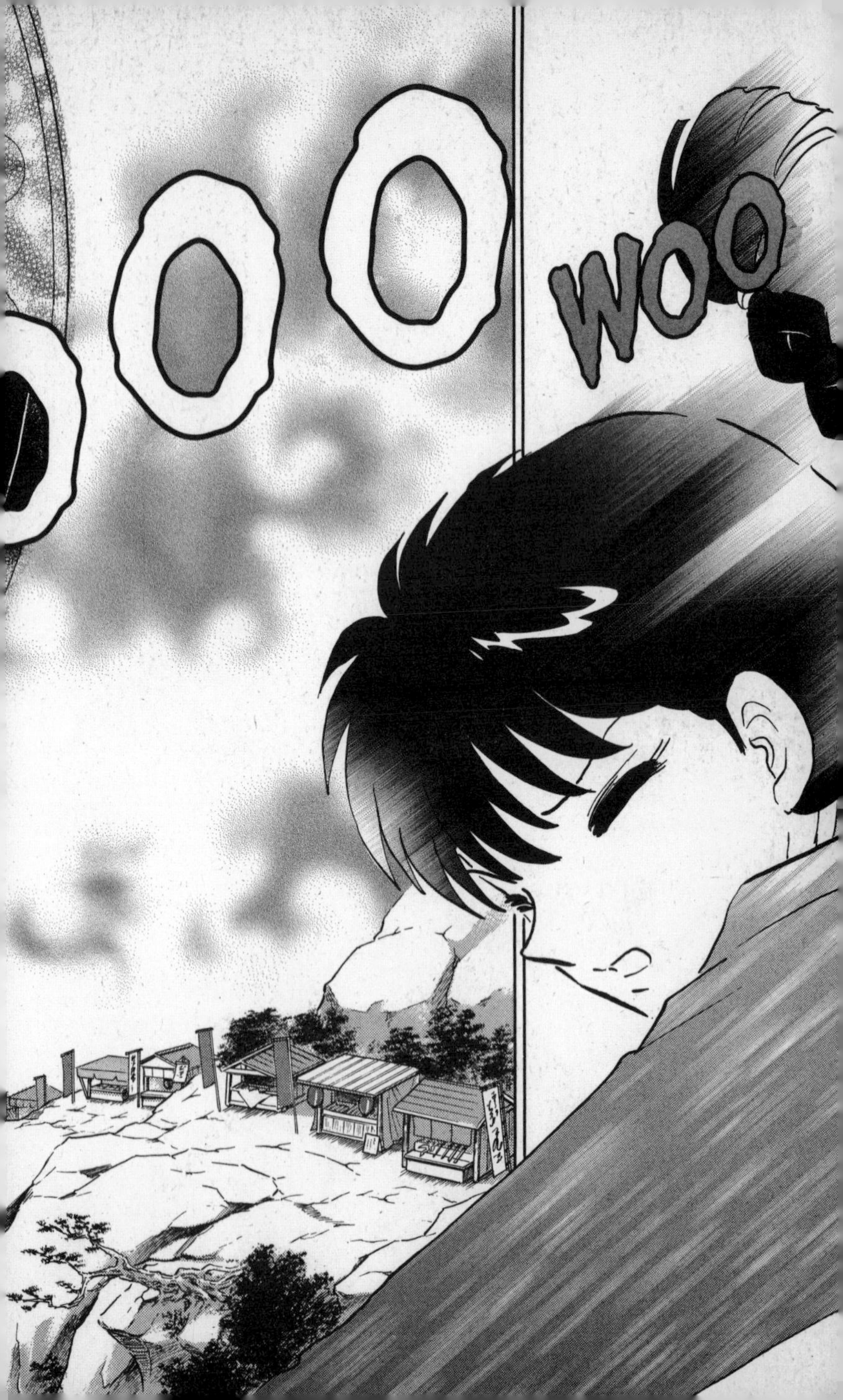
WOO
OOOO

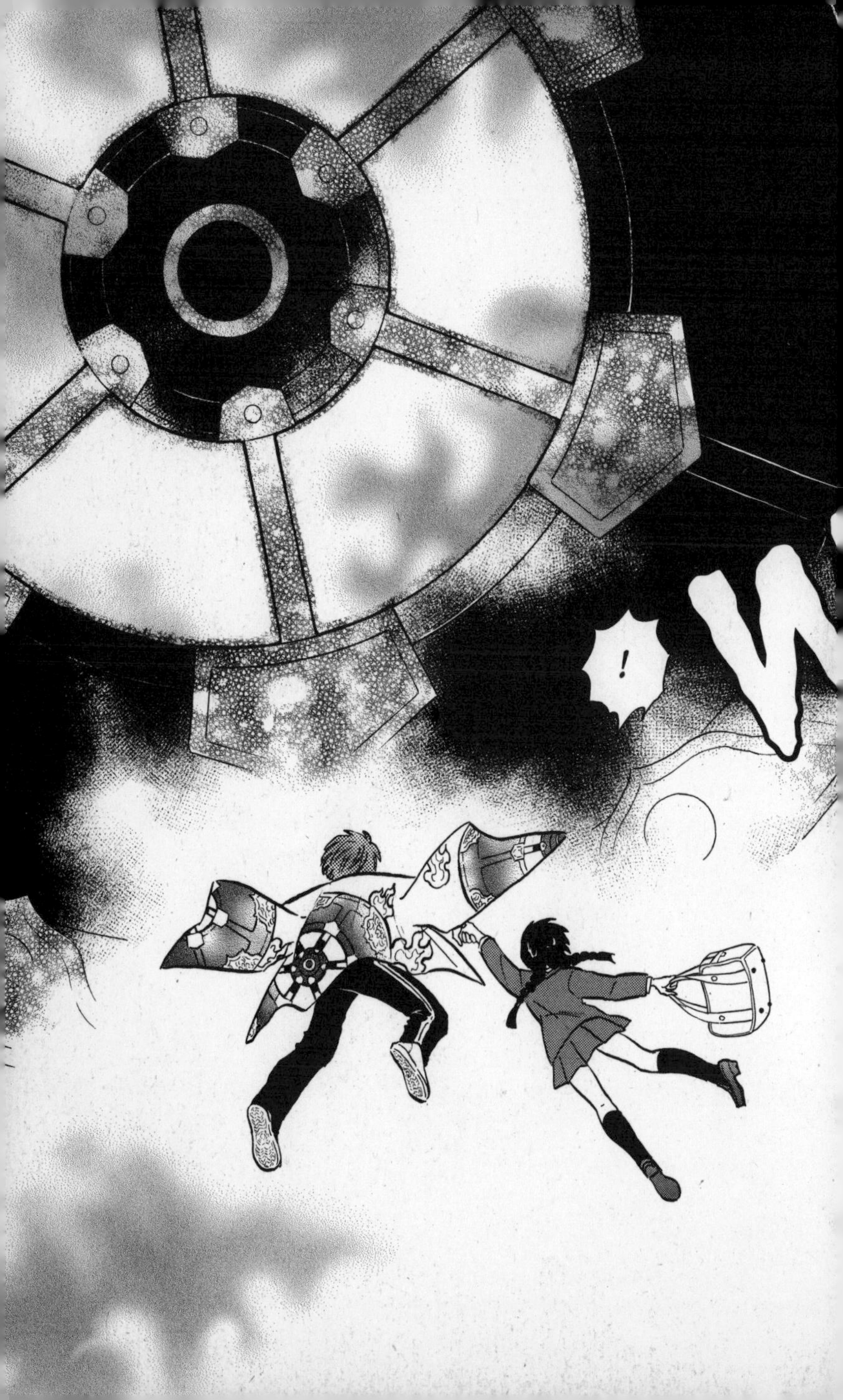
!

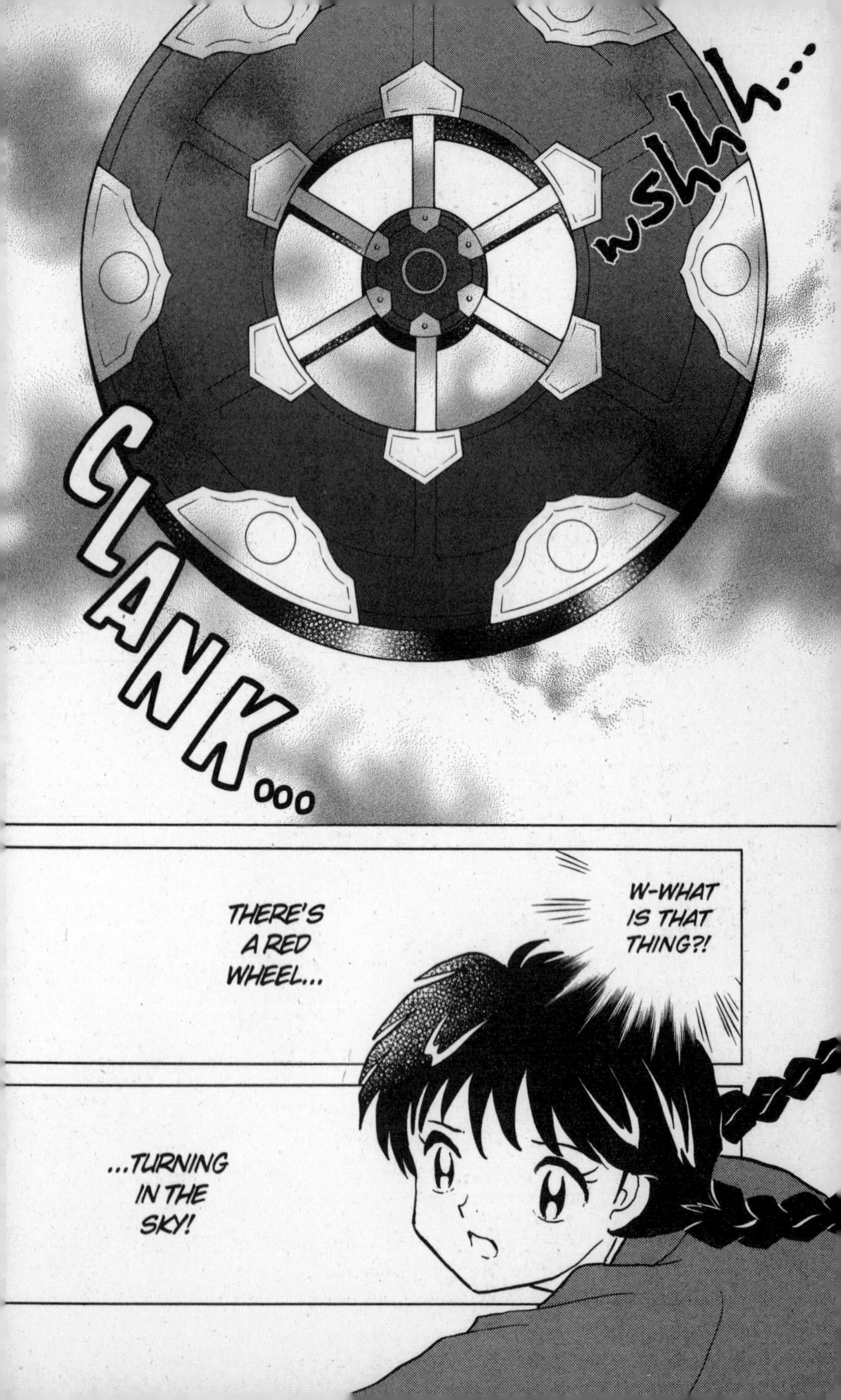
wshhh...
CLANK...
W-WHAT IS THAT THING?!
THERE'S A RED WHEEL...
...TURNING IN THE SKY!

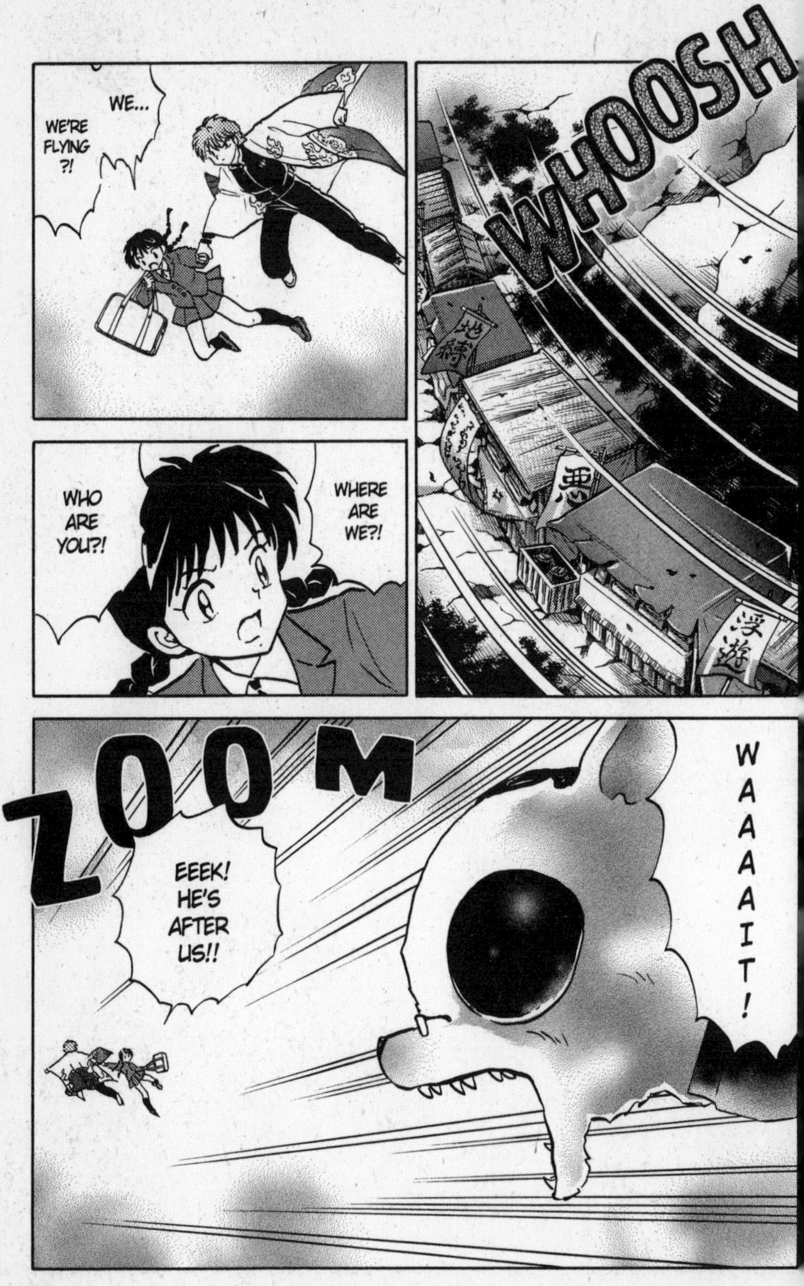
WHOOSH
WE...
WE'RE FLYING ?!
WHERE ARE WE?!
WHO ARE YOU?!
WAAAAAIT!
ZOOM
EEEK! HE'S AFTER US!!

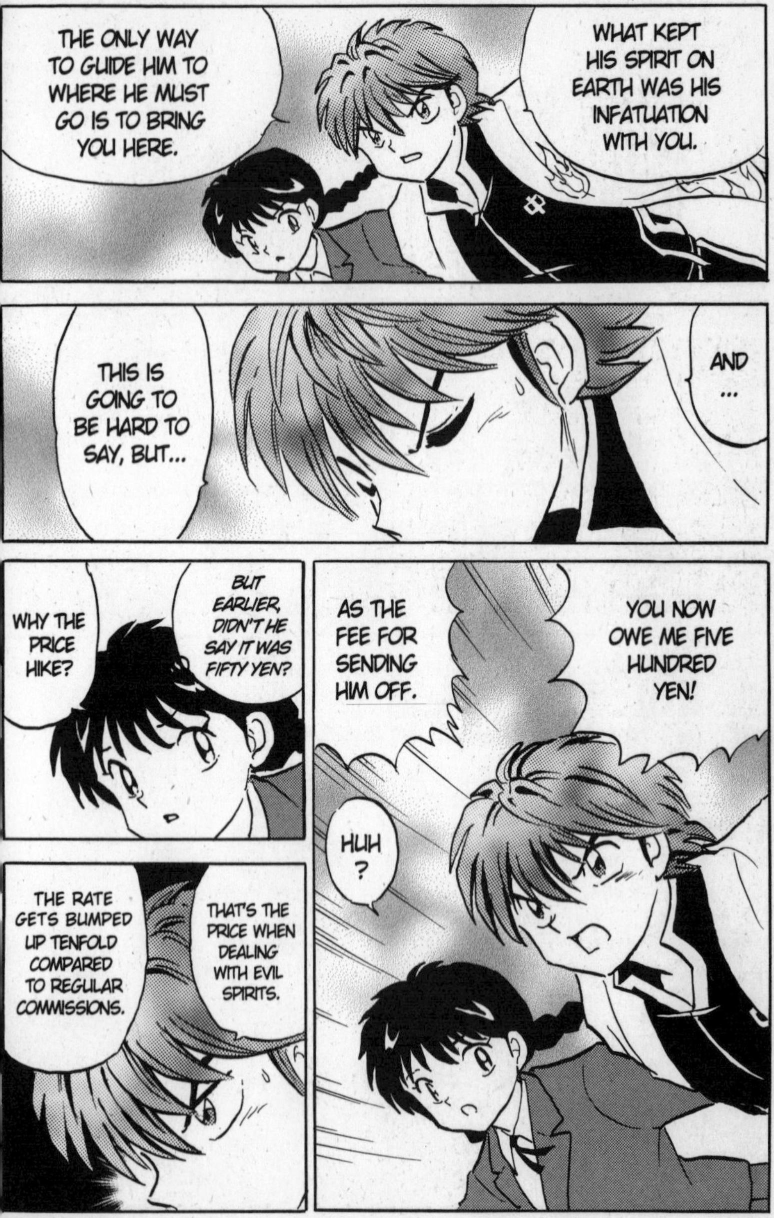
WHAT KEPT HIS SPIRIT ON EARTH WAS HIS INFATUATION WITH YOU.
THE ONLY WAY TO GUIDE HIM TO WHERE HE MUST GO IS TO BRING YOU HERE.
AND ...
THIS IS GOING TO BE HARD TO SAY, BUT...
YOU NOW OWE ME FIVE HUNDRED YEN!
AS THE FEE FOR SENDING HIM OFF.
HUH ?
BUT EARLIER, DIDN'T HE SAY IT WAS FIFTY YEN?
WHY THE PRICE HIKE?
THAT'S THE PRICE WHEN DEALING WITH EVIL SPIRITS.
THE RATE GETS BUMPED UP TENFOLD COMPARED TO REGULAR COMMISSIONS.

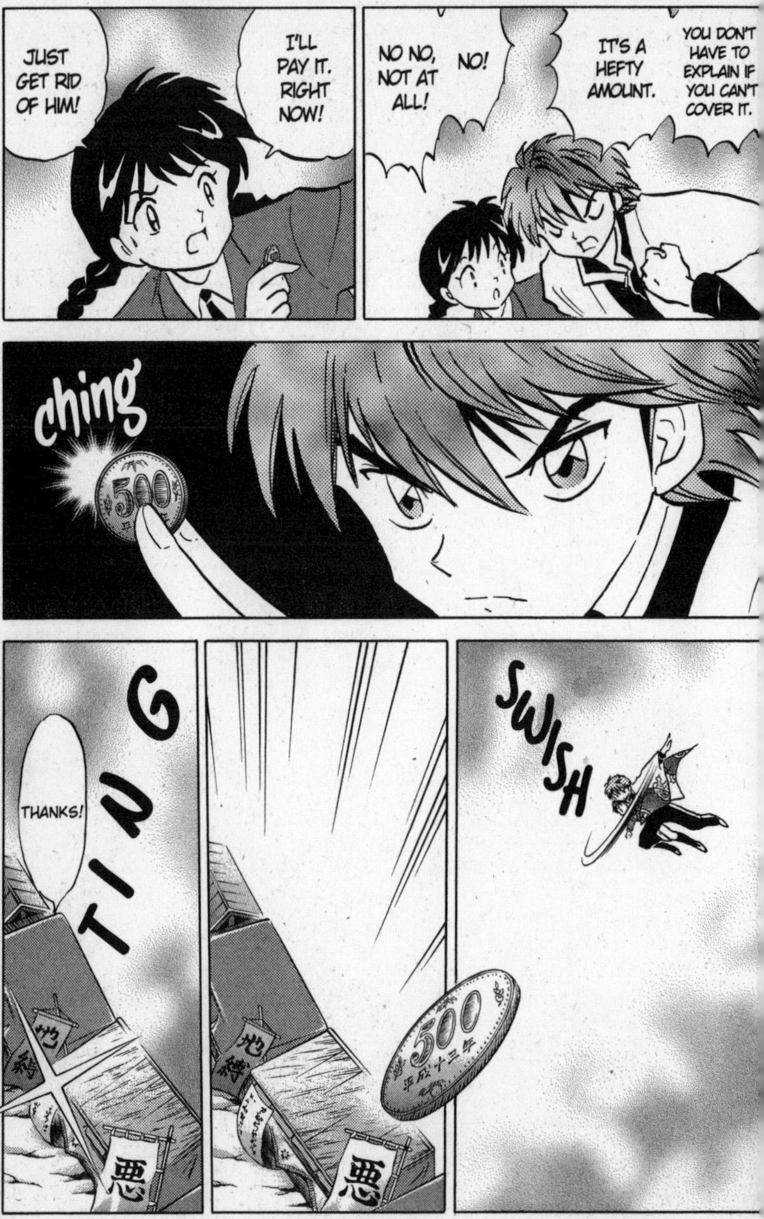
YOU DON'T HAVE TO EXPLAIN IF YOU CAN'T COVER IT.
IT'S A HEFTY AMOUNT.
NO!
NO NO, NOT AT ALL!
I'LL PAY IT. RIGHT NOW!
JUST GET RID OF HIM!
ching
SWISH
TING
THANKS!

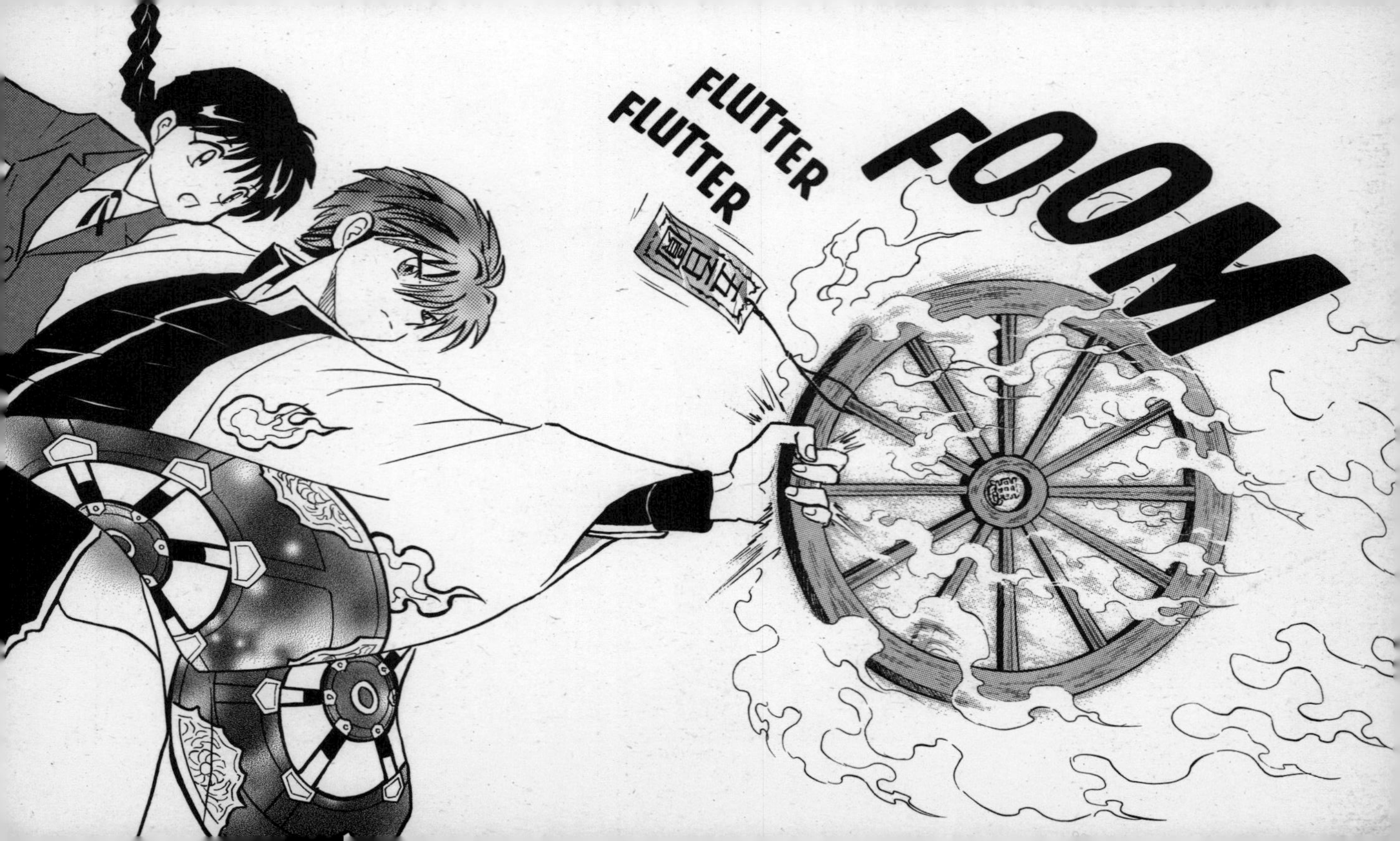
FOOM
FLUTTER
FLUTTER
五百圓

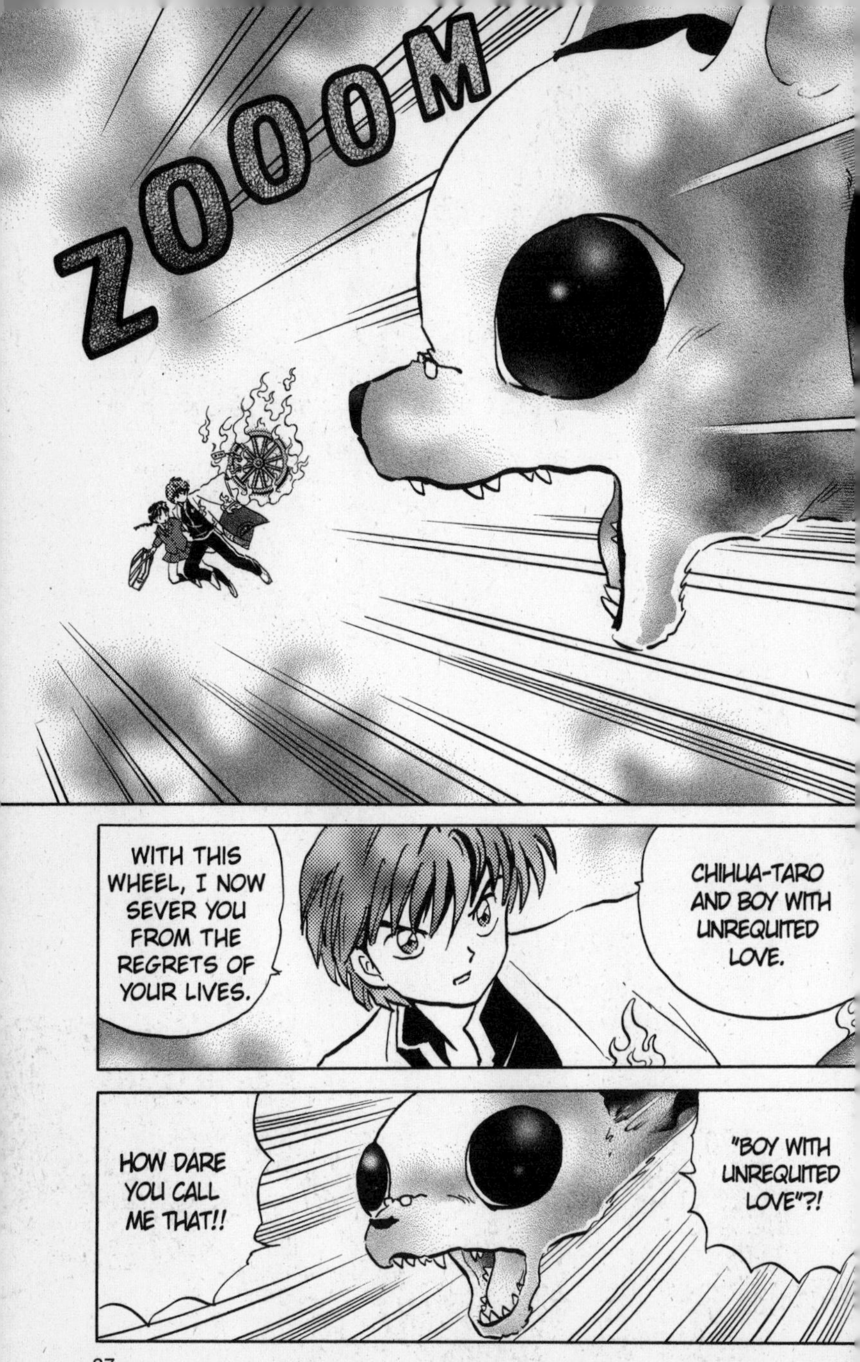
ZOOOOM
CHIHUA-TARO AND BOY WITH UNREQUITED LOVE.
WITH THIS WHEEL, I NOW SEVER YOU FROM THE REGRETS OF YOUR LIVES.
"BOY WITH UNREQUITED LOVE"?!
HOW DARE YOU CALL ME THAT!!

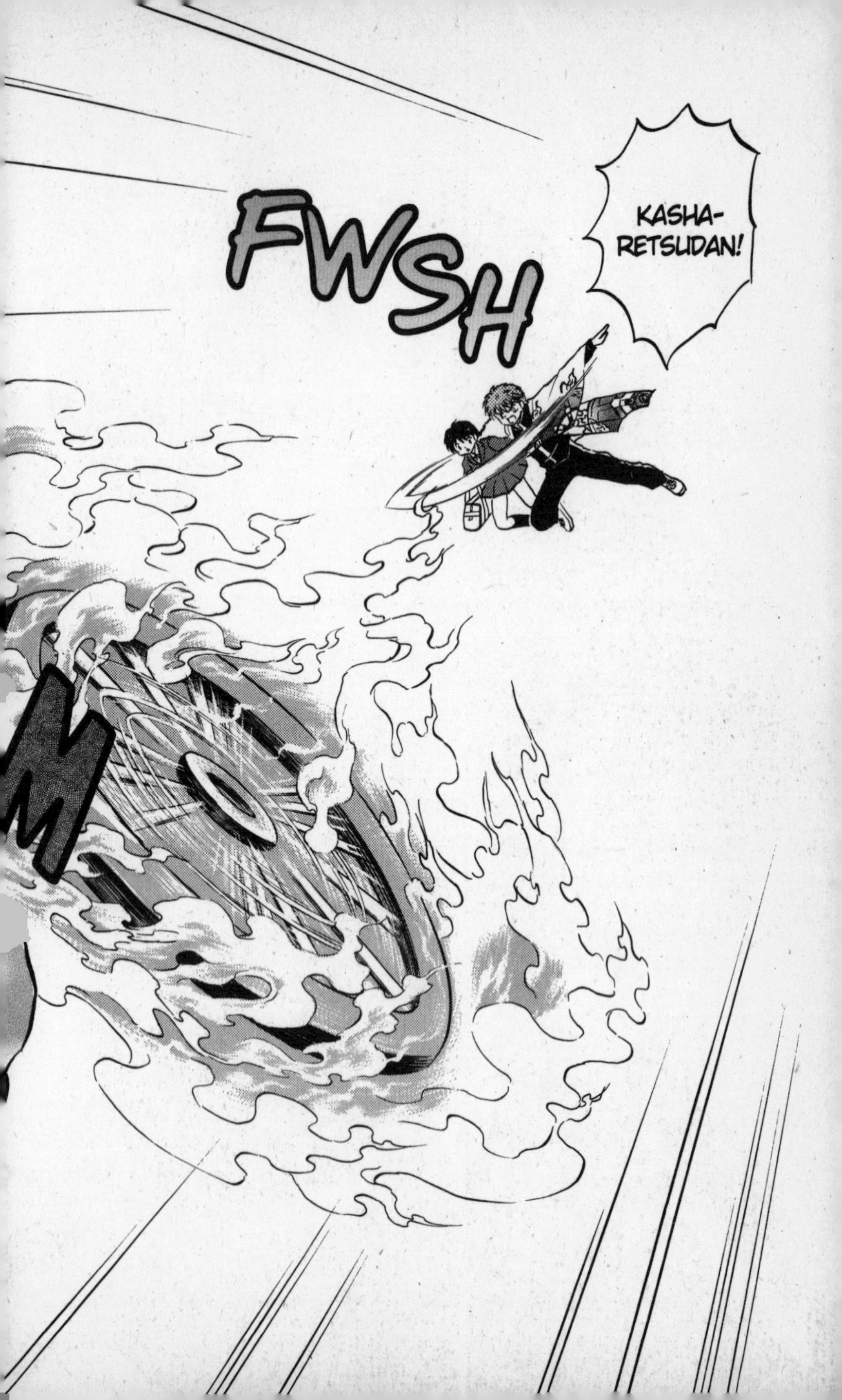
KASHA-
RETSUDAN!
FWSH

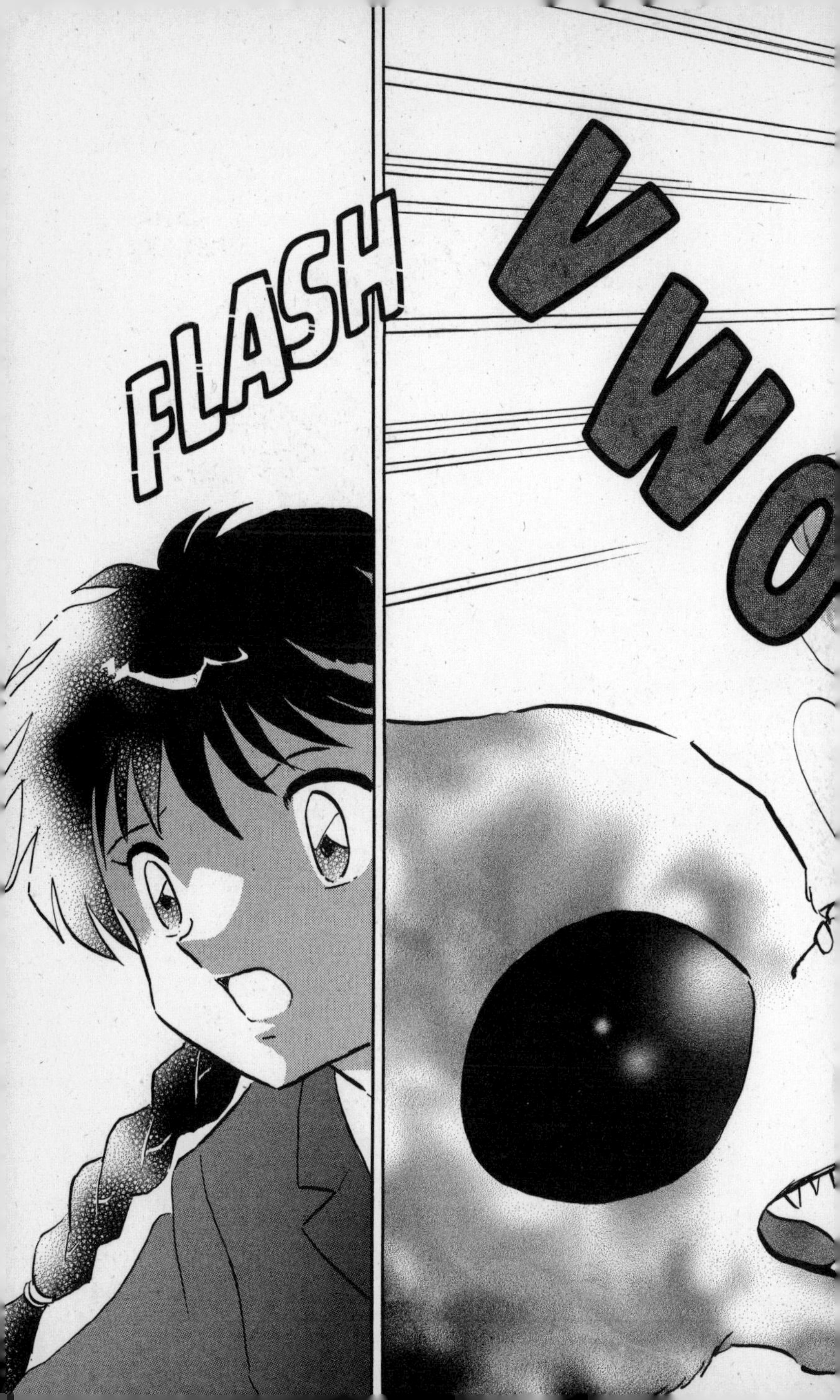
VWOO
FLASH

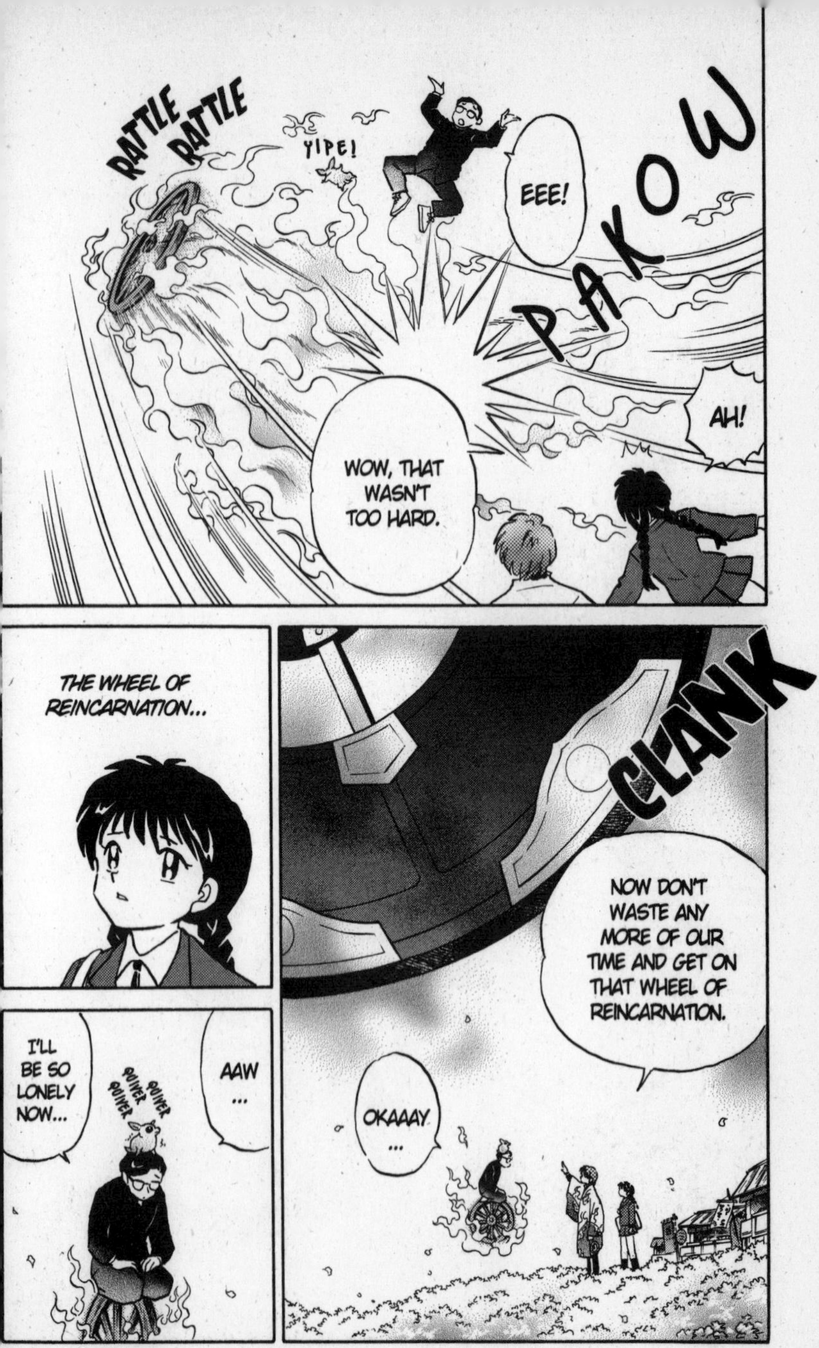
PAKOW
EEE!
AH!
YIPE!
RATTLE RATTLE
WOW, THAT WASN'T TOO HARD.
CLANK
NOW DON'T WASTE ANY MORE OF OUR TIME AND GET ON THAT WHEEL OF REINCARNATION.
OKAAAY ...
THE WHEEL OF REINCARNATION...
AAW ...
QUIVER QUIVER QUIVER
I'LL BE SO LONELY NOW...

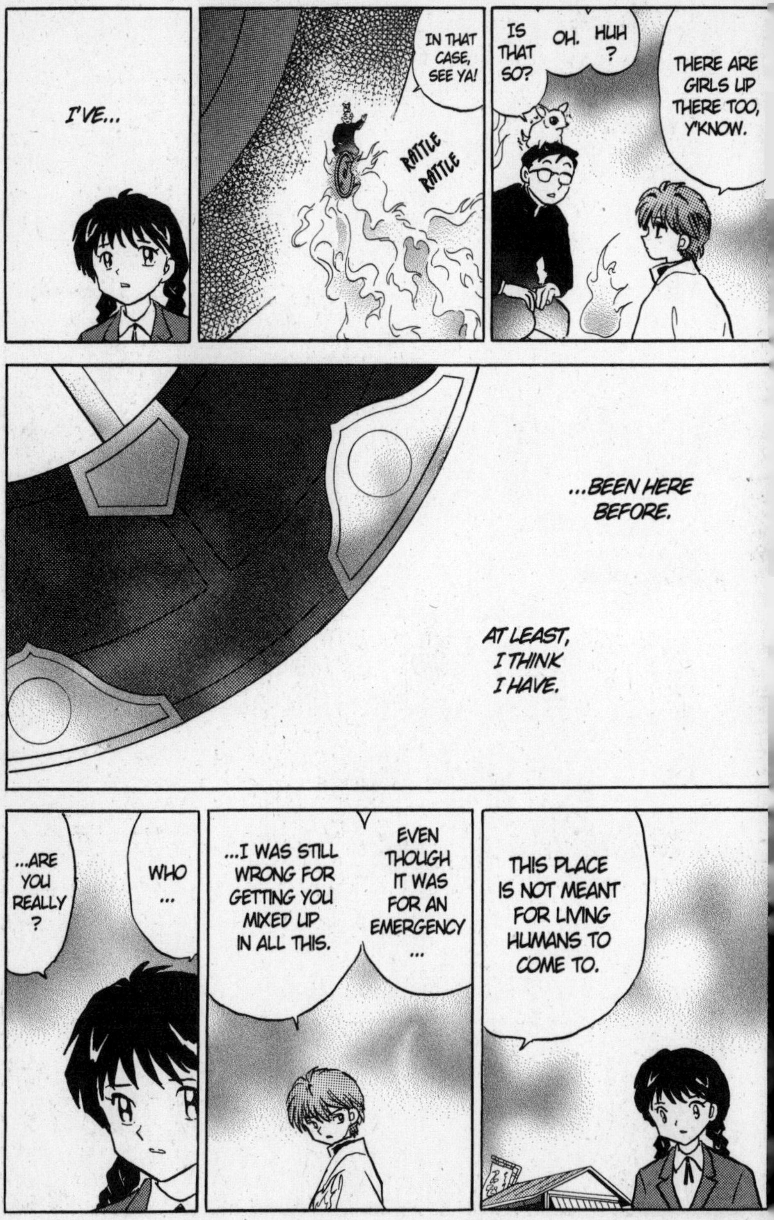
THERE ARE GIRLS UP THERE TOO, Y'KNOW.
HUH?
OH.
IS THAT SO?
IN THAT CASE, SEE YA!
RATTLE RATTLE
I'VE...
...BEEN HERE BEFORE.
AT LEAST, I THINK I HAVE.
THIS PLACE IS NOT MEANT FOR LIVING HUMANS TO COME TO.
EVEN THOUGH IT WAS FOR AN EMERGENCY...
...I WAS STILL WRONG FOR GETTING YOU MIXED UP IN ALL THIS.
WHO...
...ARE YOU REALLY?

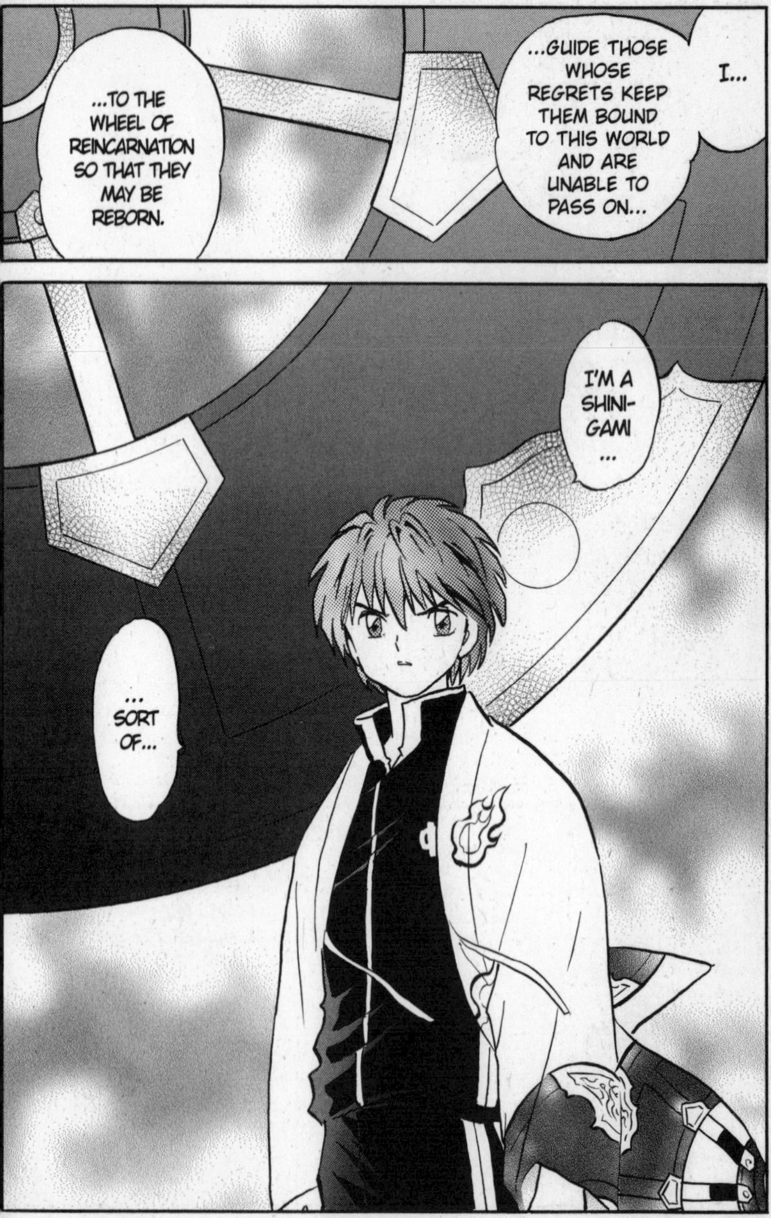
I...
...GUIDE THOSE WHOSE REGRETS KEEP THEM BOUND TO THIS WORLD AND ARE UNABLE TO PASS ON...
...TO THE WHEEL OF REINCARNATION SO THAT THEY MAY BE REBORN.
I'M A SHINI-GAMI ...
... SORT OF...

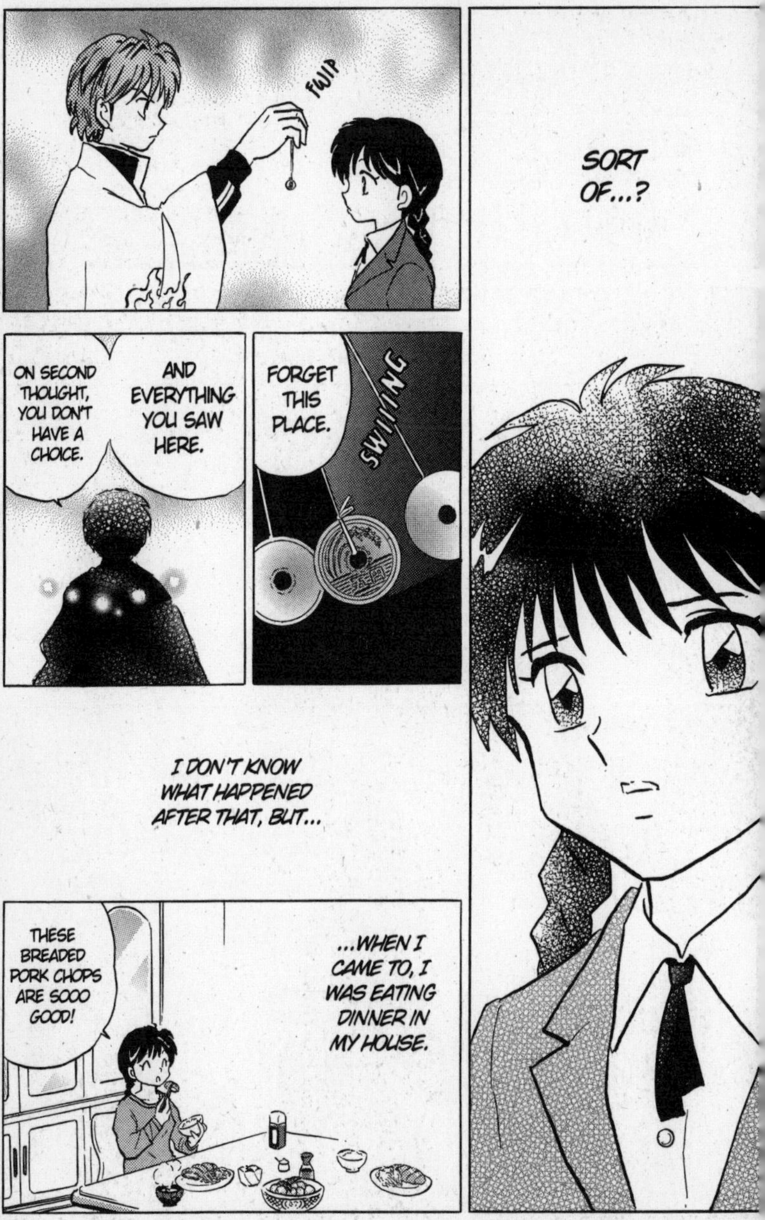
SORT OF...?
FWIP
FORGET THIS PLACE.
SWIIING
AND EVERYTHING YOU SAW HERE.
ON SECOND THOUGHT, YOU DON'T HAVE A CHOICE.
I DON'T KNOW WHAT HAPPENED AFTER THAT, BUT...
...WHEN I CAME TO, I WAS EATING DINNER IN MY HOUSE.
THESE BREADED PORK CHOPS ARE SOOO GOOD!

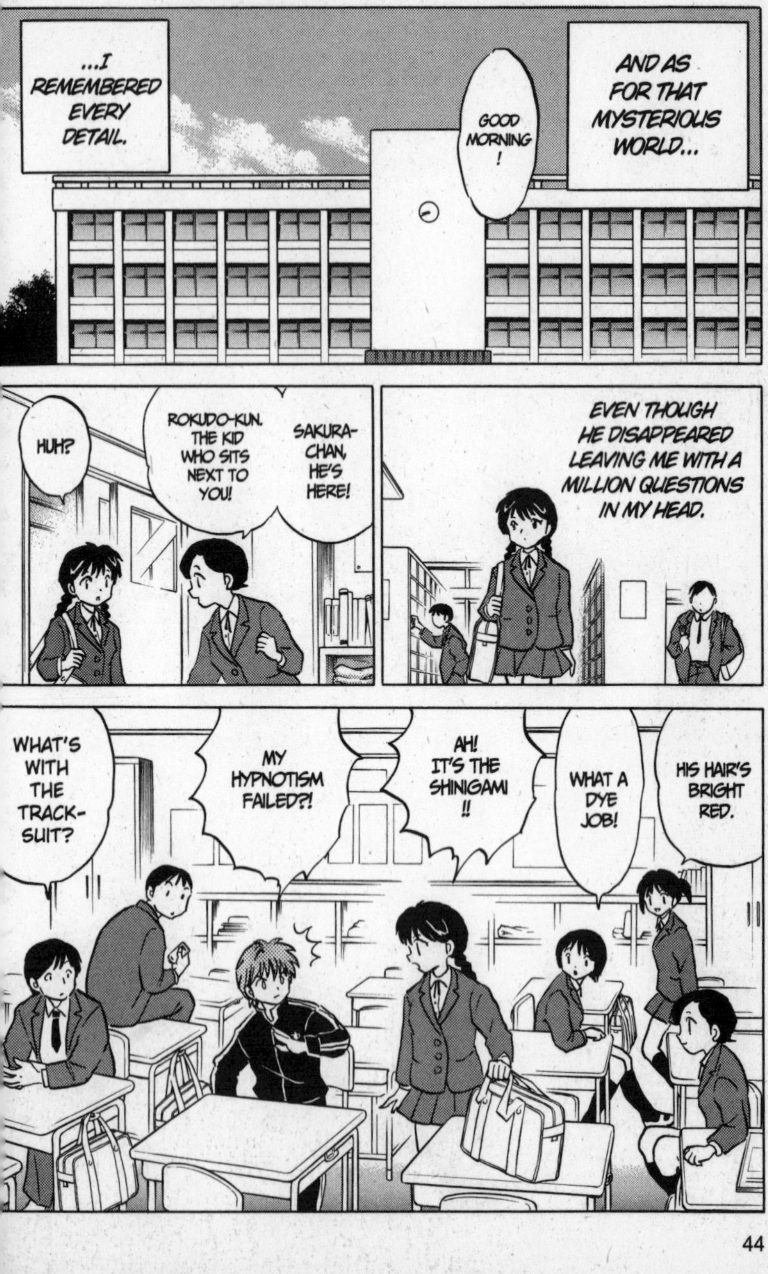
AND AS FOR THAT MYSTERIOUS WORLD...
GOOD MORNING!
...I REMEMBERED EVERY DETAIL.
EVEN THOUGH HE DISAPPEARED LEAVING ME WITH A MILLION QUESTIONS IN MY HEAD.
SAKURA-CHAN, HE'S HERE!
ROKUDO-KUN. THE KID WHO SITS NEXT TO YOU!
HUH?
HIS HAIR'S BRIGHT RED.
WHAT A DYE JOB!
AH! IT'S THE SHINIGAMI!!
MY HYPNOTISM FAILED?!
WHAT'S WITH THE TRACK-SUIT?

CHAPTER 2: THE LEGEND OF THE WEATHER HUTCH

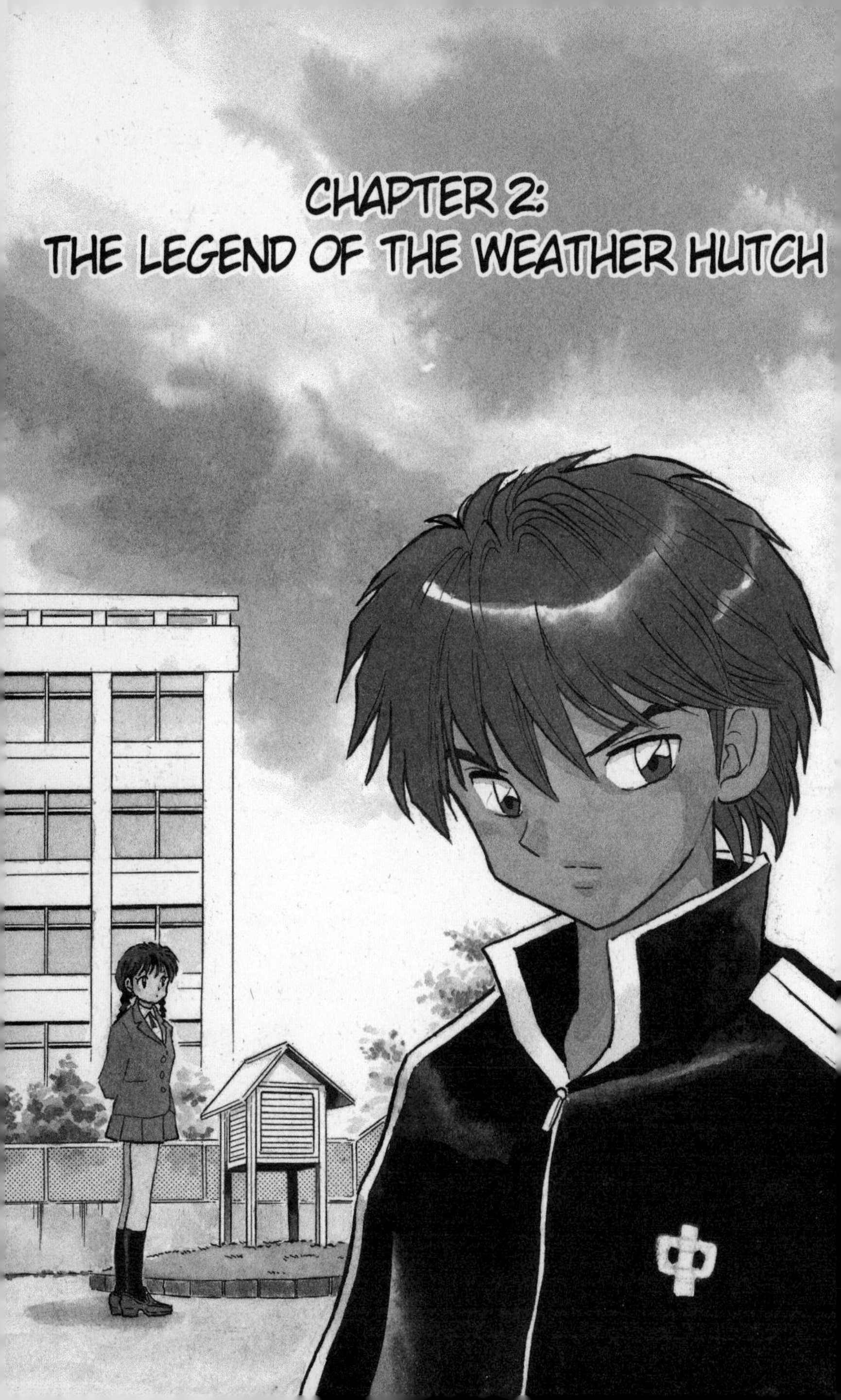

RIN-NE

雇用契約書
雇用主
被雇用者
六文

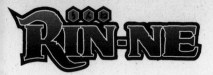

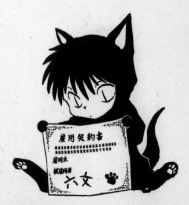

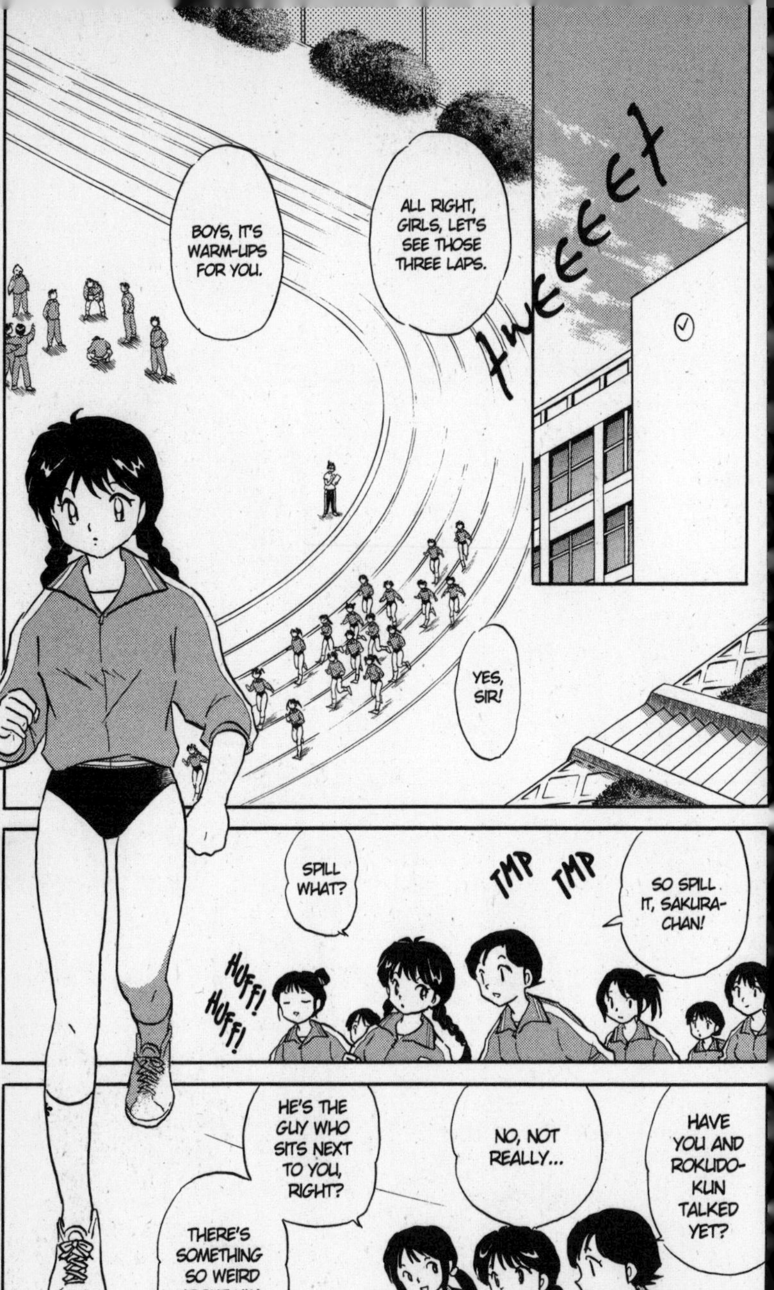
tweeeet
ALL RIGHT, GIRLS, LET'S SEE THOSE THREE LAPS.
BOYS, IT'S WARM-UPS FOR YOU.
YES, SIR!
SO SPILL IT, SAKURA-CHAN!
TMP TMP
SPILL WHAT?
HUFF! HUFF!
HAVE YOU AND ROKUDO-KUN TALKED YET?
NO, NOT REALLY...
HE'S THE GUY WHO SITS NEXT TO YOU, RIGHT?
THERE'S SOMETHING SO WEIRD ABOUT HIM.

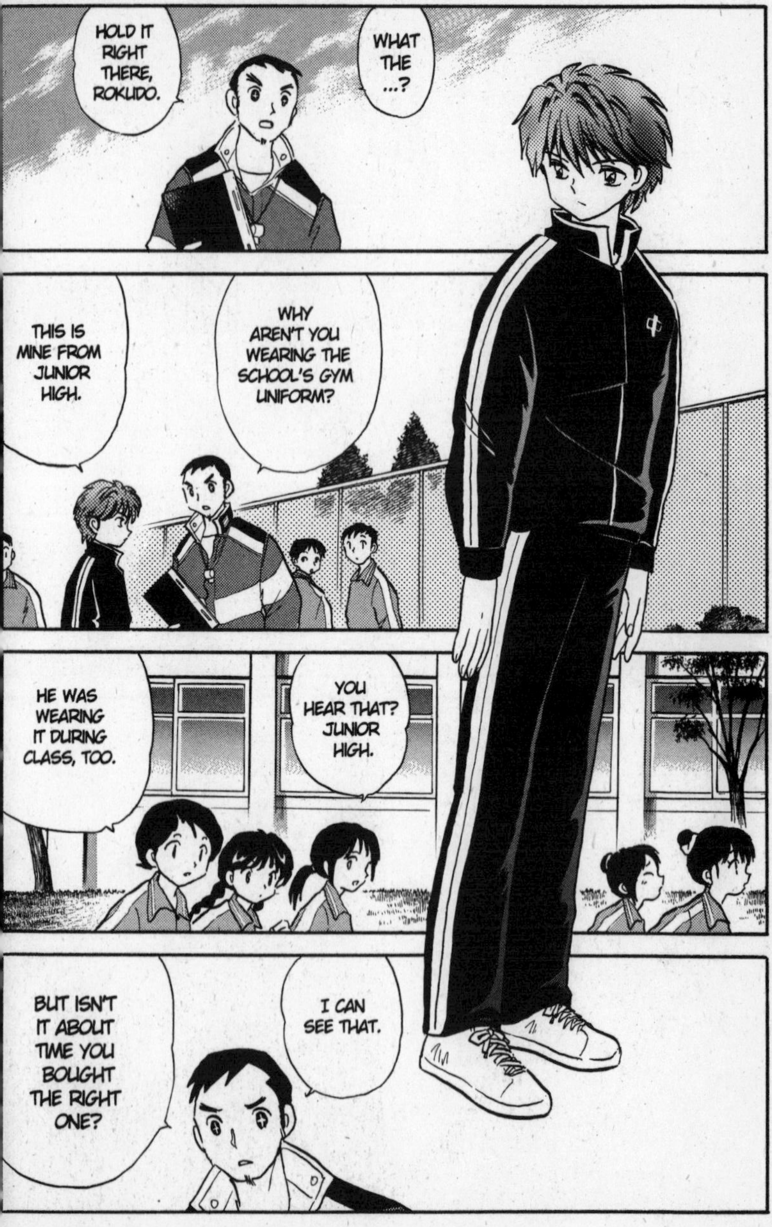
WHAT THE ...?
HOLD IT RIGHT THERE, ROKUDO.
WHY AREN'T YOU WEARING THE SCHOOL'S GYM UNIFORM?
THIS IS MINE FROM JUNIOR HIGH.
YOU HEAR THAT? JUNIOR HIGH.
HE WAS WEARING IT DURING CLASS, TOO.
I CAN SEE THAT.
BUT ISN'T IT ABOUT TIME YOU BOUGHT THE RIGHT ONE?

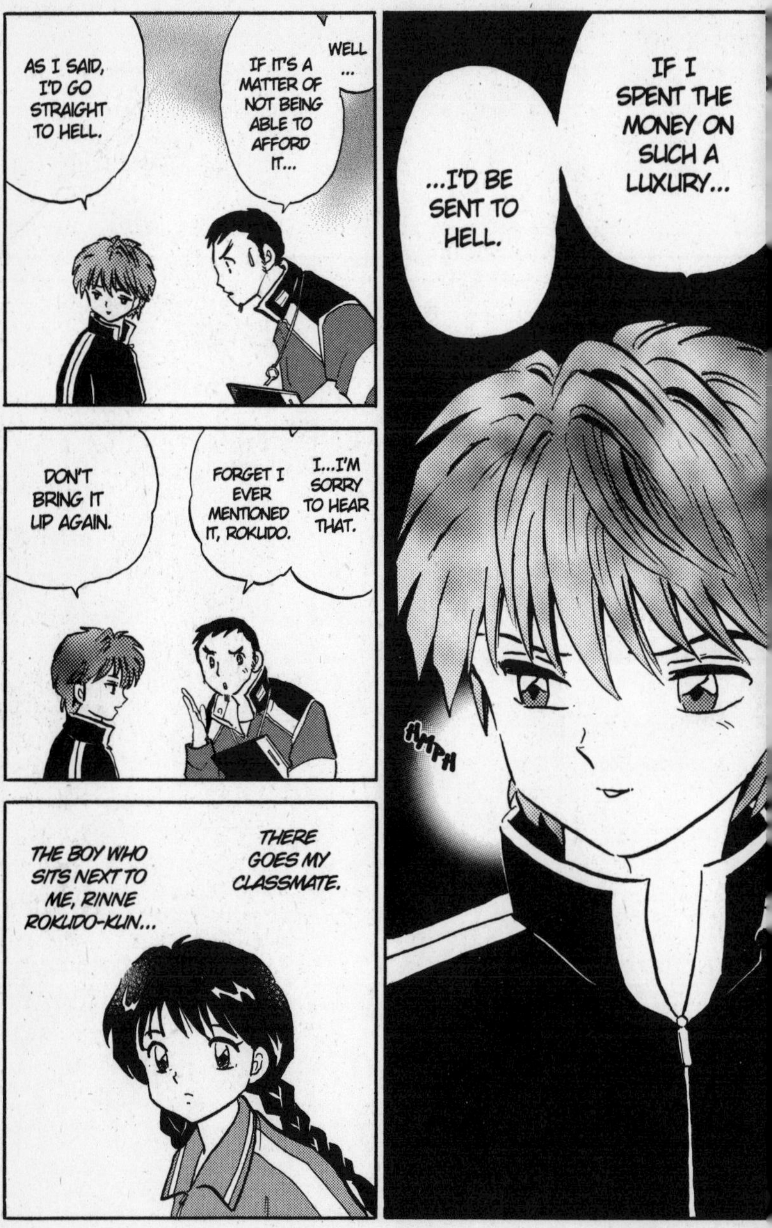
IF I SPENT THE MONEY ON SUCH A LUXURY...
...I'D BE SENT TO HELL.
HMPH
WELL ...
IF IT'S A MATTER OF NOT BEING ABLE TO AFFORD IT...
AS I SAID, I'D GO STRAIGHT TO HELL.
I...I'M SORRY TO HEAR THAT.
FORGET I EVER MENTIONED IT, ROKUDO.
DON'T BRING IT UP AGAIN.
THERE GOES MY CLASSMATE.
THE BOY WHO SITS NEXT TO ME, RINNE ROKUDO-KUN...

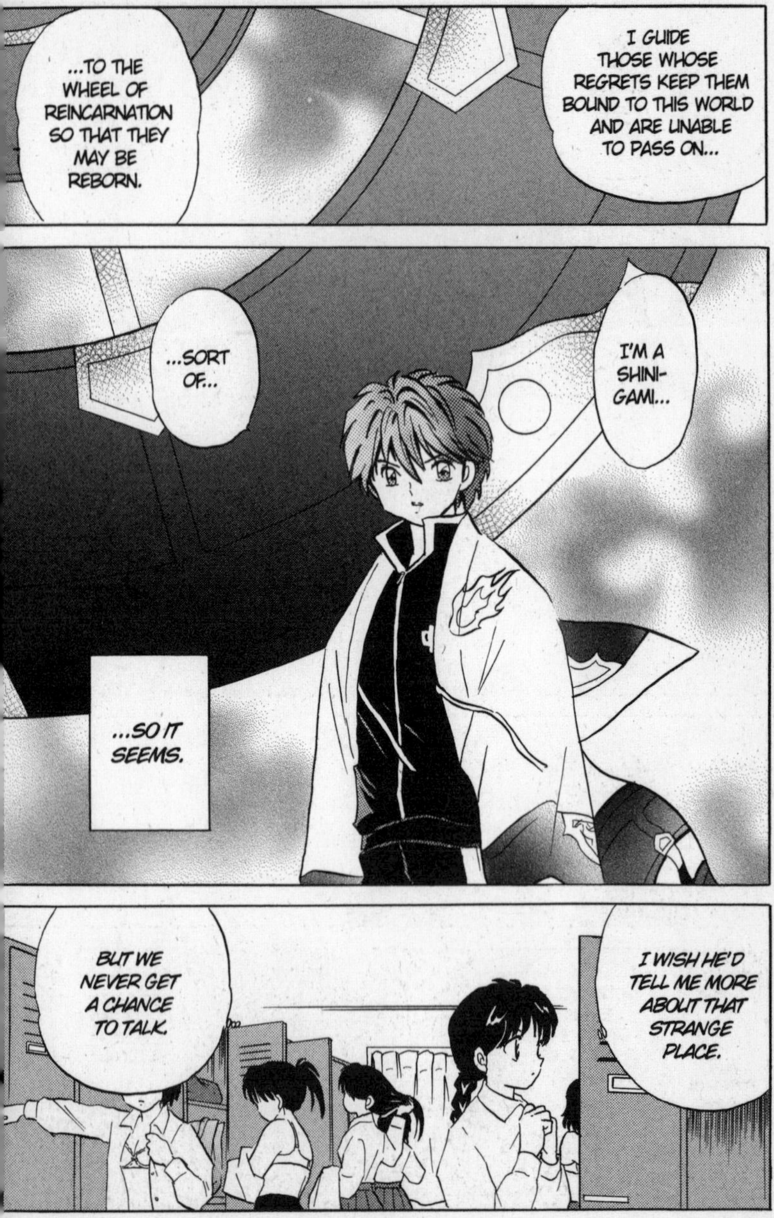
I GUIDE THOSE WHOSE REGRETS KEEP THEM BOUND TO THIS WORLD AND ARE UNABLE TO PASS ON...
...TO THE WHEEL OF REINCARNATION SO THAT THEY MAY BE REBORN.
I'M A SHINI-GAMI...
...SORT OF...
...SO IT SEEMS.
I WISH HE'D TELL ME MORE ABOUT THAT STRANGE PLACE.
BUT WE NEVER GET A CHANCE TO TALK.

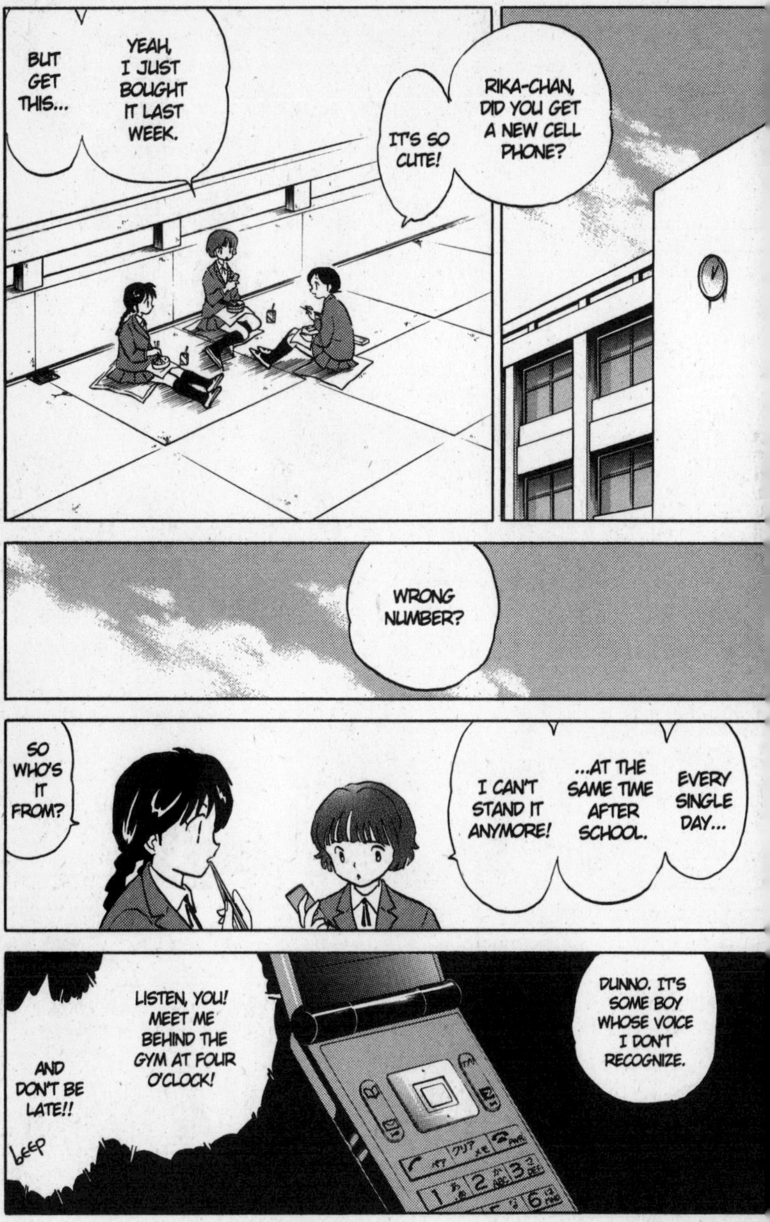
RIKA-CHAN, DID YOU GET A NEW CELL PHONE?
IT'S SO CUTE!
YEAH, I JUST BOUGHT IT LAST WEEK.
BUT GET THIS...
WRONG NUMBER?
EVERY SINGLE DAY...
...AT THE SAME TIME AFTER SCHOOL.
I CAN'T STAND IT ANYMORE!
SO WHO'S IT FROM?
DUNNO. IT'S SOME BOY WHOSE VOICE I DON'T RECOGNIZE.
LISTEN, YOU! MEET ME BEHIND THE GYM AT FOUR O'CLOCK!
AND DON'T BE LATE!!
beep

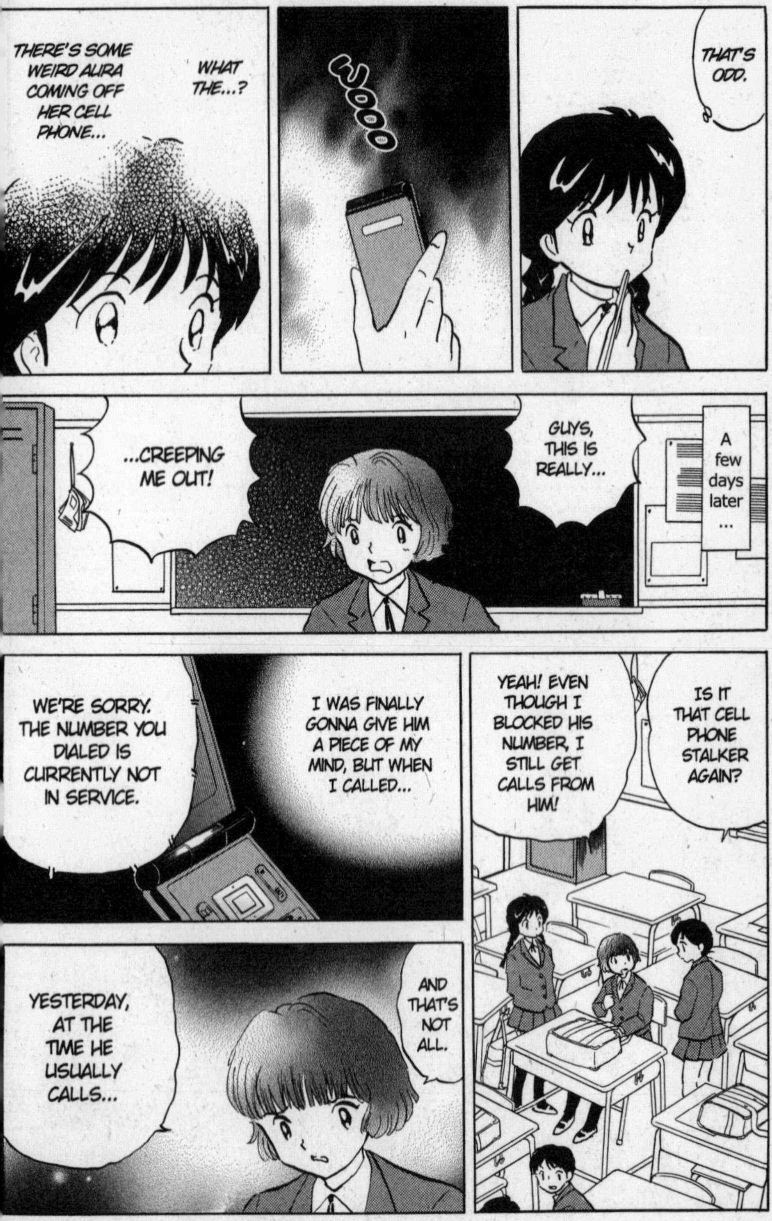
THAT'S ODD.
WOOO
WHAT THE...?
THERE'S SOME WEIRD AURA COMING OFF HER CELL PHONE...
A few days later...
GUYS, THIS IS REALLY...
...CREEPING ME OUT!
IS IT THAT CELL PHONE STALKER AGAIN?
YEAH! EVEN THOUGH I BLOCKED HIS NUMBER, I STILL GET CALLS FROM HIM!
I WAS FINALLY GONNA GIVE HIM A PIECE OF MY MIND, BUT WHEN I CALLED...
WE'RE SORRY. THE NUMBER YOU DIALED IS CURRENTLY NOT IN SERVICE.
AND THAT'S NOT ALL.
YESTERDAY, AT THE TIME HE USUALLY CALLS...

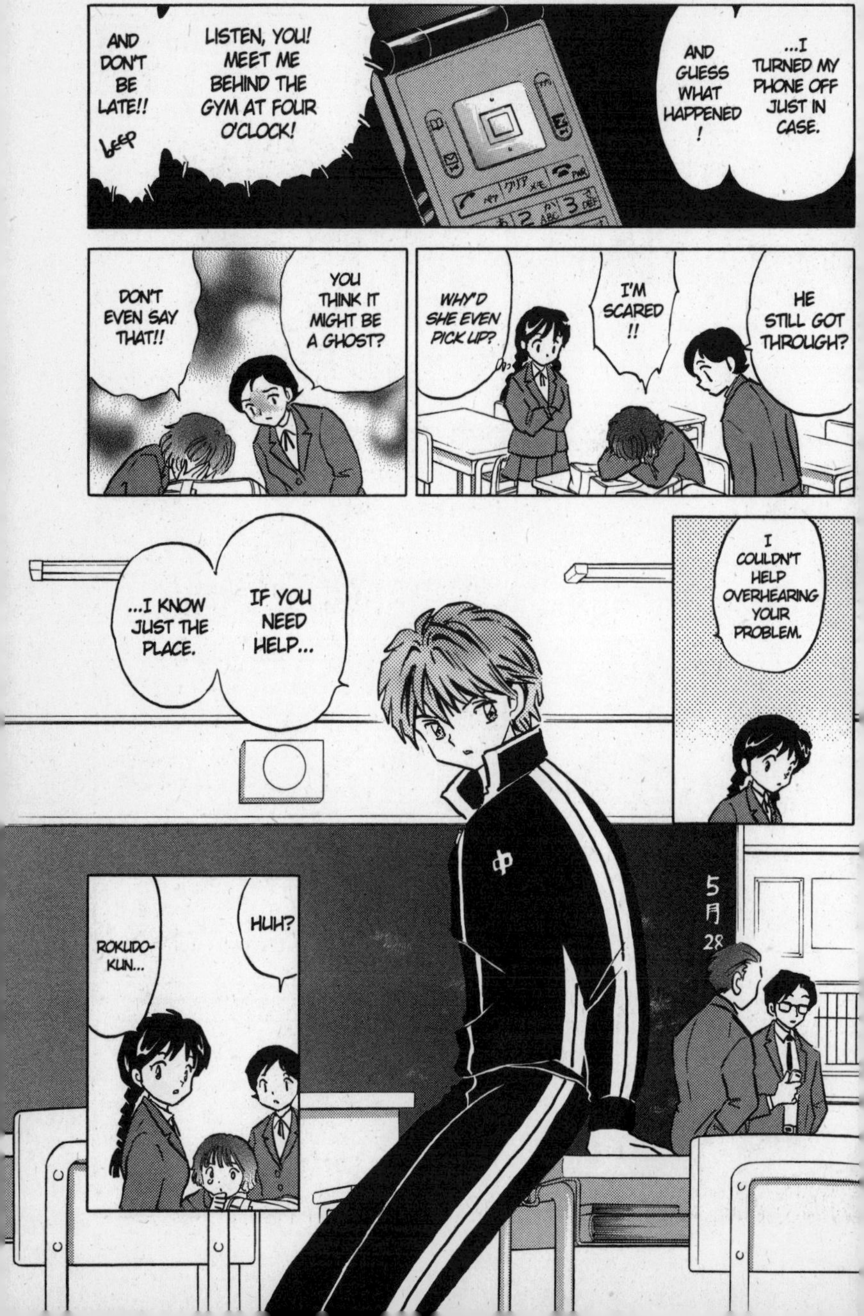
...I TURNED MY PHONE OFF JUST IN CASE.
AND GUESS WHAT HAPPENED!
LISTEN, YOU! MEET ME BEHIND THE GYM AT FOUR O'CLOCK!
AND DON'T BE LATE!!
BEEP
HE STILL GOT THROUGH?
I'M SCARED!!
WHY'D SHE EVEN PICK UP?
YOU THINK IT MIGHT BE A GHOST?
DON'T EVEN SAY THAT!!
I COULDN'T HELP OVERHEARING YOUR PROBLEM.
IF YOU NEED HELP...
...I KNOW JUST THE PLACE.
5月 28
HUH?
ROKUDO-KUN...

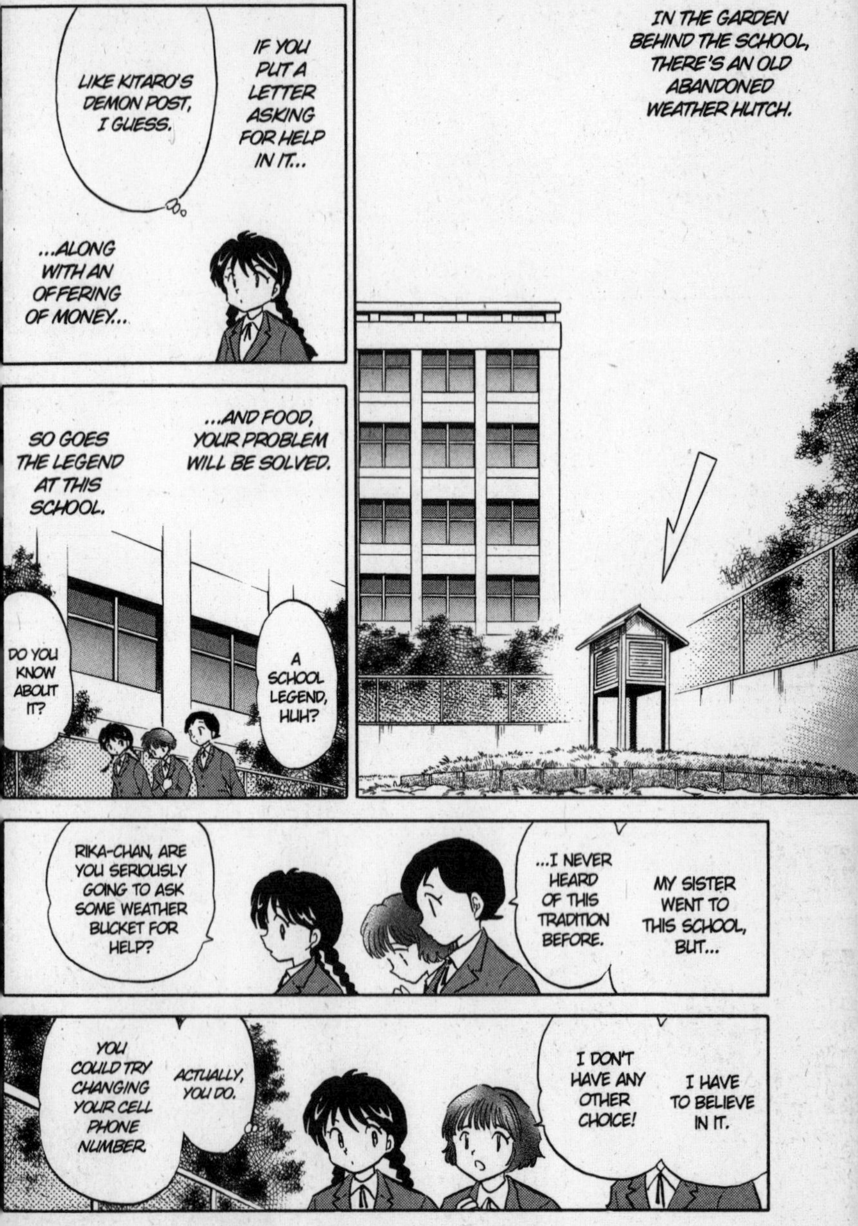

IN THE GARDEN BEHIND THE SCHOOL, THERE'S AN OLD ABANDONED WEATHER HUTCH.
IF YOU PUT A LETTER ASKING FOR HELP IN IT...
LIKE KITARO'S DEMON POST, I GUESS.
...ALONG WITH AN OFFERING OF MONEY...
...AND FOOD, YOUR PROBLEM WILL BE SOLVED.
SO GOES THE LEGEND AT THIS SCHOOL.
A SCHOOL LEGEND, HUH?
DO YOU KNOW ABOUT IT?
MY SISTER WENT TO THIS SCHOOL, BUT...
...I NEVER HEARD OF THIS TRADITION BEFORE.
RIKA-CHAN, ARE YOU SERIOUSLY GOING TO ASK SOME WEATHER BUCKET FOR HELP?
I HAVE TO BELIEVE IN IT.
I DON'T HAVE ANY OTHER CHOICE!
ACTUALLY, YOU DO.
YOU COULD TRY CHANGING YOUR CELL PHONE NUMBER.

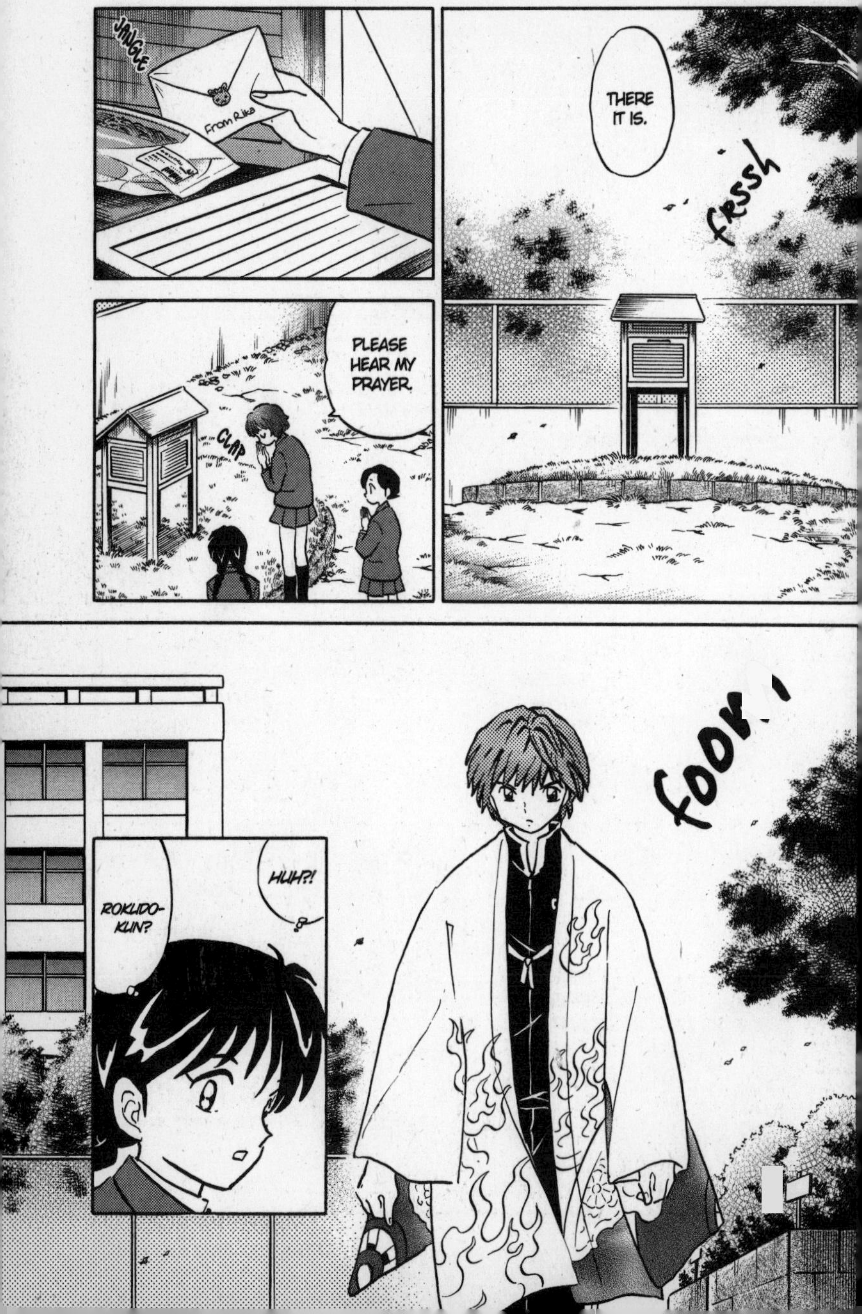
THERE IT IS.
fRSSH
JANGLE
From Rika
CLAP
PLEASE HEAR MY PRAYER.
foom
HUH?!
ROKUDO-KUN?

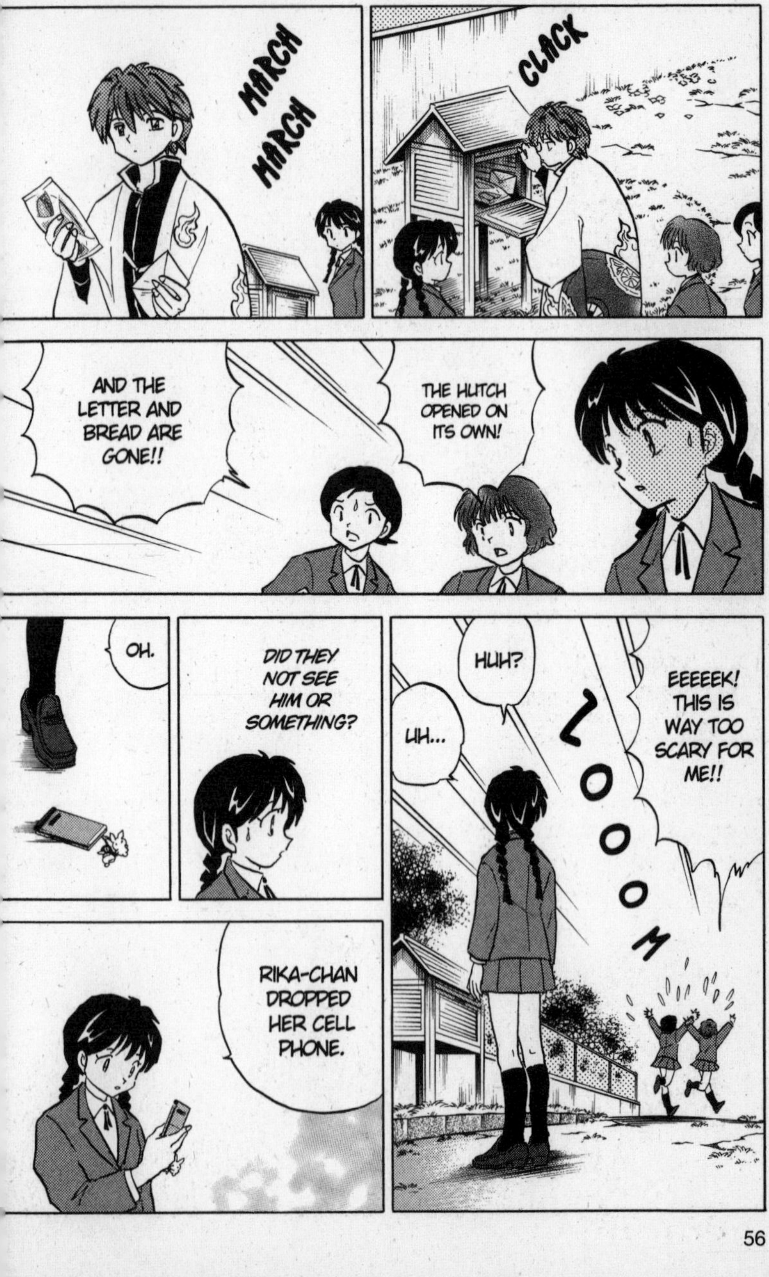
CLACK
MARCH
MARCH
THE HUTCH OPENED ON ITS OWN!
AND THE LETTER AND BREAD ARE GONE!!
EEEEEK! THIS IS WAY TOO SCARY FOR ME!!
ZOOOM
HUH?
UH...
DID THEY NOT SEE HIM OR SOMETHING?
OH.
RIKA-CHAN DROPPED HER CELL PHONE.

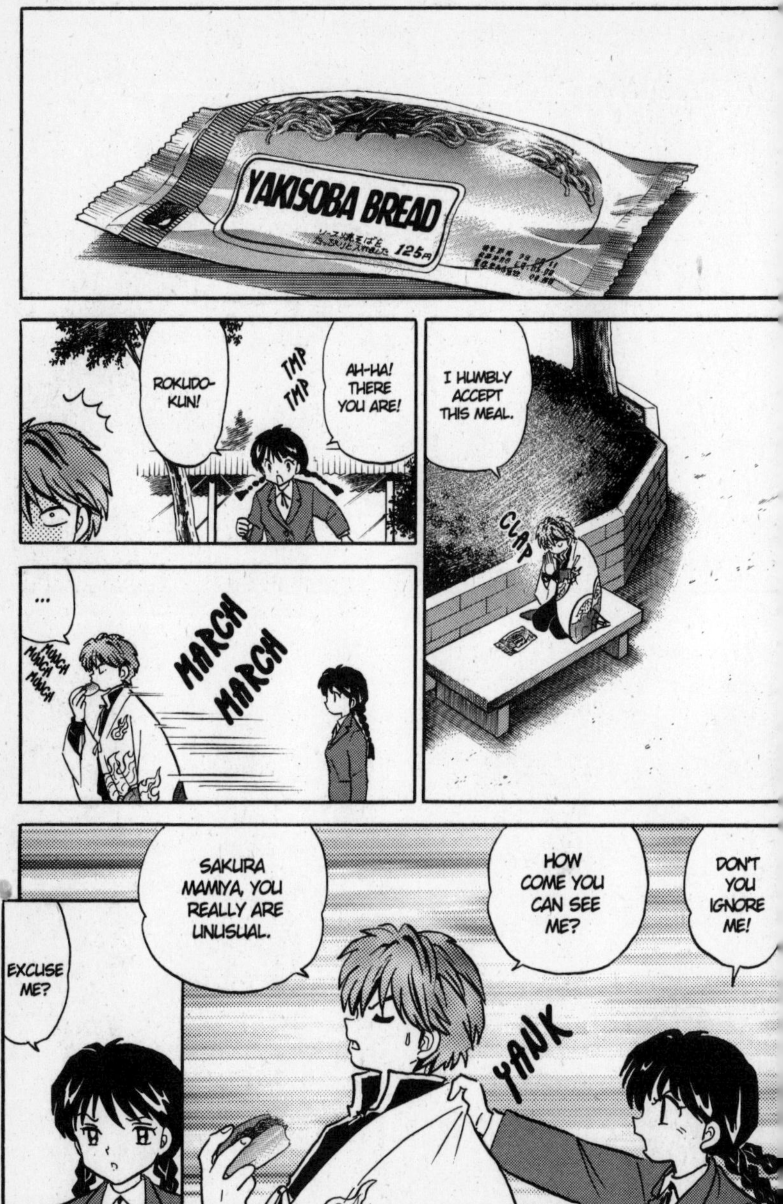
YAKISOBA BREAD
125円
I HUMBLY ACCEPT THIS MEAL.
CLAP
AH-HA! THERE YOU ARE!
TMP TMP
ROKUDO-KUN!
MARCH MARCH
MUNCH MUNCH MUNCH
...
DON'T YOU IGNORE ME!
HOW COME YOU CAN SEE ME?
YANK
SAKURA MAMIYA, YOU REALLY ARE UNUSUAL.
EXCUSE ME?

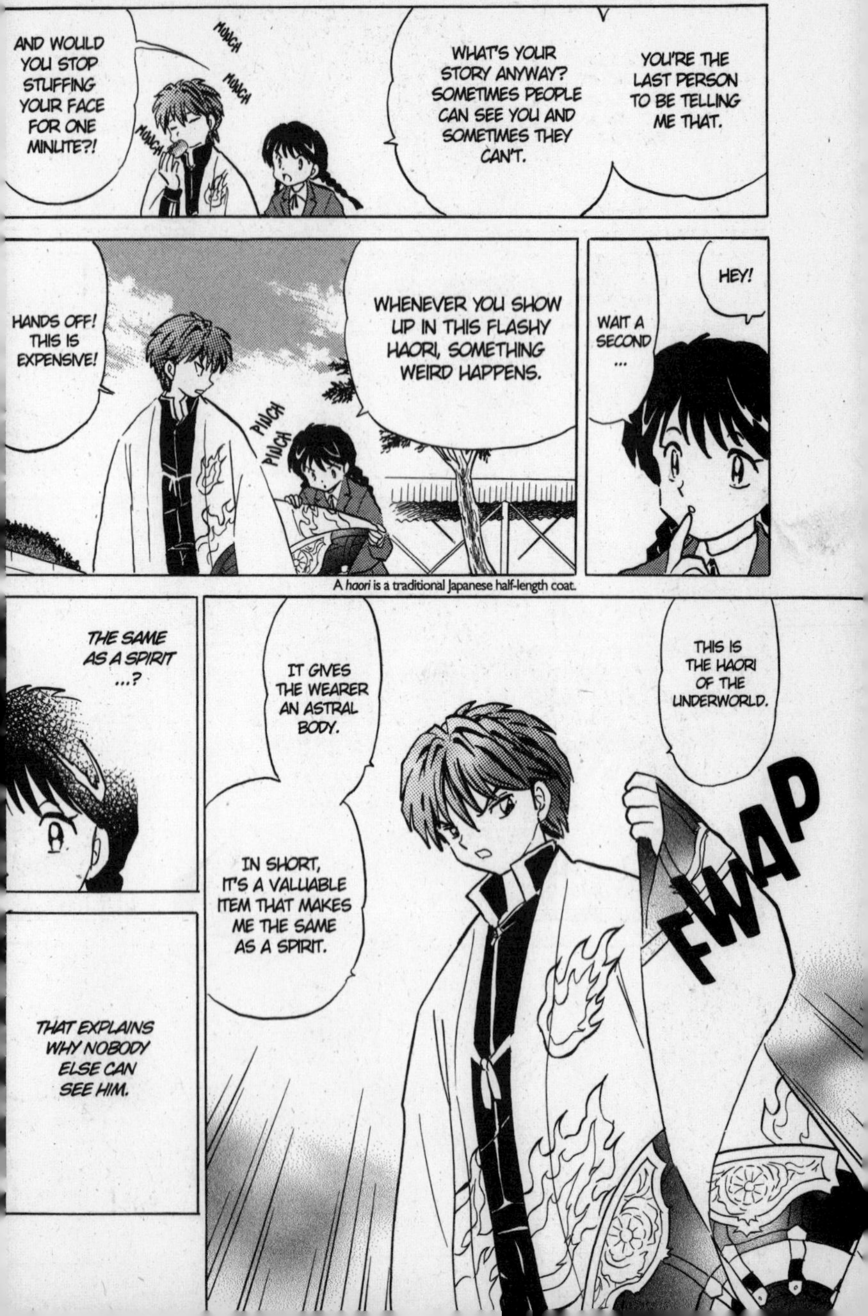
YOU'RE THE LAST PERSON TO BE TELLING ME THAT.
WHAT'S YOUR STORY ANYWAY? SOMETIMES PEOPLE CAN SEE YOU AND SOMETIMES THEY CAN'T.
MUNCH
MUNCH
MUNCH
AND WOULD YOU STOP STUFFING YOUR FACE FOR ONE MINUTE?!
HEY!
WAIT A SECOND ...
WHENEVER YOU SHOW UP IN THIS FLASHY HAORI, SOMETHING WEIRD HAPPENS.
PINCH
PINCH
HANDS OFF! THIS IS EXPENSIVE!
THIS IS THE HAORI OF THE UNDERWORLD.
FWAP
IT GIVES THE WEARER AN ASTRAL BODY.
IN SHORT, IT'S A VALUABLE ITEM THAT MAKES ME THE SAME AS A SPIRIT.
THE SAME AS A SPIRIT ...?
THAT EXPLAINS WHY NOBODY ELSE CAN SEE HIM.
A *haori* is a traditional Japanese half-length coat.

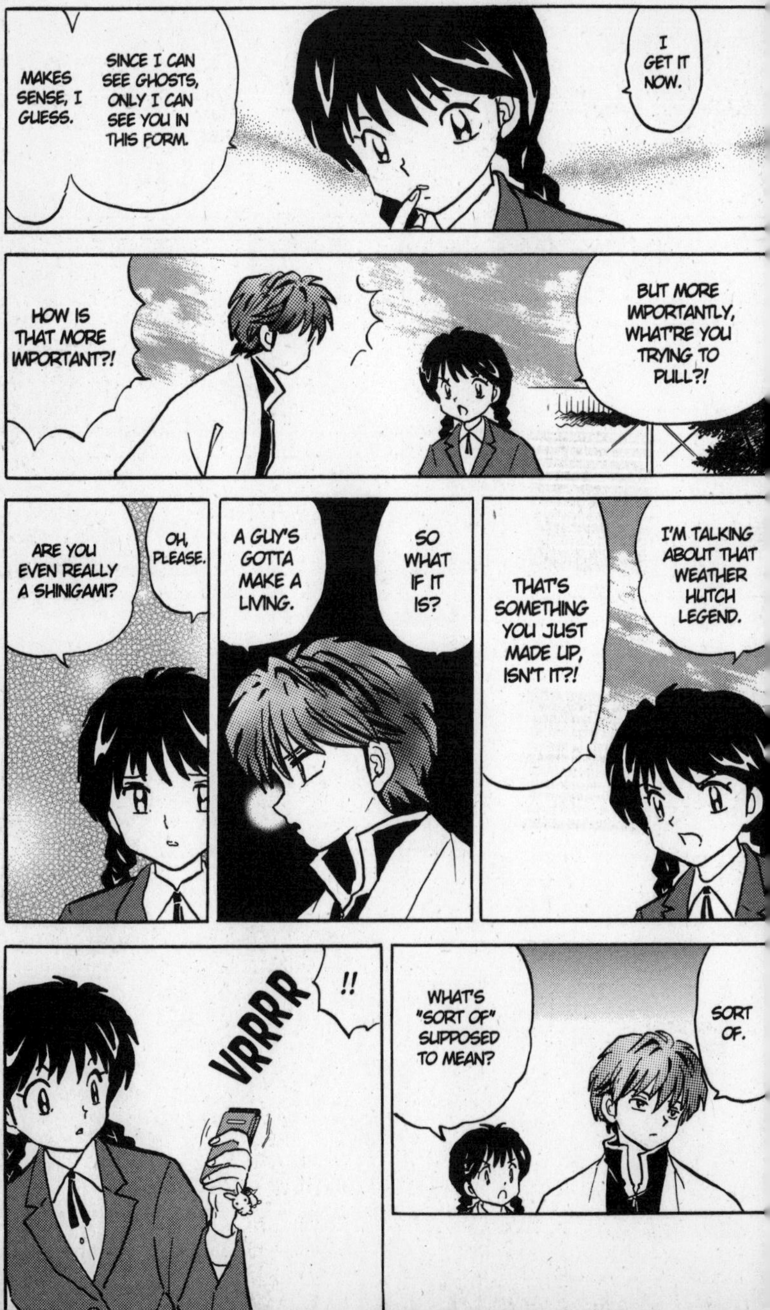
I GET IT NOW.
SINCE I CAN SEE GHOSTS, ONLY I CAN SEE YOU IN THIS FORM.
MAKES SENSE, I GUESS.
BUT MORE IMPORTANTLY, WHAT'RE YOU TRYING TO PULL?!
HOW IS THAT MORE IMPORTANT?!
I'M TALKING ABOUT THAT WEATHER HUTCH LEGEND.
THAT'S SOMETHING YOU JUST MADE UP, ISN'T IT?!
SO WHAT IF IT IS?
A GUY'S GOTTA MAKE A LIVING.
OH, PLEASE.
ARE YOU EVEN REALLY A SHINIGAMI?
SORT OF.
WHAT'S "SORT OF" SUPPOSED TO MEAN?
!!
VRRRR

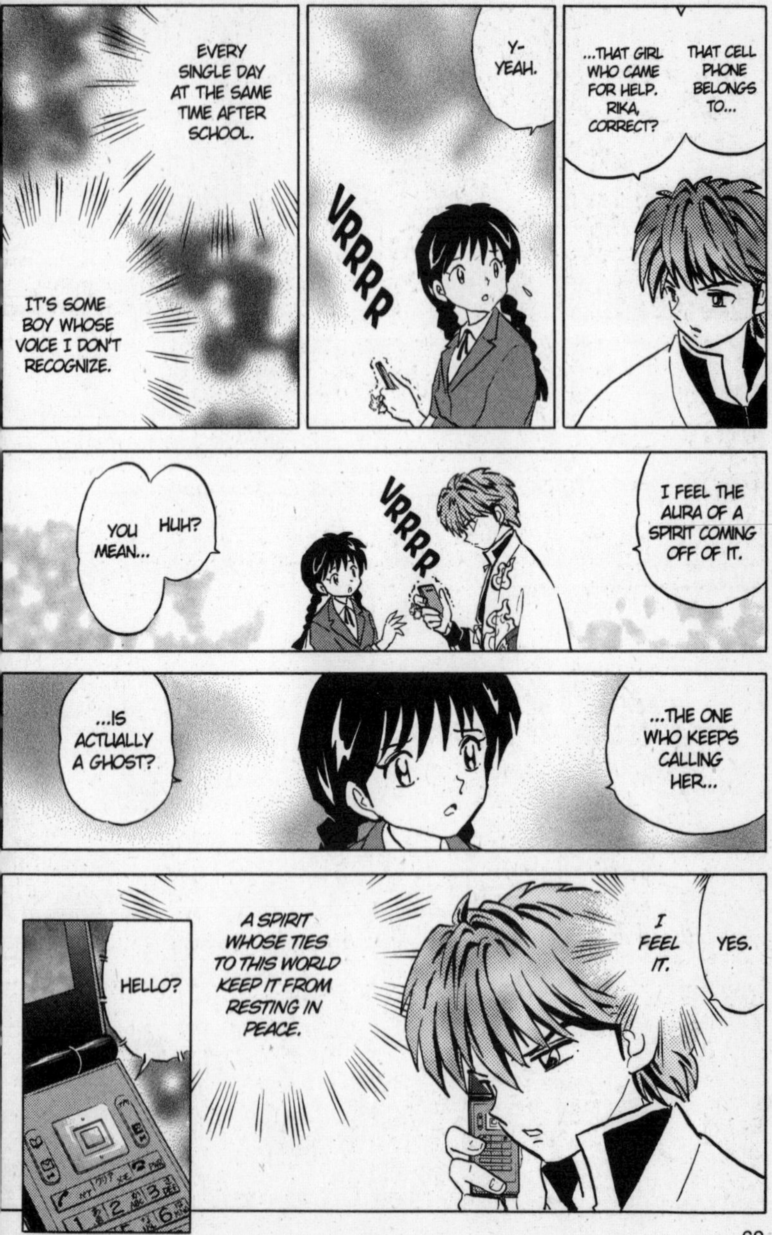
THAT CELL PHONE BELONGS TO...
...THAT GIRL WHO CAME FOR HELP. RIKA, CORRECT?
Y-YEAH.
VRRRR
EVERY SINGLE DAY AT THE SAME TIME AFTER SCHOOL.
IT'S SOME BOY WHOSE VOICE I DON'T RECOGNIZE.
I FEEL THE AURA OF A SPIRIT COMING OFF OF IT.
VRRRR
HUH?
YOU MEAN...
...THE ONE WHO KEEPS CALLING HER...
...IS ACTUALLY A GHOST?
YES.
I FEEL IT.
A SPIRIT WHOSE TIES TO THIS WORLD KEEP IT FROM RESTING IN PEACE.
HELLO?

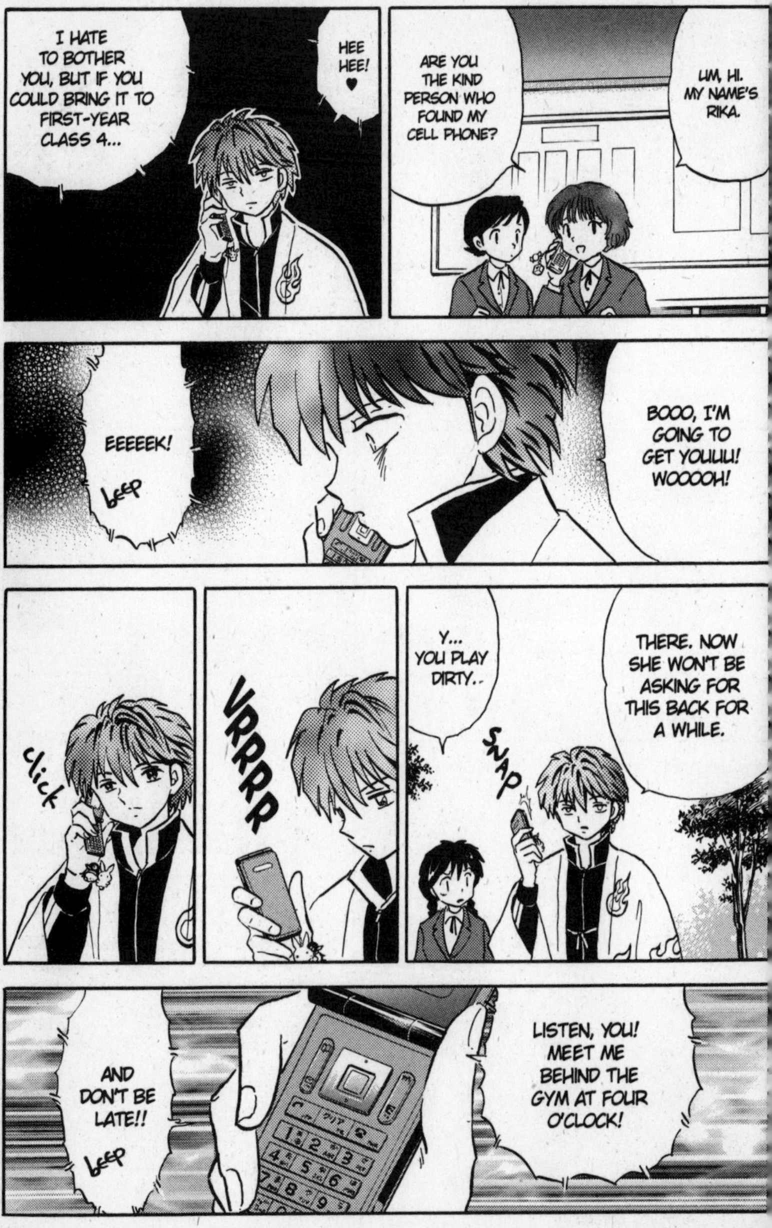
UM, HI. MY NAME'S RIKA.
ARE YOU THE KIND PERSON WHO FOUND MY CELL PHONE?
HEE HEE! ♥
I HATE TO BOTHER YOU, BUT IF YOU COULD BRING IT TO FIRST-YEAR CLASS 4...
BOOO, I'M GOING TO GET YOUUU! WOOOOH!
EEEEEK!
beep
THERE. NOW SHE WON'T BE ASKING FOR THIS BACK FOR A WHILE.
SNAP
Y... YOU PLAY DIRTY..
VRRRR
click
LISTEN, YOU! MEET ME BEHIND THE GYM AT FOUR O'CLOCK!
AND DON'T BE LATE!!
beep

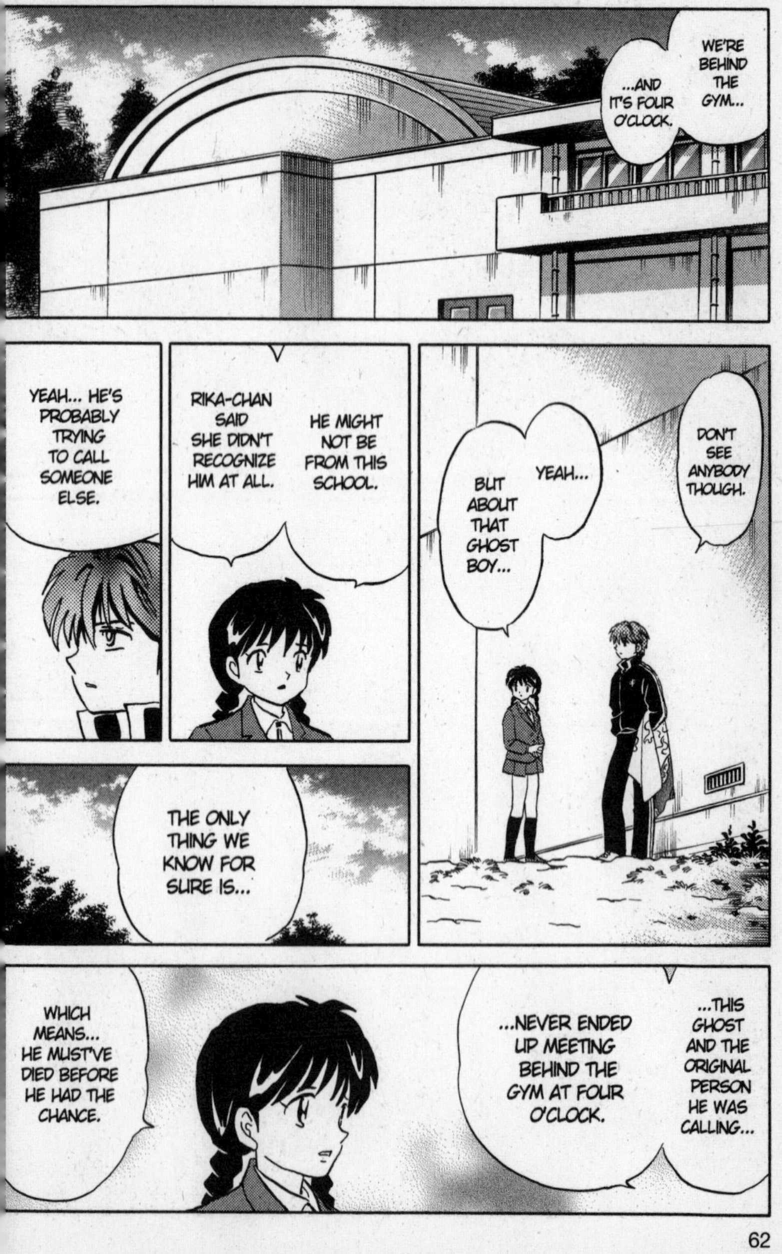
WE'RE BEHIND THE GYM...
...AND IT'S FOUR O'CLOCK.
DON'T SEE ANYBODY THOUGH.
YEAH...
BUT ABOUT THAT GHOST BOY...
RIKA-CHAN SAID SHE DIDN'T RECOGNIZE HIM AT ALL.
HE MIGHT NOT BE FROM THIS SCHOOL.
YEAH... HE'S PROBABLY TRYING TO CALL SOMEONE ELSE.
THE ONLY THING WE KNOW FOR SURE IS...
...THIS GHOST AND THE ORIGINAL PERSON HE WAS CALLING...
...NEVER ENDED UP MEETING BEHIND THE GYM AT FOUR O'CLOCK.
WHICH MEANS... HE MUST'VE DIED BEFORE HE HAD THE CHANCE.

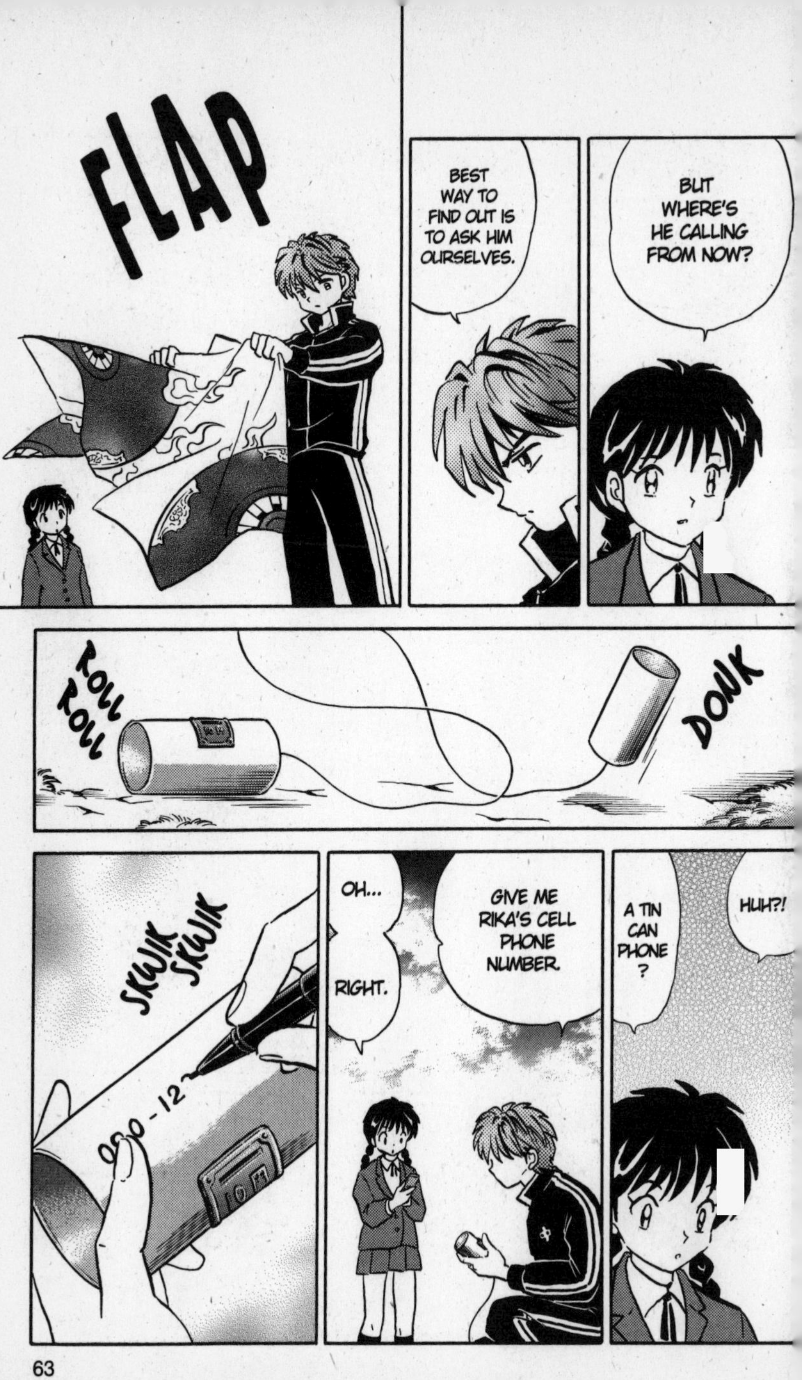
BUT WHERE'S HE CALLING FROM NOW?
BEST WAY TO FIND OUT IS TO ASK HIM OURSELVES.
FLAP
DONK
ROLL ROLL
HUH?!
A TIN CAN PHONE ?
GIVE ME RIKA'S CELL PHONE NUMBER.
OH...
RIGHT.
SKWIK SKWIK

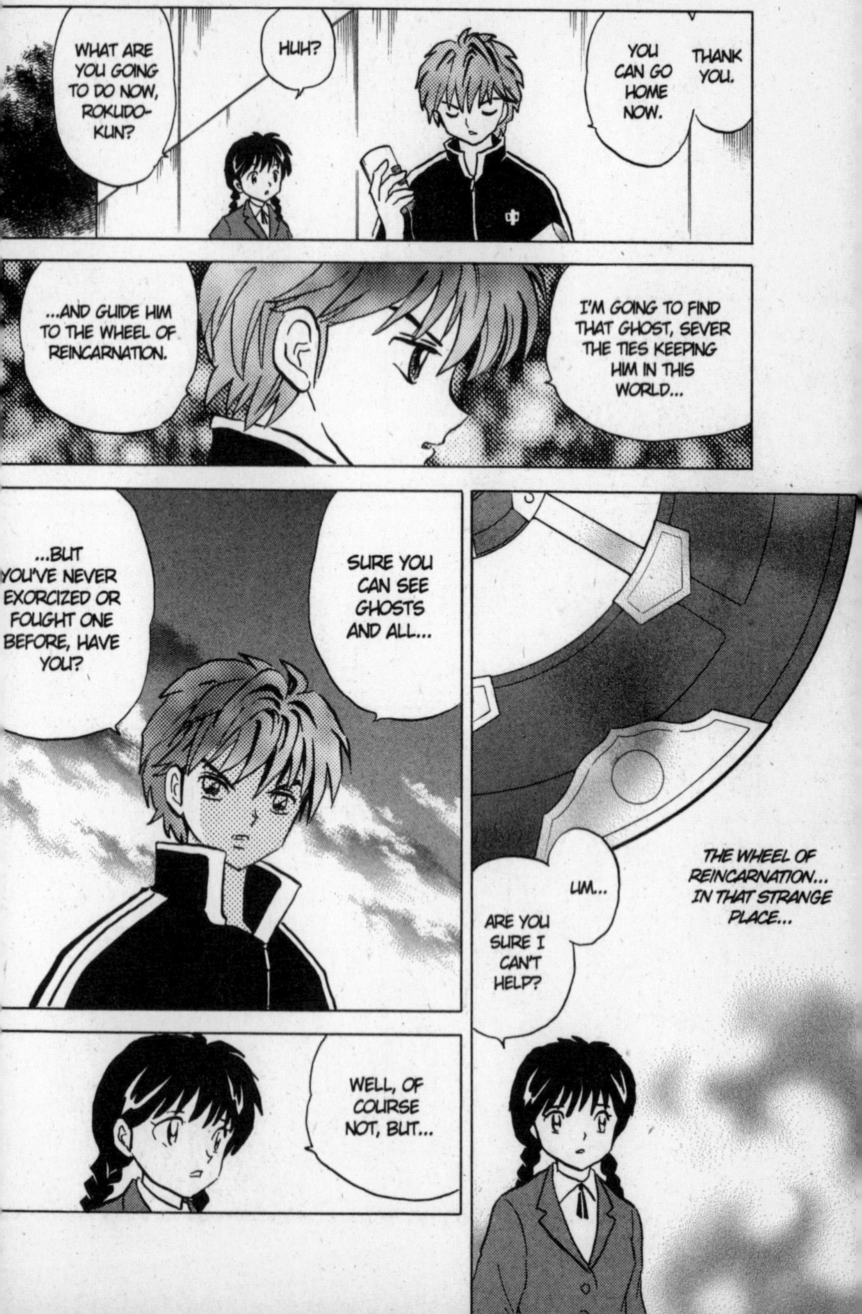
THANK YOU.
YOU CAN GO HOME NOW.
HUH?
WHAT ARE YOU GOING TO DO NOW, ROKUDO-KUN?
I'M GOING TO FIND THAT GHOST, SEVER THE TIES KEEPING HIM IN THIS WORLD...
...AND GUIDE HIM TO THE WHEEL OF REINCARNATION.
THE WHEEL OF REINCARNATION... IN THAT STRANGE PLACE...
UM...
ARE YOU SURE I CAN'T HELP?
SURE YOU CAN SEE GHOSTS AND ALL...
...BUT YOU'VE NEVER EXORCIZED OR FOUGHT ONE BEFORE, HAVE YOU?
WELL, OF COURSE NOT, BUT...

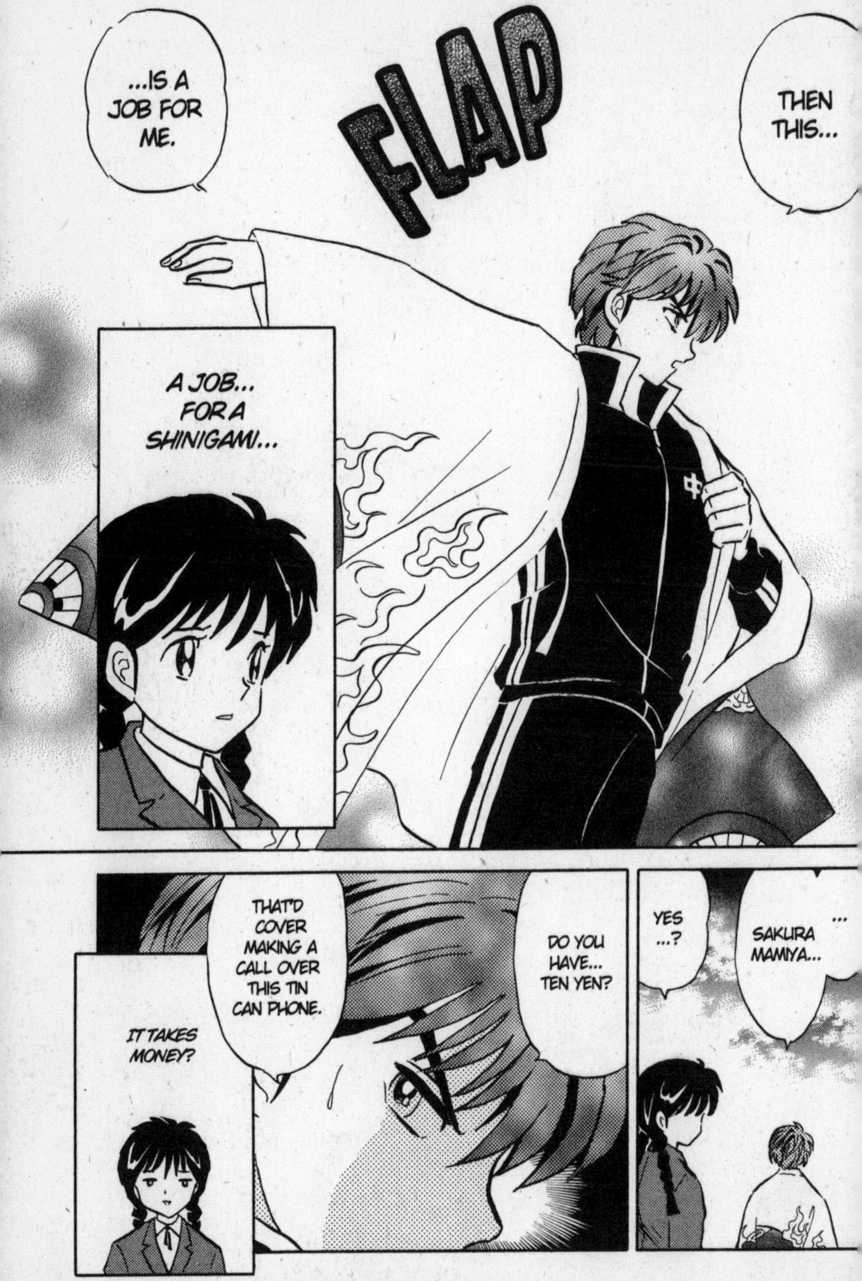
THEN THIS...
FLAP
...IS A JOB FOR ME.
A JOB... FOR A SHINIGAMI...
...
SAKURA MAMIYA...
YES ...?
DO YOU HAVE... TEN YEN?
THAT'D COVER MAKING A CALL OVER THIS TIN CAN PHONE.
IT TAKES MONEY?

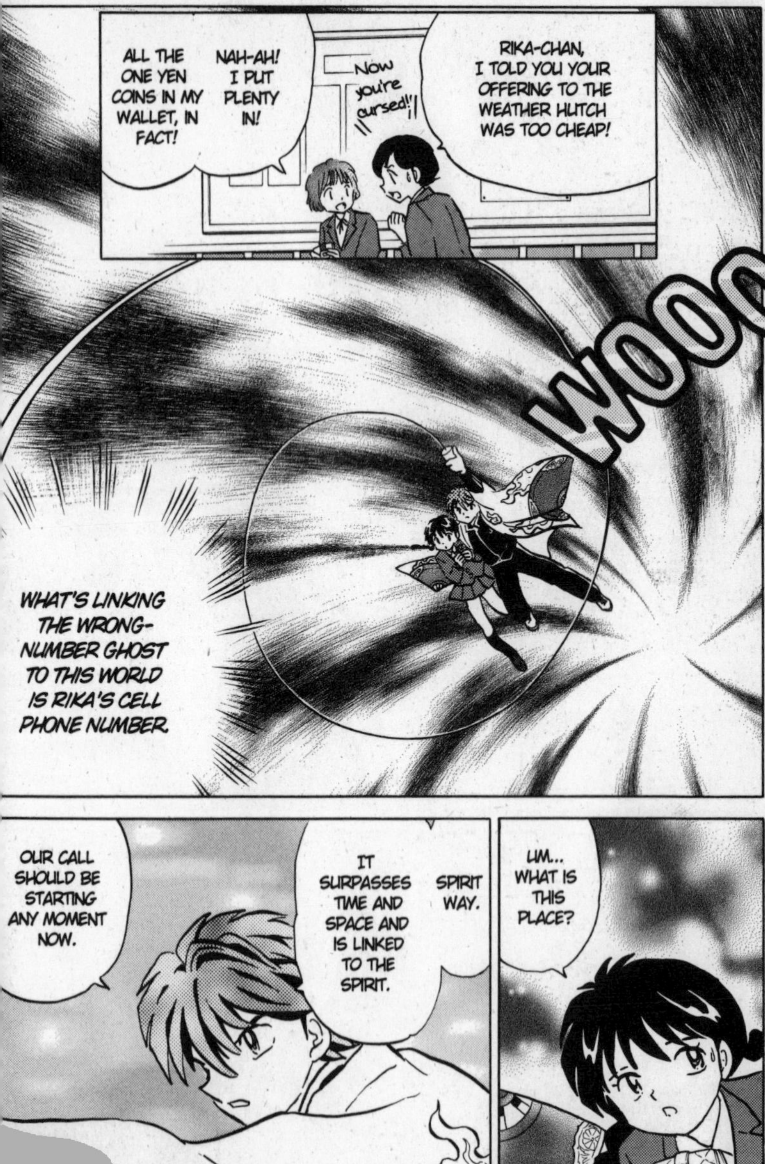
RIKA-CHAN, I TOLD YOU YOUR OFFERING TO THE WEATHER HUTCH WAS TOO CHEAP!
Now you're cursed!
NAH-AH! I PUT PLENTY IN!
ALL THE ONE YEN COINS IN MY WALLET, IN FACT!
WOOO
WHAT'S LINKING THE WRONG-NUMBER GHOST TO THIS WORLD IS RIKA'S CELL PHONE NUMBER.
UM... WHAT IS THIS PLACE?
SPIRIT WAY.
IT SURPASSES TIME AND SPACE AND IS LINKED TO THE SPIRIT.
OUR CALL SHOULD BE STARTING ANY MOMENT NOW.

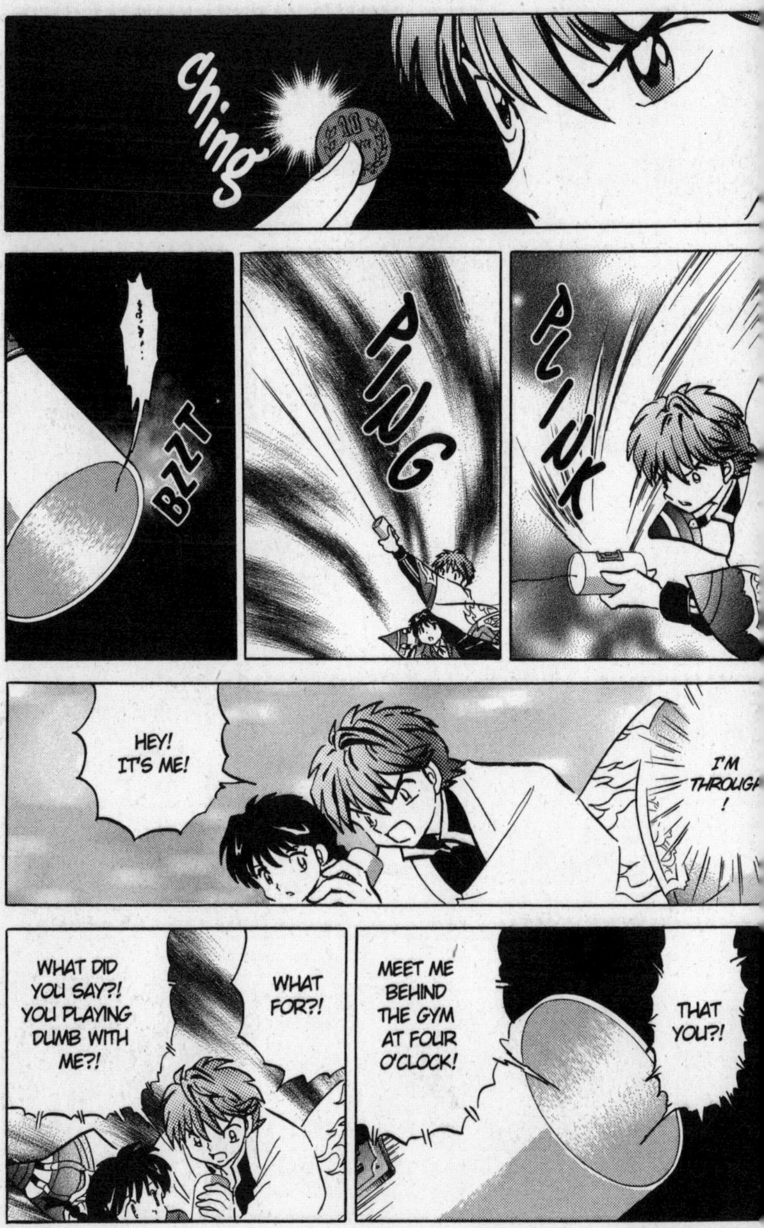
ching
PLINK
PLING
BZZT
I'M THROUG !
HEY! IT'S ME!
THAT YOU?!
MEET ME BEHIND THE GYM AT FOUR O'CLOCK!
WHAT FOR?!
WHAT DID YOU SAY?! YOU PLAYING DUMB WITH ME?!

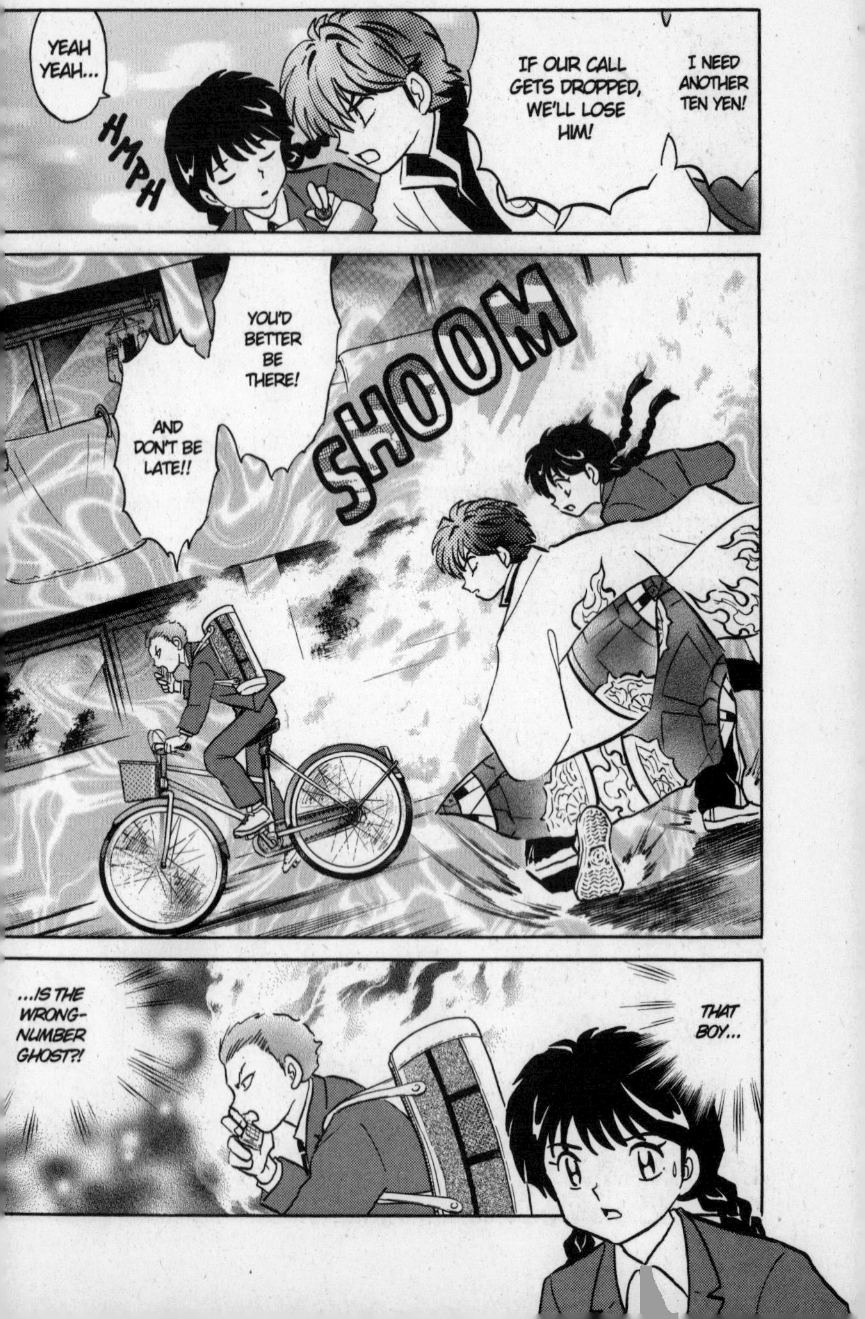
I NEED ANOTHER TEN YEN!
IF OUR CALL GETS DROPPED, WE'LL LOSE HIM!
HMPH
YEAH YEAH...
SHOOM
YOU'D BETTER BE THERE!
AND DON'T BE LATE!!
THAT BOY...
...IS THE WRONG-NUMBER GHOST?!

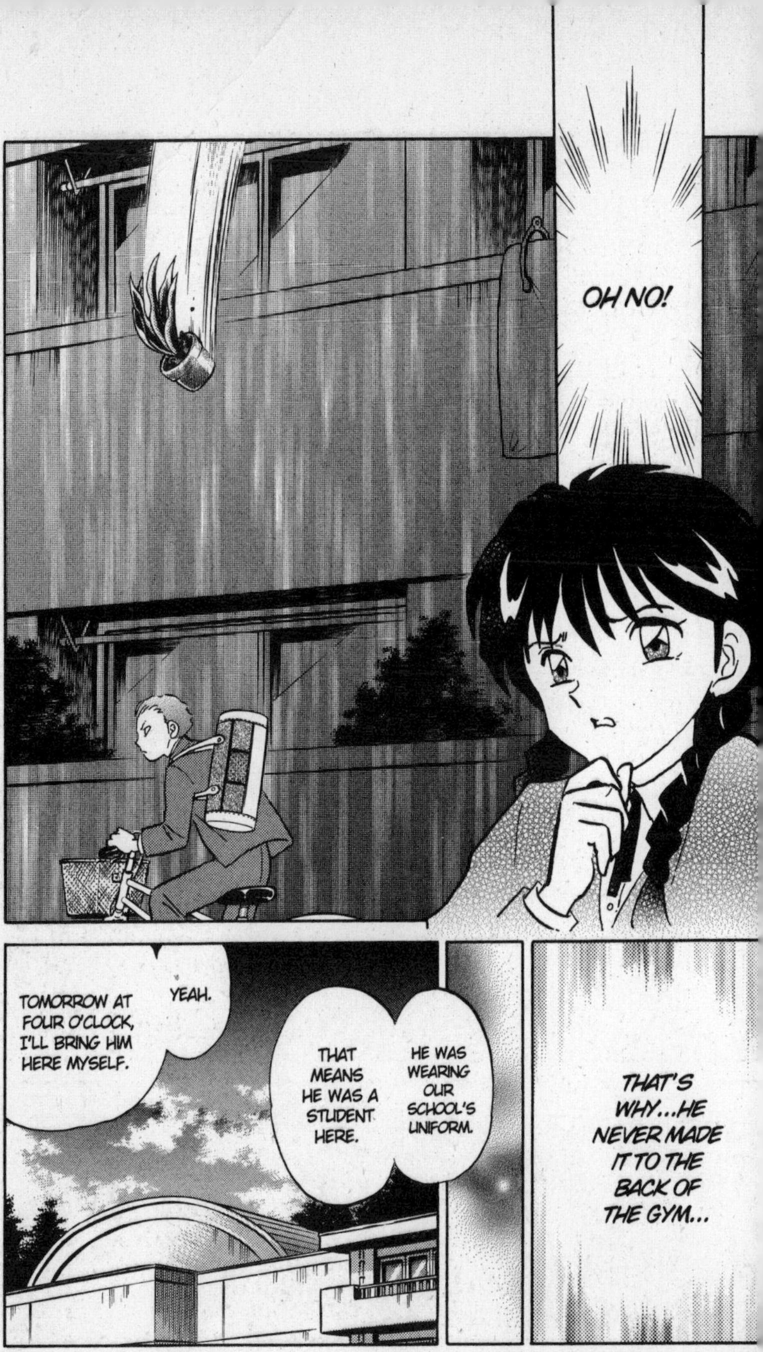
OH NO!
THAT'S WHY...HE NEVER MADE IT TO THE BACK OF THE GYM...
TOMORROW AT FOUR O'CLOCK, I'LL BRING HIM HERE MYSELF.
YEAH.
HE WAS WEARING OUR SCHOOL'S UNIFORM.
THAT MEANS HE WAS A STUDENT HERE.

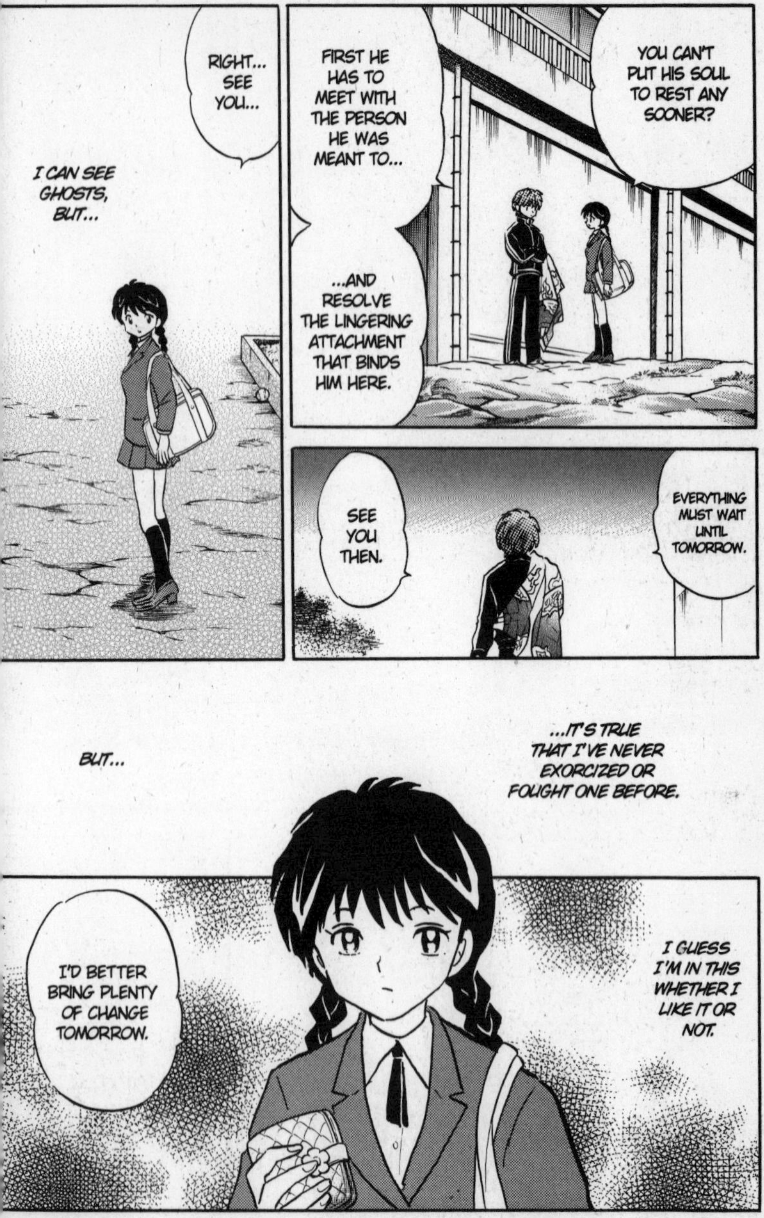
YOU CAN'T PUT HIS SOUL TO REST ANY SOONER?
FIRST HE HAS TO MEET WITH THE PERSON HE WAS MEANT TO...
...AND RESOLVE THE LINGERING ATTACHMENT THAT BINDS HIM HERE.
EVERYTHING MUST WAIT UNTIL TOMORROW.
SEE YOU THEN.
RIGHT... SEE YOU...
I CAN SEE GHOSTS, BUT...
...IT'S TRUE THAT I'VE NEVER EXORCIZED OR FOUGHT ONE BEFORE.
BUT...
I GUESS I'M IN THIS WHETHER I LIKE IT OR NOT.
I'D BETTER BRING PLENTY OF CHANGE TOMORROW.

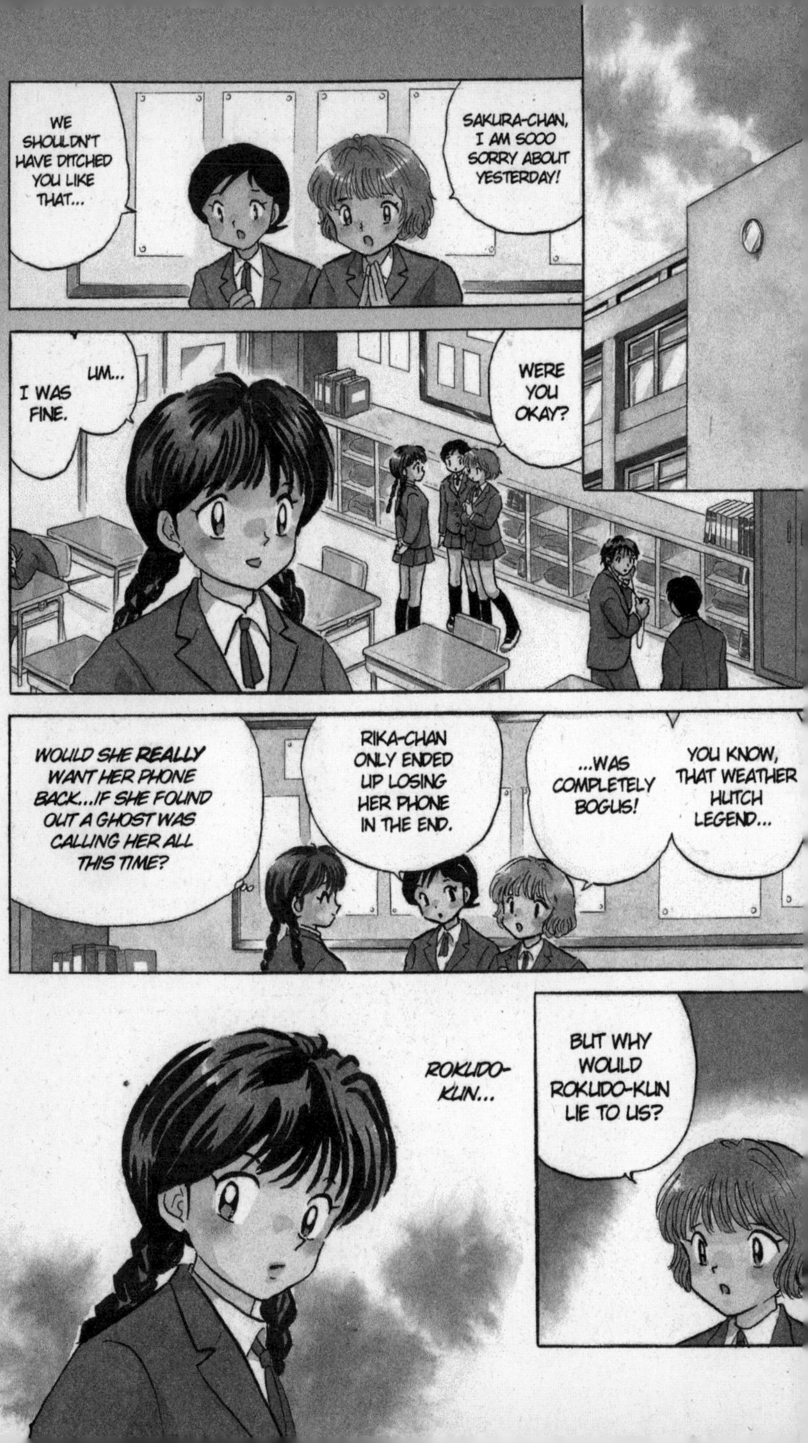
SAKURA-CHAN, I AM SOOO SORRY ABOUT YESTERDAY!
WE SHOULDN'T HAVE DITCHED YOU LIKE THAT...
WERE YOU OKAY?
UM... I WAS FINE.
YOU KNOW, THAT WEATHER HUTCH LEGEND...
...WAS COMPLETELY BOGUS!
RIKA-CHAN ONLY ENDED UP LOSING HER PHONE IN THE END.
WOULD SHE REALLY WANT HER PHONE BACK...IF SHE FOUND OUT A GHOST WAS CALLING HER ALL THIS TIME?
BUT WHY WOULD ROKUDO-KUN LIE TO US?
ROKUDO-KUN...

CHAPTER 3:
FOUR O'CLOCK BEHIND THE GYM

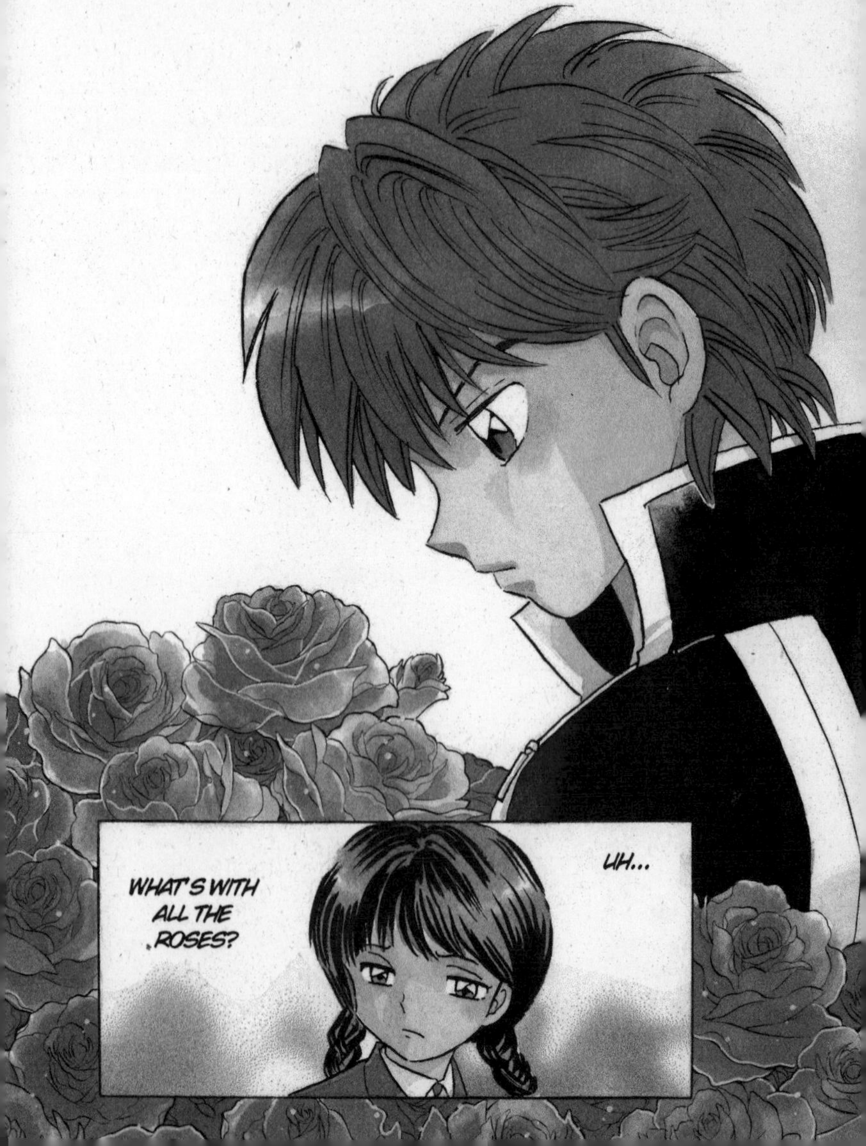

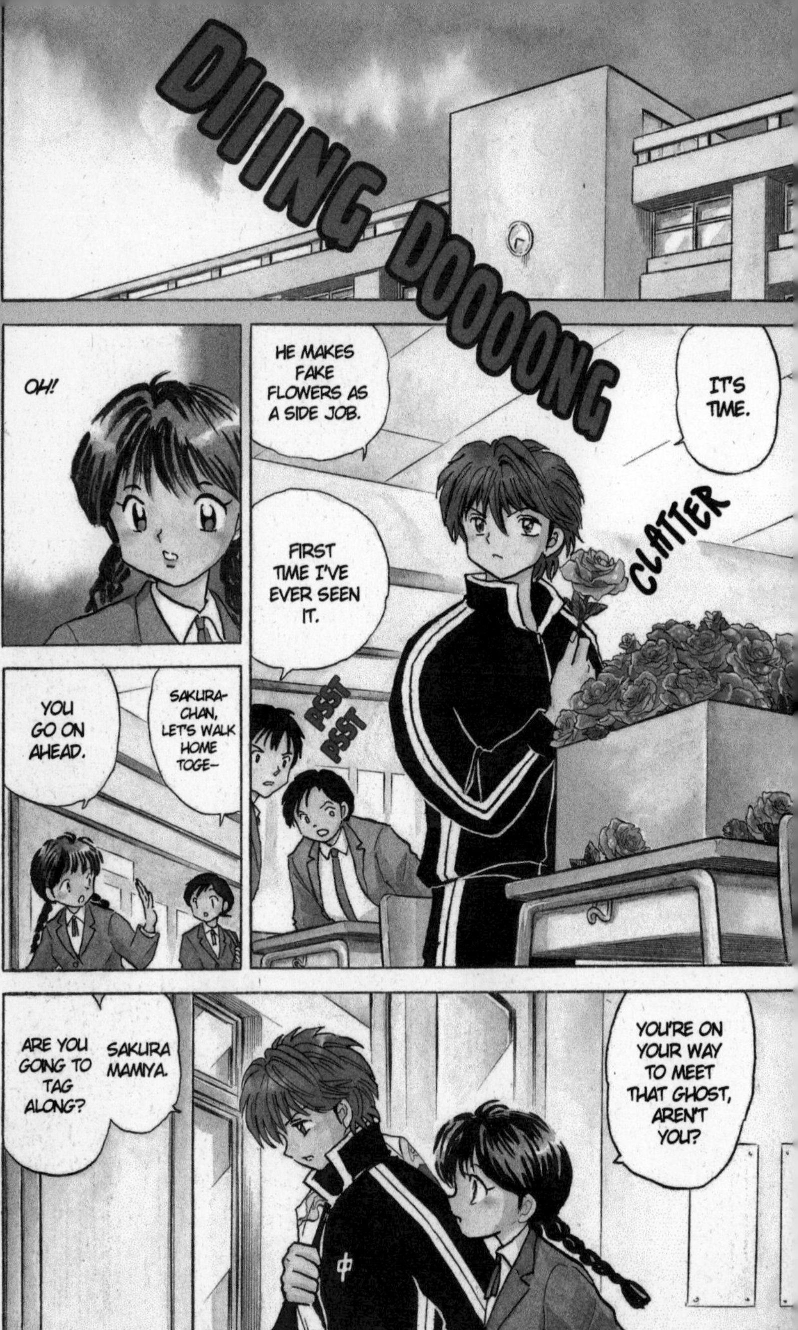
DIIING DOOOOONG
IT'S TIME.
CLATTER
HE MAKES FAKE FLOWERS AS A SIDE JOB.
FIRST TIME I'VE EVER SEEN IT.
PSST PSST
OH!
SAKURA-CHAN, LET'S WALK HOME TOGE-
YOU GO ON AHEAD.
YOU'RE ON YOUR WAY TO MEET THAT GHOST, AREN'T YOU?
SAKURA MAMIYA.
ARE YOU GOING TO TAG ALONG?

RIN-NE

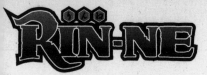

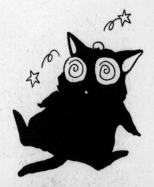

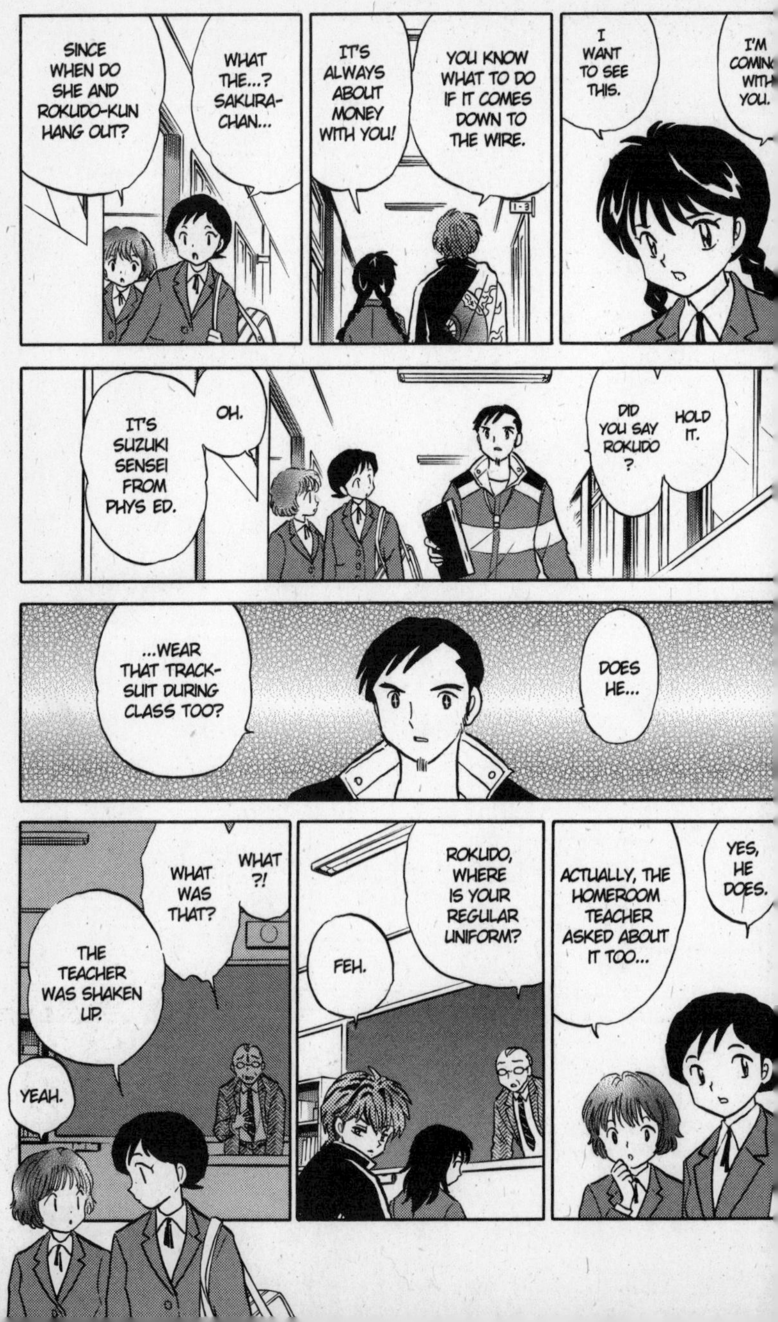
I'M COMIN WITH YOU.
I WANT TO SEE THIS.
YOU KNOW WHAT TO DO IF IT COMES DOWN TO THE WIRE.
IT'S ALWAYS ABOUT MONEY WITH YOU!
WHAT THE...? SAKURA-CHAN...
SINCE WHEN DO SHE AND ROKUDO-KUN HANG OUT?
HOLD IT.
DID YOU SAY ROKUDO?
OH.
IT'S SUZUKI SENSEI FROM PHYS ED.
DOES HE...
...WEAR THAT TRACK-SUIT DURING CLASS TOO?
YES, HE DOES.
ACTUALLY, THE HOMEROOM TEACHER ASKED ABOUT IT TOO...
ROKUDO, WHERE IS YOUR REGULAR UNIFORM?
FEH.
WHAT ?!
WHAT WAS THAT?
THE TEACHER WAS SHAKEN UP.
YEAH.

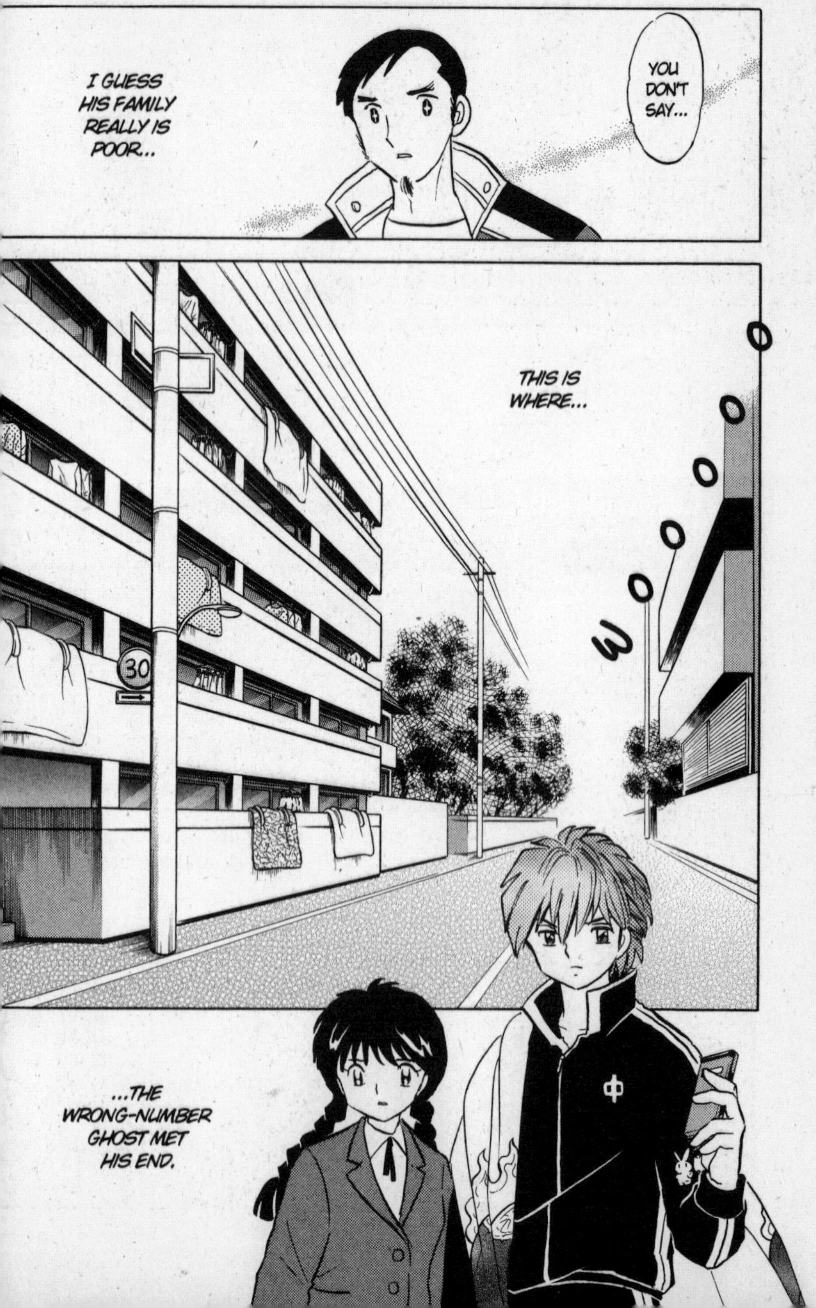
YOU DON'T SAY...
I GUESS HIS FAMILY REALLY IS POOR...
THIS IS WHERE...
WOOOOO
...THE WRONG-NUMBER GHOST MET HIS END.

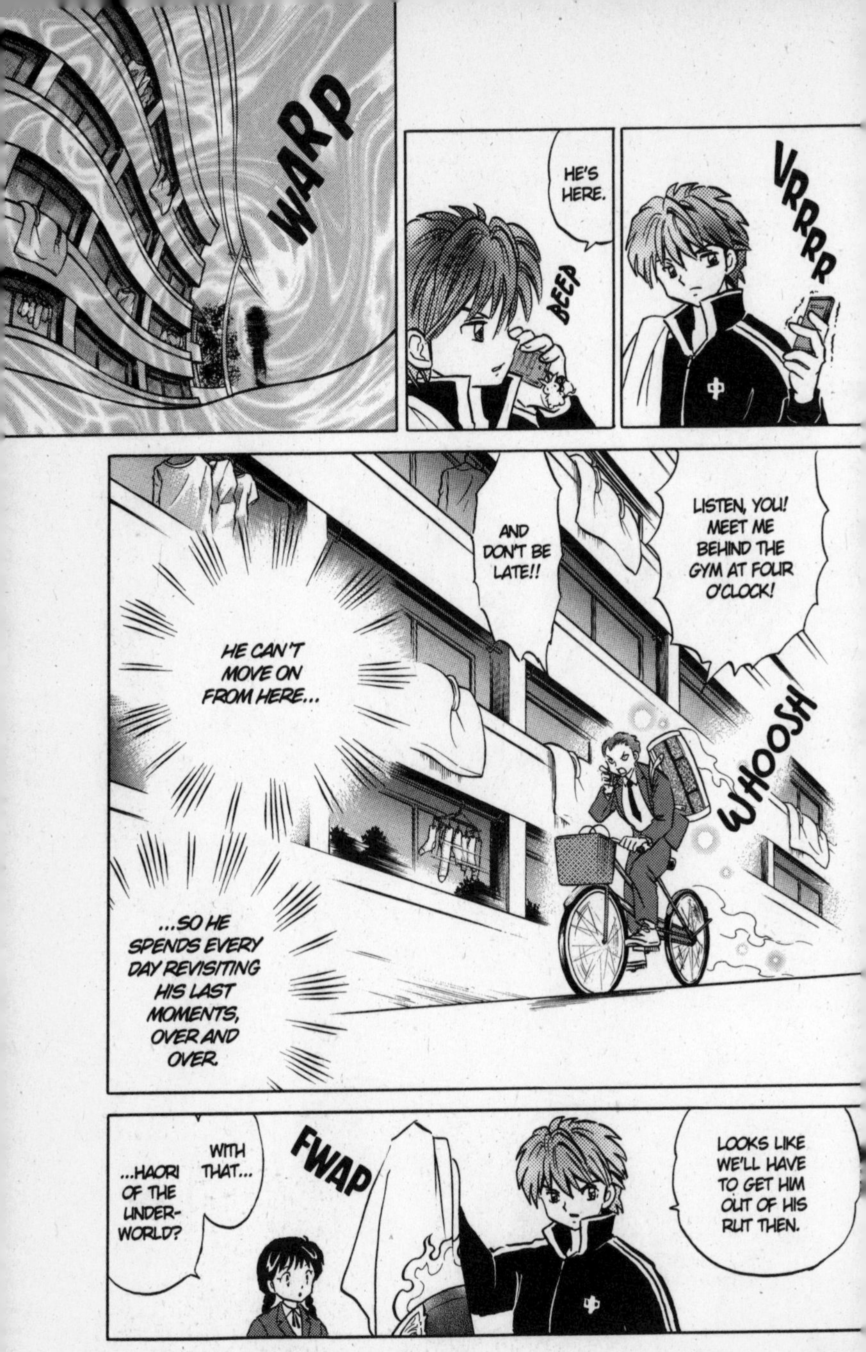
VRRRR
HE'S HERE.
BEEP
WARP
LISTEN, YOU! MEET ME BEHIND THE GYM AT FOUR O'CLOCK!
AND DON'T BE LATE!!
WHOOSH
HE CAN'T MOVE ON FROM HERE...
...SO HE SPENDS EVERY DAY REVISITING HIS LAST MOMENTS, OVER AND OVER.
LOOKS LIKE WE'LL HAVE TO GET HIM OUT OF HIS RUT THEN.
FWAP
WITH THAT...
...HAORI OF THE UNDER-WORLD?

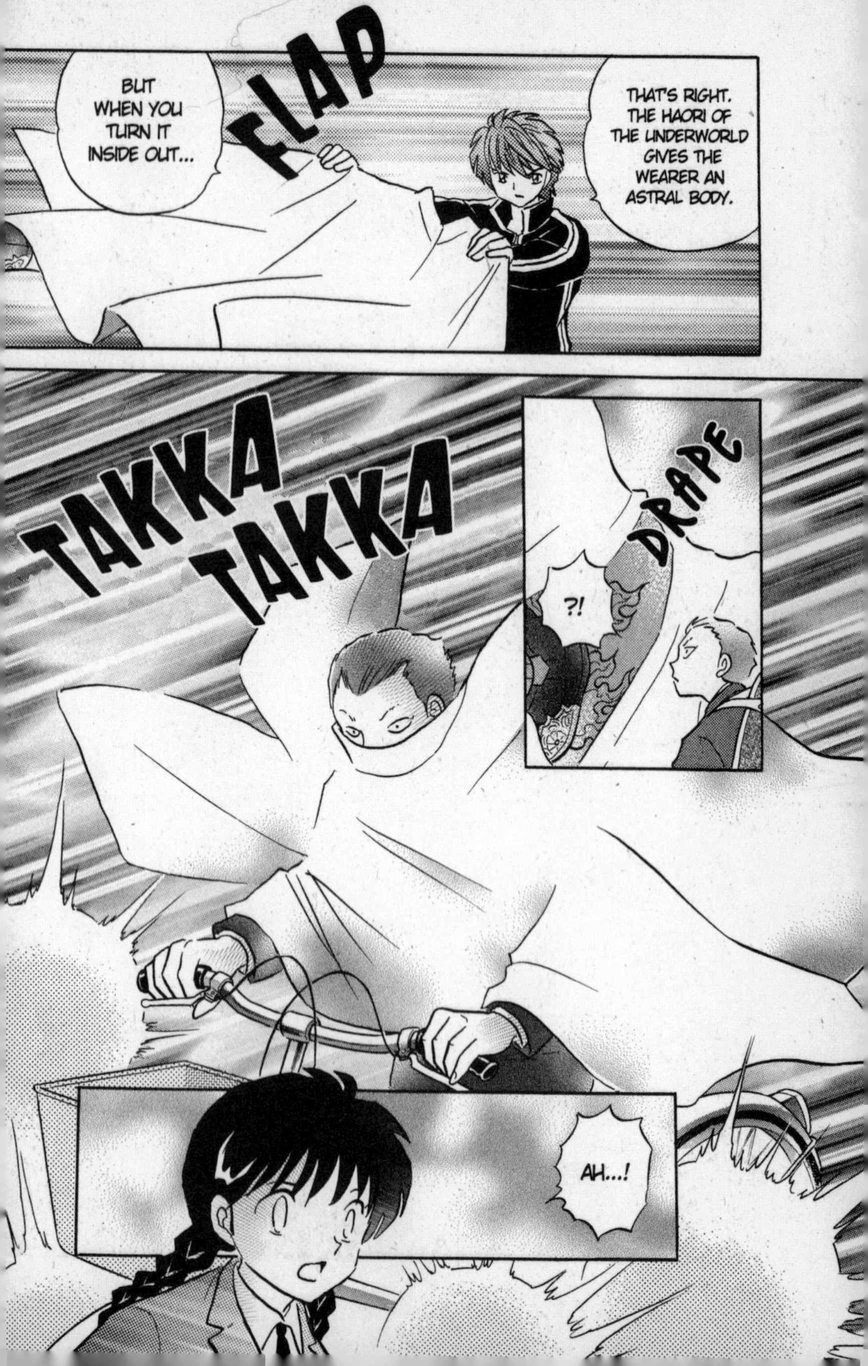
THAT'S RIGHT. THE HAORI OF THE UNDERWORLD GIVES THE WEARER AN ASTRAL BODY.
FLAP
BUT WHEN YOU TURN IT INSIDE OUT...
DRAPE
?!
TAKKA TAKKA
AH...!

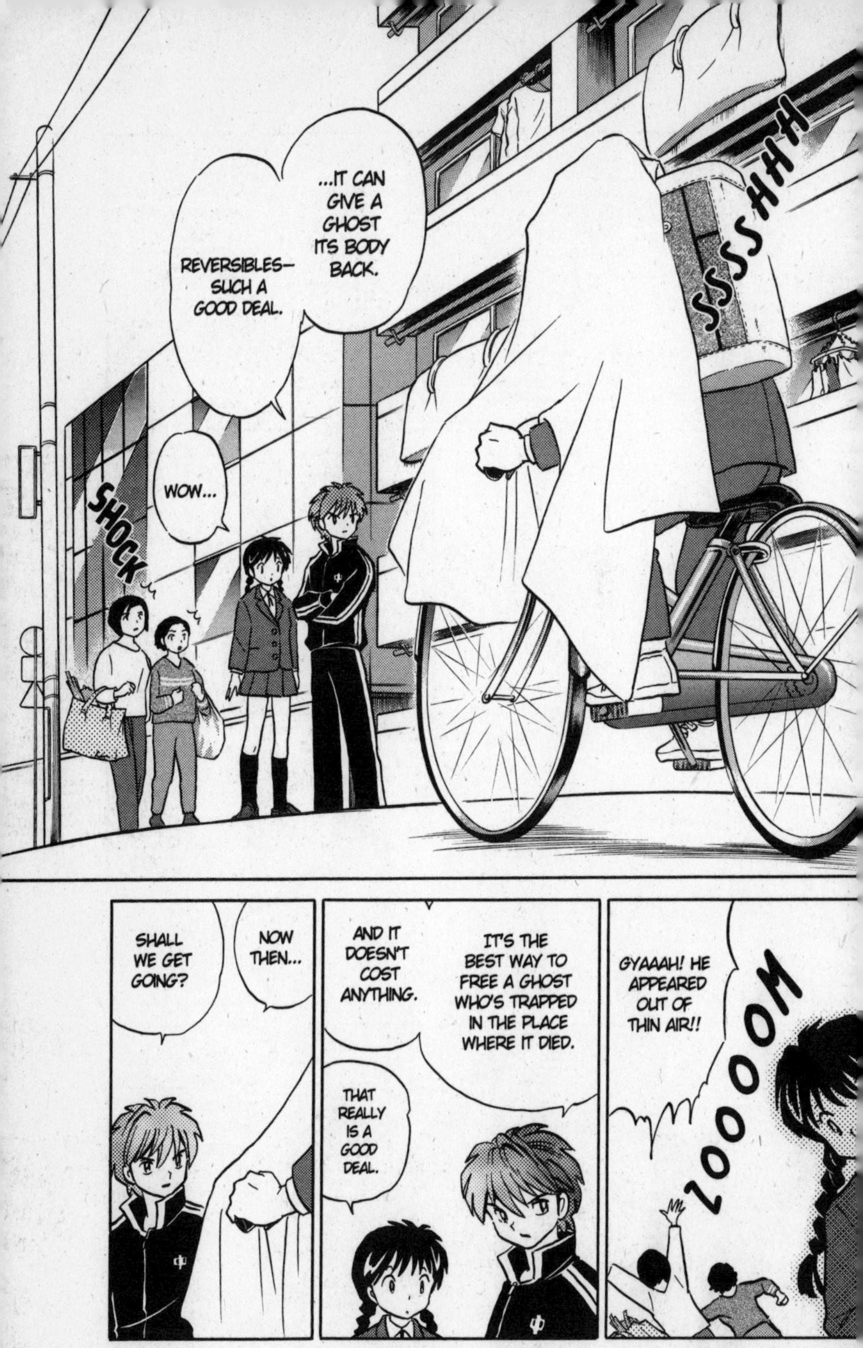
SSSSHHH
...IT CAN GIVE A GHOST ITS BODY BACK.
REVERSIBLES— SUCH A GOOD DEAL.
WOW...
SHOCK
ZOOOOM
GYAAAH! HE APPEARED OUT OF THIN AIR!!
IT'S THE BEST WAY TO FREE A GHOST WHO'S TRAPPED IN THE PLACE WHERE IT DIED.
AND IT DOESN'T COST ANYTHING.
THAT REALLY IS A GOOD DEAL.
NOW THEN...
SHALL WE GET GOING?

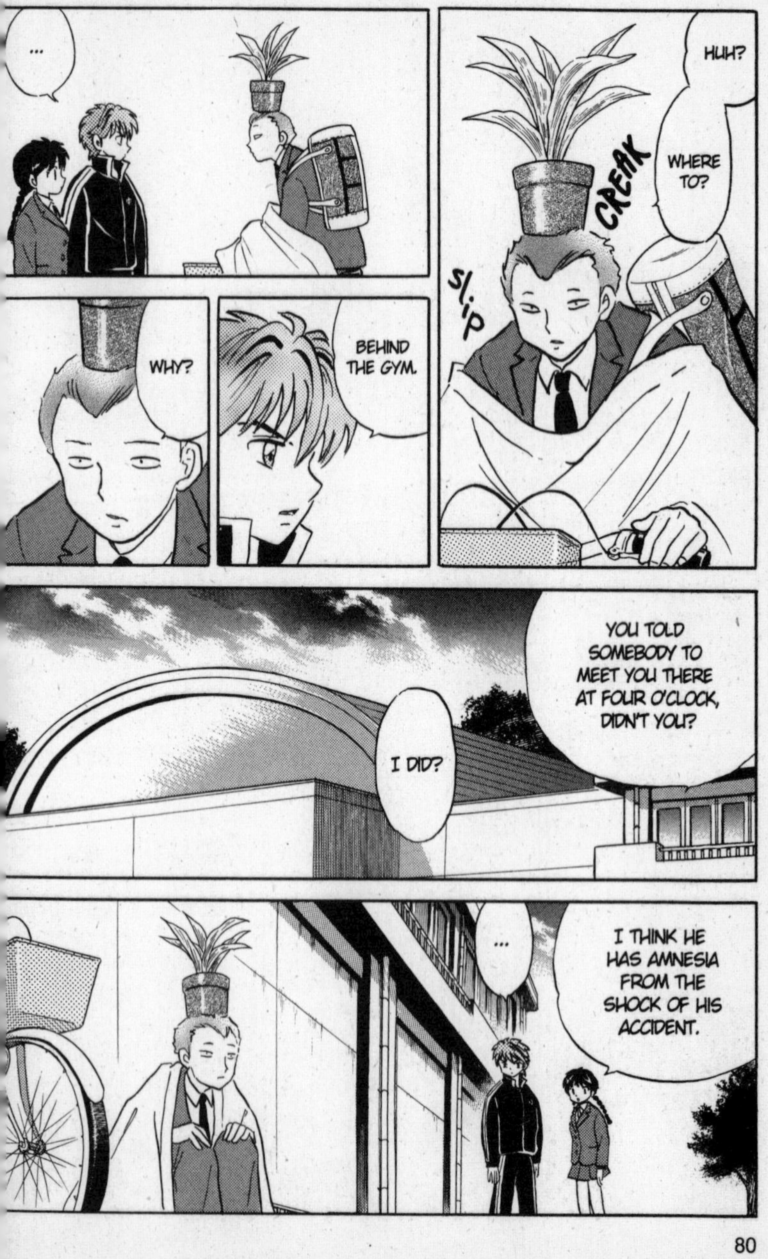
HUH?
WHERE TO?
CREAK
slip
...
BEHIND THE GYM.
WHY?
YOU TOLD SOMEBODY TO MEET YOU THERE AT FOUR O'CLOCK, DIDN'T YOU?
I DID?
I THINK HE HAS AMNESIA FROM THE SHOCK OF HIS ACCIDENT.
...

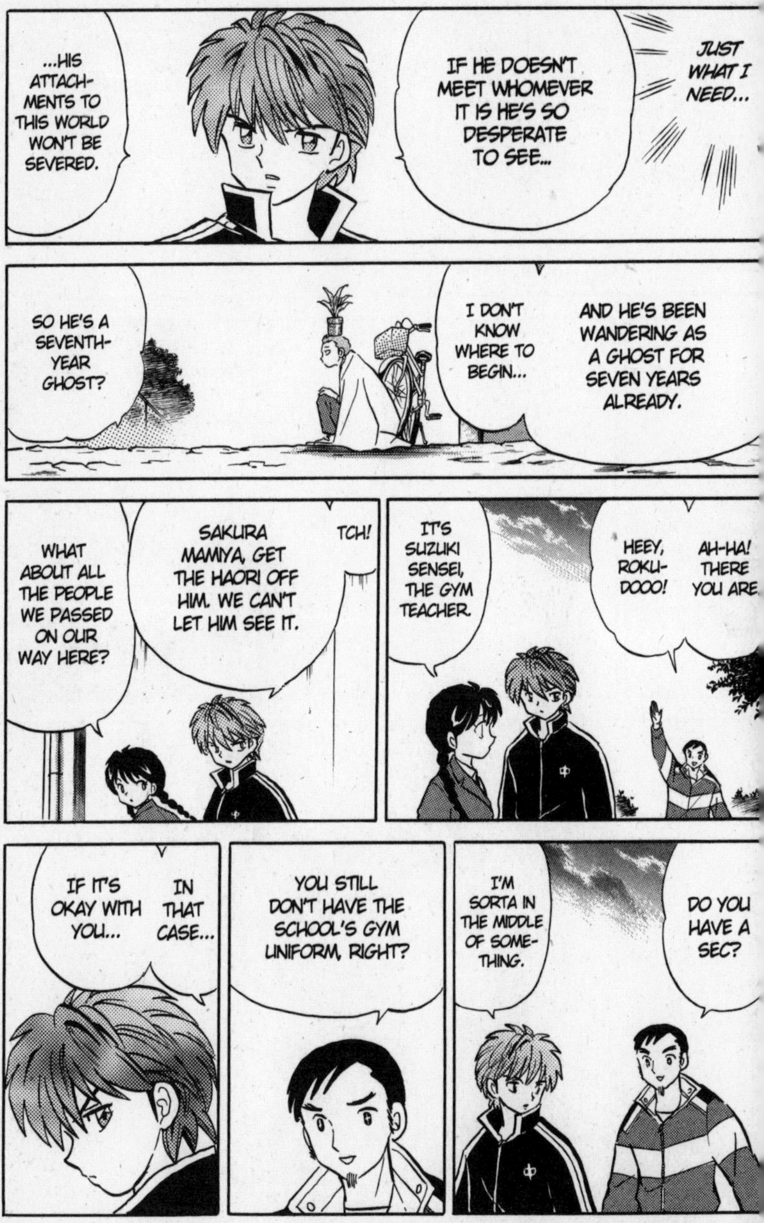
JUST WHAT I NEED...
IF HE DOESN'T MEET WHOMEVER IT IS HE'S SO DESPERATE TO SEE...
...HIS ATTACHMENTS TO THIS WORLD WON'T BE SEVERED.
AND HE'S BEEN WANDERING AS A GHOST FOR SEVEN YEARS ALREADY.
I DON'T KNOW WHERE TO BEGIN...
SO HE'S A SEVENTH-YEAR GHOST?
AH-HA! THERE YOU ARE.
HEEY, ROKU-DOOO!
IT'S SUZUKI SENSEI, THE GYM TEACHER.
TCH!
SAKURA MAMIYA, GET THE HAORI OFF HIM. WE CAN'T LET HIM SEE IT.
WHAT ABOUT ALL THE PEOPLE WE PASSED ON OUR WAY HERE?
DO YOU HAVE A SEC?
I'M SORTA IN THE MIDDLE OF SOMETHING.
YOU STILL DON'T HAVE THE SCHOOL'S GYM UNIFORM, RIGHT?
IN THAT CASE...
IF IT'S OKAY WITH YOU...

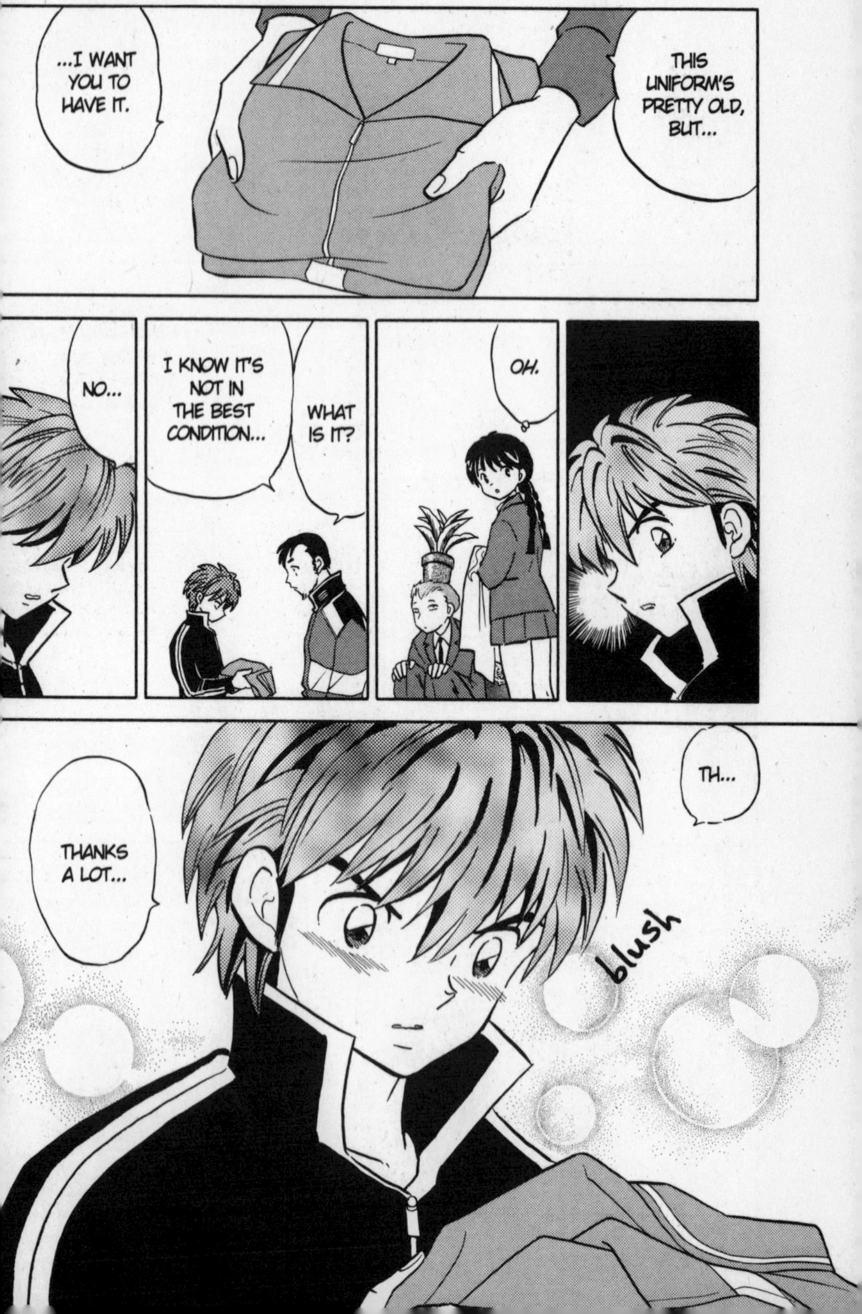
THIS UNIFORM'S PRETTY OLD, BUT...
...I WANT YOU TO HAVE IT.
OH.
WHAT IS IT?
I KNOW IT'S NOT IN THE BEST CONDITION...
NO...
TH...
THANKS A LOT...
blush

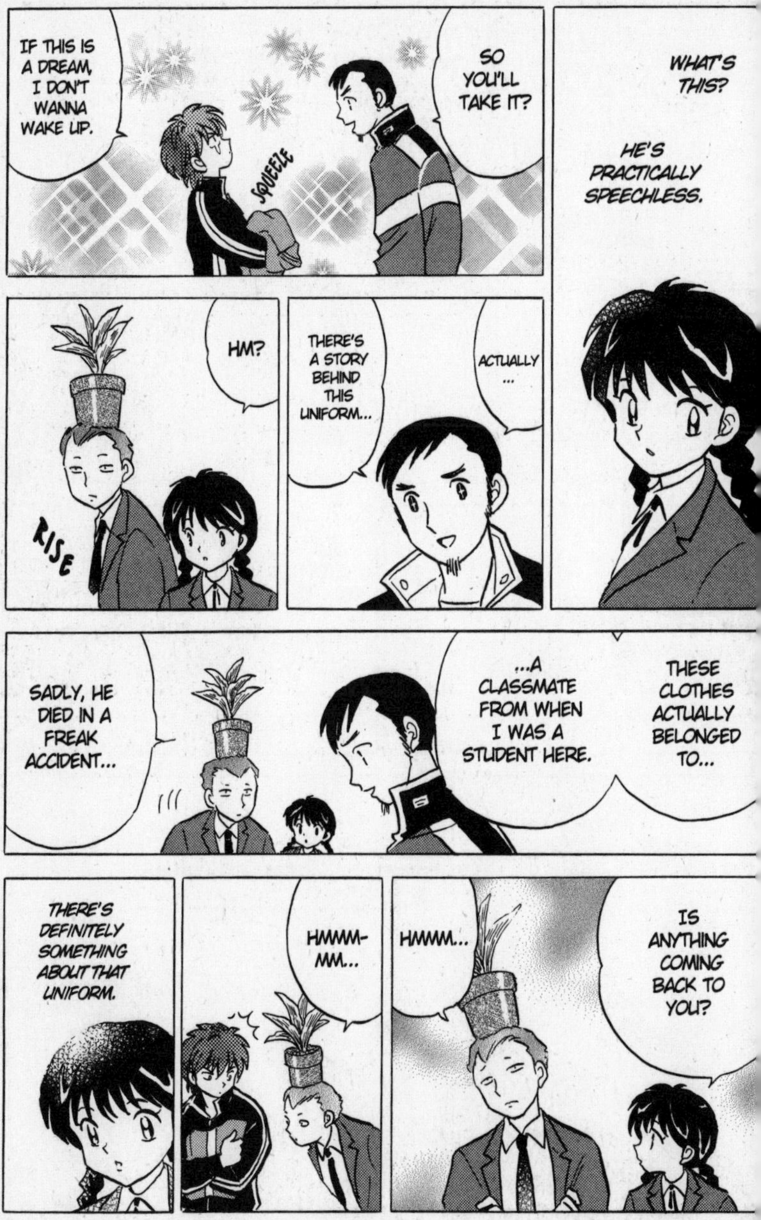
WHAT'S THIS?
HE'S PRACTICALLY SPEECHLESS.
SO YOU'LL TAKE IT?
IF THIS IS A DREAM, I DON'T WANNA WAKE UP.
SQUEEZE
ACTUALLY...
THERE'S A STORY BEHIND THIS UNIFORM...
HM?
RISE
THESE CLOTHES ACTUALLY BELONGED TO...
...A CLASSMATE FROM WHEN I WAS A STUDENT HERE.
SADLY, HE DIED IN A FREAK ACCIDENT...
IS ANYTHING COMING BACK TO YOU?
HMMMM...
HMMMM-MM...
THERE'S DEFINITELY SOMETHING ABOUT THAT UNIFORM.

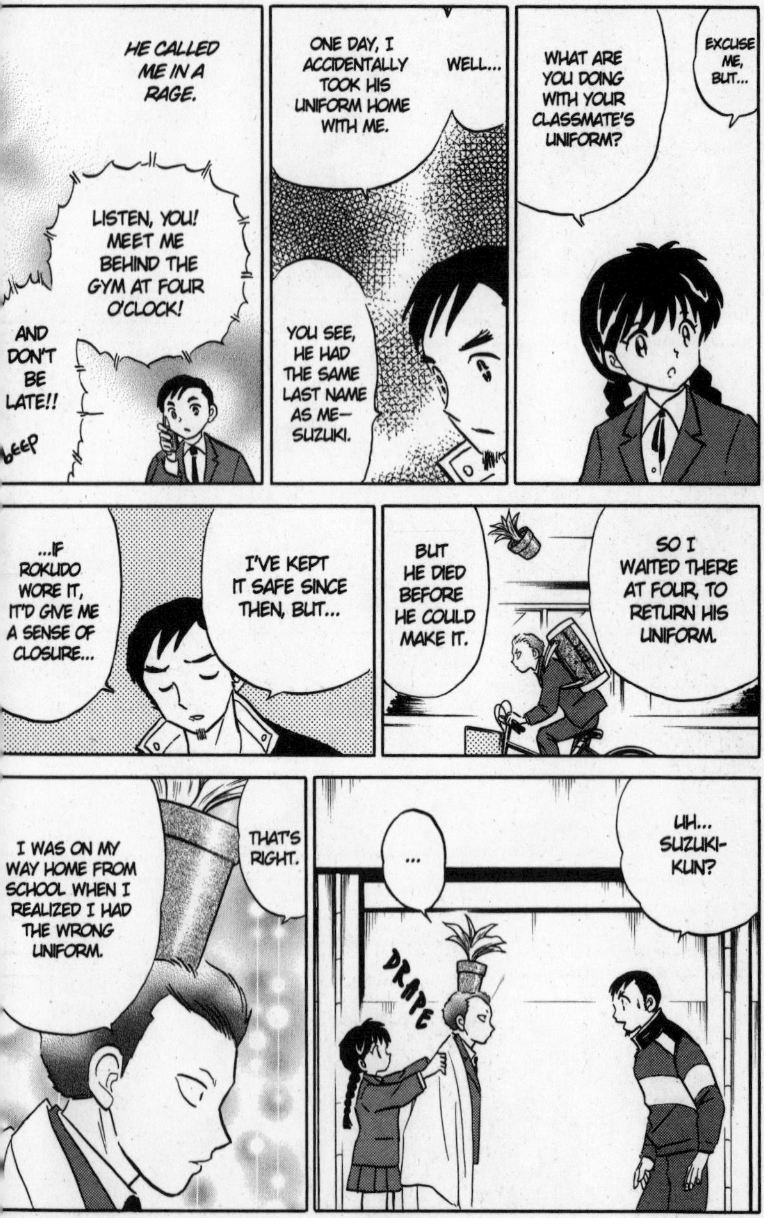
EXCUSE ME, BUT...
WHAT ARE YOU DOING WITH YOUR CLASSMATE'S UNIFORM?
WELL...
ONE DAY, I ACCIDENTALLY TOOK HIS UNIFORM HOME WITH ME.
YOU SEE, HE HAD THE SAME LAST NAME AS ME— SUZUKI.
HE CALLED ME IN A RAGE.
LISTEN, YOU! MEET ME BEHIND THE GYM AT FOUR O'CLOCK!
AND DON'T BE LATE!!
beep
SO I WAITED THERE AT FOUR, TO RETURN HIS UNIFORM.
BUT HE DIED BEFORE HE COULD MAKE IT.
I'VE KEPT IT SAFE SINCE THEN, BUT...
...IF ROKUDO WORE IT, IT'D GIVE ME A SENSE OF CLOSURE...
UH... SUZUKI-KUN?
...
DRAPE
THAT'S RIGHT.
I WAS ON MY WAY HOME FROM SCHOOL WHEN I REALIZED I HAD THE WRONG UNIFORM.

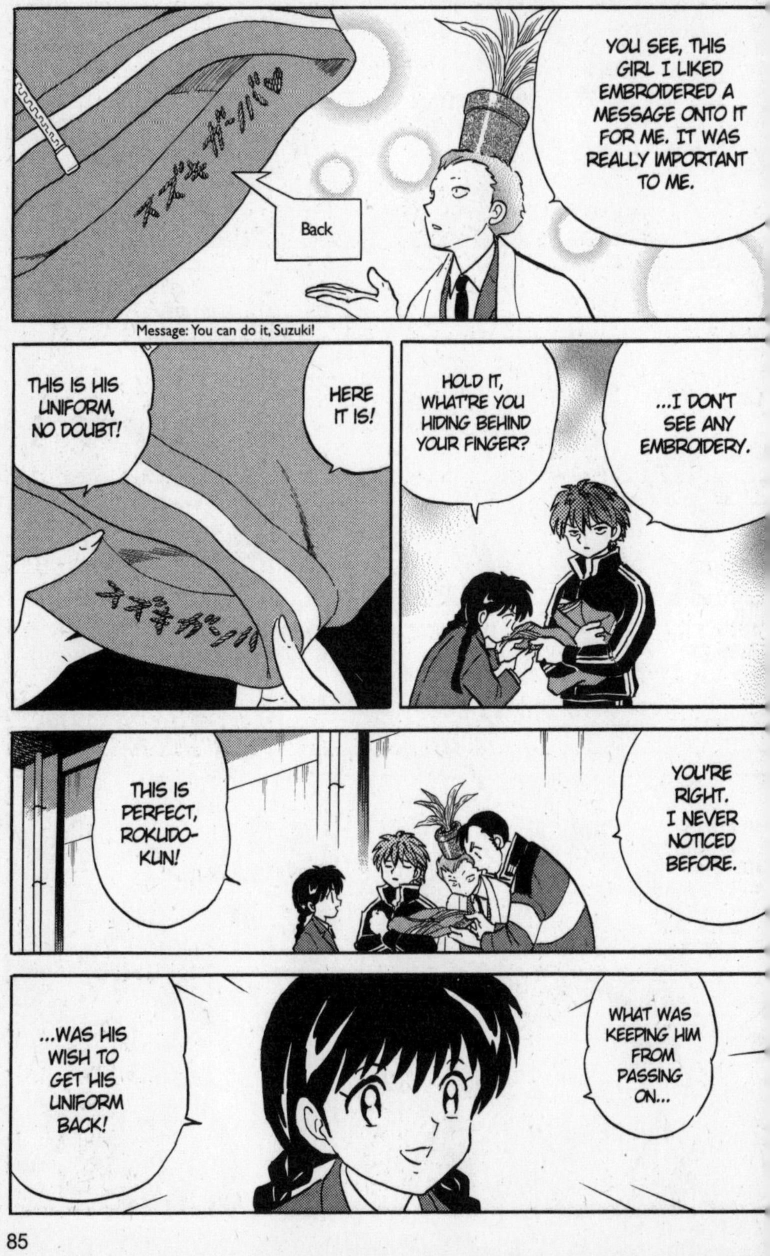
YOU SEE, THIS GIRL I LIKED EMBROIDERED A MESSAGE ONTO IT FOR ME. IT WAS REALLY IMPORTANT TO ME.
Back
Message: You can do it, Suzuki!
...I DON'T SEE ANY EMBROIDERY.
HOLD IT, WHAT'RE YOU HIDING BEHIND YOUR FINGER?
HERE IT IS!
THIS IS HIS UNIFORM, NO DOUBT!
YOU'RE RIGHT. I NEVER NOTICED BEFORE.
THIS IS PERFECT, ROKUDO-KUN!
WHAT WAS KEEPING HIM FROM PASSING ON...
...WAS HIS WISH TO GET HIS UNIFORM BACK!

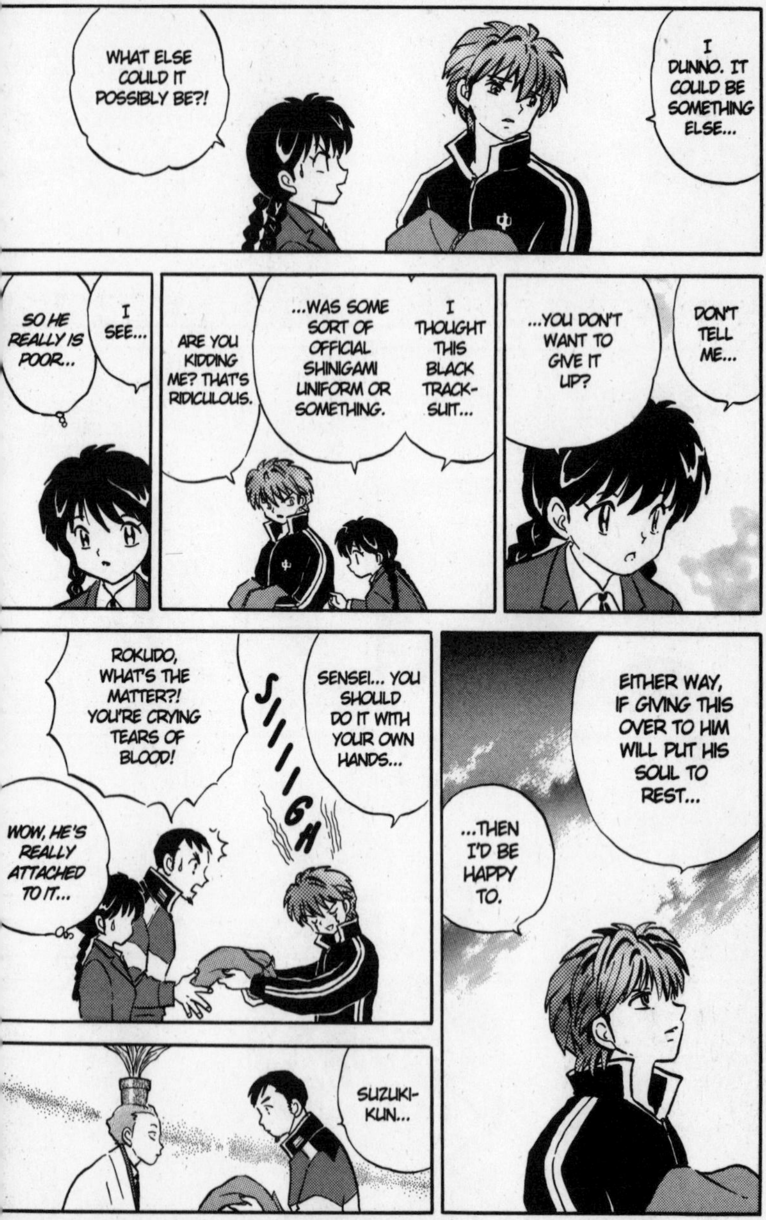
I DUNNO. IT COULD BE SOMETHING ELSE...
WHAT ELSE COULD IT POSSIBLY BE?!
DON'T TELL ME...
...YOU DON'T WANT TO GIVE IT UP?
I THOUGHT THIS BLACK TRACK-SUIT...
...WAS SOME SORT OF OFFICIAL SHINIGAMI UNIFORM OR SOMETHING.
ARE YOU KIDDING ME? THAT'S RIDICULOUS.
I SEE...
SO HE REALLY IS POOR...
EITHER WAY, IF GIVING THIS OVER TO HIM WILL PUT HIS SOUL TO REST...
...THEN I'D BE HAPPY TO.
SENSEI... YOU SHOULD DO IT WITH YOUR OWN HANDS...
SIIIIGH
ROKUDO, WHAT'S THE MATTER?! YOU'RE CRYING TEARS OF BLOOD!
WOW, HE'S REALLY ATTACHED TO IT...
SUZUKI-KUN...

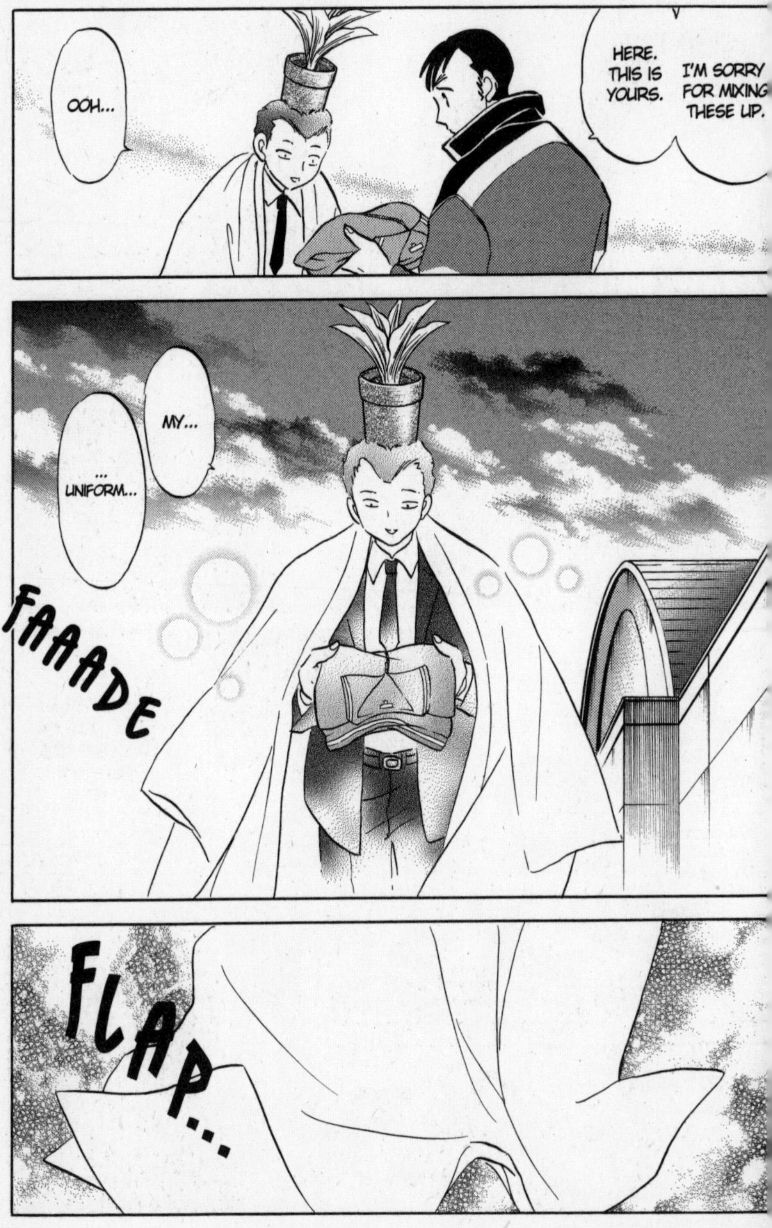
HERE. THIS IS YOURS.
I'M SORRY FOR MIXING THESE UP.
OOH...
MY...
...UNIFORM...
FAAADE
FLAP...

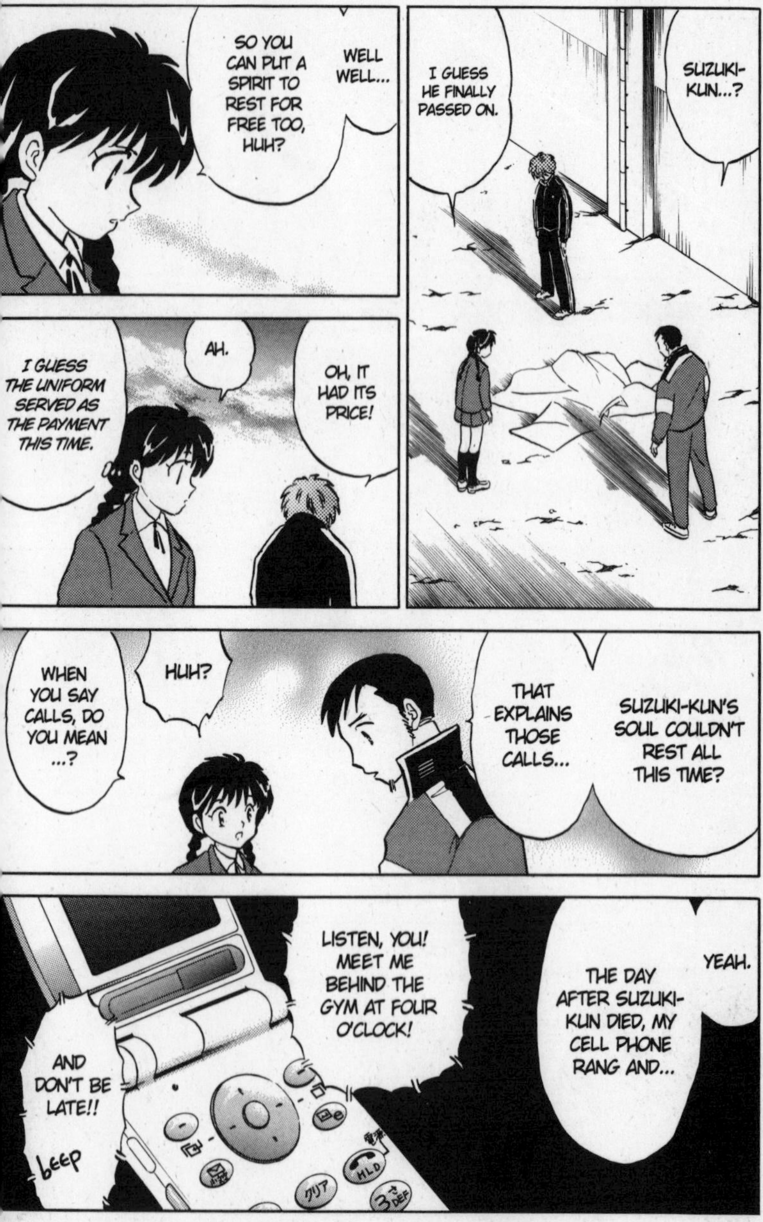
SUZUKI-KUN...?
I GUESS HE FINALLY PASSED ON.
WELL WELL...
SO YOU CAN PUT A SPIRIT TO REST FOR FREE TOO, HUH?
OH, IT HAD ITS PRICE!
AH.
I GUESS THE UNIFORM SERVED AS THE PAYMENT THIS TIME.
SUZUKI-KUN'S SOUL COULDN'T REST ALL THIS TIME?
THAT EXPLAINS THOSE CALLS...
HUH?
WHEN YOU SAY CALLS, DO YOU MEAN ...?
YEAH.
THE DAY AFTER SUZUKI-KUN DIED, MY CELL PHONE RANG AND...
LISTEN, YOU! MEET ME BEHIND THE GYM AT FOUR O'CLOCK!
AND DON'T BE LATE!!
beep

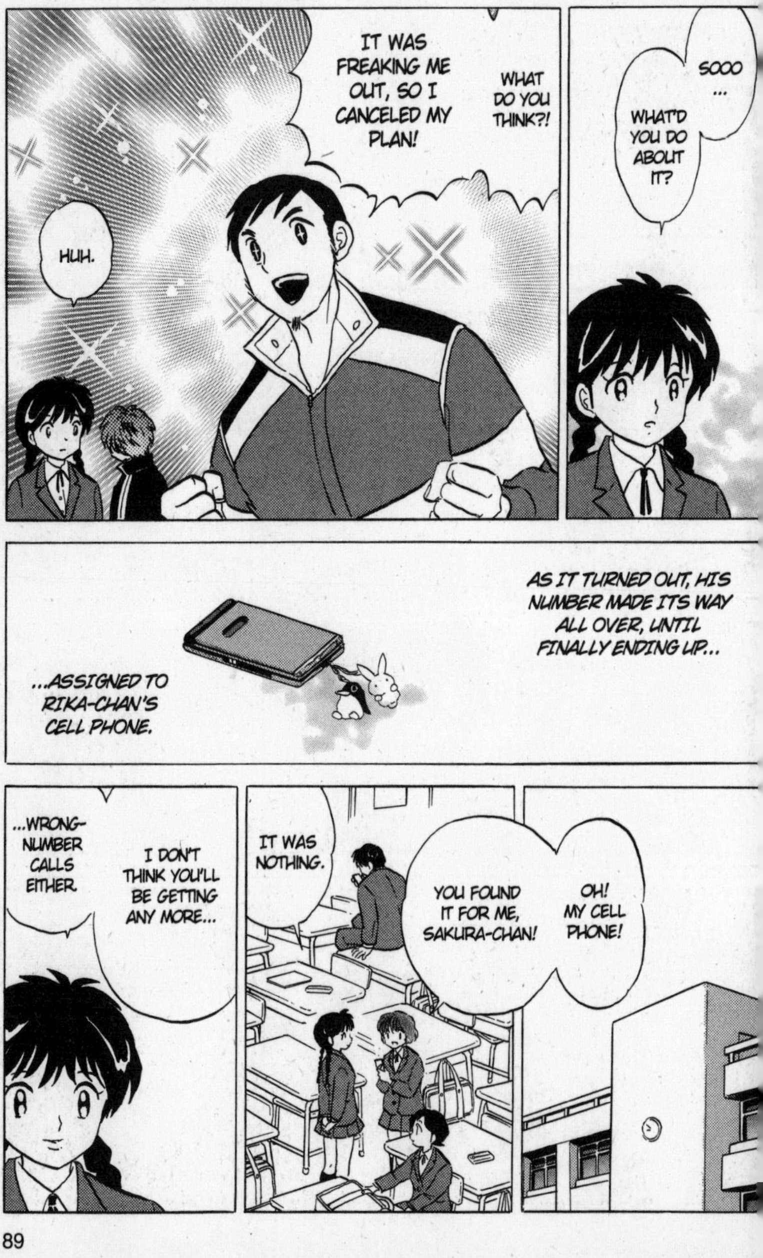
SOOO ...
WHAT'D YOU DO ABOUT IT?
WHAT DO YOU THINK?!
IT WAS FREAKING ME OUT, SO I CANCELED MY PLAN!
HUH.
AS IT TURNED OUT, HIS NUMBER MADE ITS WAY ALL OVER, UNTIL FINALLY ENDING UP...
...ASSIGNED TO RIKA-CHAN'S CELL PHONE.
OH! MY CELL PHONE!
YOU FOUND IT FOR ME, SAKURA-CHAN!
IT WAS NOTHING.
I DON'T THINK YOU'LL BE GETTING ANY MORE...
...WRONG-NUMBER CALLS EITHER.

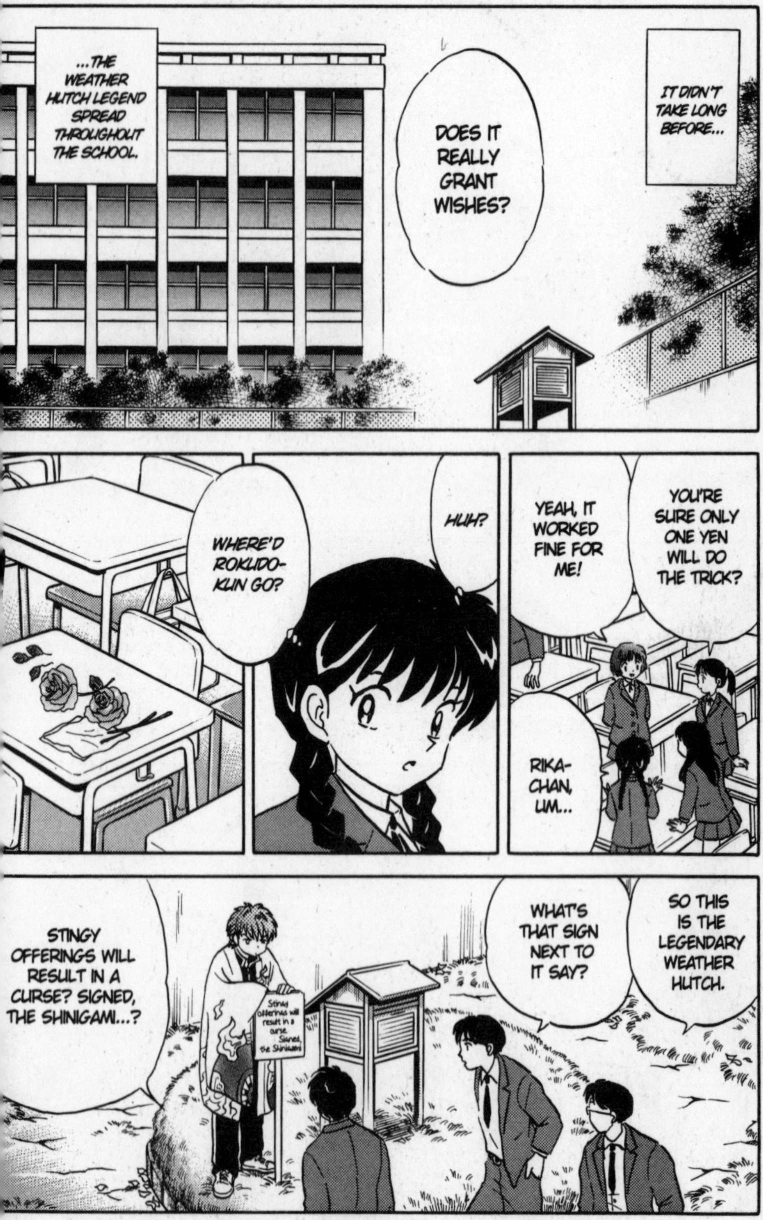
IT DIDN'T TAKE LONG BEFORE...
DOES IT REALLY GRANT WISHES?
...THE WEATHER HUTCH LEGEND SPREAD THROUGHOUT THE SCHOOL.
YOU'RE SURE ONLY ONE YEN WILL DO THE TRICK?
YEAH, IT WORKED FINE FOR ME!
RIKA-CHAN, UM...
HUH?
WHERE'D ROKUDO-KUN GO?
SO THIS IS THE LEGENDARY WEATHER HUTCH.
WHAT'S THAT SIGN NEXT TO IT SAY?
Stingy Offerings will result in a curse. Signed, the Shinigami
STINGY OFFERINGS WILL RESULT IN A CURSE? SIGNED, THE SHINIGAMI...?

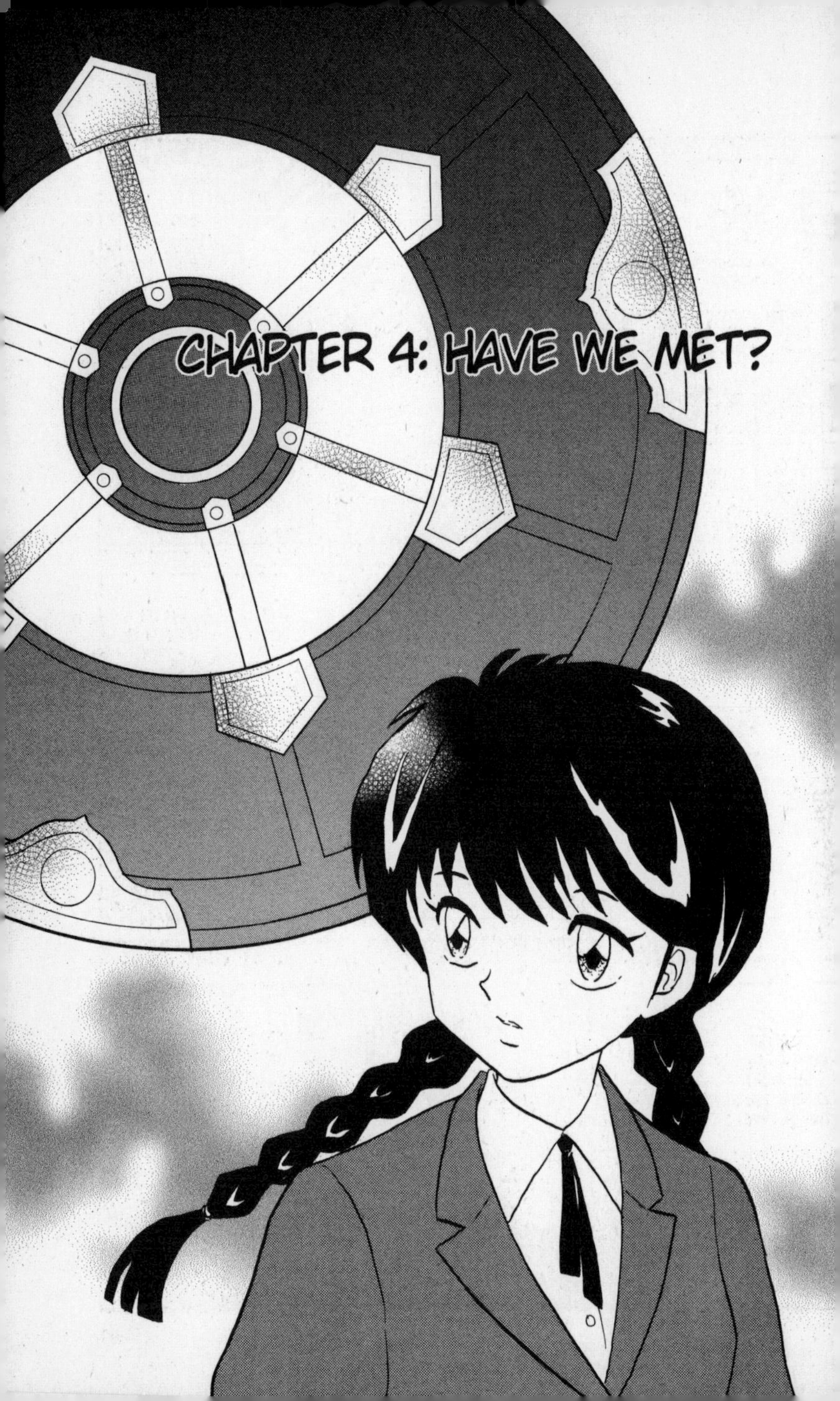
CHAPTER 4: HAVE WE MET?

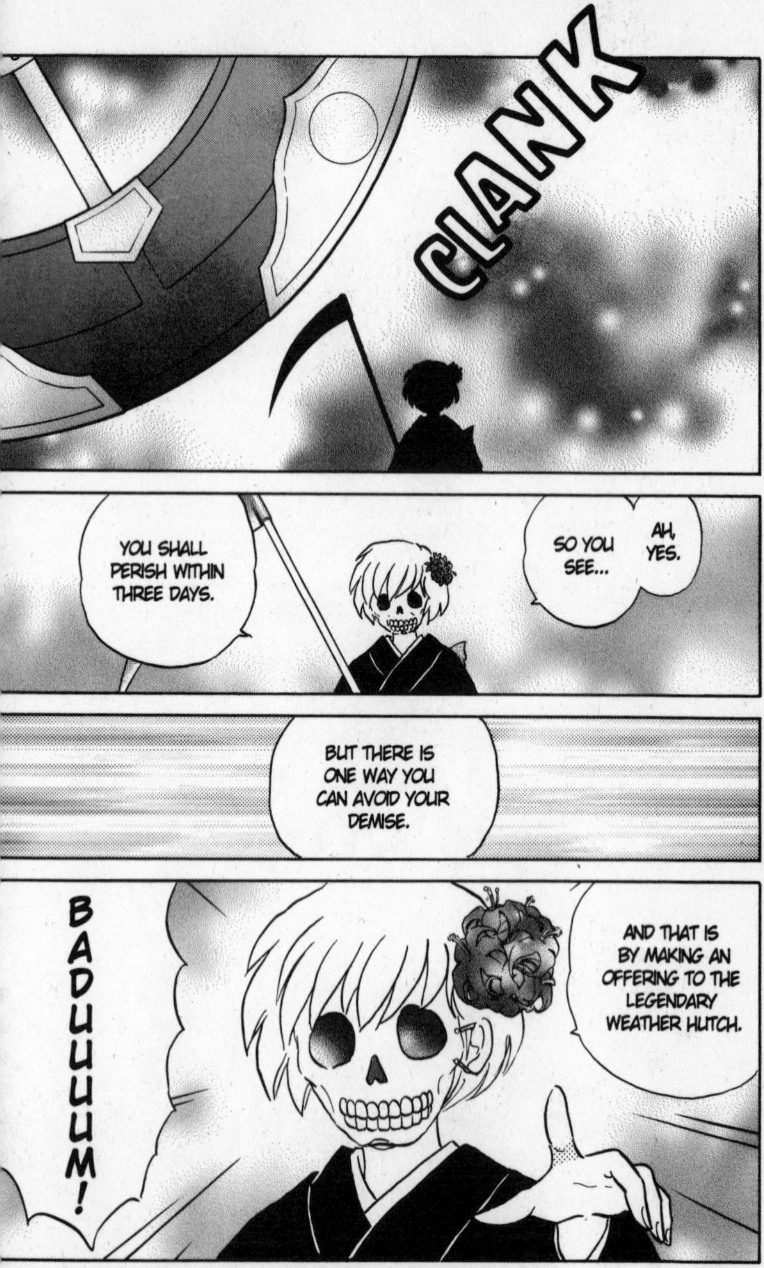
CLANK
AH, YES.
SO YOU SEE...
YOU SHALL PERISH WITHIN THREE DAYS.
BUT THERE IS ONE WAY YOU CAN AVOID YOUR DEMISE.
AND THAT IS BY MAKING AN OFFERING TO THE LEGENDARY WEATHER HUTCH.
BADUUUUM!

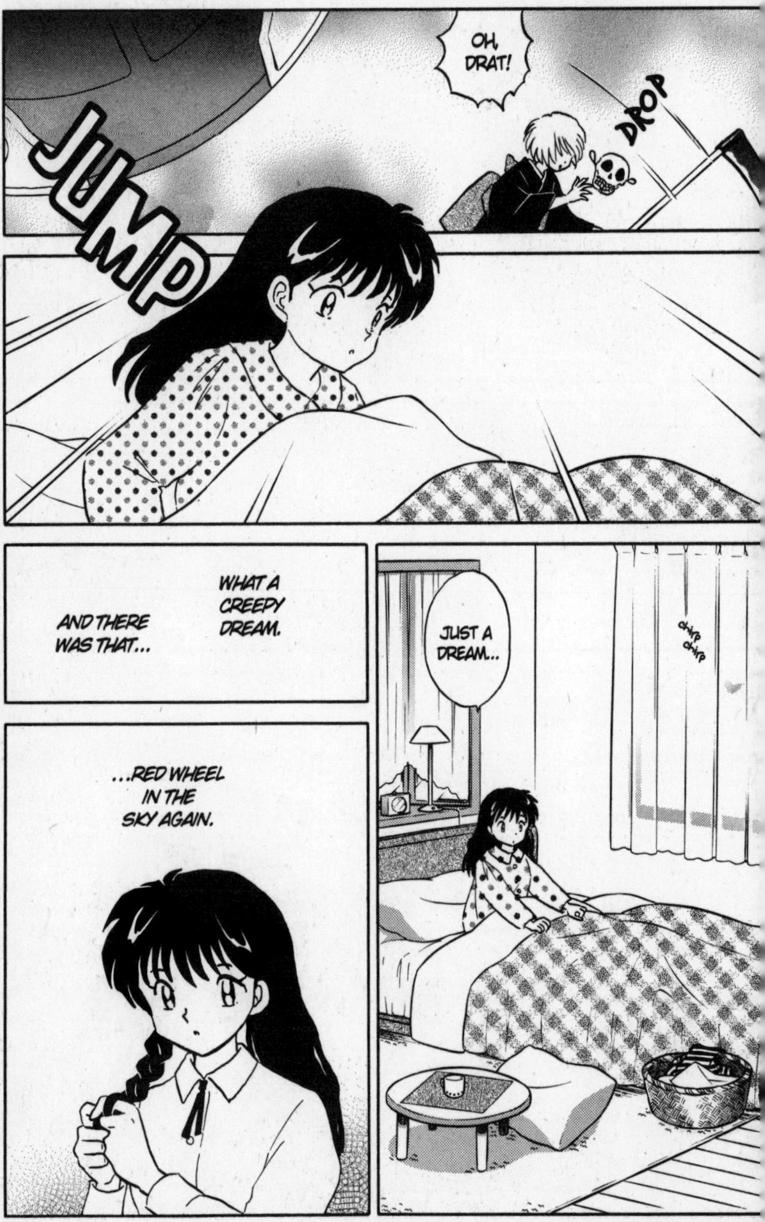
OH, DRAT!
DROP
JUMP
JUST A DREAM...
chirp chirp
WHAT A CREEPY DREAM.
AND THERE WAS THAT...
...RED WHEEL IN THE SKY AGAIN.

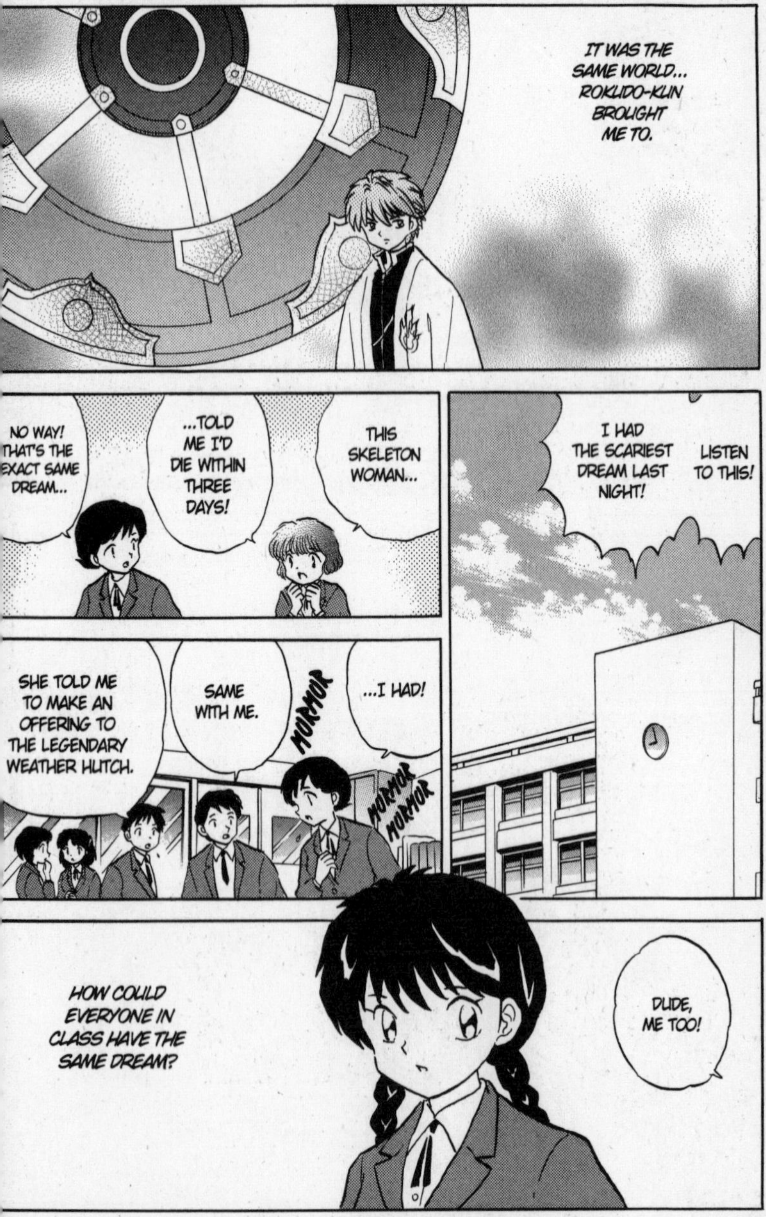
IT WAS THE SAME WORLD... ROKUDO-KUN BROUGHT ME TO.
LISTEN TO THIS!
I HAD THE SCARIEST DREAM LAST NIGHT!
THIS SKELETON WOMAN...
...TOLD ME I'D DIE WITHIN THREE DAYS!
NO WAY! THAT'S THE EXACT SAME DREAM...
...I HAD!
MORMOR
SAME WITH ME.
SHE TOLD ME TO MAKE AN OFFERING TO THE LEGENDARY WEATHER HUTCH.
MORMOR MORMOR
DUDE, ME TOO!
HOW COULD EVERYONE IN CLASS HAVE THE SAME DREAM?

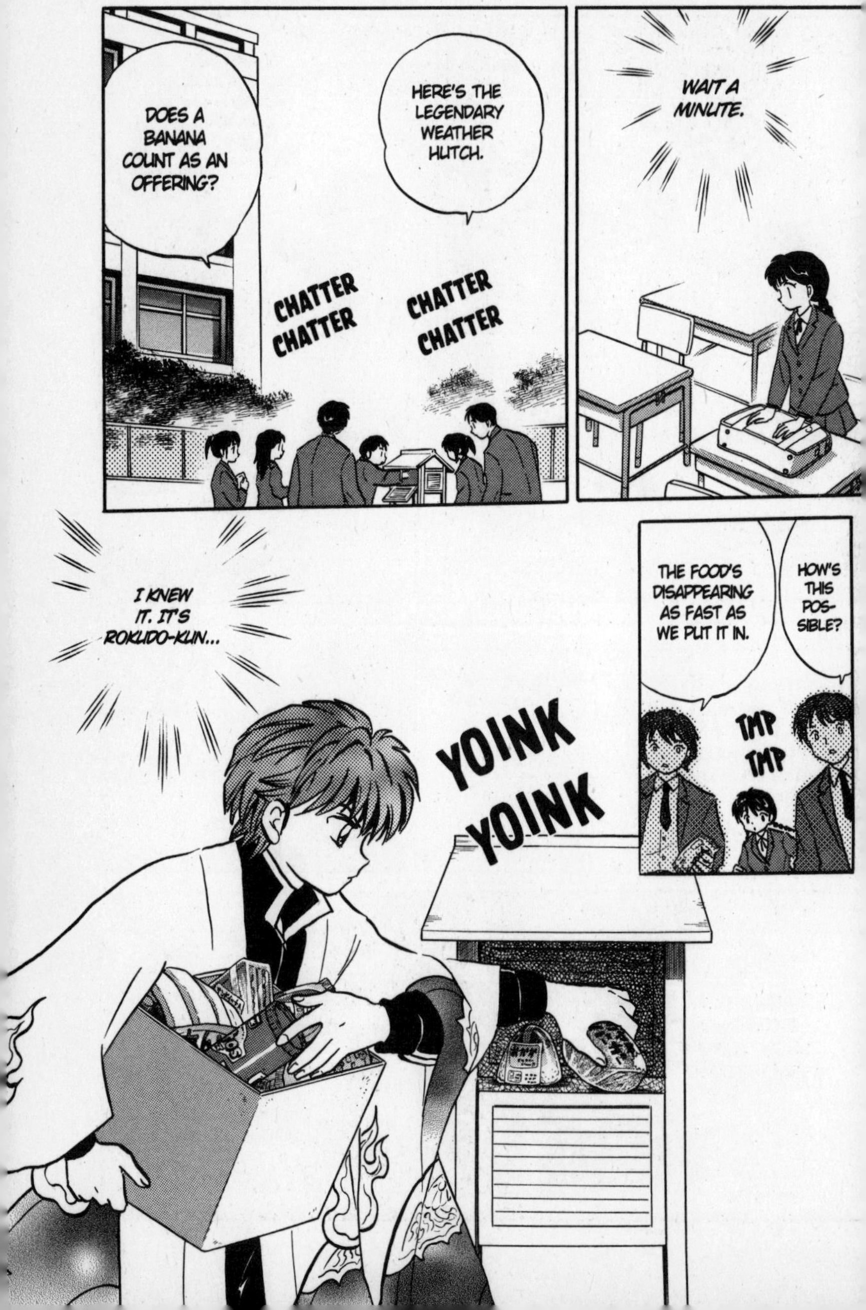
WAIT A MINUTE.
HERE'S THE LEGENDARY WEATHER HUTCH.
DOES A BANANA COUNT AS AN OFFERING?
CHATTER CHATTER
CHATTER CHATTER
HOW'S THIS POS-SIBLE?
THE FOOD'S DISAPPEARING AS FAST AS WE PUT IT IN.
TMP TMP
I KNEW IT. IT'S ROKUDO-KUN...
YOINK YOINK

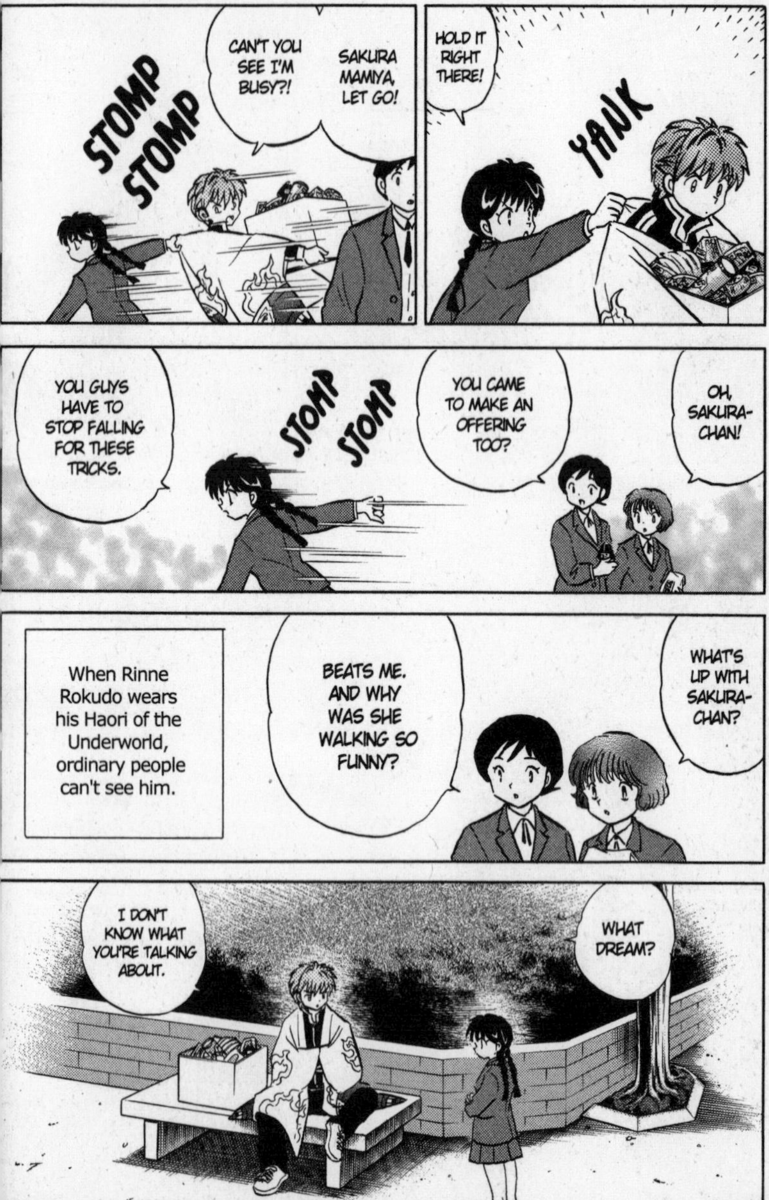
HOLD IT RIGHT THERE!
YANK
SAKURA MAMIYA, LET GO!
CAN'T YOU SEE I'M BUSY?!
STOMP STOMP
OH, SAKURA-CHAN!
YOU CAME TO MAKE AN OFFERING TOO?
STOMP STOMP
YOU GUYS HAVE TO STOP FALLING FOR THESE TRICKS.
WHAT'S UP WITH SAKURA-CHAN?
BEATS ME. AND WHY WAS SHE WALKING SO FUNNY?
When Rinne Rokudo wears his Haori of the Underworld, ordinary people can't see him.
WHAT DREAM?
I DON'T KNOW WHAT YOU'RE TALKING ABOUT.

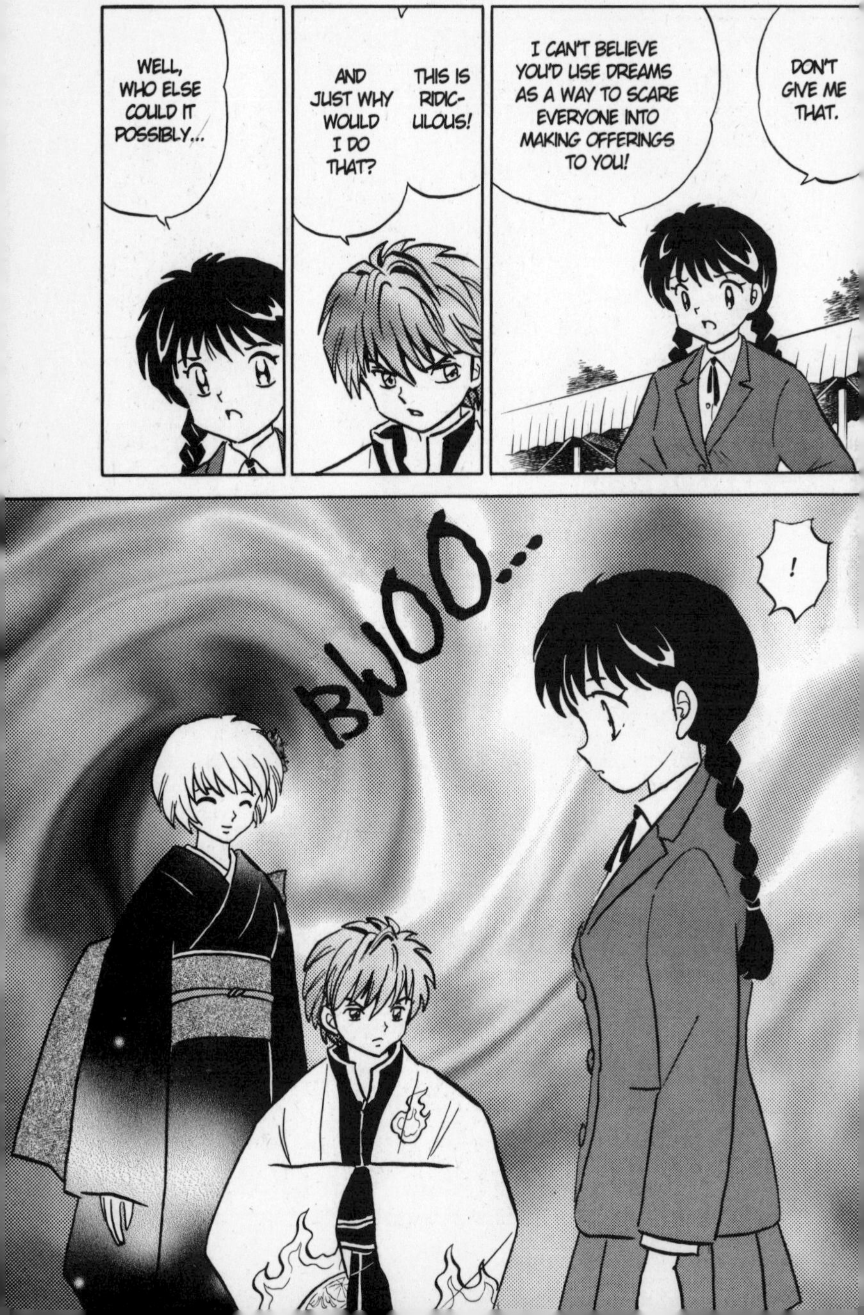
DON'T GIVE ME THAT.
I CAN'T BELIEVE YOU'D USE DREAMS AS A WAY TO SCARE EVERYONE INTO MAKING OFFERINGS TO YOU!
THIS IS RIDIC-ULOUS!
AND JUST WHY WOULD I DO THAT?
WELL, WHO ELSE COULD IT POSSIBLY...
!
BWOO...

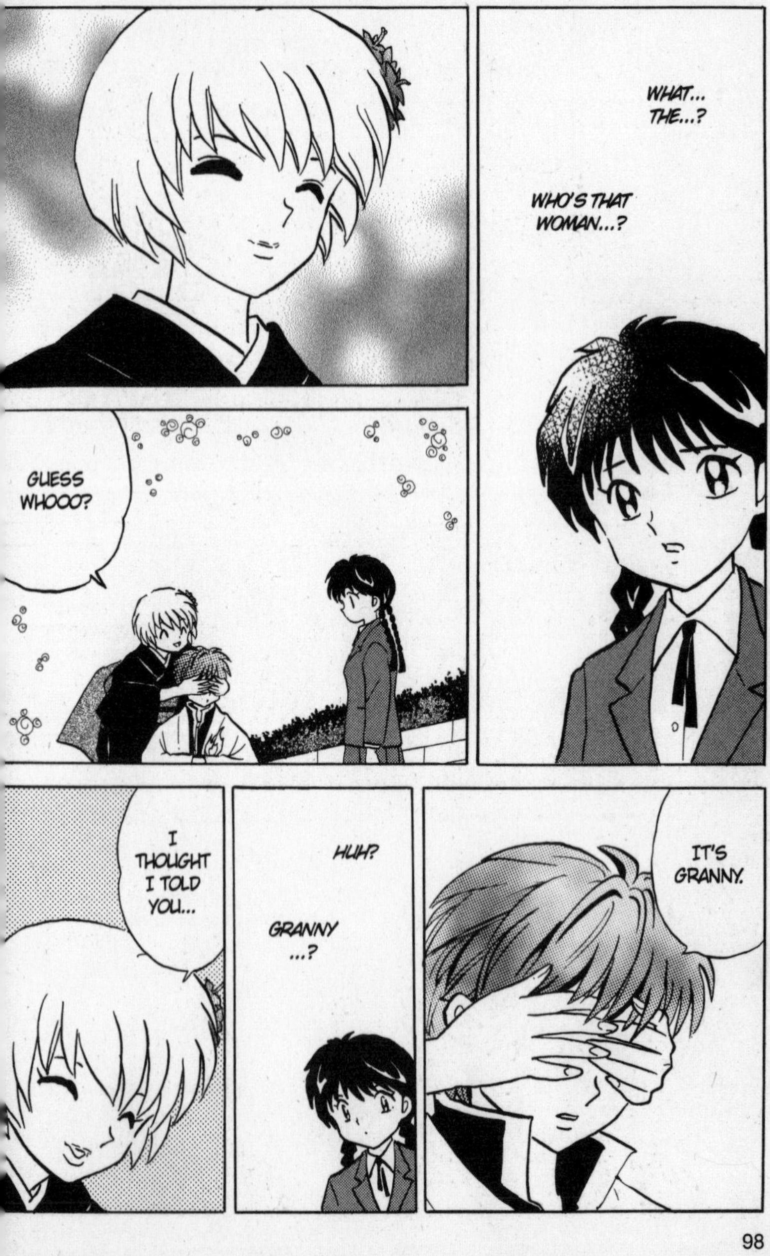
WHAT... THE...?
WHO'S THAT WOMAN...?
GUESS WHOOO?
IT'S GRANNY.
HUH?
GRANNY ...?
I THOUGHT I TOLD YOU...

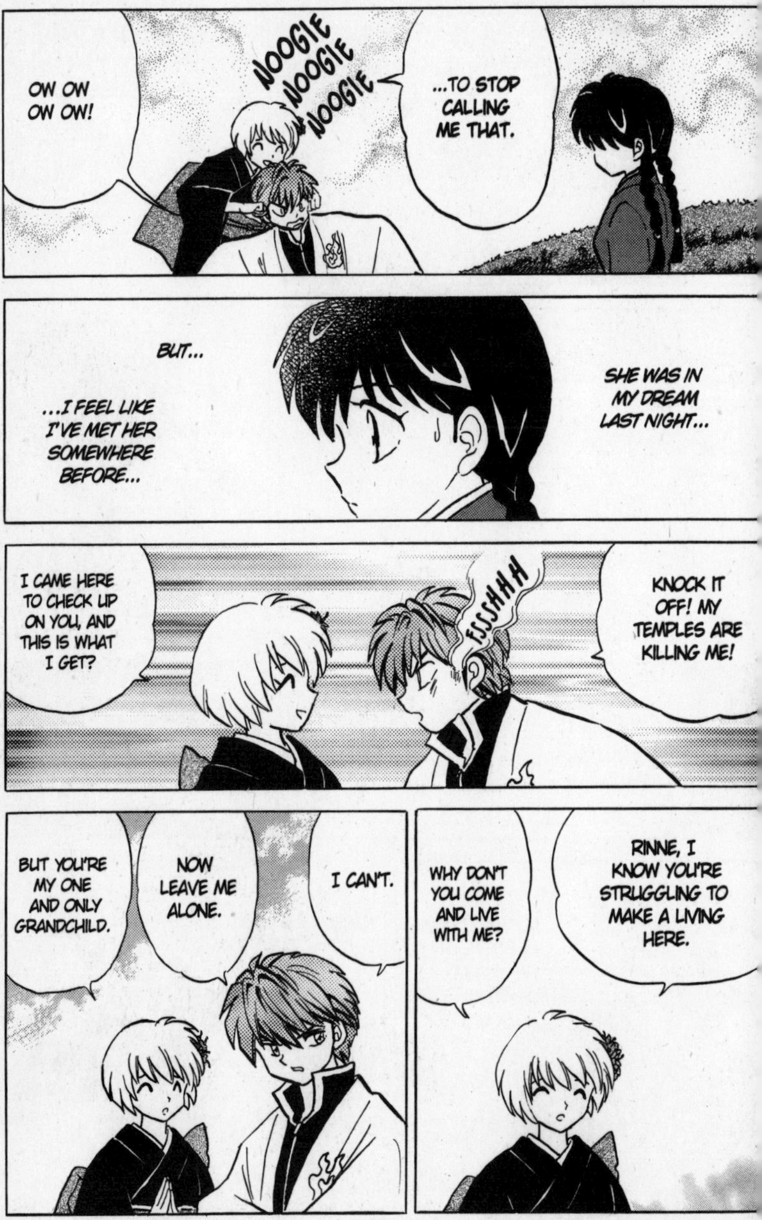
...TO STOP CALLING ME THAT.
NOOGIE NOOGIE NOOGIE
OW OW OW OW!
SHE WAS IN MY DREAM LAST NIGHT...
BUT...
...I FEEL LIKE I'VE MET HER SOMEWHERE BEFORE...
KNOCK IT OFF! MY TEMPLES ARE KILLING ME!
FSSSHHH
I CAME HERE TO CHECK UP ON YOU, AND THIS IS WHAT I GET?
RINNE, I KNOW YOU'RE STRUGGLING TO MAKE A LIVING HERE.
WHY DON'T YOU COME AND LIVE WITH ME?
I CAN'T.
NOW LEAVE ME ALONE.
BUT YOU'RE MY ONE AND ONLY GRANDCHILD.

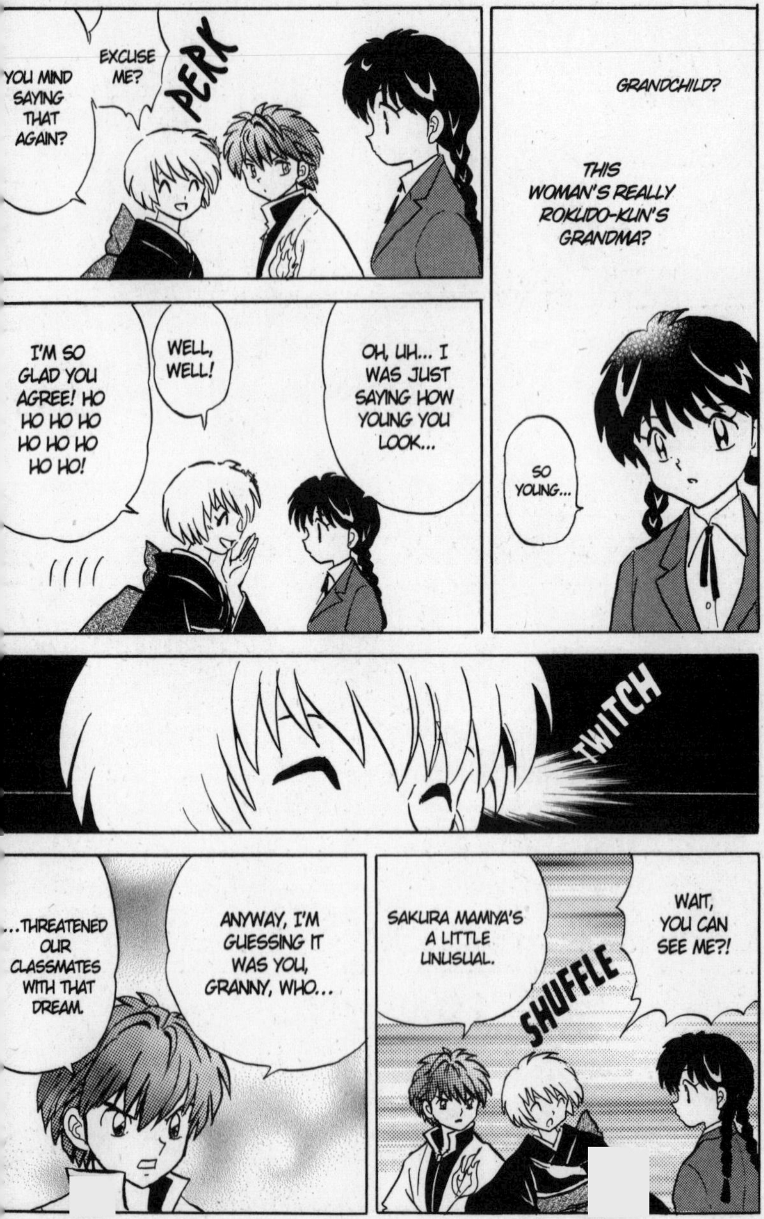
GRANDCHILD?
THIS WOMAN'S REALLY ROKUDO-KUN'S GRANDMA?
SO YOUNG...
PERK
EXCUSE ME?
YOU MIND SAYING THAT AGAIN?
OH, UH... I WAS JUST SAYING HOW YOUNG YOU LOOK...
WELL, WELL!
I'M SO GLAD YOU AGREE! HO HO HO HO HO HO HO HO HO!
TWITCH
WAIT, YOU CAN SEE ME?!
SHUFFLE
SAKURA MAMIYA'S A LITTLE UNUSUAL.
ANYWAY, I'M GUESSING IT WAS YOU, GRANNY, WHO...
...THREATENED OUR CLASSMATES WITH THAT DREAM.

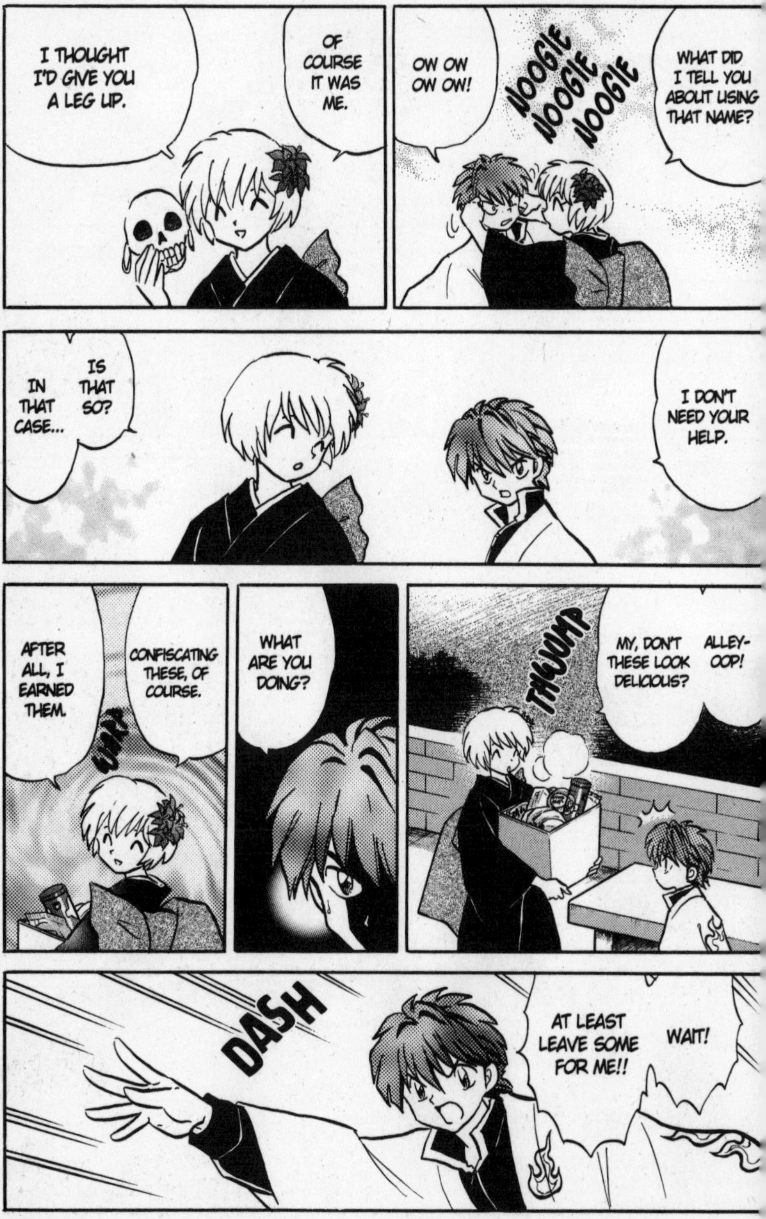
WHAT DID I TELL YOU ABOUT USING THAT NAME?
NOOGIE NOOGIE NOOGIE
OW OW OW OW!
OF COURSE IT WAS ME.
I THOUGHT I'D GIVE YOU A LEG UP.
I DON'T NEED YOUR HELP.
IS THAT SO?
IN THAT CASE...
ALLEY-OOP!
MY, DON'T THESE LOOK DELICIOUS?
THWUMP
WHAT ARE YOU DOING?
CONFISCATING THESE, OF COURSE.
AFTER ALL, I EARNED THEM.
WAIT!
AT LEAST LEAVE SOME FOR ME!!
DASH

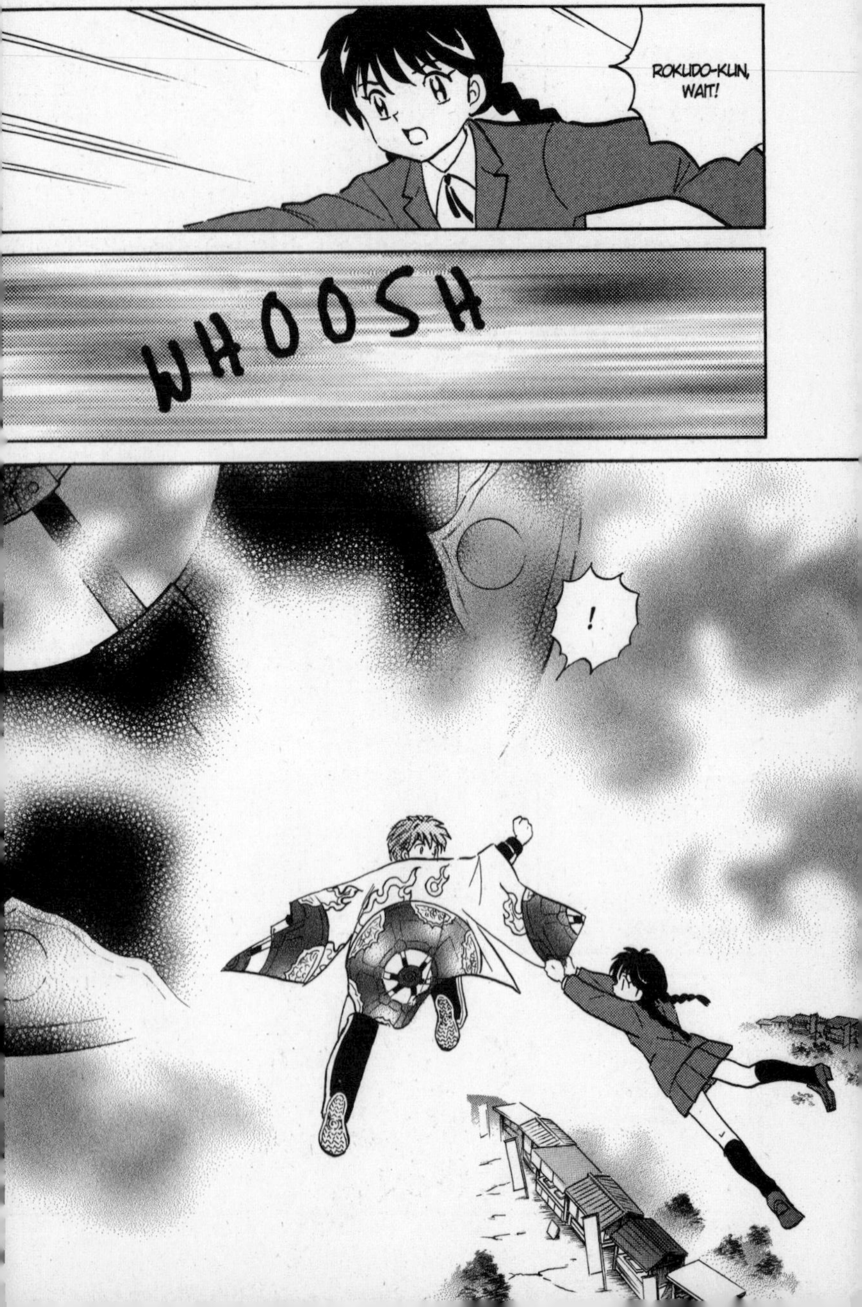
ROKUDO-KUN, WAIT!
WHOOSH
!

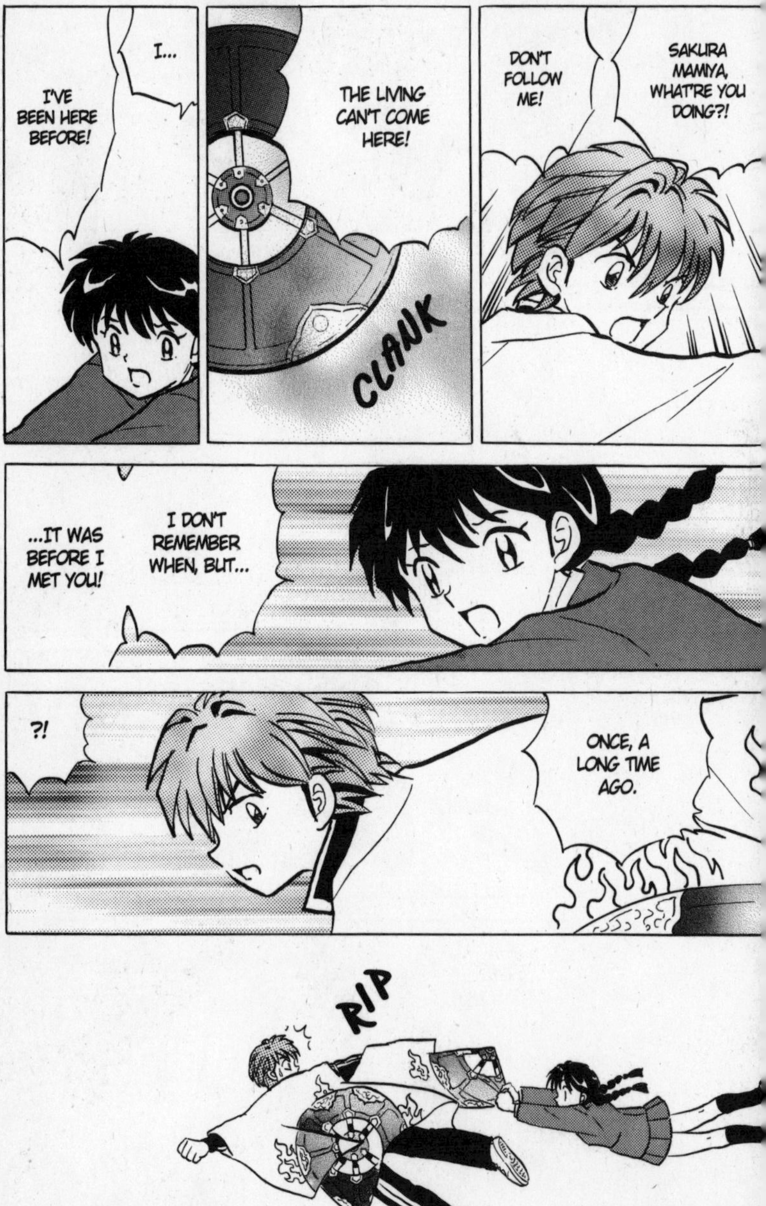
SAKURA MAMIYA, WHAT'RE YOU DOING?!
DON'T FOLLOW ME!
THE LIVING CAN'T COME HERE!
CLANK
I...
I'VE BEEN HERE BEFORE!
I DON'T REMEMBER WHEN, BUT...
...IT WAS BEFORE I MET YOU!
ONCE, A LONG TIME AGO.
?!
RIP

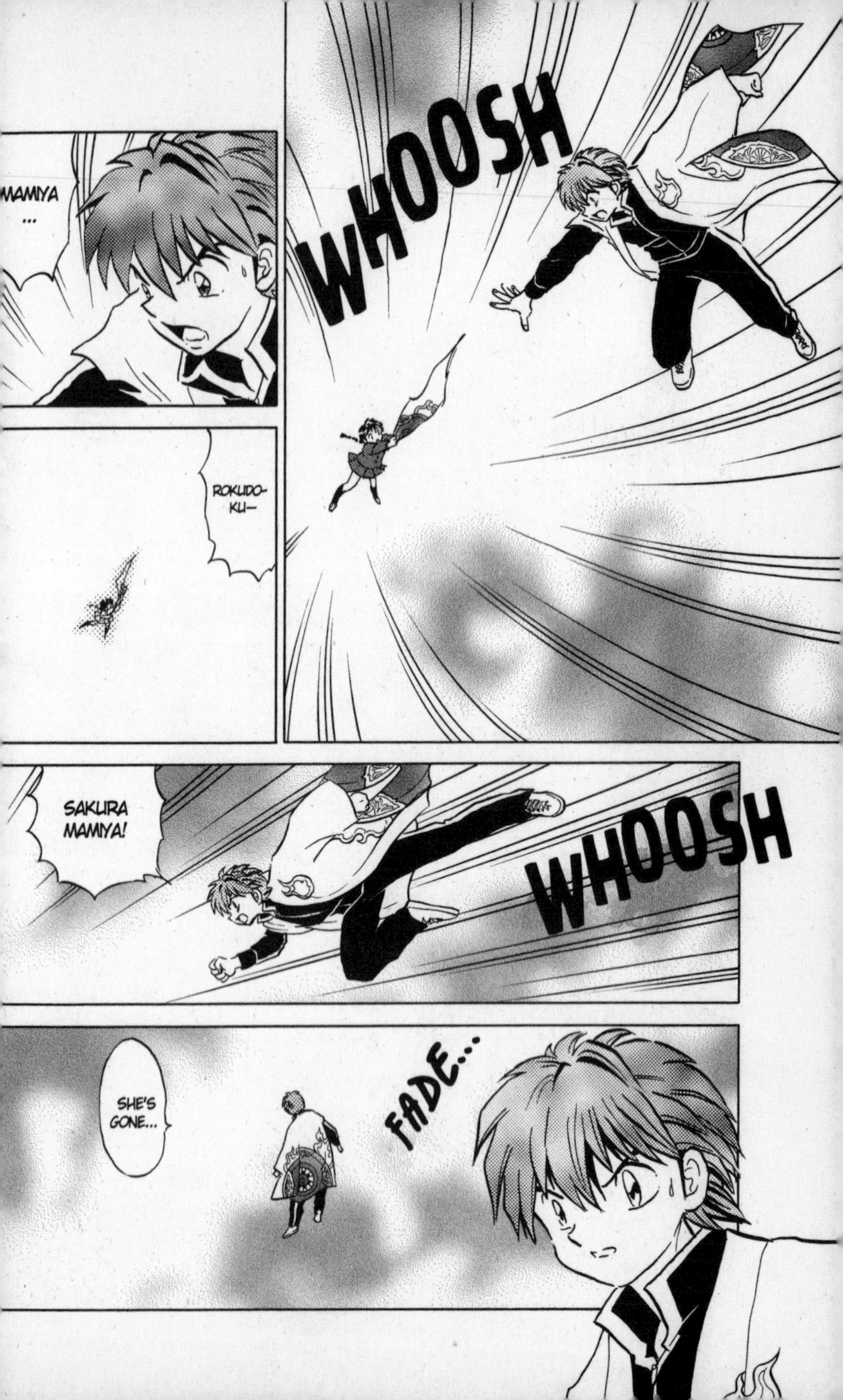
WHOOSH
MAMIYA ...
ROKUDO-KU—
WHOOSH
SAKURA MAMIYA!
FADE...
SHE'S GONE...

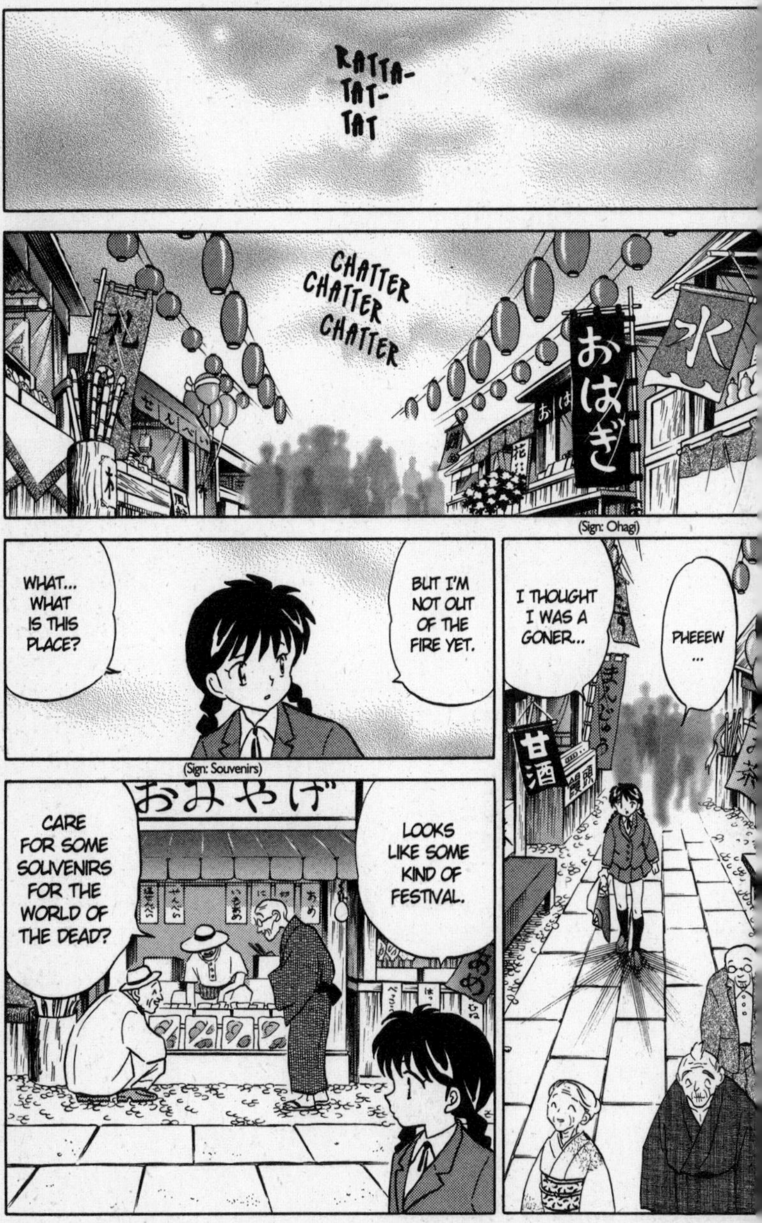
RATTA-TAT-TAT
CHATTER CHATTER CHATTER
水
おはぎ
(Sign: Ohagi)
PHEEEW...
I THOUGHT I WAS A GONER...
甘酒
BUT I'M NOT OUT OF THE FIRE YET.
WHAT... WHAT IS THIS PLACE?
(Sign: Souvenirs)
おみやげ
LOOKS LIKE SOME KIND OF FESTIVAL.
CARE FOR SOME SOUVENIRS FOR THE WORLD OF THE DEAD?

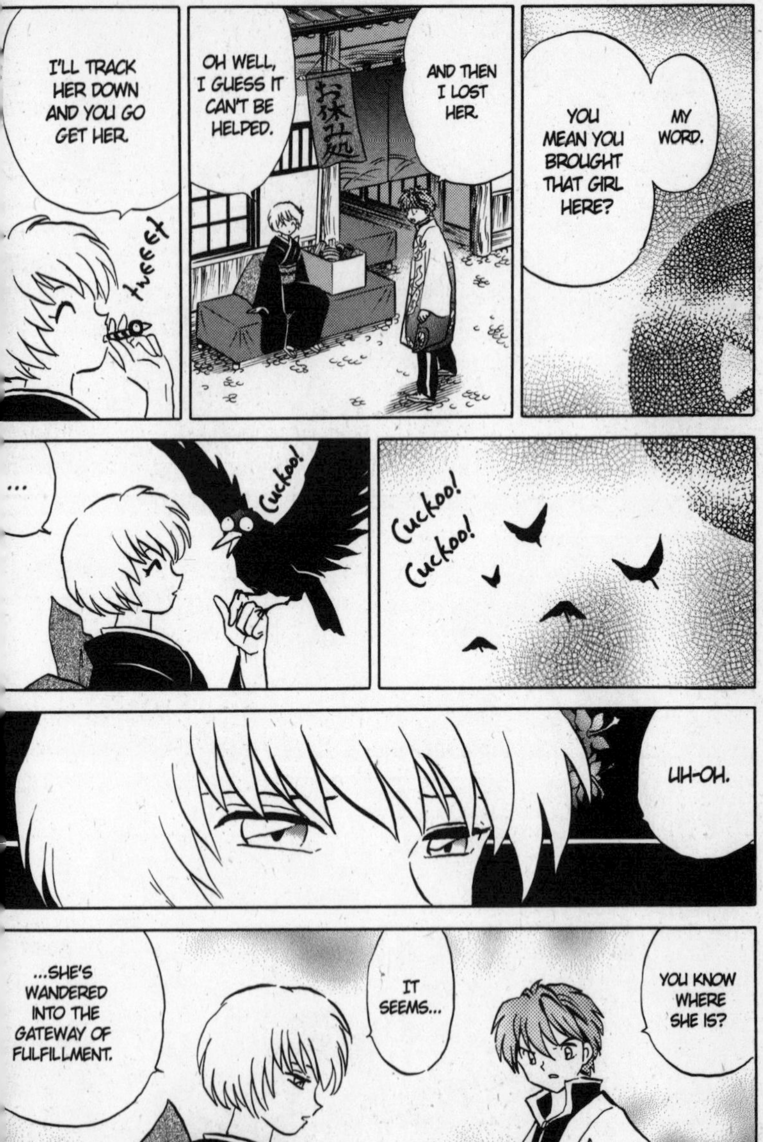
MY WORD.
YOU MEAN YOU BROUGHT THAT GIRL HERE?
AND THEN I LOST HER.
お休み処
OH WELL, I GUESS IT CAN'T BE HELPED.
I'LL TRACK HER DOWN AND YOU GO GET HER.
tweeet
Cuckoo! Cuckoo!
Cuckoo!
...
UH-OH.
YOU KNOW WHERE SHE IS?
IT SEEMS...
...SHE'S WANDERED INTO THE GATEWAY OF FULFILLMENT.

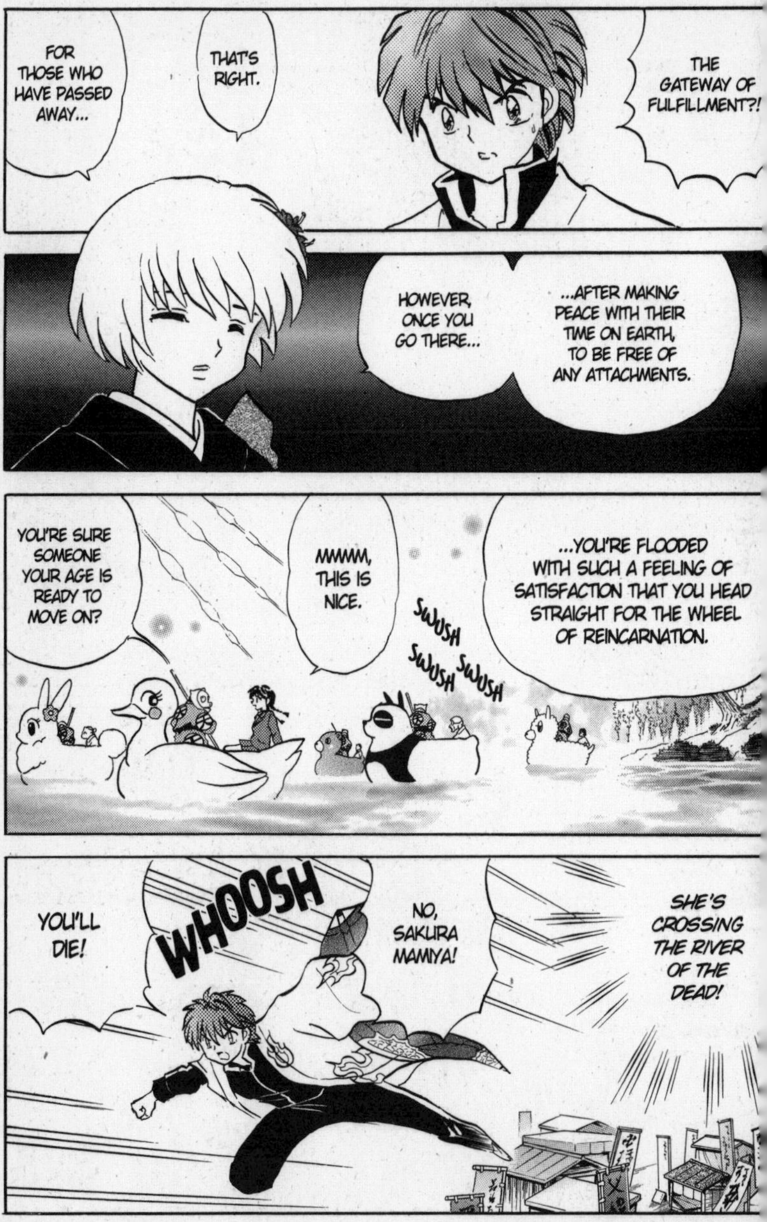
THE GATEWAY OF FULFILLMENT?!
THAT'S RIGHT.
FOR THOSE WHO HAVE PASSED AWAY...
...AFTER MAKING PEACE WITH THEIR TIME ON EARTH, TO BE FREE OF ANY ATTACHMENTS.
HOWEVER, ONCE YOU GO THERE...
...YOU'RE FLOODED WITH SUCH A FEELING OF SATISFACTION THAT YOU HEAD STRAIGHT FOR THE WHEEL OF REINCARNATION.
SWUSH SWUSH SWUSH
MMMM, THIS IS NICE.
YOU'RE SURE SOMEONE YOUR AGE IS READY TO MOVE ON?
SHE'S CROSSING THE RIVER OF THE DEAD!
NO, SAKURA MAMIYA!
WHOOSH
YOU'LL DIE!

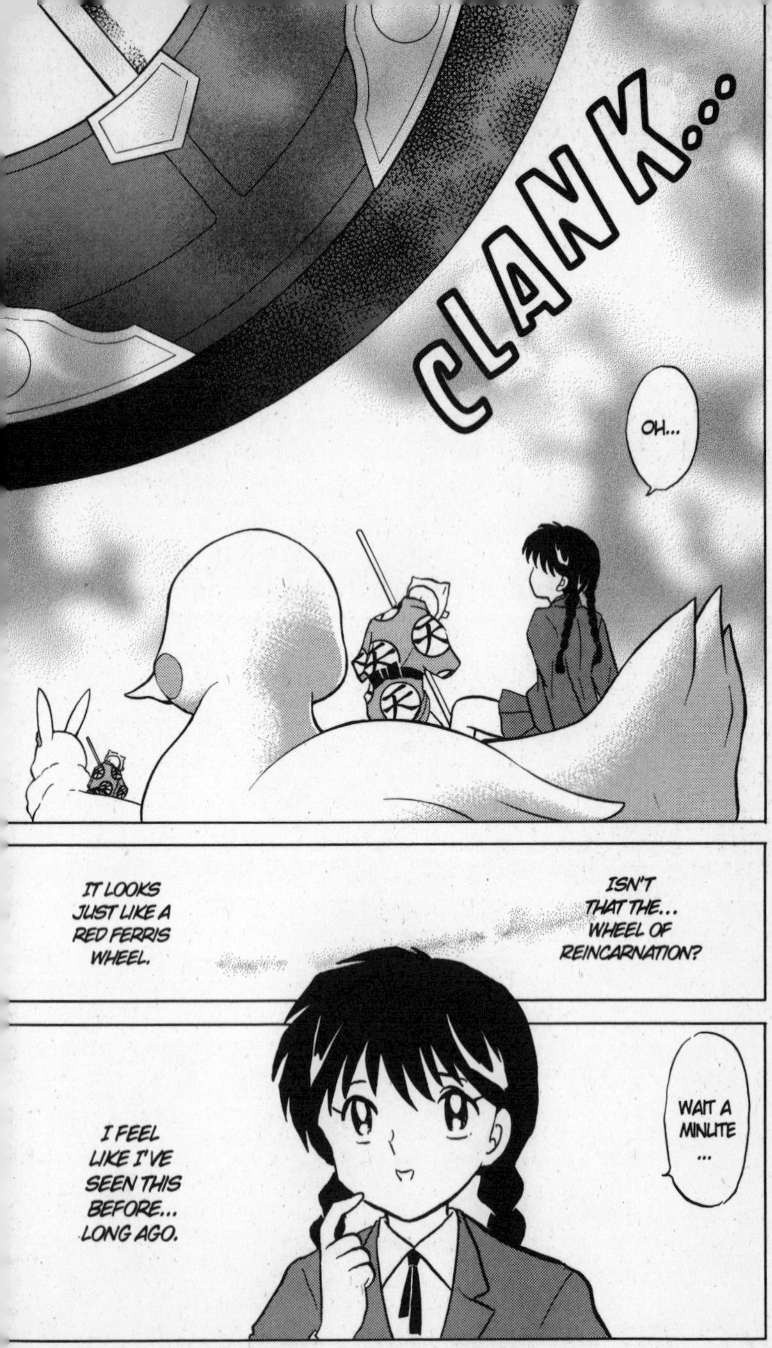
CLANK...
OH...
ISN'T THAT THE... WHEEL OF REINCARNATION?
IT LOOKS JUST LIKE A RED FERRIS WHEEL.
WAIT A MINUTE...
I FEEL LIKE I'VE SEEN THIS BEFORE... LONG AGO.

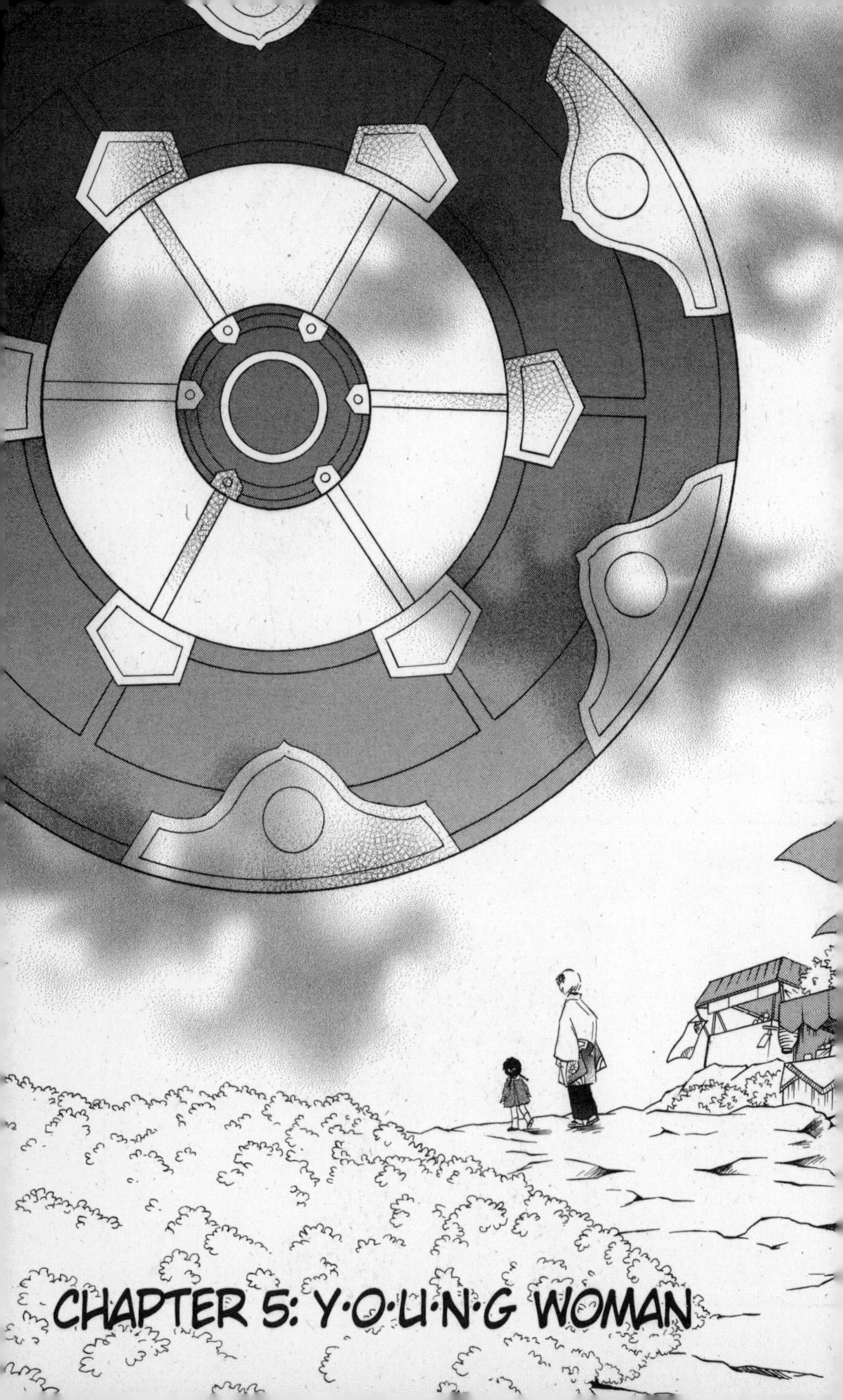

CHAPTER 5: Y·O·U·N·G WOMAN

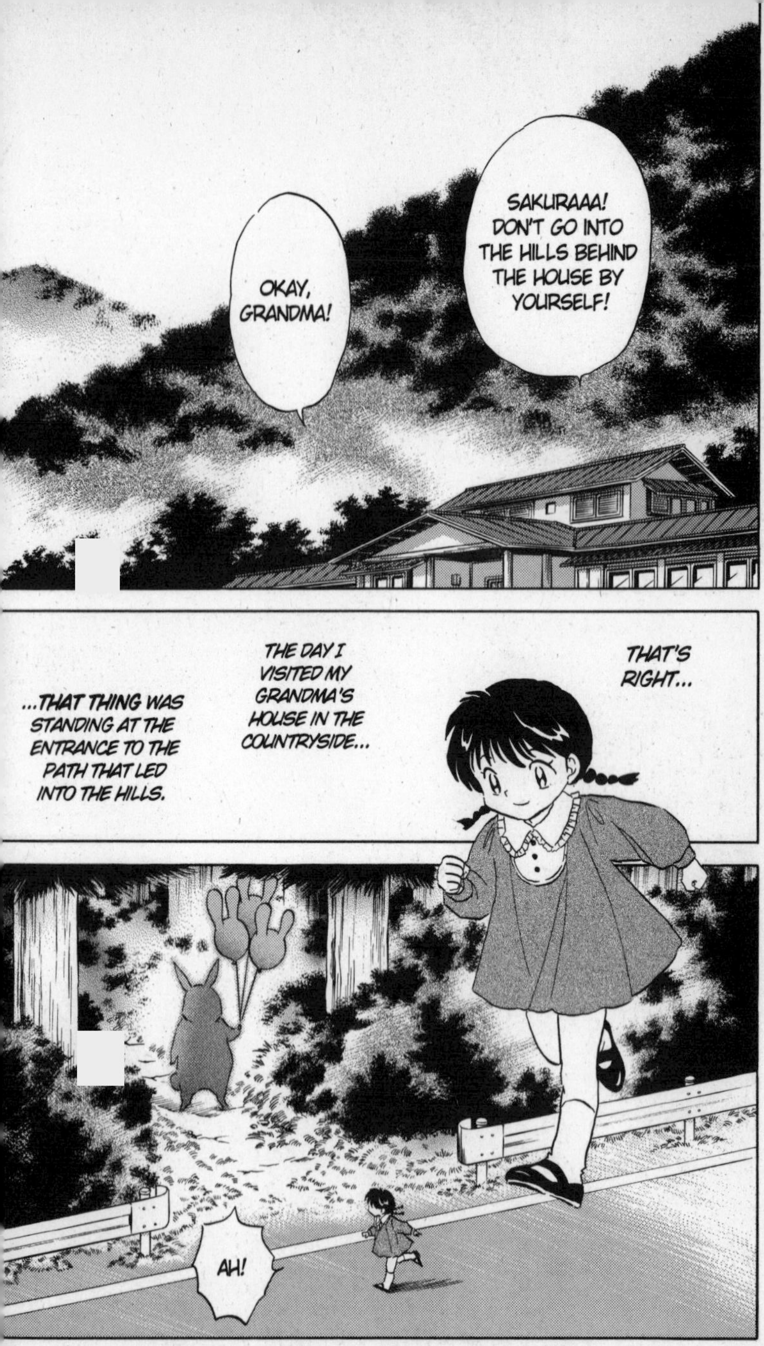
SAKURAAA! DON'T GO INTO THE HILLS BEHIND THE HOUSE BY YOURSELF!
OKAY, GRANDMA!
THAT'S RIGHT...
THE DAY I VISITED MY GRANDMA'S HOUSE IN THE COUNTRYSIDE...
...THAT THING WAS STANDING AT THE ENTRANCE TO THE PATH THAT LED INTO THE HILLS.
AH!

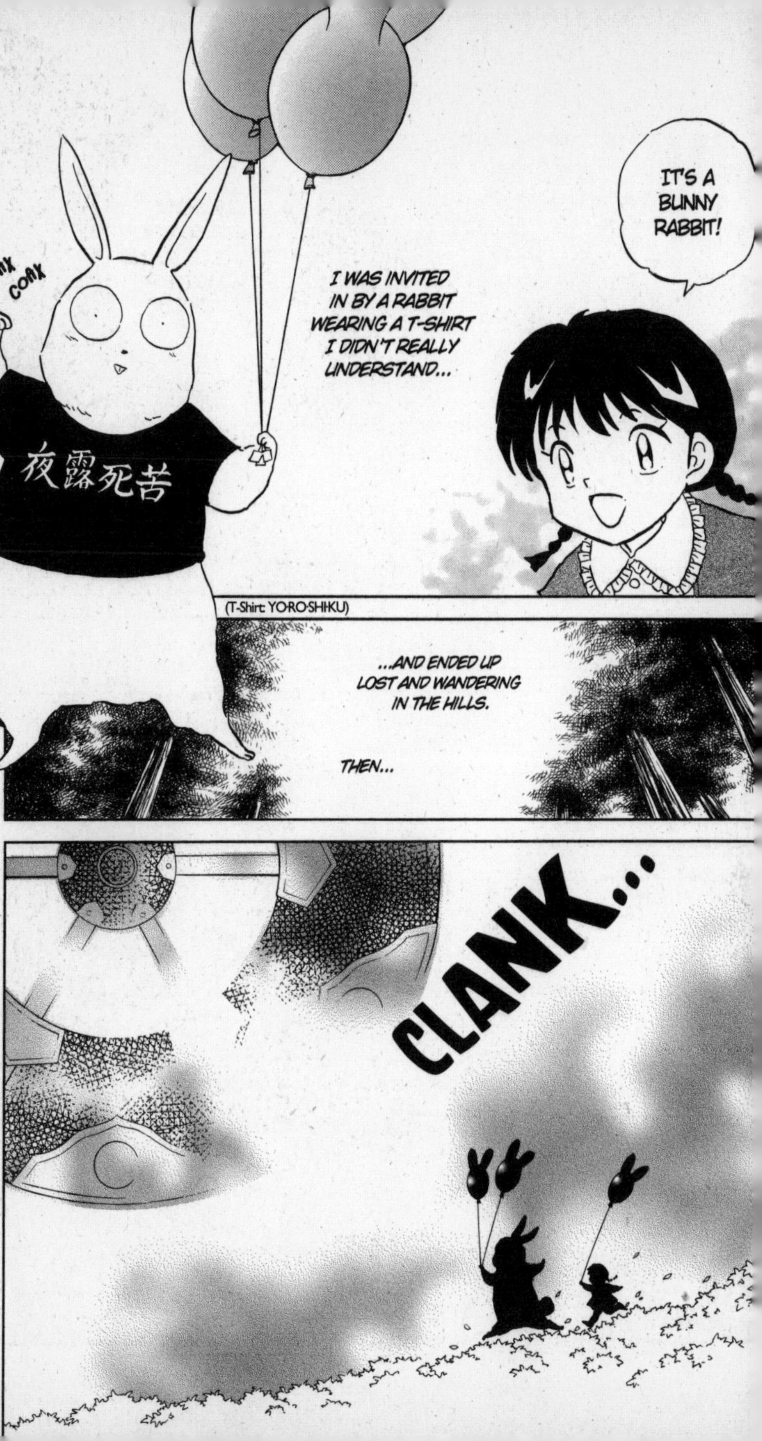
IT'S A BUNNY RABBIT!
I WAS INVITED IN BY A RABBIT WEARING A T-SHIRT I DIDN'T REALLY UNDERSTAND...
COAX COAX
夜露死苦
(T-Shirt: YO·RO·SHIKU)
...AND ENDED UP LOST AND WANDERING IN THE HILLS.
THEN...
CLANK...

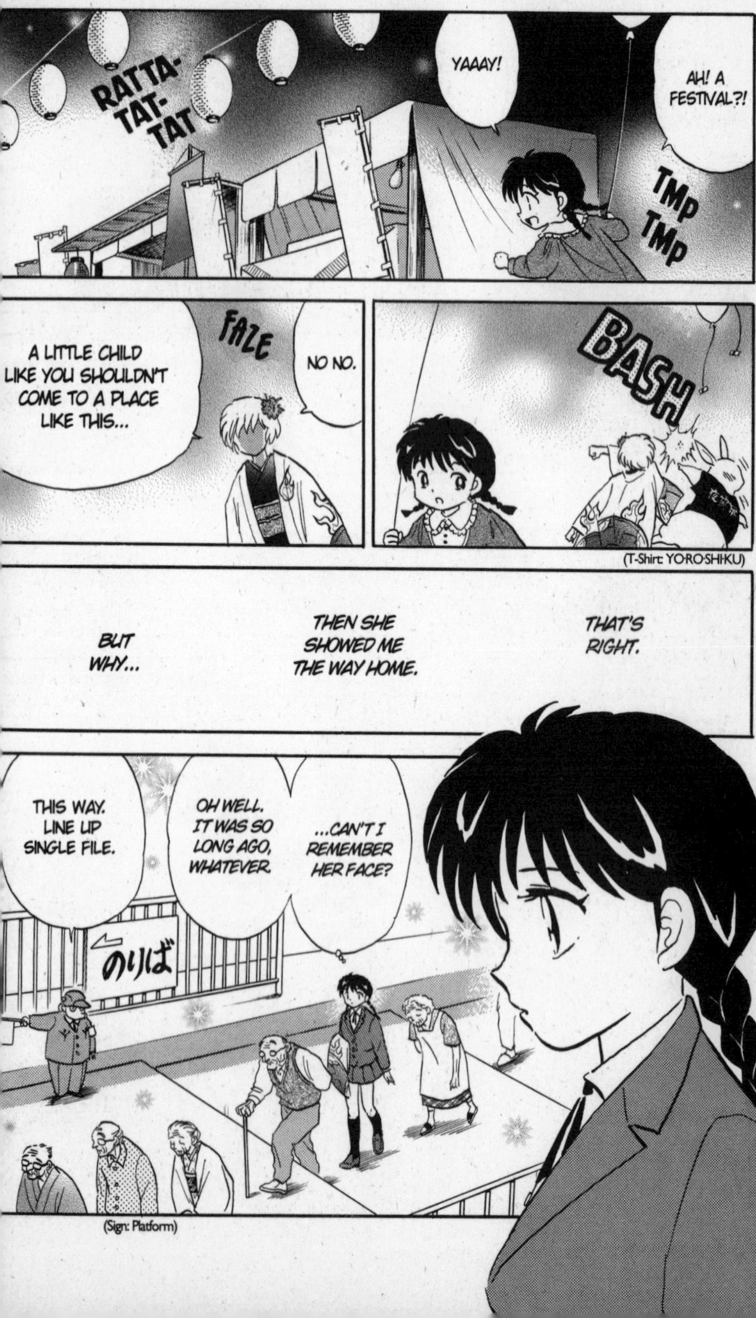
AH! A FESTIVAL?!
TMP TMP
YAAAY!
RATTA-TAT-TAT
BASH
(T-Shirt: YO·RO·SHI·KU)
NO NO.
FAZE
A LITTLE CHILD LIKE YOU SHOULDN'T COME TO A PLACE LIKE THIS...
THAT'S RIGHT.
THEN SHE SHOWED ME THE WAY HOME.
BUT WHY...
...CAN'T I REMEMBER HER FACE?
OH WELL. IT WAS SO LONG AGO, WHATEVER.
THIS WAY. LINE UP SINGLE FILE.
のりば
(Sign: Platform)

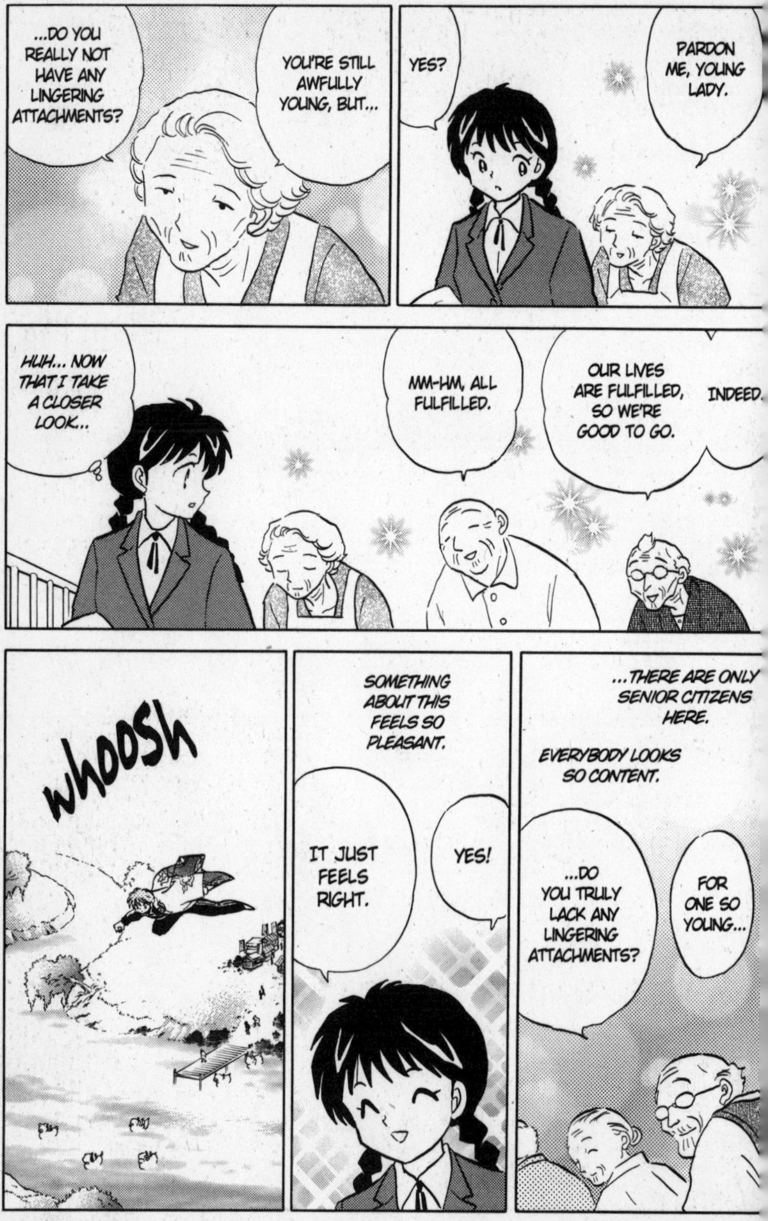
PARDON ME, YOUNG LADY.
YES?
YOU'RE STILL AWFULLY YOUNG, BUT...
...DO YOU REALLY NOT HAVE ANY LINGERING ATTACHMENTS?
INDEED.
OUR LIVES ARE FULFILLED, SO WE'RE GOOD TO GO.
MM-HM, ALL FULFILLED.
HUH... NOW THAT I TAKE A CLOSER LOOK...
...THERE ARE ONLY SENIOR CITIZENS HERE.
EVERYBODY LOOKS SO CONTENT.
FOR ONE SO YOUNG...
...DO YOU TRULY LACK ANY LINGERING ATTACHMENTS?
SOMETHING ABOUT THIS FEELS SO PLEASANT.
YES!
IT JUST FEELS RIGHT.
whoosh

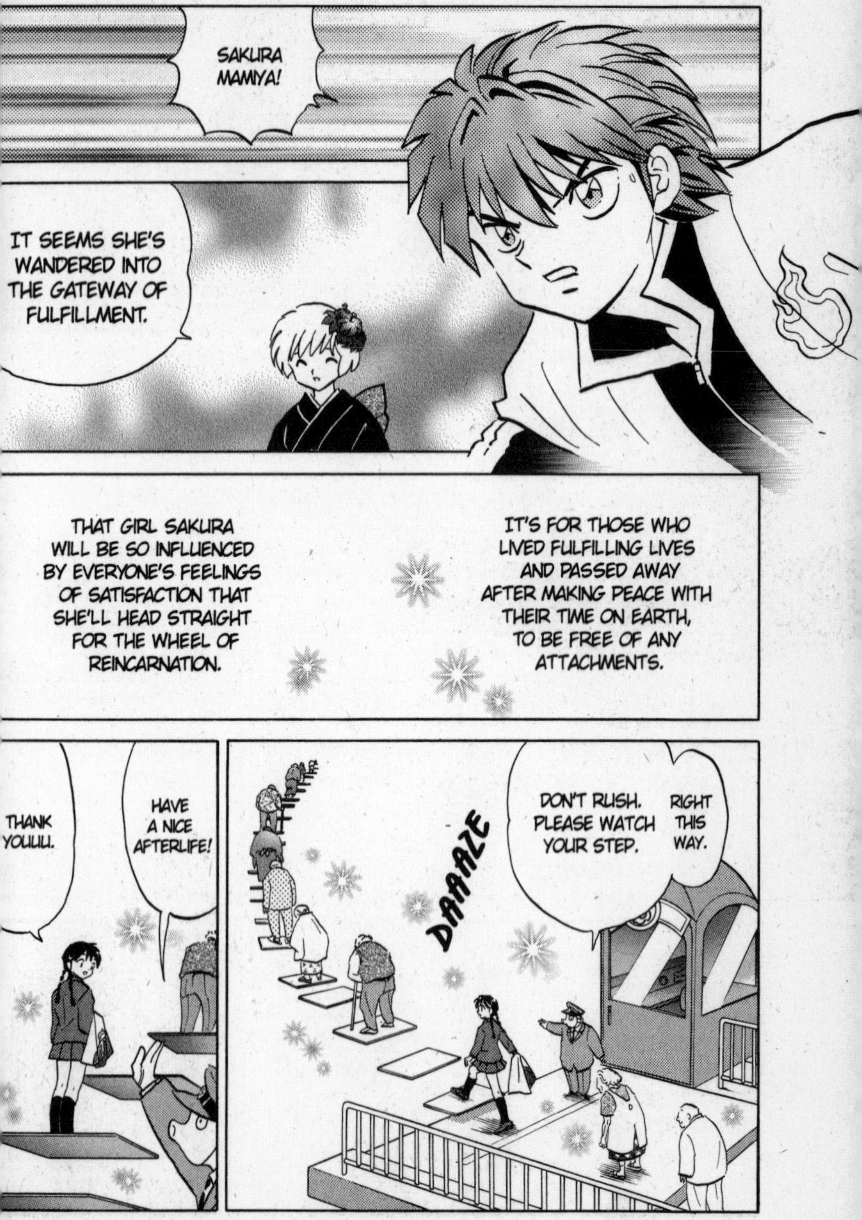
SAKURA MAMIYA!
IT SEEMS SHE'S WANDERED INTO THE GATEWAY OF FULFILLMENT.
IT'S FOR THOSE WHO LIVED FULFILLING LIVES AND PASSED AWAY AFTER MAKING PEACE WITH THEIR TIME ON EARTH, TO BE FREE OF ANY ATTACHMENTS.
THAT GIRL SAKURA WILL BE SO INFLUENCED BY EVERYONE'S FEELINGS OF SATISFACTION THAT SHE'LL HEAD STRAIGHT FOR THE WHEEL OF REINCARNATION.
RIGHT THIS WAY.
DON'T RUSH. PLEASE WATCH YOUR STEP.
DAAAZE
HAVE A NICE AFTERLIFE!
THANK YOUUU.

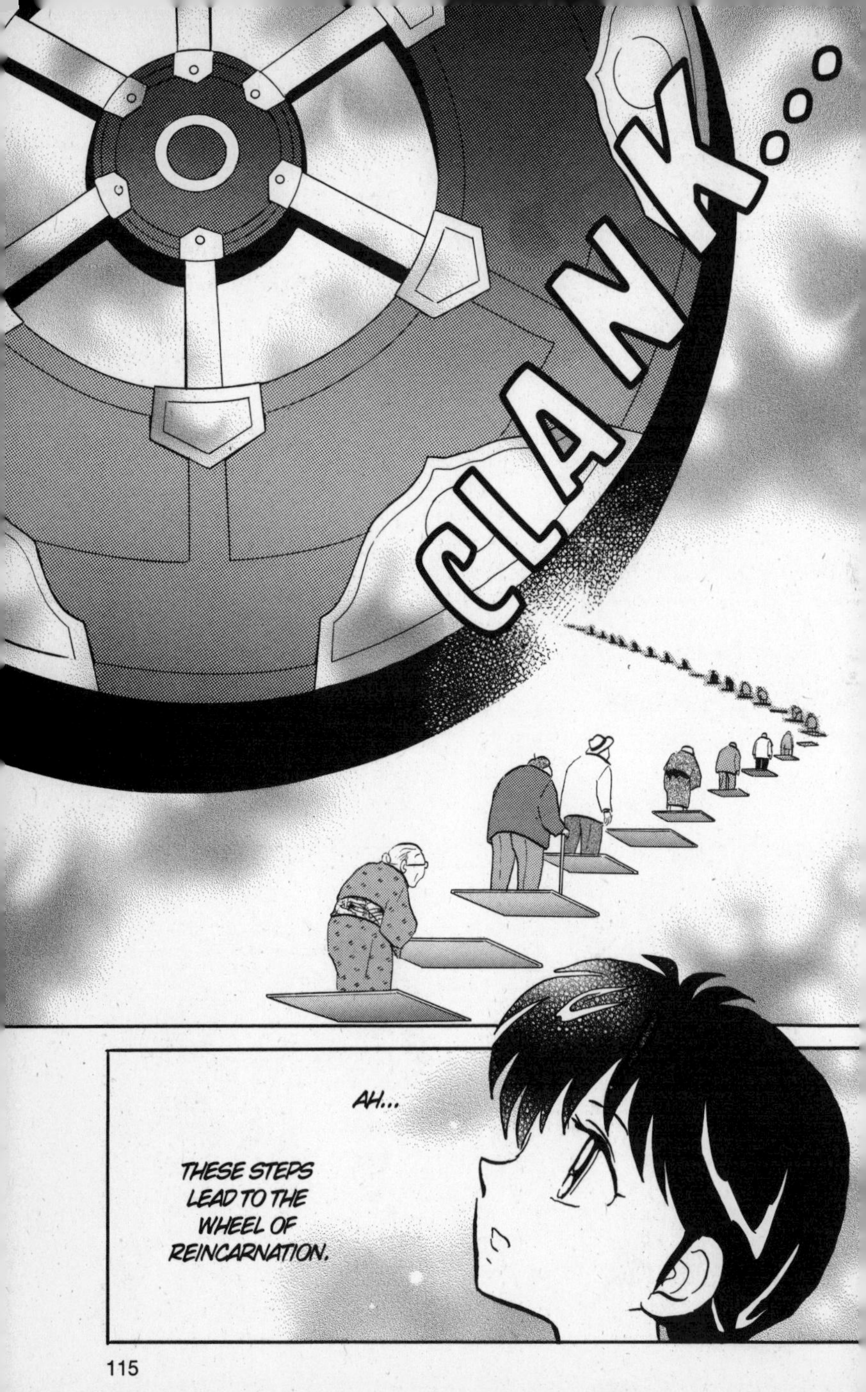
CLANK...
AH...
THESE STEPS LEAD TO THE WHEEL OF REINCARNATION.

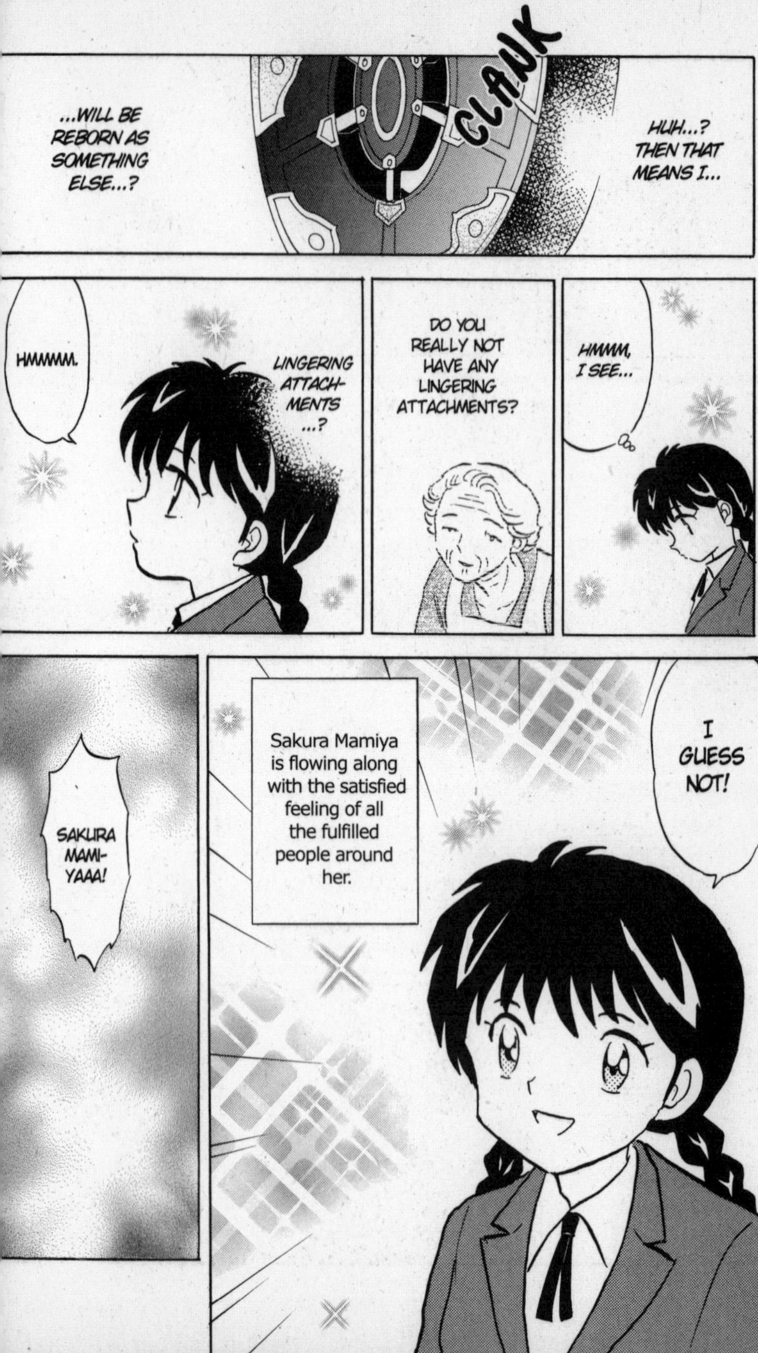
CLANK
HUH...? THEN THAT MEANS I...
...WILL BE REBORN AS SOMETHING ELSE...?
HMMM, I SEE...
DO YOU REALLY NOT HAVE ANY LINGERING ATTACHMENTS?
LINGERING ATTACH-MENTS ...?
HMMMM.
I GUESS NOT!
Sakura Mamiya is flowing along with the satisfied feeling of all the fulfilled people around her.
SAKURA MAMI-YAAA!

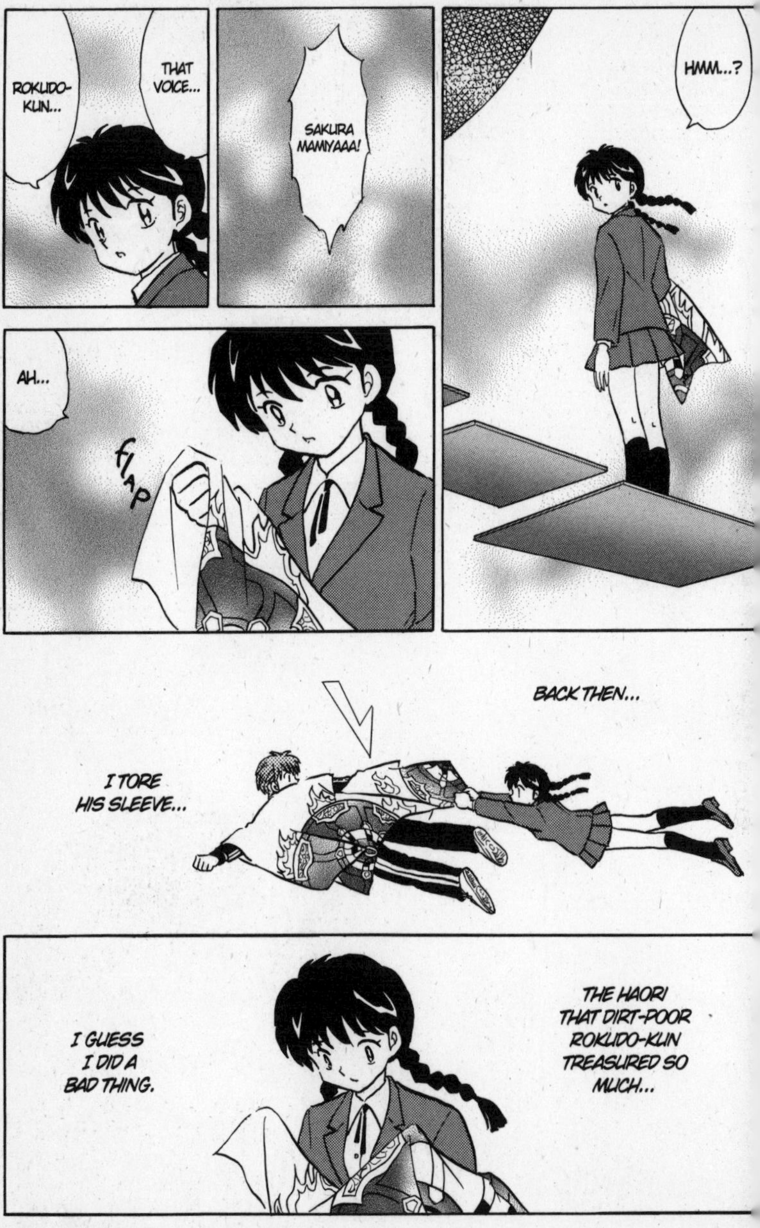
HMM...?
SAKURA MAMIYAAA!
THAT VOICE...
ROKUDO-KUN...
AH...
flap
BACK THEN...
I TORE HIS SLEEVE...
THE HAORI THAT DIRT-POOR ROKUDO-KUN TREASURED SO MUCH...
I GUESS I DID A BAD THING.

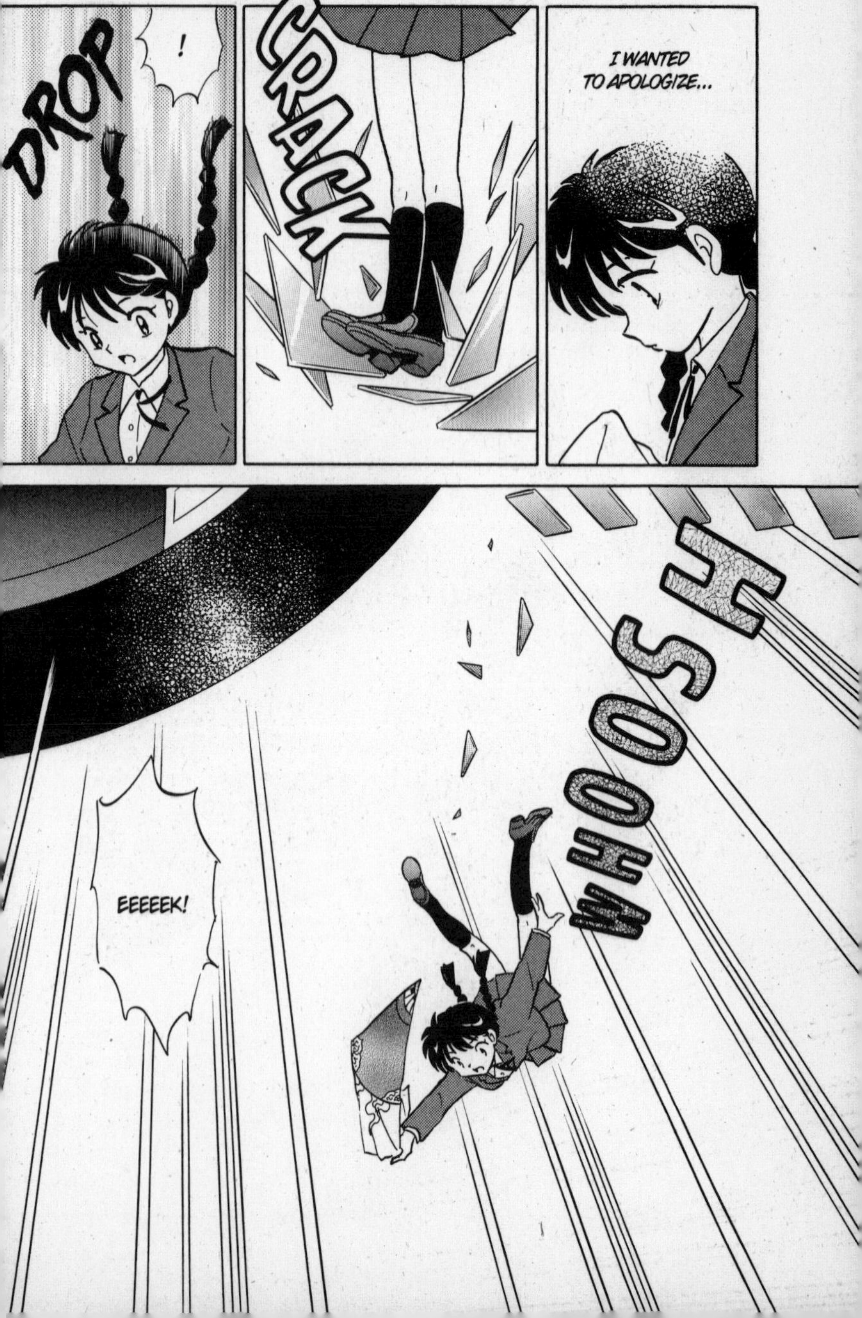
I WANTED TO APOLOGIZE...
CRACK
DROP
!
WHOOSH
EEEEEK!

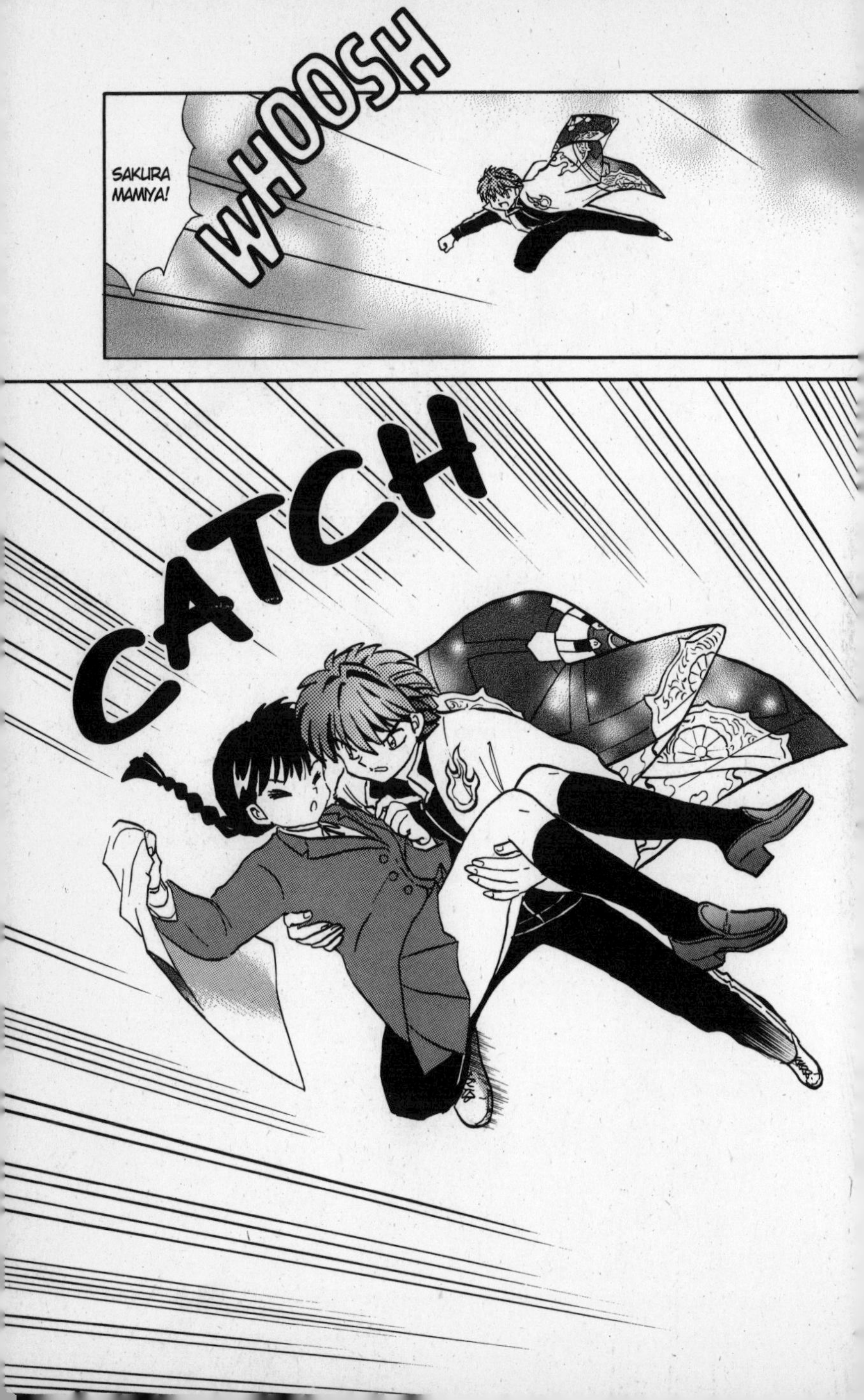
WHOOSH
SAKURA MAMIYA!
CATCH

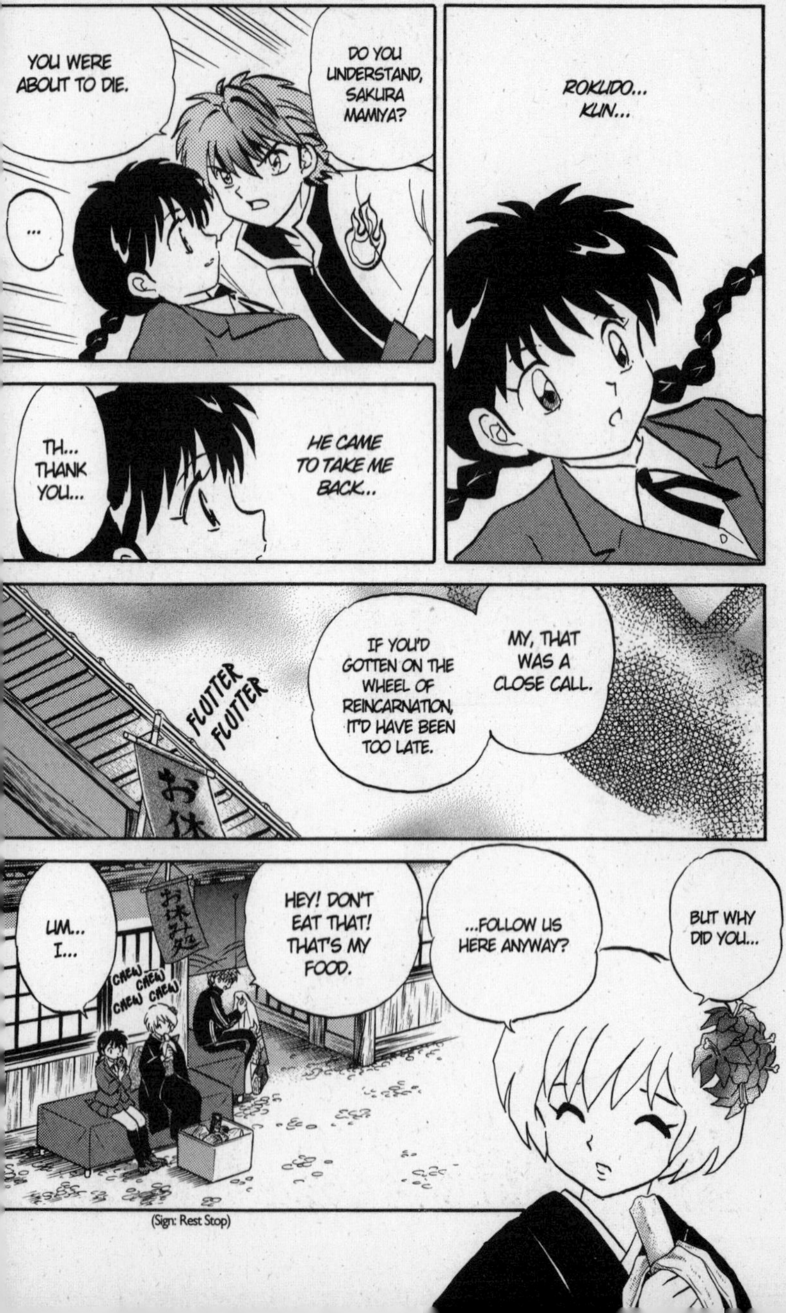
ROKUDO... KUN...
DO YOU UNDERSTAND, SAKURA MAMIYA?
YOU WERE ABOUT TO DIE.
...
HE CAME TO TAKE ME BACK...
TH... THANK YOU...
MY, THAT WAS A CLOSE CALL.
IF YOU'D GOTTEN ON THE WHEEL OF REINCARNATION, IT'D HAVE BEEN TOO LATE.
FLUTTER FLUTTER
BUT WHY DID YOU...
...FOLLOW US HERE ANYWAY?
HEY! DON'T EAT THAT! THAT'S MY FOOD.
UM... I...
CHEW CHEW CHEW CHEW
(Sign: Rest Stop)

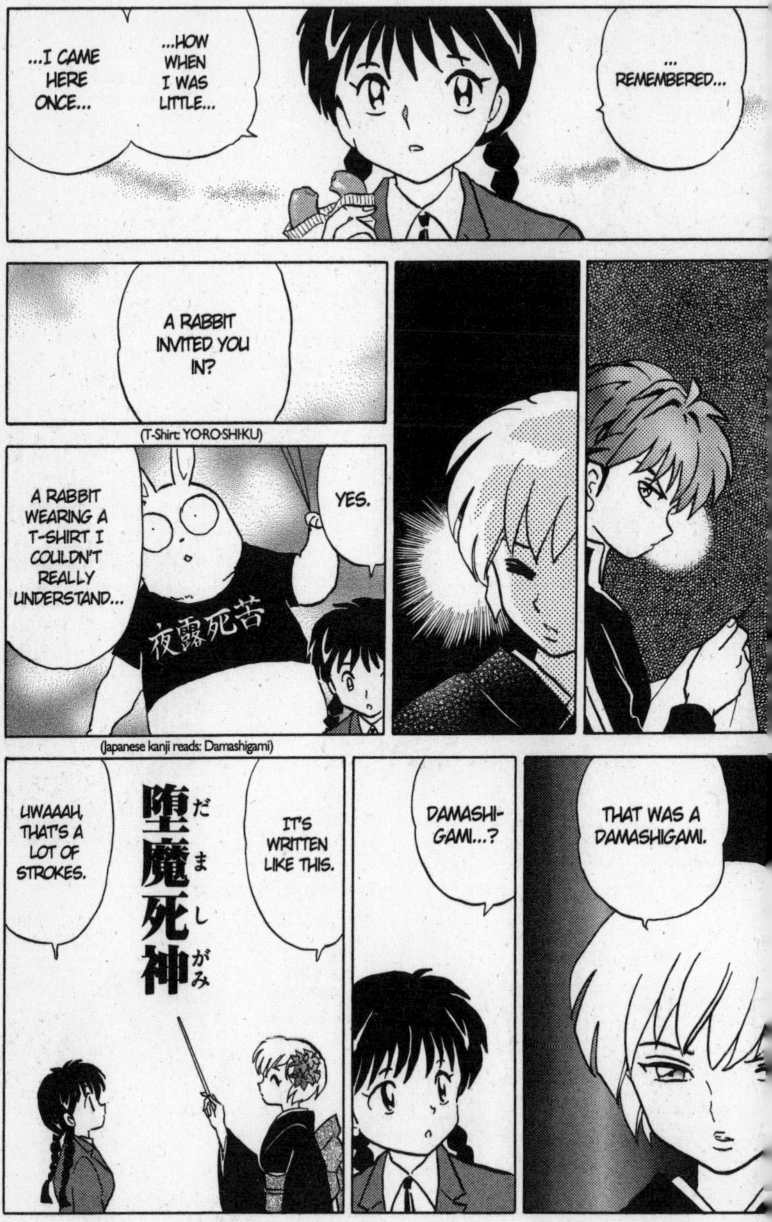
...REMEMBERED...
...HOW WHEN I WAS LITTLE...
...I CAME HERE ONCE...
A RABBIT INVITED YOU IN?
(T-Shirt: YO·RO·SHI·KU)
YES.
A RABBIT WEARING A T-SHIRT I COULDN'T REALLY UNDERSTAND...
夜露死苦
(Japanese kanji reads: Damashigami)
THAT WAS A DAMASHIGAMI.
DAMASHI-GAMI...?
IT'S WRITTEN LIKE THIS.
堕魔死神
だましがみ
UWAAAH, THAT'S A LOT OF STROKES.

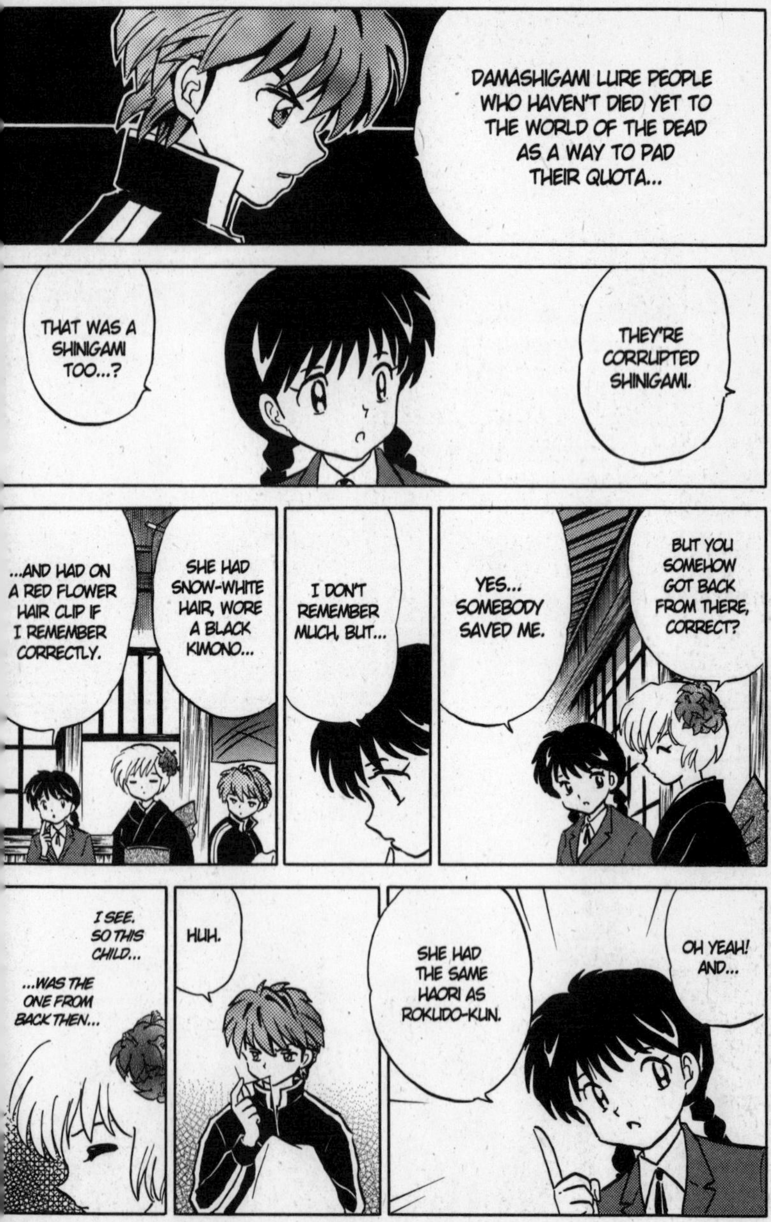
DAMASHIGAMI LURE PEOPLE WHO HAVEN'T DIED YET TO THE WORLD OF THE DEAD AS A WAY TO PAD THEIR QUOTA...
THAT WAS A SHINIGAMI TOO...?
THEY'RE CORRUPTED SHINIGAMI.
BUT YOU SOMEHOW GOT BACK FROM THERE, CORRECT?
YES... SOMEBODY SAVED ME.
I DON'T REMEMBER MUCH, BUT...
SHE HAD SNOW-WHITE HAIR, WORE A BLACK KIMONO...
...AND HAD ON A RED FLOWER HAIR CLIP IF I REMEMBER CORRECTLY.
OH YEAH! AND...
SHE HAD THE SAME HAORI AS ROKUDO-KUN.
HUH.
I SEE. SO THIS CHILD...
...WAS THE ONE FROM BACK THEN...

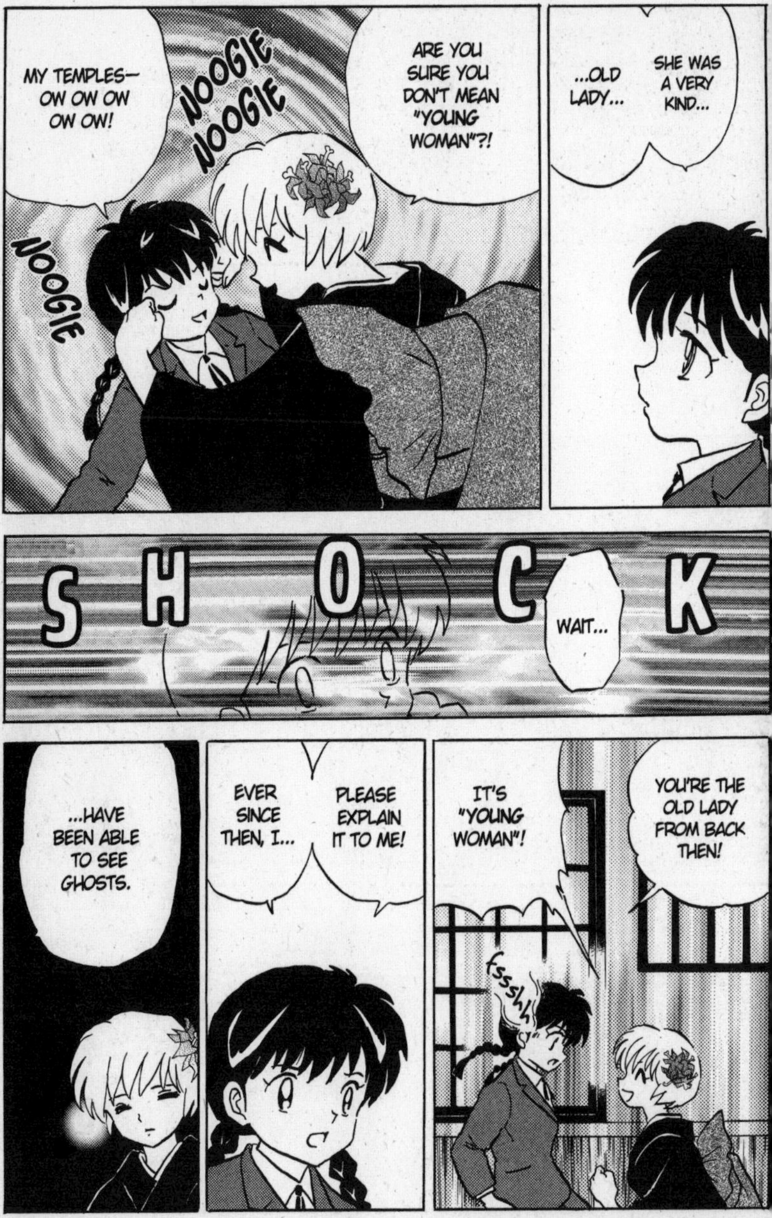
SHE WAS A VERY KIND...
...OLD LADY...
ARE YOU SURE YOU DON'T MEAN "YOUNG WOMAN"?!
NOOGIE NOOGIE
MY TEMPLES— OW OW OW OW OW!
NOOGIE
SHOCK
WAIT...
YOU'RE THE OLD LADY FROM BACK THEN!
IT'S "YOUNG WOMAN"!
fssshh
PLEASE EXPLAIN IT TO ME!
EVER SINCE THEN, I...
...HAVE BEEN ABLE TO SEE GHOSTS.

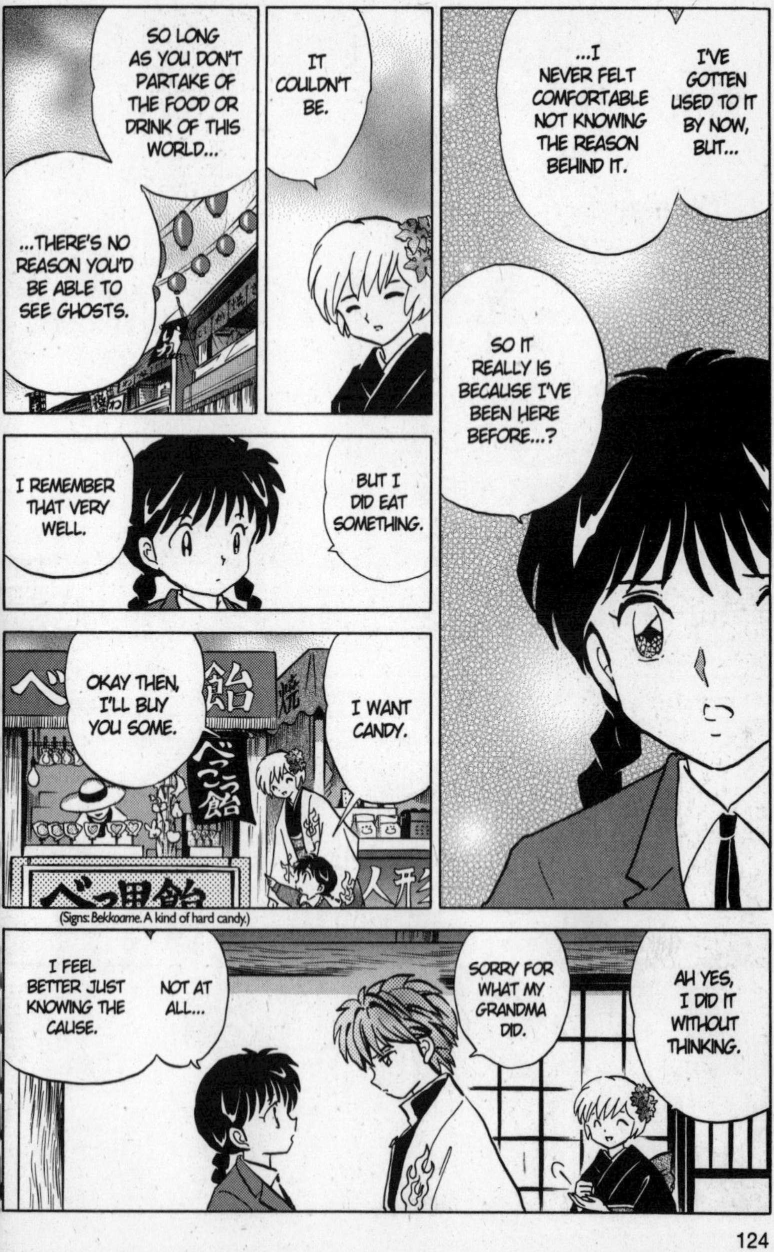
I'VE GOTTEN USED TO IT BY NOW, BUT...
...I NEVER FELT COMFORTABLE NOT KNOWING THE REASON BEHIND IT.
SO IT REALLY IS BECAUSE I'VE BEEN HERE BEFORE...?
IT COULDN'T BE.
SO LONG AS YOU DON'T PARTAKE OF THE FOOD OR DRINK OF THIS WORLD...
...THERE'S NO REASON YOU'D BE ABLE TO SEE GHOSTS.
BUT I DID EAT SOMETHING.
I REMEMBER THAT VERY WELL.
I WANT CANDY.
OKAY THEN, I'LL BUY YOU SOME.
(Signs: Bekkoame. A kind of hard candy.)
AH YES, I DID IT WITHOUT THINKING.
SORRY FOR WHAT MY GRANDMA DID.
NOT AT ALL...
I FEEL BETTER JUST KNOWING THE CAUSE.

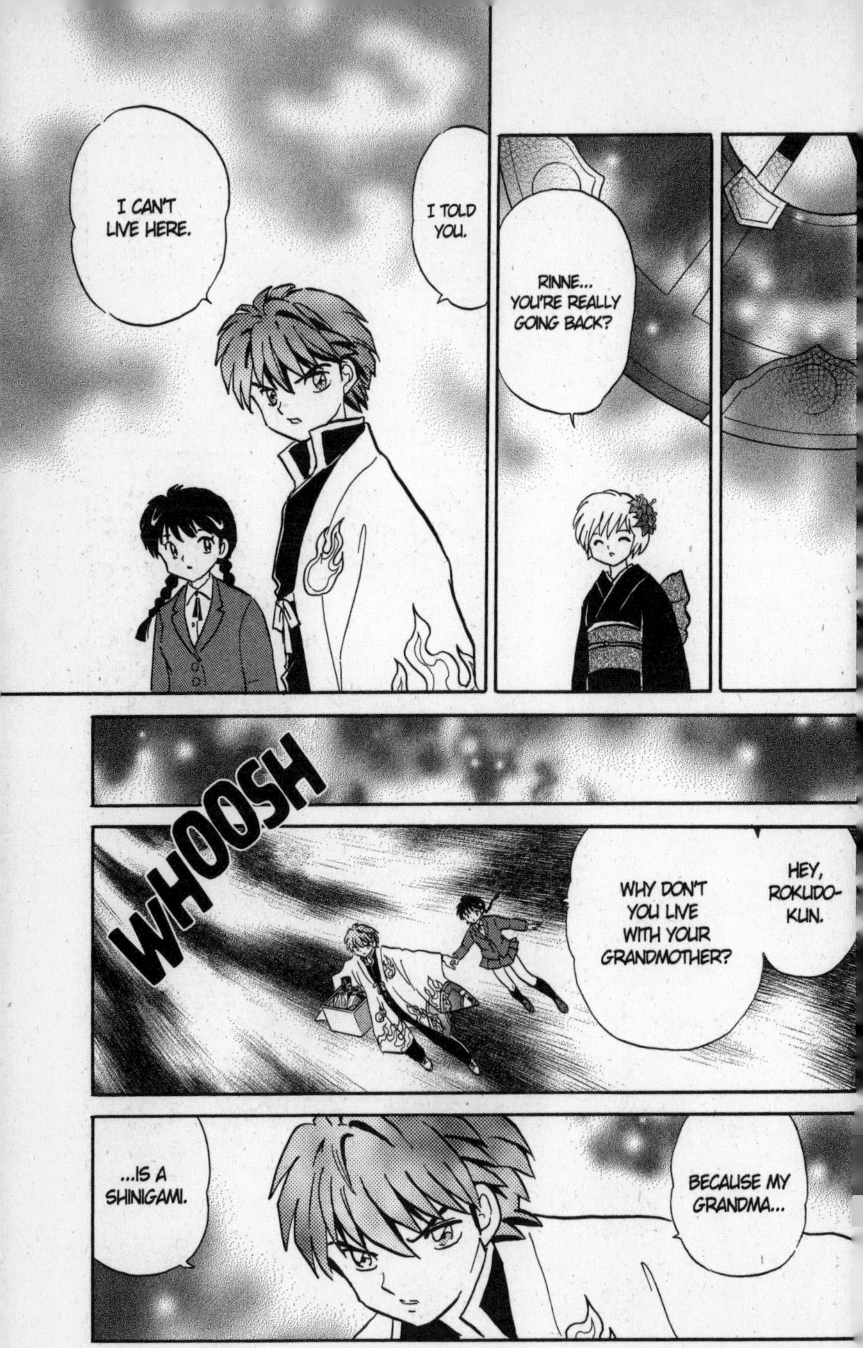
RINNE... YOU'RE REALLY GOING BACK?
I TOLD YOU.
I CAN'T LIVE HERE.
HEY, ROKUDO-KUN.
WHY DON'T YOU LIVE WITH YOUR GRANDMOTHER?
WHOOSH
BECAUSE MY GRANDMA...
...IS A SHINIGAMI.

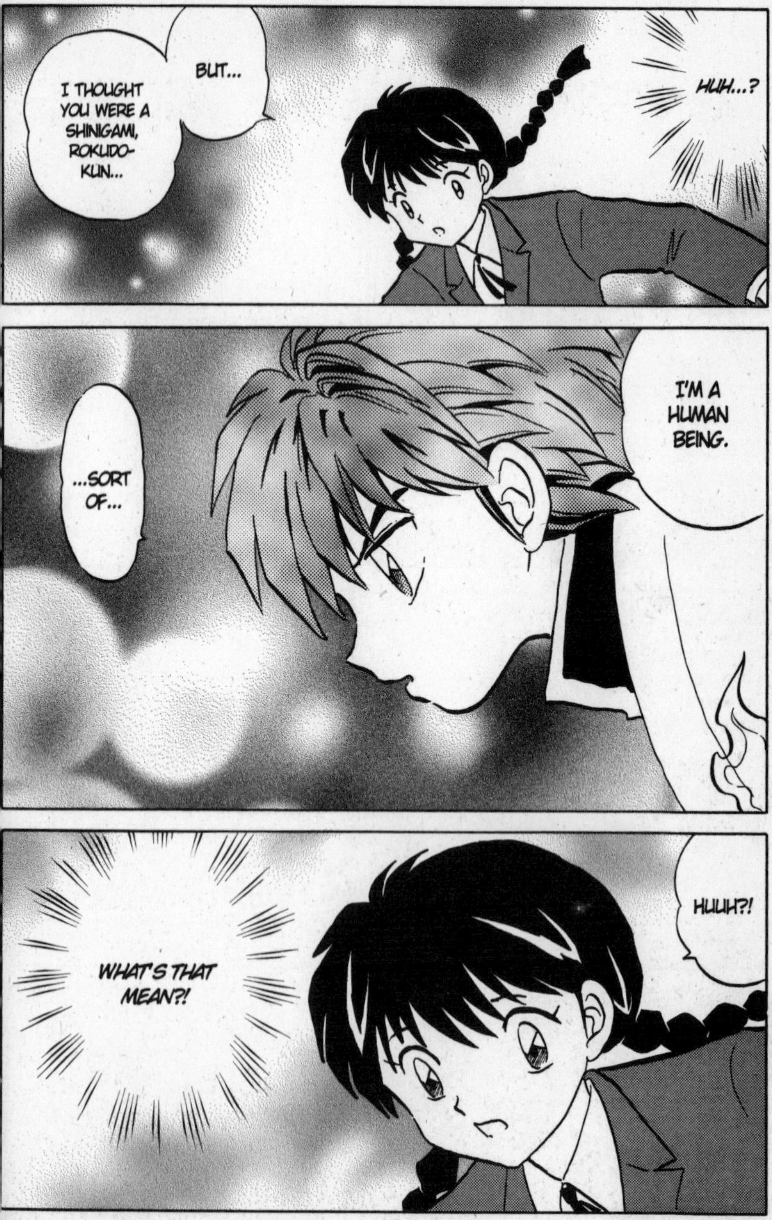
HUH...?
BUT...
I THOUGHT YOU WERE A SHINIGAMI, ROKUDO-KUN...
I'M A HUMAN BEING.
...SORT OF...
HUUH?!
WHAT'S THAT MEAN?!

CHAPTER 6:
MYSTERY IN THE CLUB BUILDING

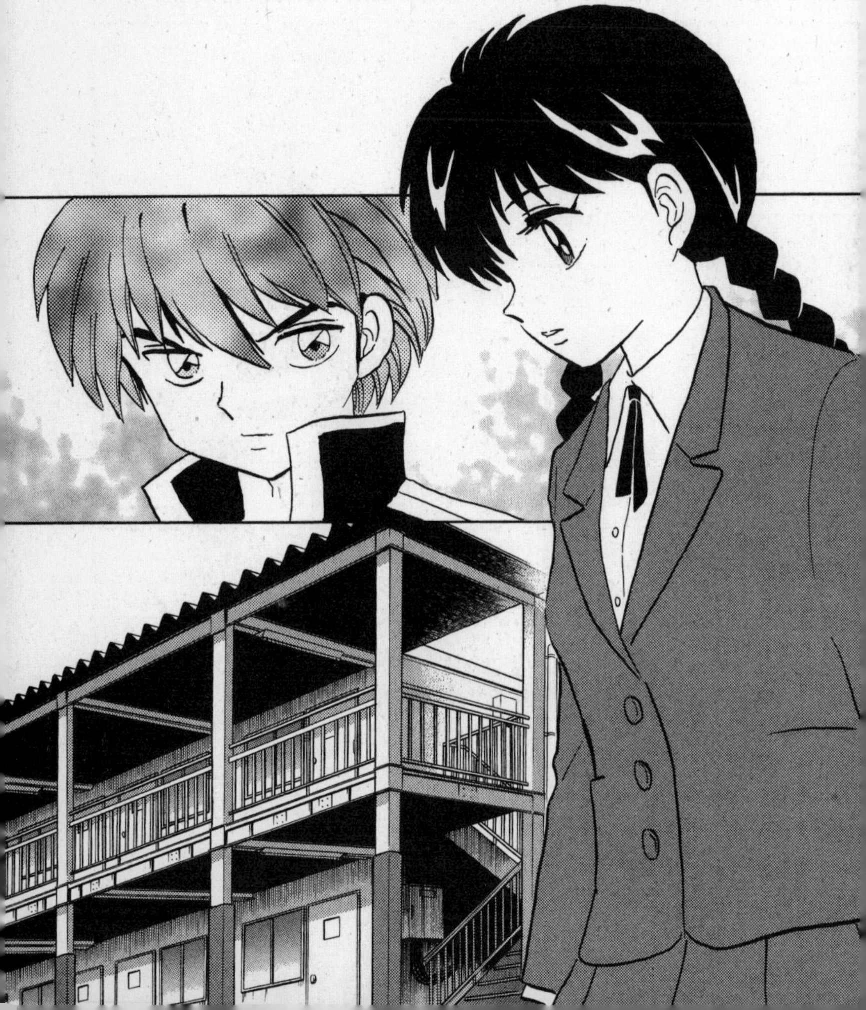

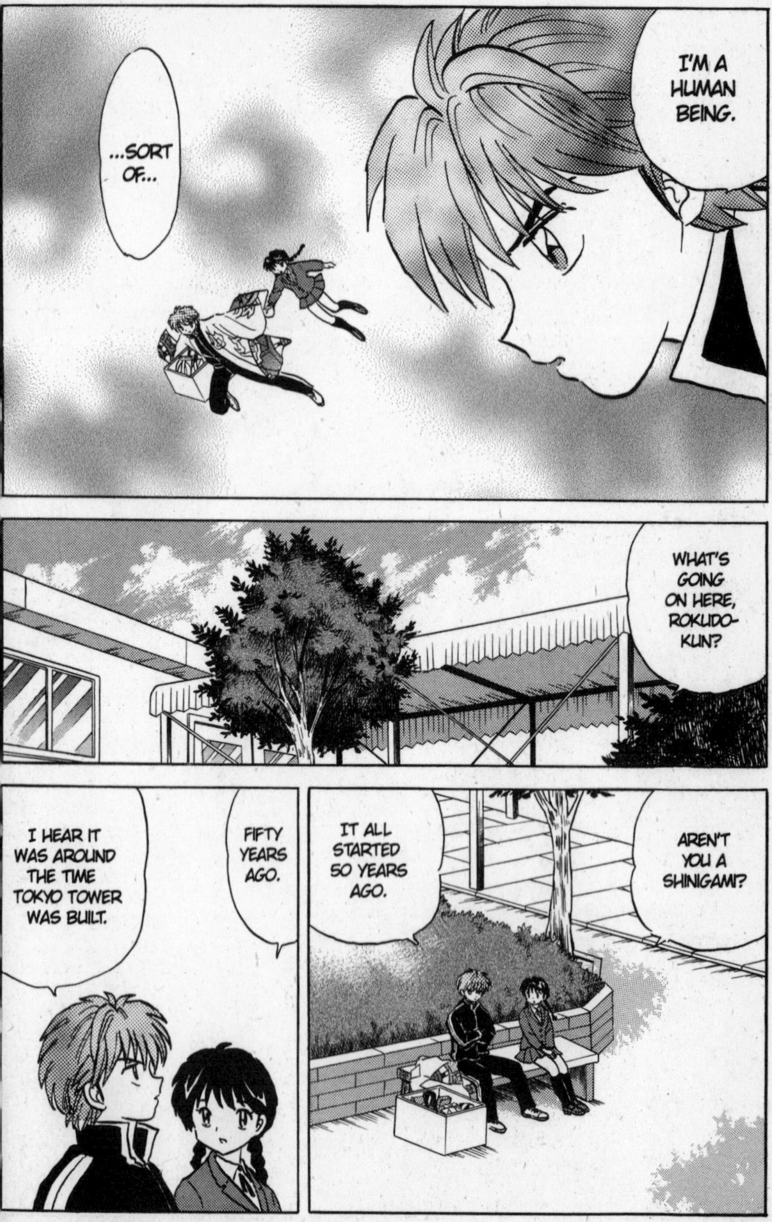
I'M A HUMAN BEING.
...SORT OF...
WHAT'S GOING ON HERE, ROKUDO-KUN?
AREN'T YOU A SHINIGAMI?
IT ALL STARTED 50 YEARS AGO.
FIFTY YEARS AGO.
I HEAR IT WAS AROUND THE TIME TOKYO TOWER WAS BUILT.

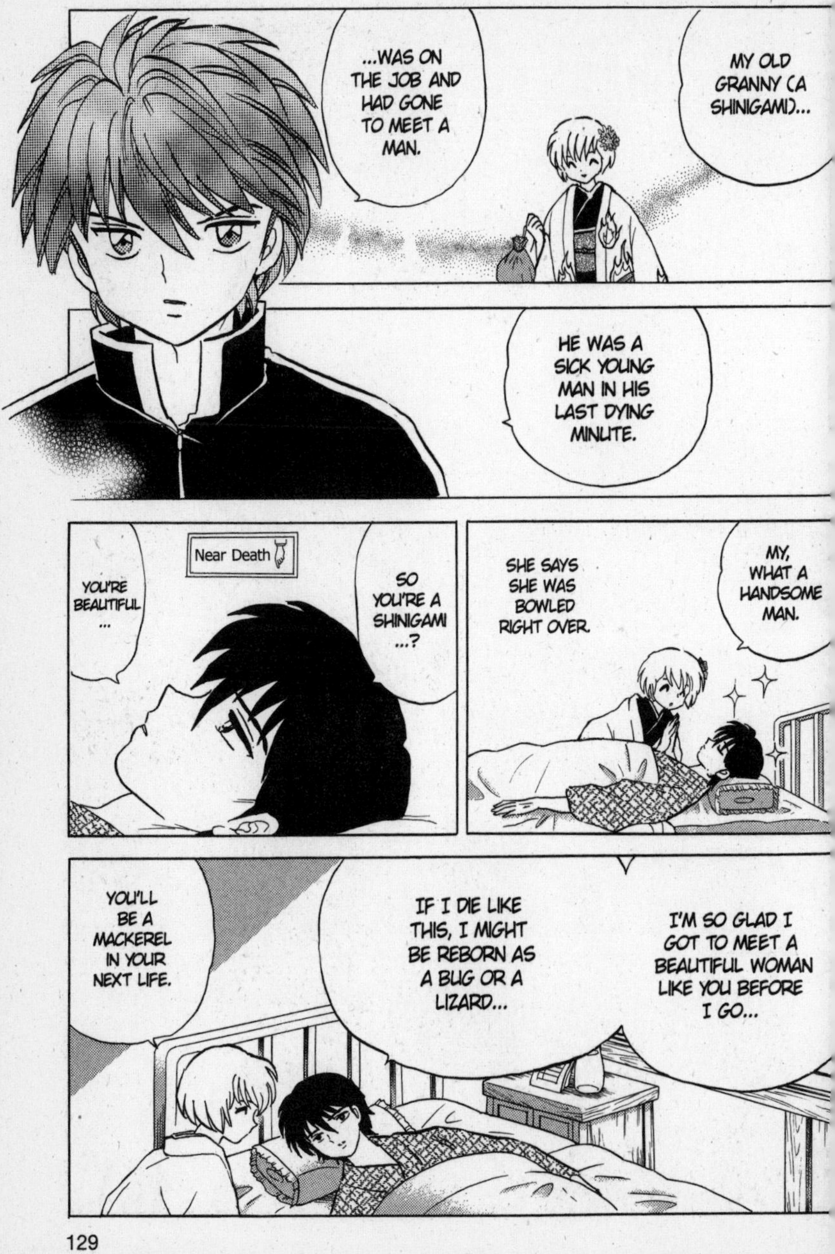
MY OLD GRANNY (A SHINIGAMI)...
...WAS ON THE JOB AND HAD GONE TO MEET A MAN.
HE WAS A SICK YOUNG MAN IN HIS LAST DYING MINUTE.
MY, WHAT A HANDSOME MAN.
SHE SAYS SHE WAS BOWLED RIGHT OVER.
SO YOU'RE A SHINIGAMI...?
Near Death
YOU'RE BEAUTIFUL...
I'M SO GLAD I GOT TO MEET A BEAUTIFUL WOMAN LIKE YOU BEFORE I GO...
IF I DIE LIKE THIS, I MIGHT BE REBORN AS A BUG OR A LIZARD...
YOU'LL BE A MACKEREL IN YOUR NEXT LIFE.

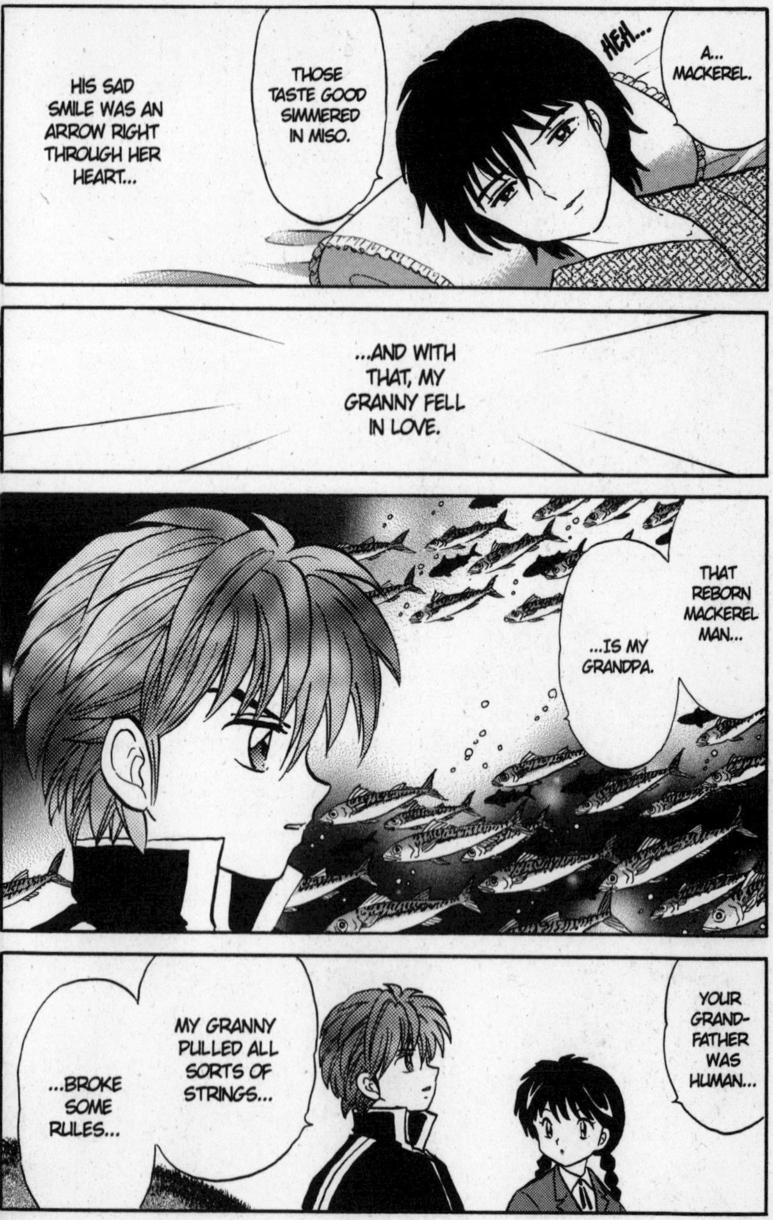
A... MACKEREL.
HEH...
THOSE TASTE GOOD SIMMERED IN MISO.
HIS SAD SMILE WAS AN ARROW RIGHT THROUGH HER HEART...
...AND WITH THAT, MY GRANNY FELL IN LOVE.
THAT REBORN MACKEREL MAN...
...IS MY GRANDPA.
YOUR GRAND-FATHER WAS HUMAN...
MY GRANNY PULLED ALL SORTS OF STRINGS...
...BROKE SOME RULES...

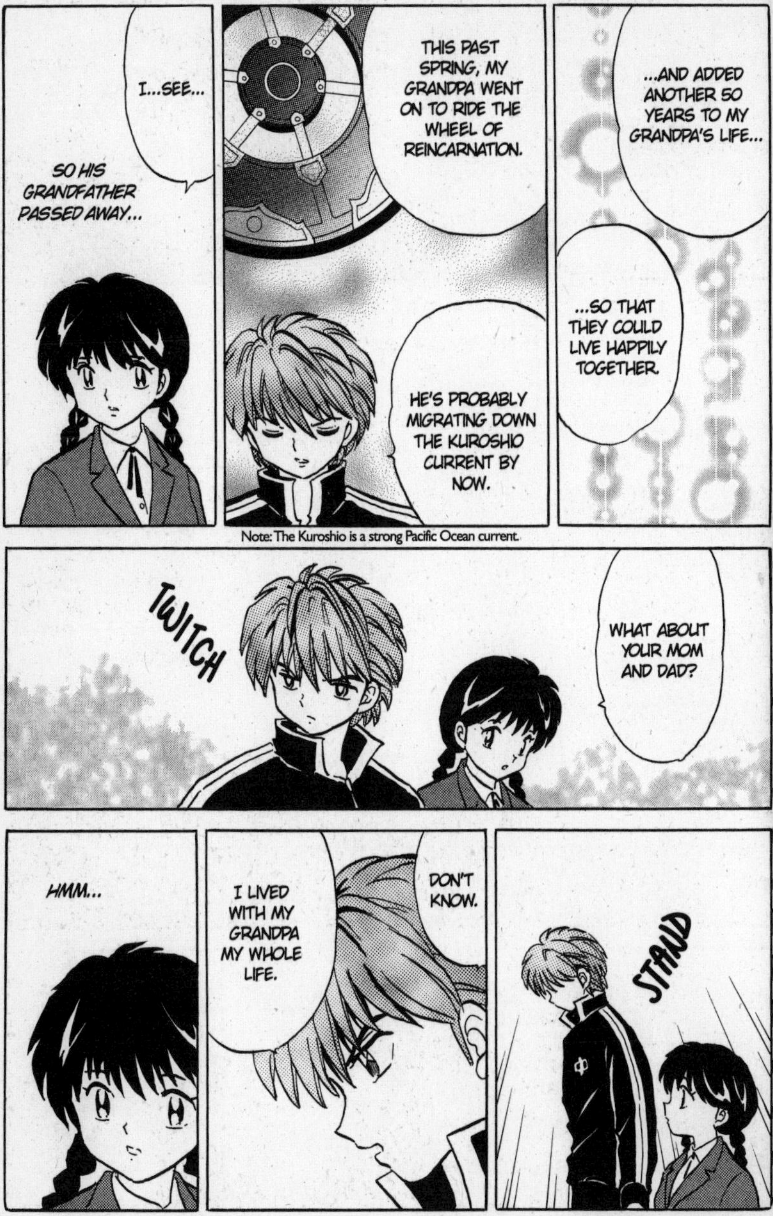
...AND ADDED ANOTHER 50 YEARS TO MY GRANDPA'S LIFE...
...SO THAT THEY COULD LIVE HAPPILY TOGETHER.
THIS PAST SPRING, MY GRANDPA WENT ON TO RIDE THE WHEEL OF REINCARNATION.
HE'S PROBABLY MIGRATING DOWN THE KUROSHIO CURRENT BY NOW.
I...SEE...
SO HIS GRANDFATHER PASSED AWAY...
WHAT ABOUT YOUR MOM AND DAD?
TWITCH
STAND
DON'T KNOW.
I LIVED WITH MY GRANDPA MY WHOLE LIFE.
HMM...

Note: The Kuroshio is a strong Pacific Ocean current.

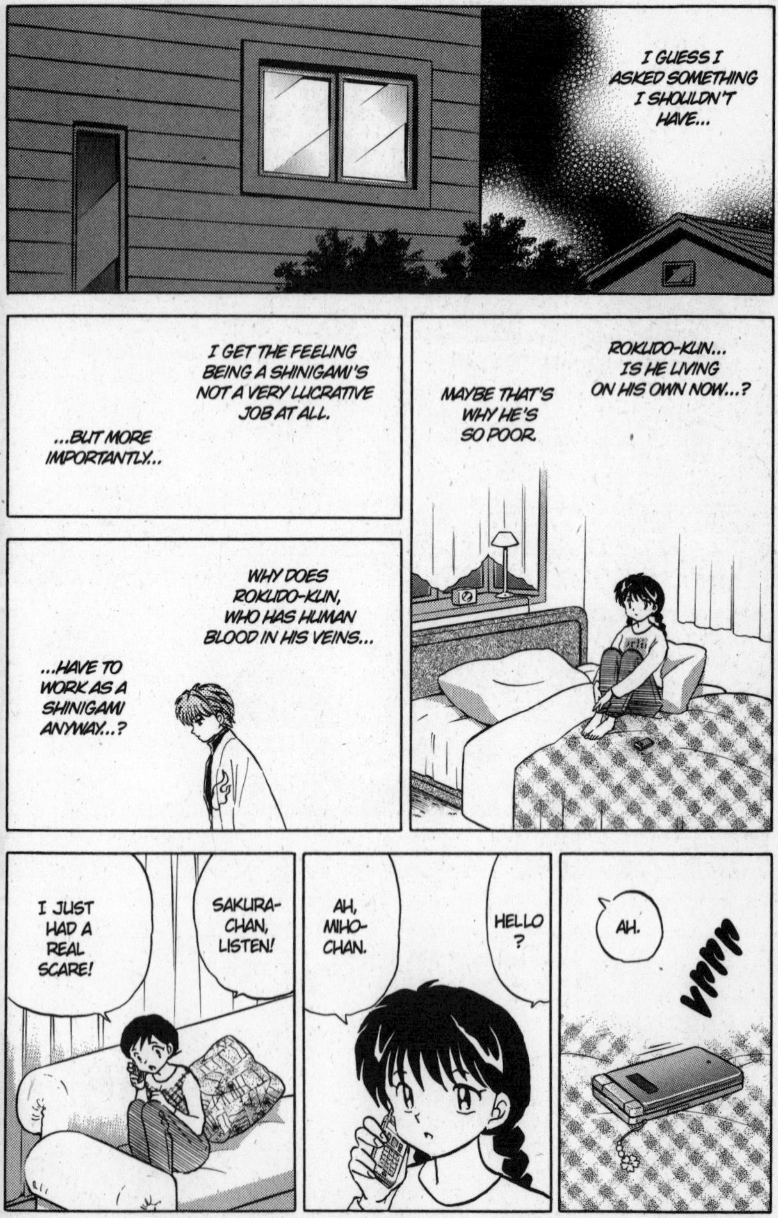
I GUESS I ASKED SOMETHING I SHOULDN'T HAVE...
ROKUDO-KUN... IS HE LIVING ON HIS OWN NOW...?
MAYBE THAT'S WHY HE'S SO POOR.
I GET THE FEELING BEING A SHINIGAMI'S NOT A VERY LUCRATIVE JOB AT ALL.
...BUT MORE IMPORTANTLY...
WHY DOES ROKUDO-KUN, WHO HAS HUMAN BLOOD IN HIS VEINS...
...HAVE TO WORK AS A SHINIGAMI ANYWAY...?
VRRRR
AH.
HELLO?
AH, MIHO-CHAN.
SAKURA-CHAN, LISTEN!
I JUST HAD A REAL SCARE!

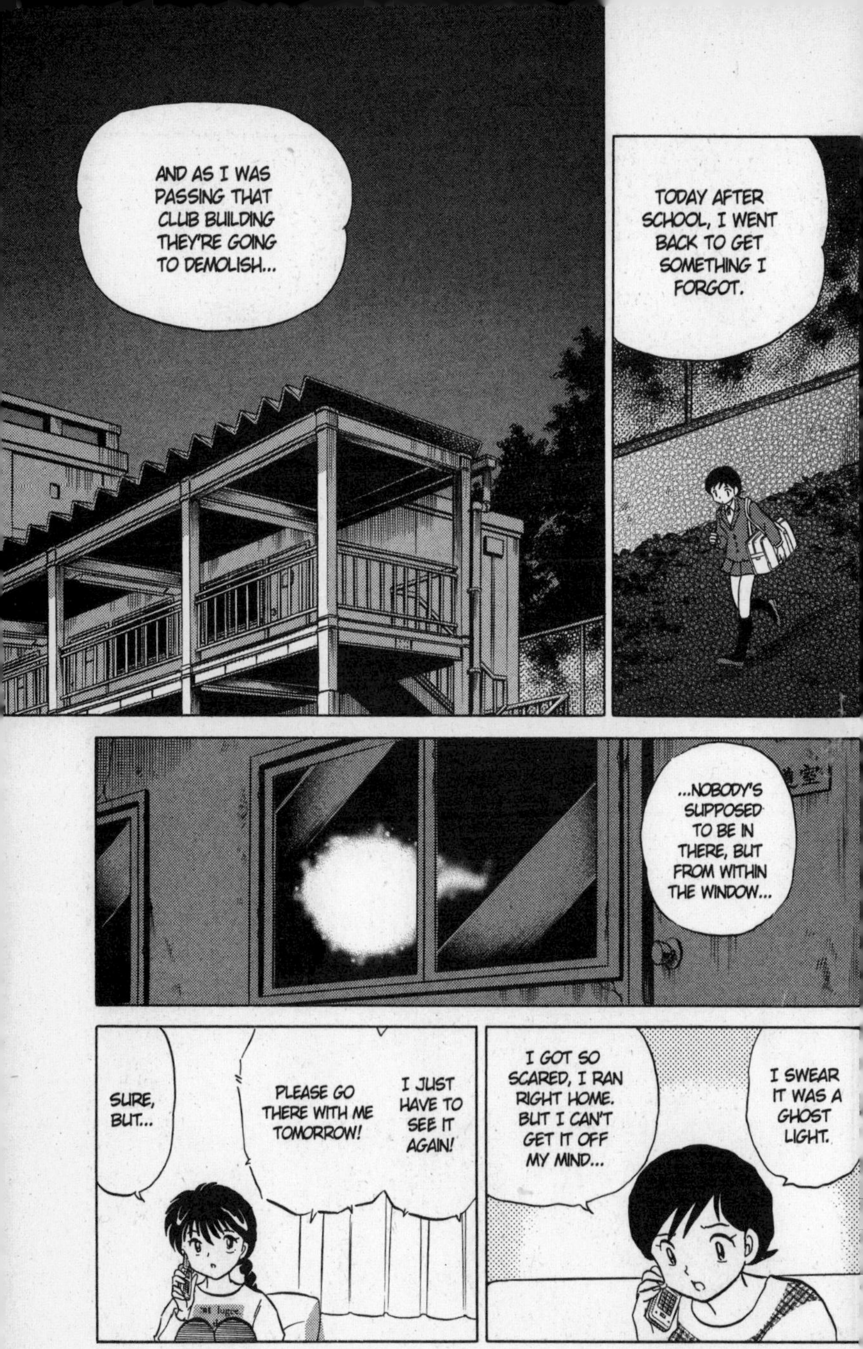
TODAY AFTER SCHOOL, I WENT BACK TO GET SOMETHING I FORGOT.
AND AS I WAS PASSING THAT CLUB BUILDING THEY'RE GOING TO DEMOLISH...
...NOBODY'S SUPPOSED TO BE IN THERE, BUT FROM WITHIN THE WINDOW...
I SWEAR IT WAS A GHOST LIGHT.
I GOT SO SCARED, I RAN RIGHT HOME. BUT I CAN'T GET IT OFF MY MIND...
I JUST HAVE TO SEE IT AGAIN!
PLEASE GO THERE WITH ME TOMORROW!
SURE, BUT...

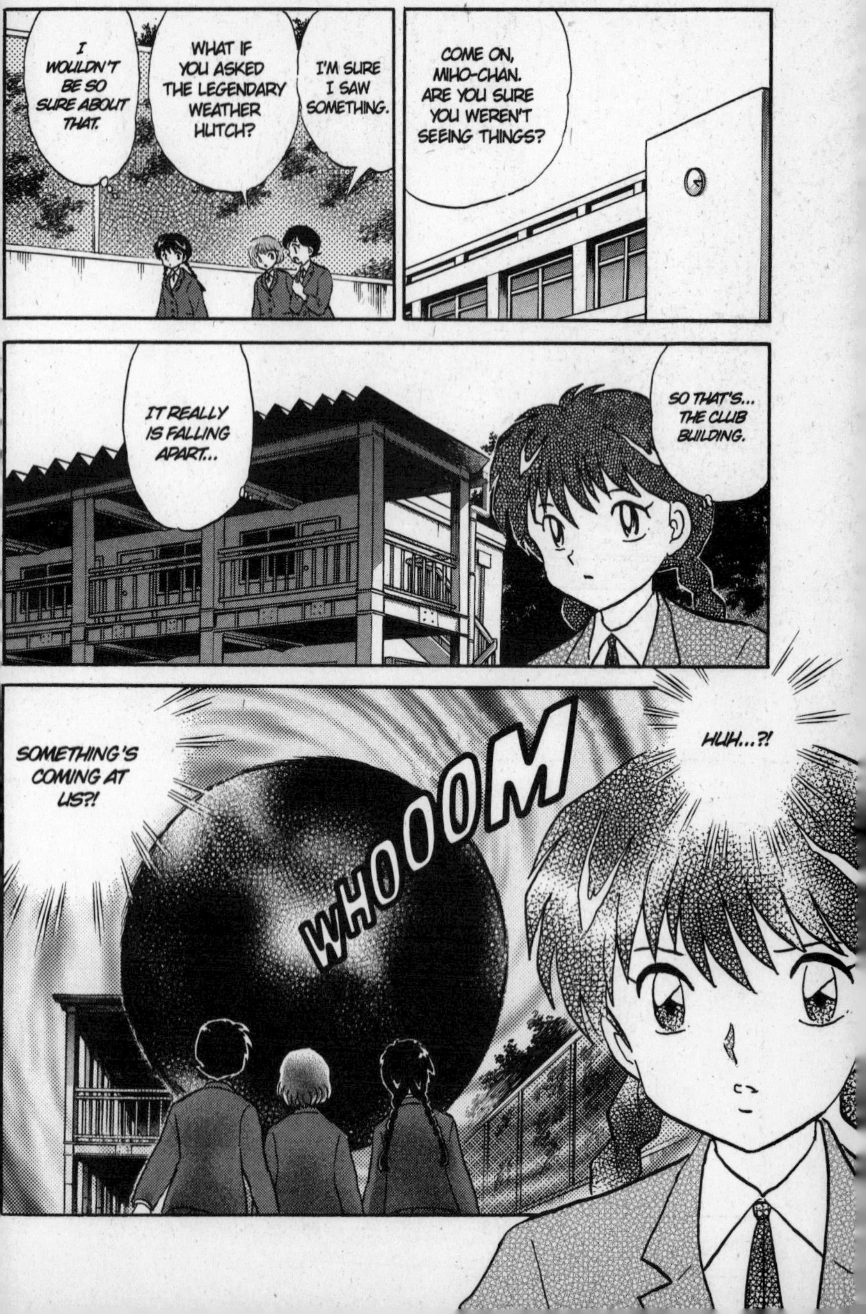
COME ON, MIHO-CHAN. ARE YOU SURE YOU WEREN'T SEEING THINGS?
I'M SURE I SAW SOMETHING.
WHAT IF YOU ASKED THE LEGENDARY WEATHER HUTCH?
I WOULDN'T BE SO SURE ABOUT THAT.
SO THAT'S... THE CLUB BUILDING.
IT REALLY IS FALLING APART...
HUH...?!
WHOOOM
SOMETHING'S COMING AT US?!

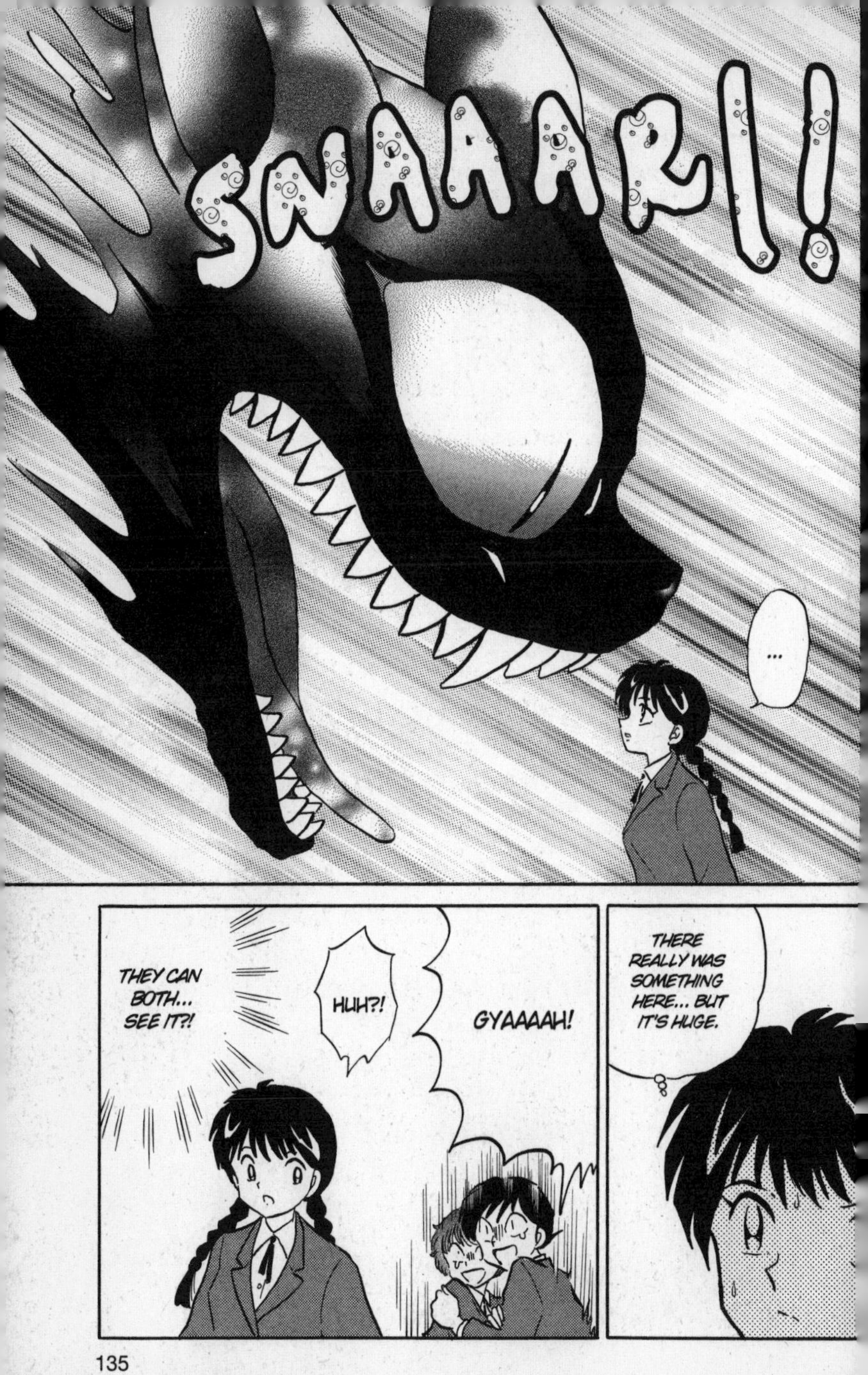
SNAAARL!!
...
THERE REALLY WAS SOMETHING HERE... BUT IT'S HUGE.
GYAAAAH!
HUH?!
THEY CAN BOTH... SEE IT?!

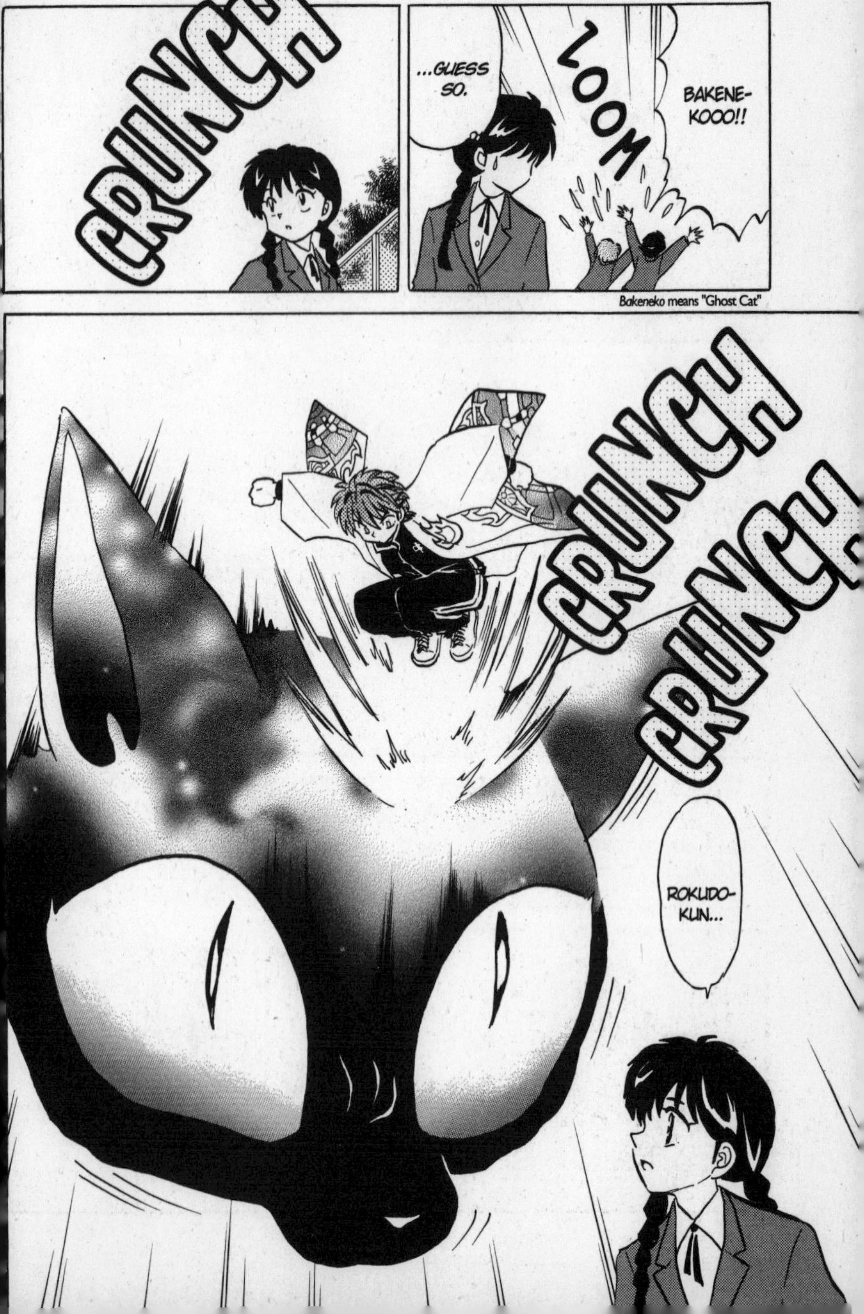
BAKENE-KOOO!!
LOOM
...GUESS SO.
CRUNCH
Bakeneko means "Ghost Cat"
CRUNCH
CRUNCH
ROKUDO-KUN...

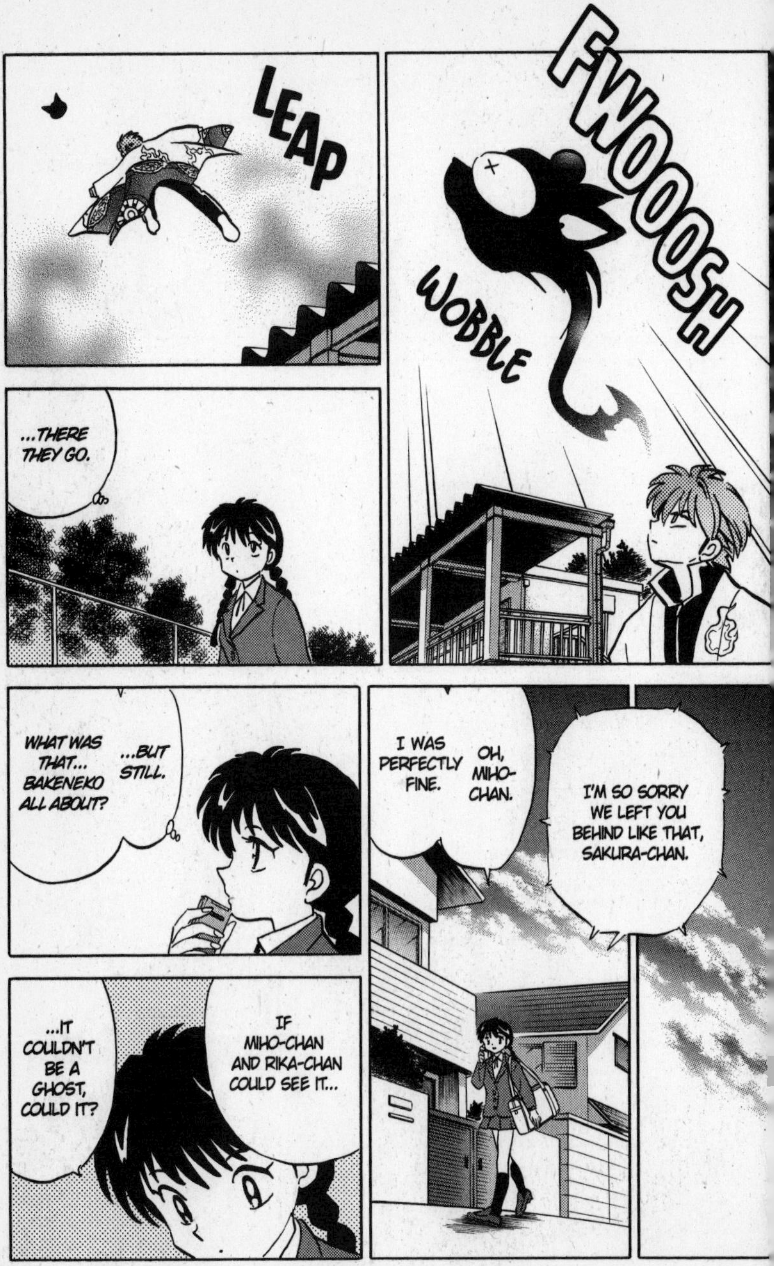
FWOOOSH
WOBBLE
LEAP
...THERE THEY GO.
I'M SO SORRY WE LEFT YOU BEHIND LIKE THAT, SAKURA-CHAN.
OH, MIHO-CHAN.
I WAS PERFECTLY FINE.
...BUT STILL.
WHAT WAS THAT... BAKENEKO ALL ABOUT?
IF MIHO-CHAN AND RIKA-CHAN COULD SEE IT...
...IT COULDN'T BE A GHOST, COULD IT?

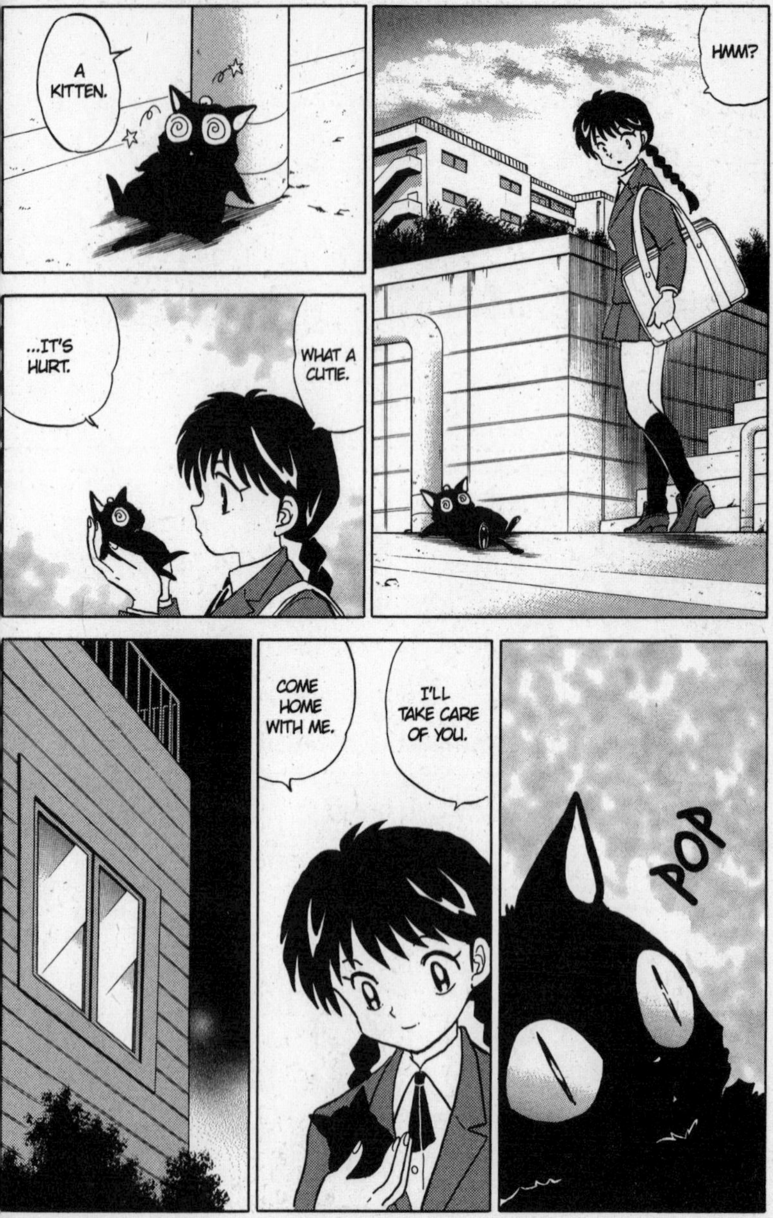
HMM?
A KITTEN.
WHAT A CUTIE.
...IT'S HURT.
POP
I'LL TAKE CARE OF YOU.
COME HOME WITH ME.

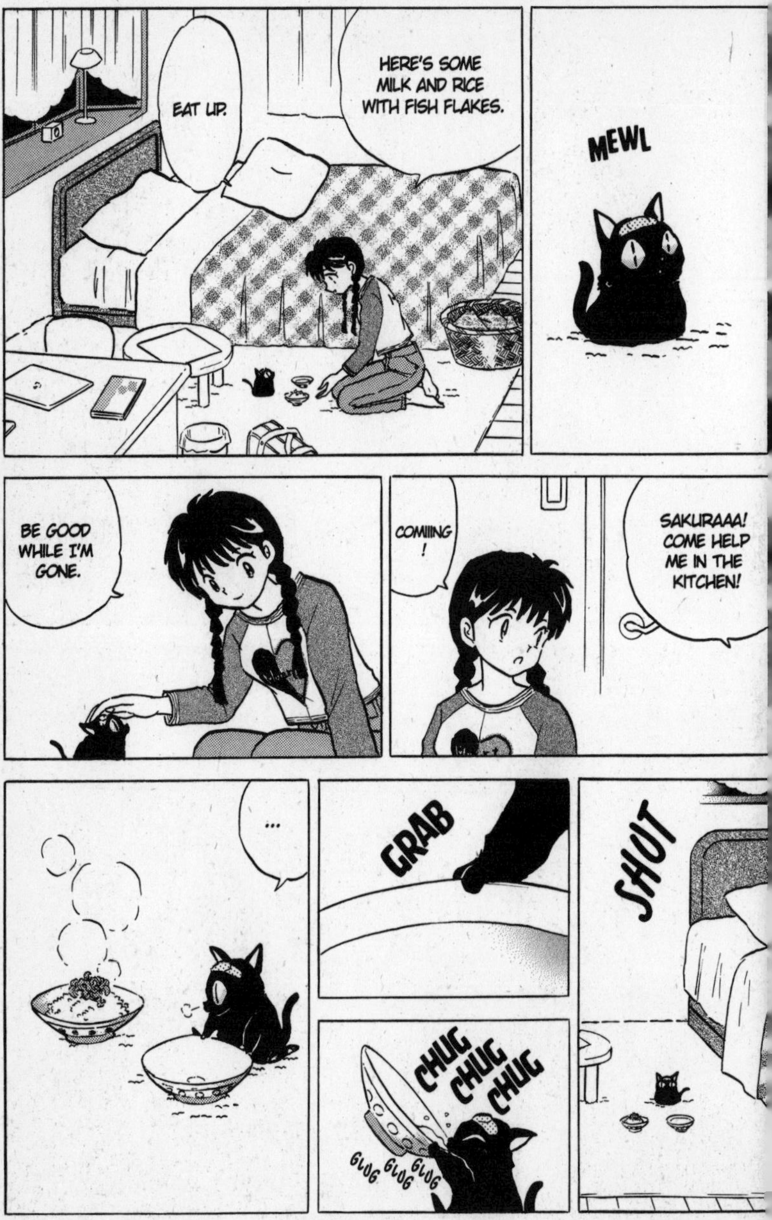
MEWL
HERE'S SOME MILK AND RICE WITH FISH FLAKES.
EAT UP.
SAKURAAA! COME HELP ME IN THE KITCHEN!
COMIIING!
BE GOOD WHILE I'M GONE.
SHUT
GRAB
CHUG CHUG CHUG
GLUG GLUG GLUG
...

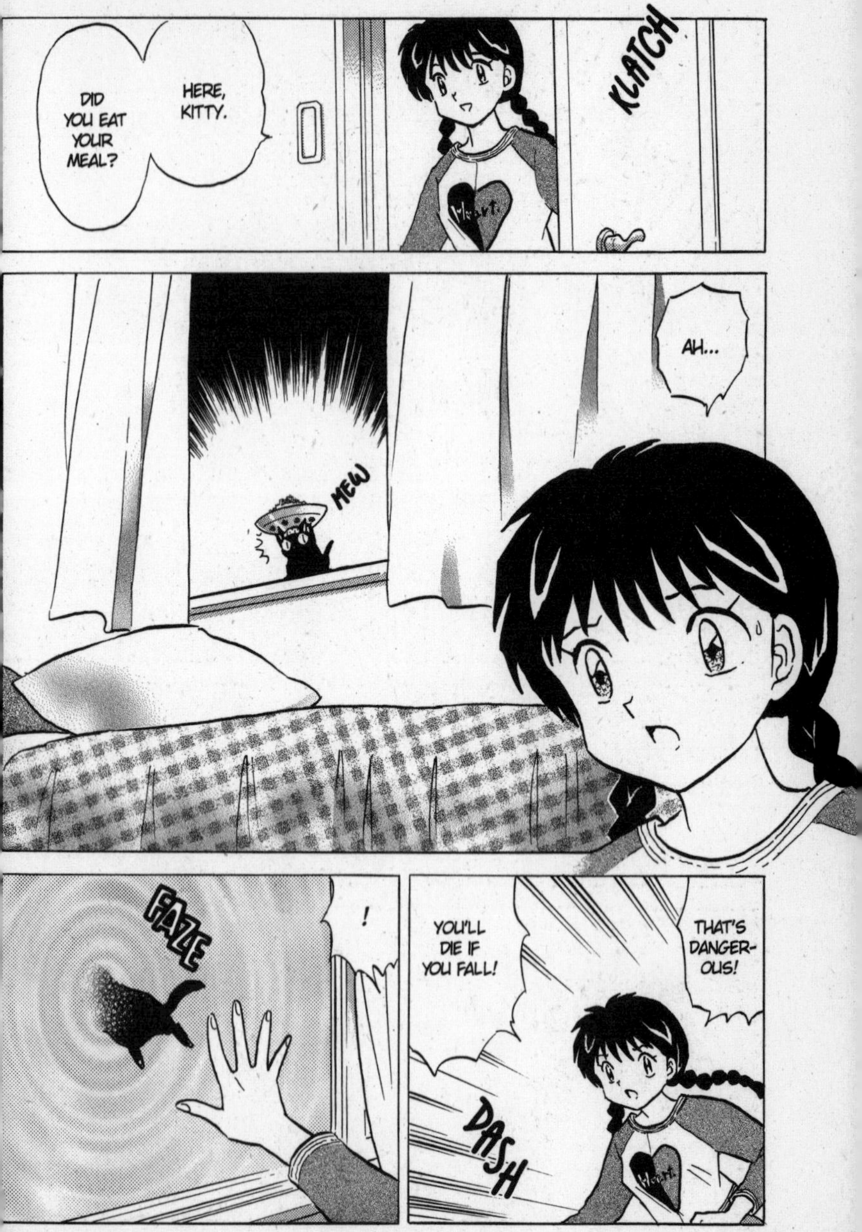
KLATCH
HERE, KITTY.
DID YOU EAT YOUR MEAL?
AH...
MEW
THAT'S DANGER-OUS!
YOU'LL DIE IF YOU FALL!
DASH
!
FAZE

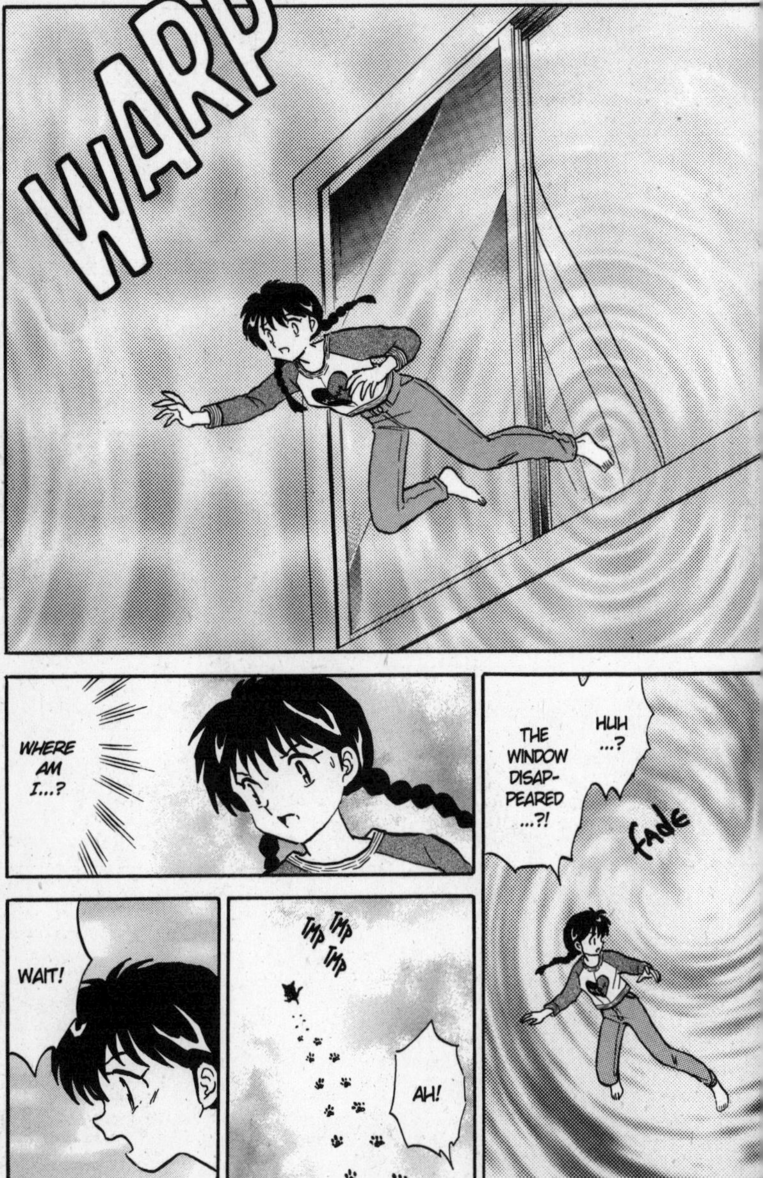
WARP
HUH ...?
THE WINDOW DISAP-PEARED ...?!
fade
WHERE AM I...?
TMP TMP TMP
AH!
WAIT!

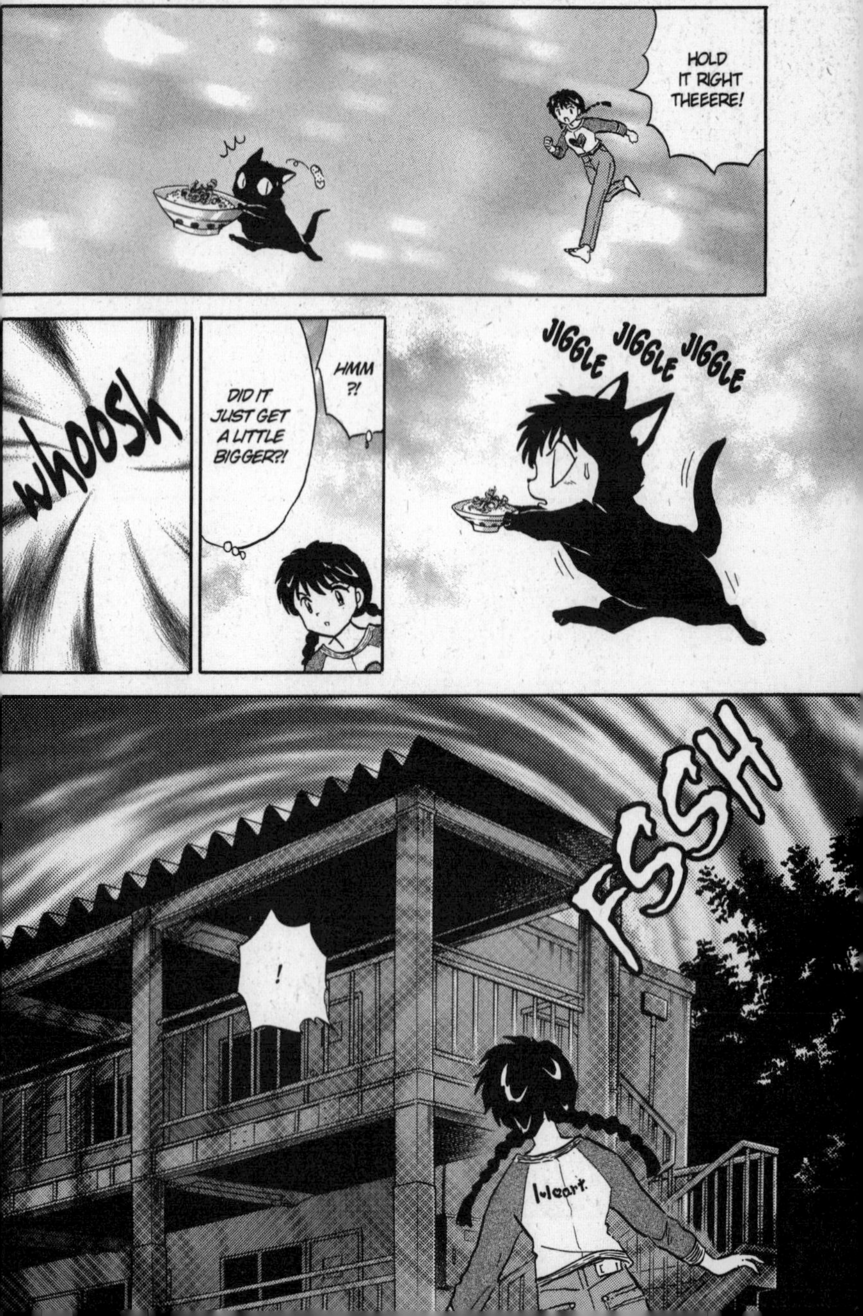
HOLD IT RIGHT THEEERE!
JIGGLE JIGGLE JIGGLE
HMM ?!
DID IT JUST GET A LITTLE BIGGER?!
whoosh
FSSH
!
Heart.

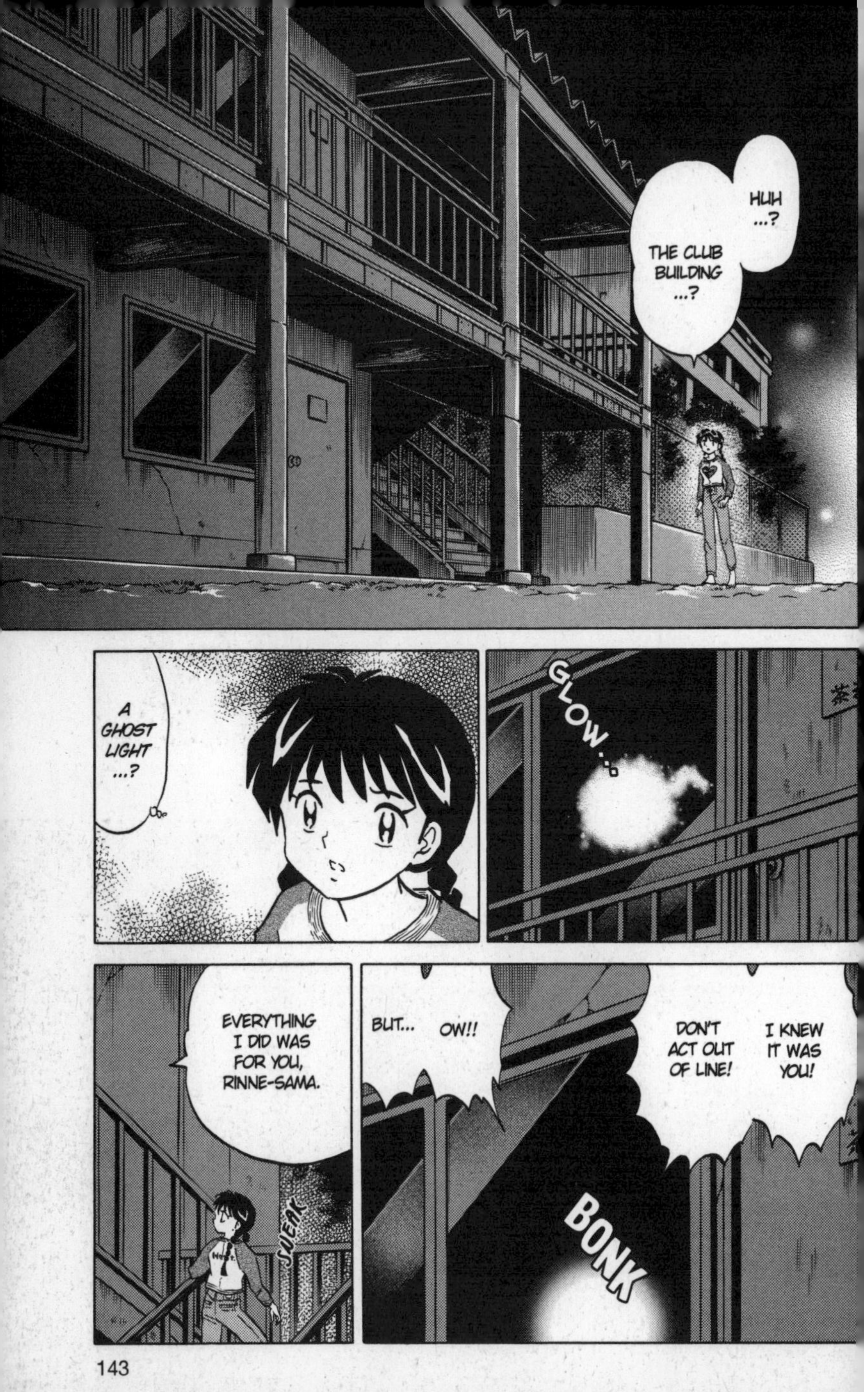
HUH ...?
THE CLUB BUILDING ...?
GLOW...
A GHOST LIGHT ...?
I KNEW IT WAS YOU!
DON'T ACT OUT OF LINE!
BONK
OW!!
BUT...
EVERYTHING I DID WAS FOR YOU, RINNE-SAMA.
SQUEAK

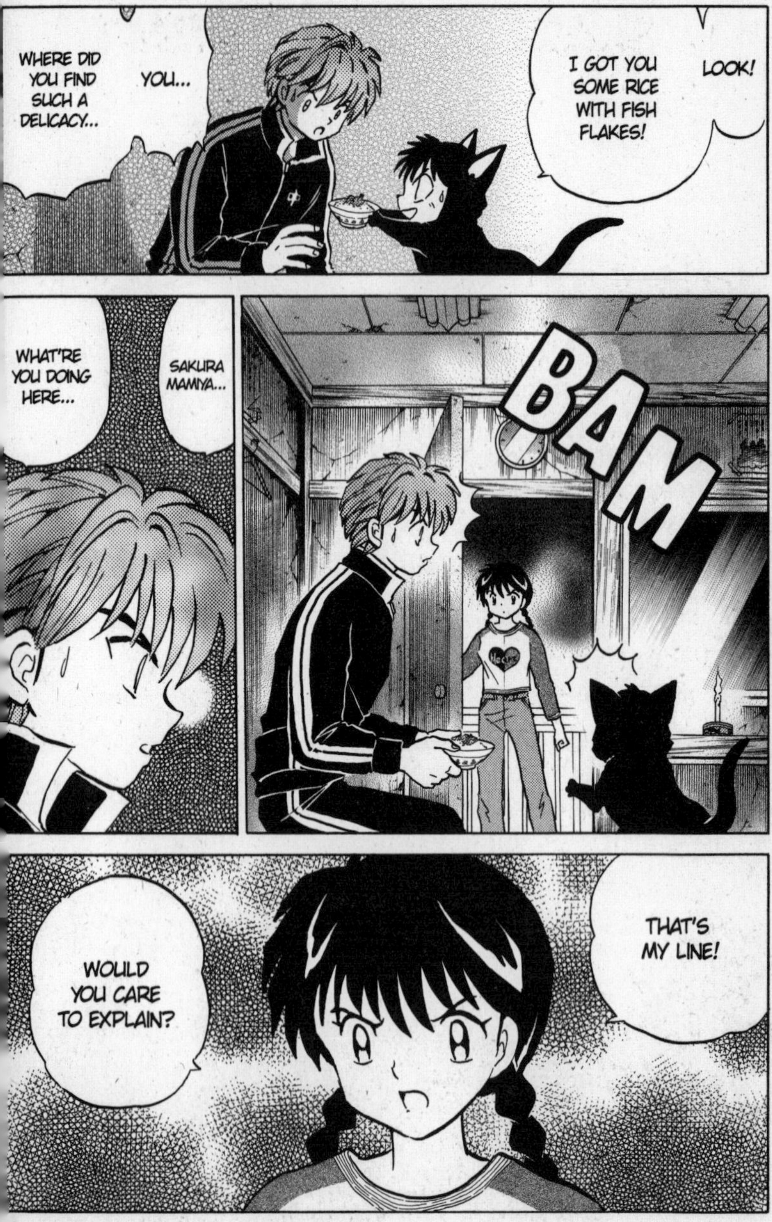
LOOK!
I GOT YOU SOME RICE WITH FISH FLAKES!
YOU...
WHERE DID YOU FIND SUCH A DELICACY...
BAM
SAKURA MAMIYA...
WHAT'RE YOU DOING HERE...
THAT'S MY LINE!
WOULD YOU CARE TO EXPLAIN?

CHAPTER 7: BLACK CAT BY CONTRACT

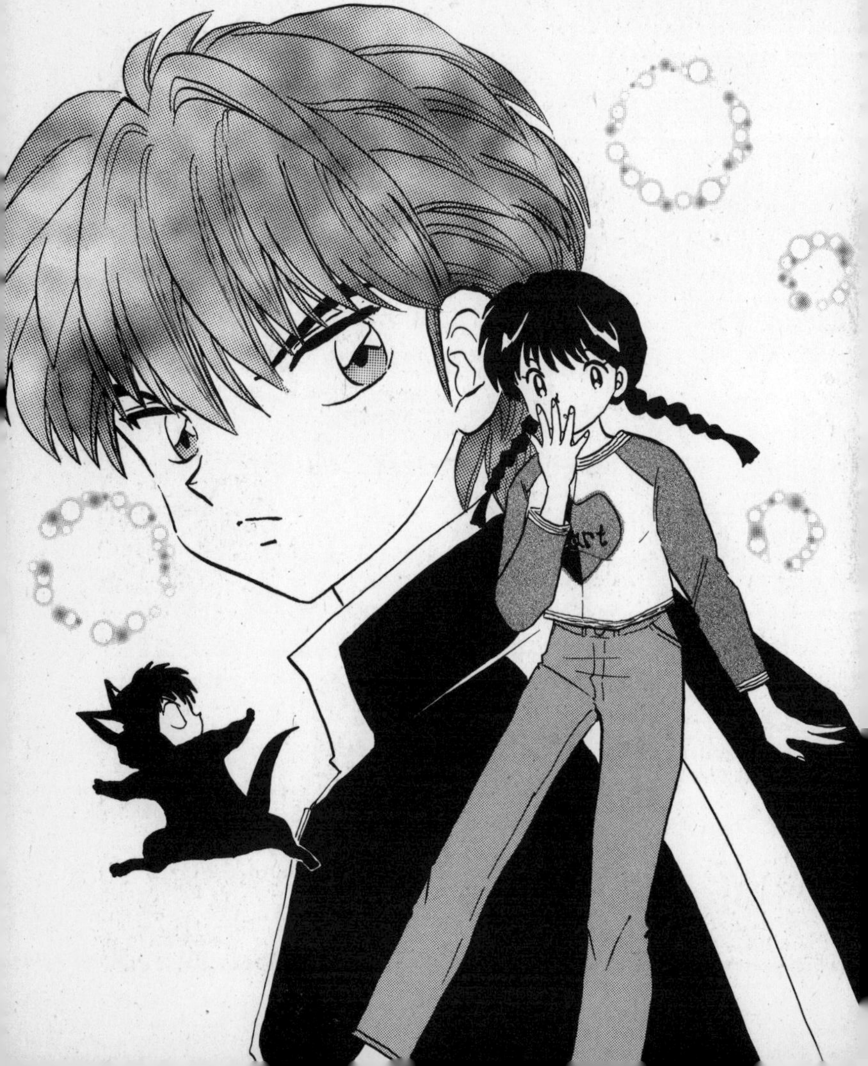

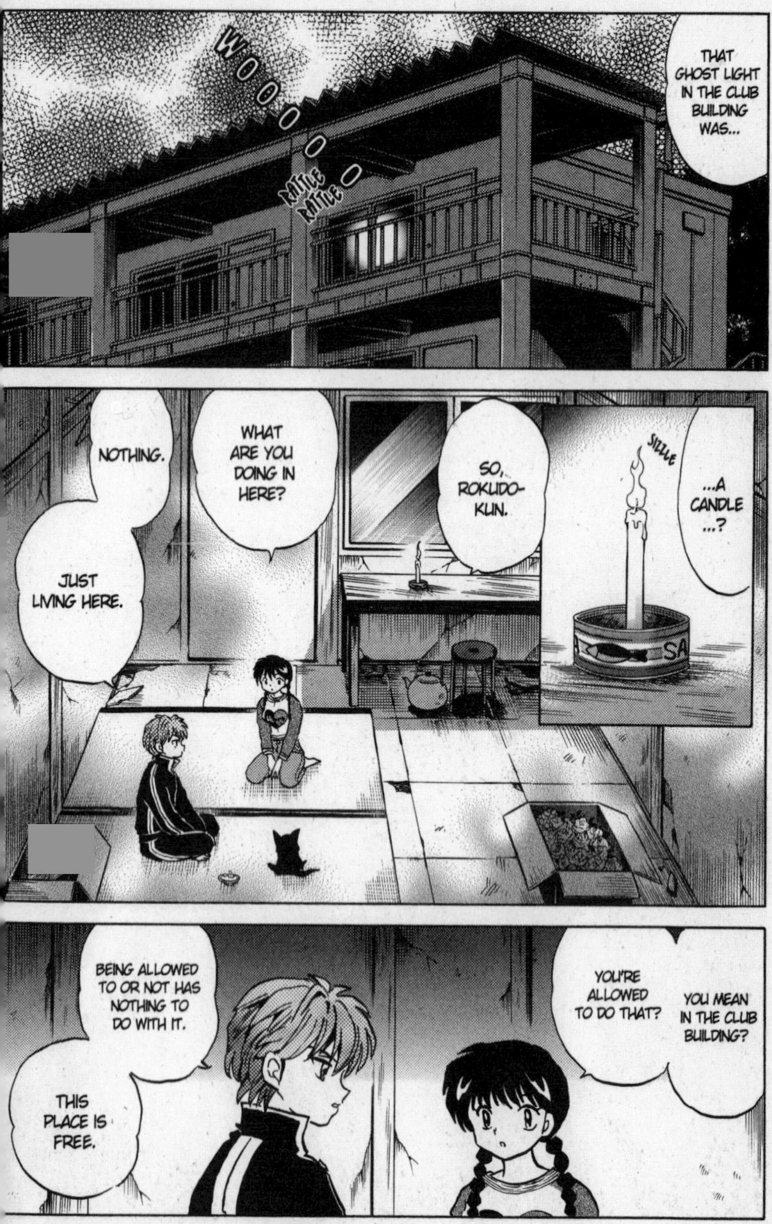
THAT GHOST LIGHT IN THE CLUB BUILDING WAS...
WOOOOOOO
RATTLE RATTLE
SIZZLE
...A CANDLE ...?
SA
SO, ROKUDO-KUN.
WHAT ARE YOU DOING IN HERE?
NOTHING.
JUST LIVING HERE.
YOU MEAN IN THE CLUB BUILDING?
YOU'RE ALLOWED TO DO THAT?
BEING ALLOWED TO OR NOT HAS NOTHING TO DO WITH IT.
THIS PLACE IS FREE.

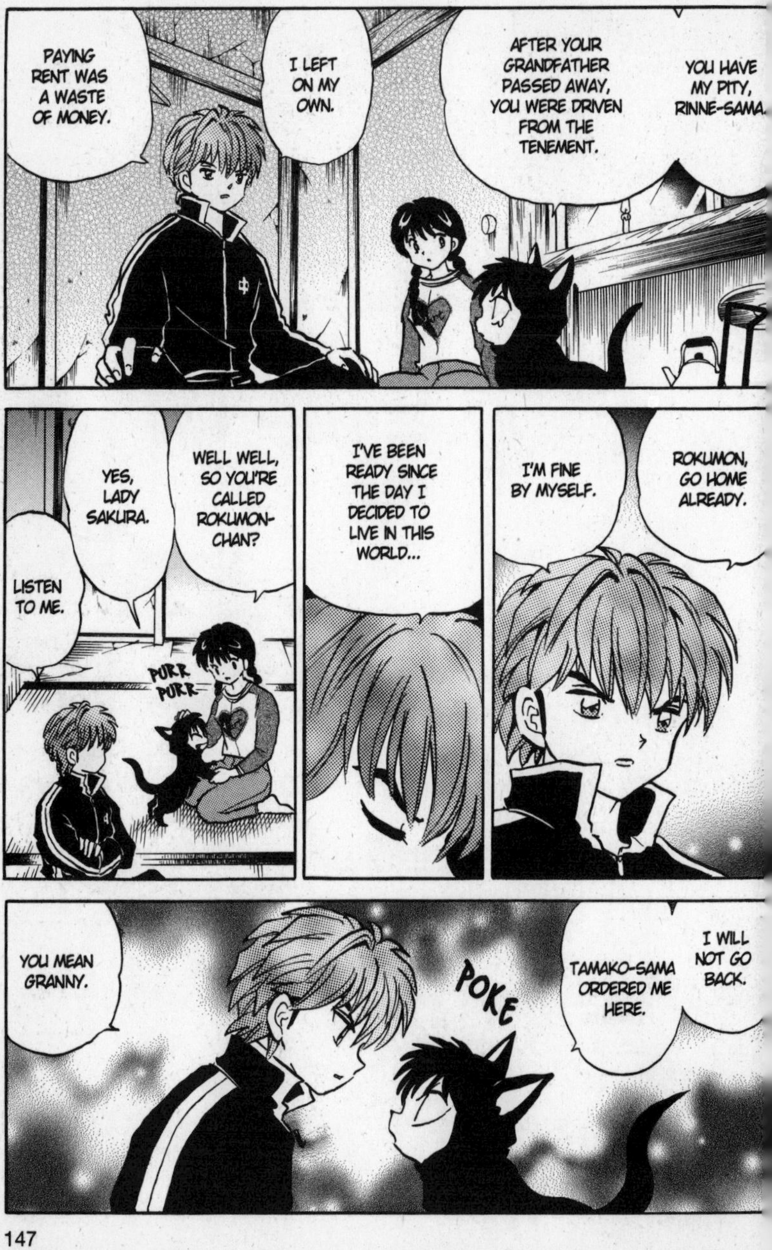
YOU HAVE MY PITY, RINNE-SAMA.
AFTER YOUR GRANDFATHER PASSED AWAY, YOU WERE DRIVEN FROM THE TENEMENT.
I LEFT ON MY OWN.
PAYING RENT WAS A WASTE OF MONEY.
ROKUMON, GO HOME ALREADY.
I'M FINE BY MYSELF.
I'VE BEEN READY SINCE THE DAY I DECIDED TO LIVE IN THIS WORLD...
WELL WELL, SO YOU'RE CALLED ROKUMON-CHAN?
YES, LADY SAKURA.
LISTEN TO ME.
PURR PURR
I WILL NOT GO BACK.
TAMAKO-SAMA ORDERED ME HERE.
POKE
YOU MEAN GRANNY.

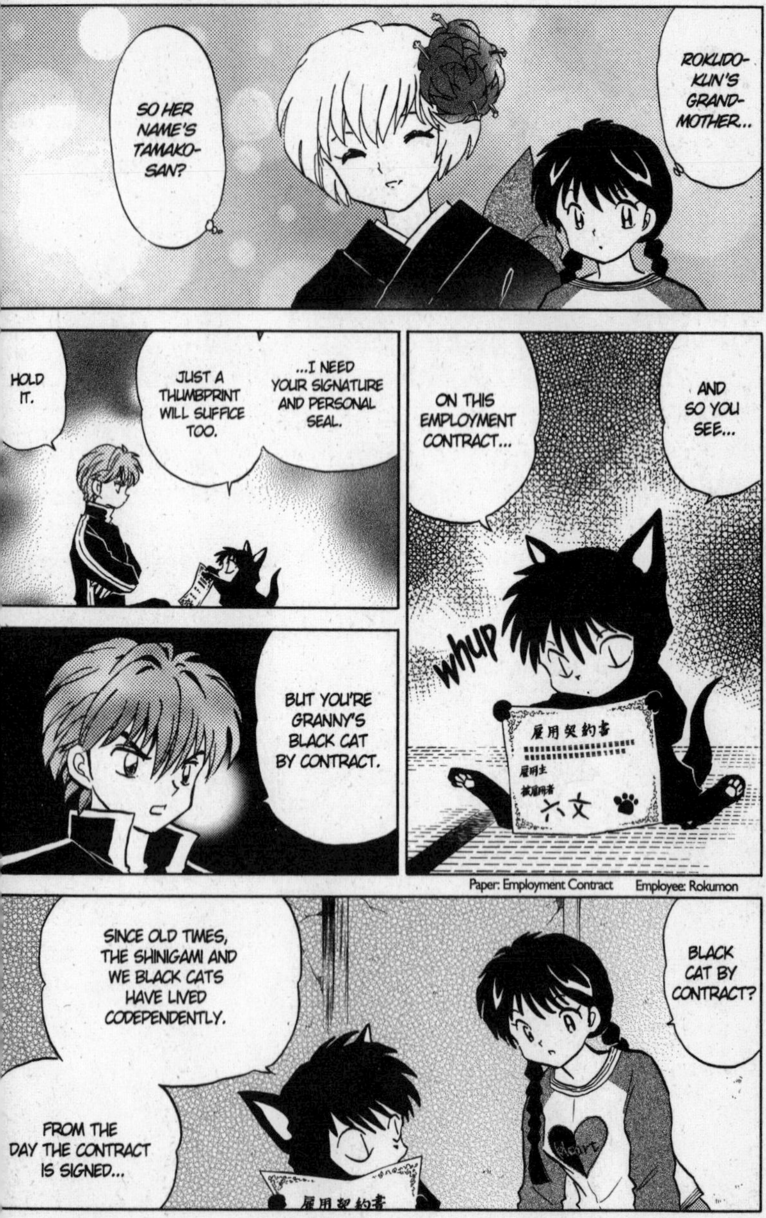
ROKUDO-KUN'S GRAND-MOTHER...
SO HER NAME'S TAMAKO-SAN?
AND SO YOU SEE...
ON THIS EMPLOYMENT CONTRACT...
whup
雇用契約書
六文
...I NEED YOUR SIGNATURE AND PERSONAL SEAL.
JUST A THUMBPRINT WILL SUFFICE TOO.
HOLD IT.
BUT YOU'RE GRANNY'S BLACK CAT BY CONTRACT.
Paper: Employment Contract
Employee: Rokumon
BLACK CAT BY CONTRACT?
SINCE OLD TIMES, THE SHINIGAMI AND WE BLACK CATS HAVE LIVED CODEPENDENTLY.
FROM THE DAY THE CONTRACT IS SIGNED...
雇用契約書

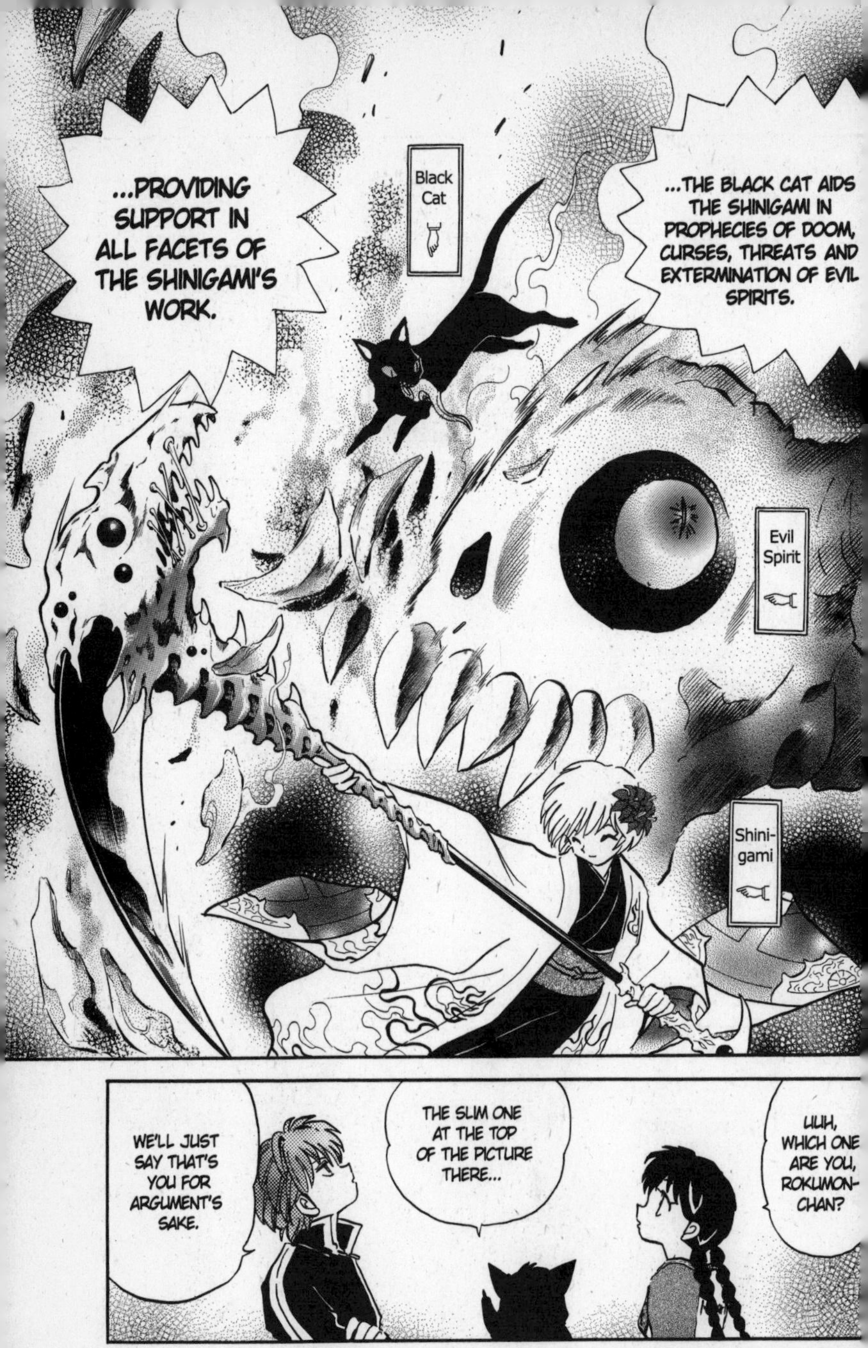
...THE BLACK CAT AIDS THE SHINIGAMI IN PROPHECIES OF DOOM, CURSES, THREATS AND EXTERMINATION OF EVIL SPIRITS.
Black Cat
...PROVIDING SUPPORT IN ALL FACETS OF THE SHINIGAMI'S WORK.
Evil Spirit
Shinigami
UUH, WHICH ONE ARE YOU, ROKUMON-CHAN?
THE SLIM ONE AT THE TOP OF THE PICTURE THERE...
WE'LL JUST SAY THAT'S YOU FOR ARGUMENT'S SAKE.

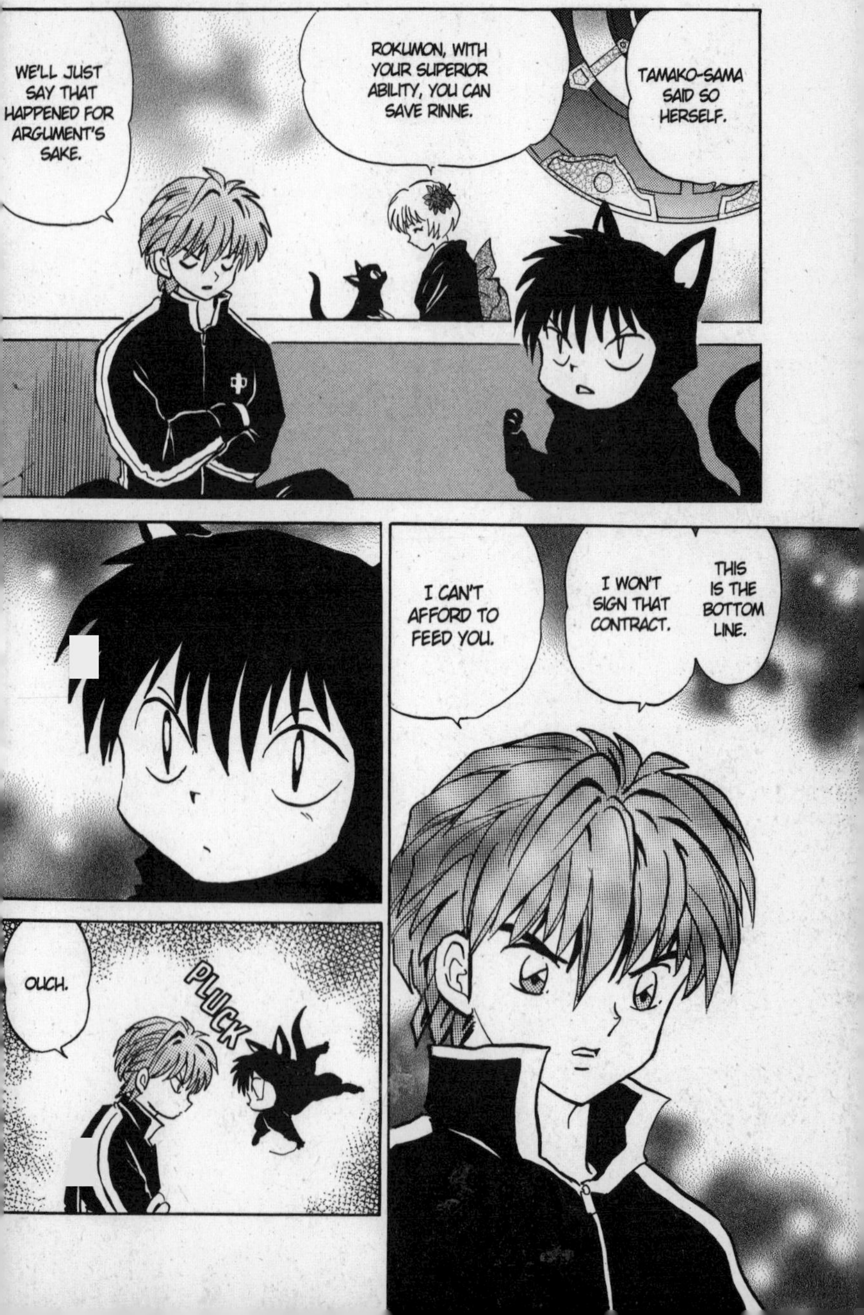
TAMAKO-SAMA SAID SO HERSELF.
ROKUMON, WITH YOUR SUPERIOR ABILITY, YOU CAN SAVE RINNE.
WE'LL JUST SAY THAT HAPPENED FOR ARGUMENT'S SAKE.
THIS IS THE BOTTOM LINE.
I WON'T SIGN THAT CONTRACT.
I CAN'T AFFORD TO FEED YOU.
PLUCK
OUCH.

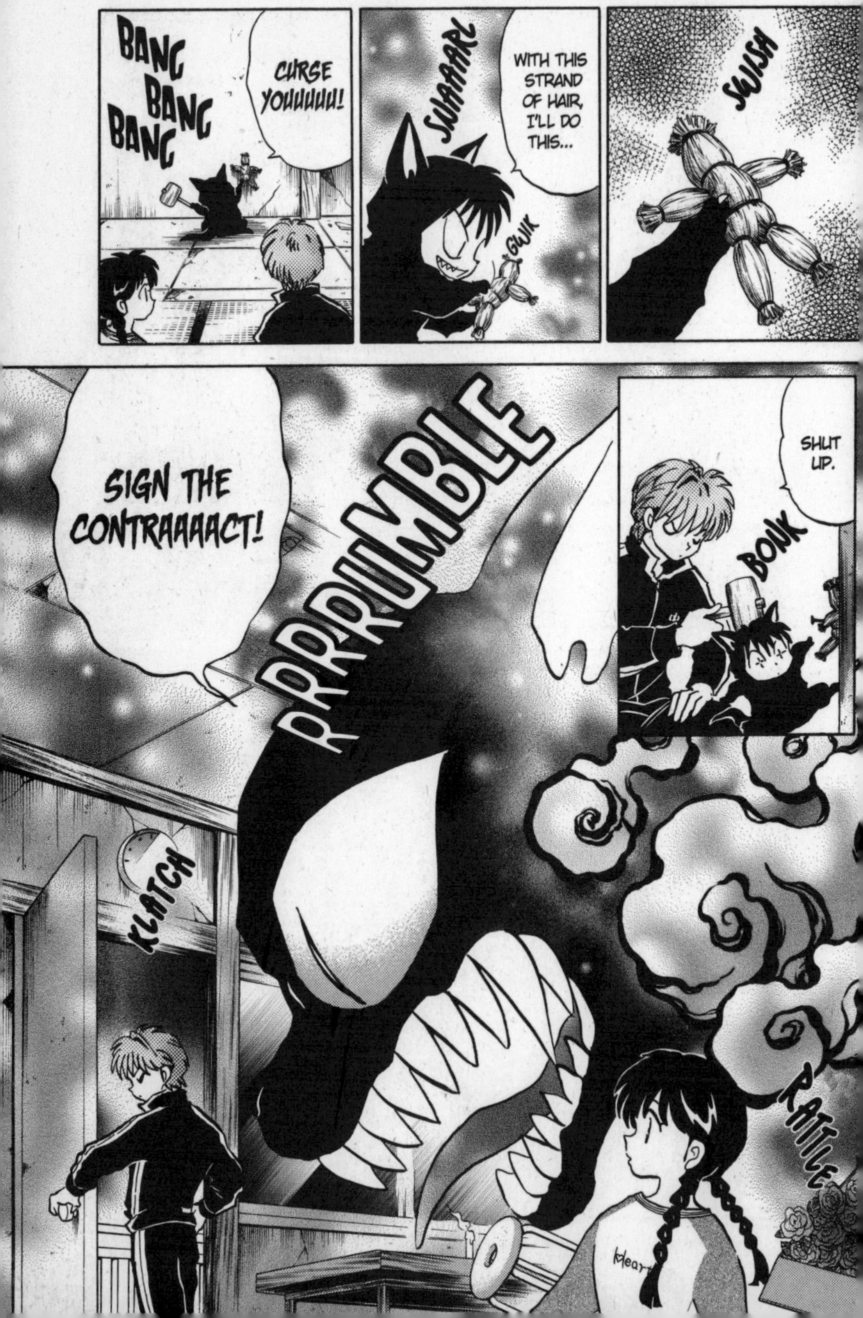
SWISH
WITH THIS STRAND OF HAIR, I'LL DO THIS...
SWAAARL
GWIK
CURSE YOUUUUU!
BANG BANG BANG
SHUT UP.
BONK
SIGN THE CONTRAAAACT!
PRRRUMBLE
KLATCH
RATTLE

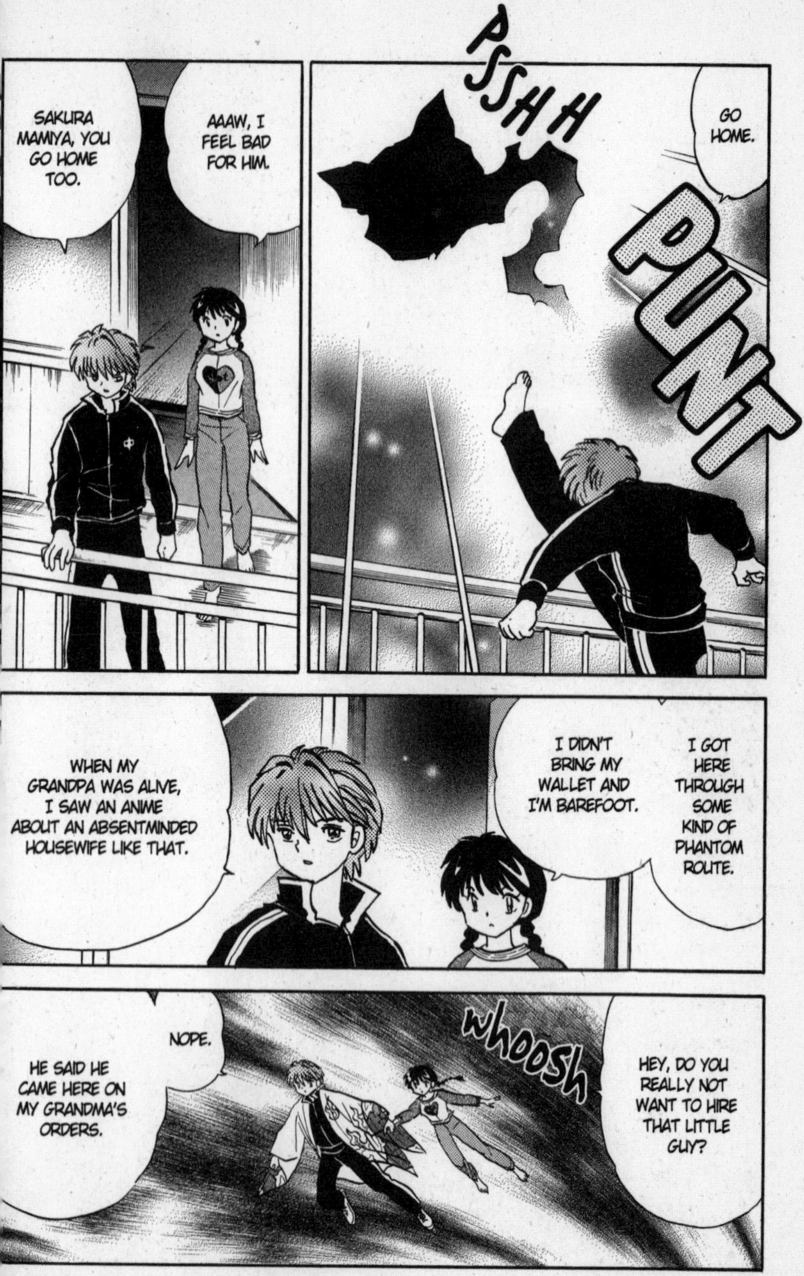
GO HOME.
PSSH
PUNT
AAAW, I FEEL BAD FOR HIM.
SAKURA MAMIYA, YOU GO HOME TOO.
I GOT HERE THROUGH SOME KIND OF PHANTOM ROUTE.
I DIDN'T BRING MY WALLET AND I'M BAREFOOT.
WHEN MY GRANDPA WAS ALIVE, I SAW AN ANIME ABOUT AN ABSENTMINDED HOUSEWIFE LIKE THAT.
HEY, DO YOU REALLY NOT WANT TO HIRE THAT LITTLE GUY?
whoosh
NOPE.
HE SAID HE CAME HERE ON MY GRANDMA'S ORDERS.

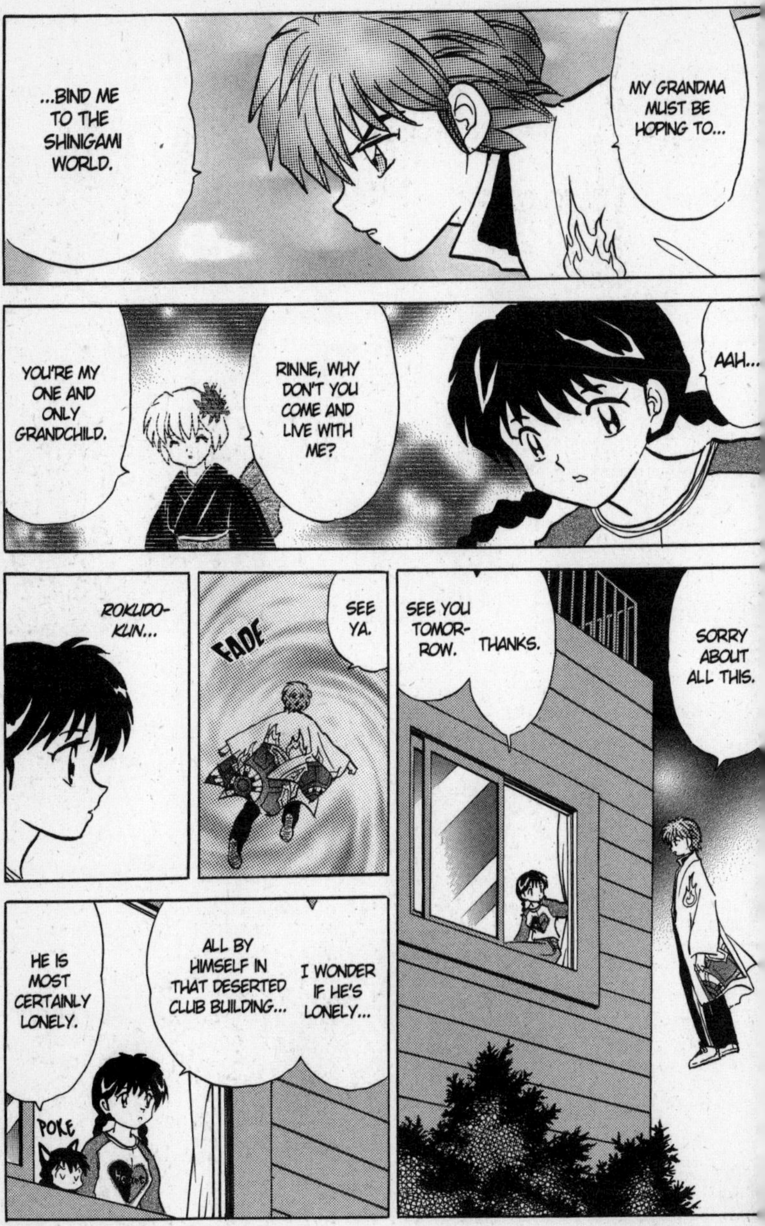
MY GRANDMA MUST BE HOPING TO...
...BIND ME TO THE SHINIGAMI WORLD.
AAH...
RINNE, WHY DON'T YOU COME AND LIVE WITH ME?
YOU'RE MY ONE AND ONLY GRANDCHILD.
SORRY ABOUT ALL THIS.
THANKS.
SEE YOU TOMOR-ROW.
SEE YA.
FADE
ROKUDO-KUN...
I WONDER IF HE'S LONELY...
ALL BY HIMSELF IN THAT DESERTED CLUB BUILDING...
HE IS MOST CERTAINLY LONELY.
POKE

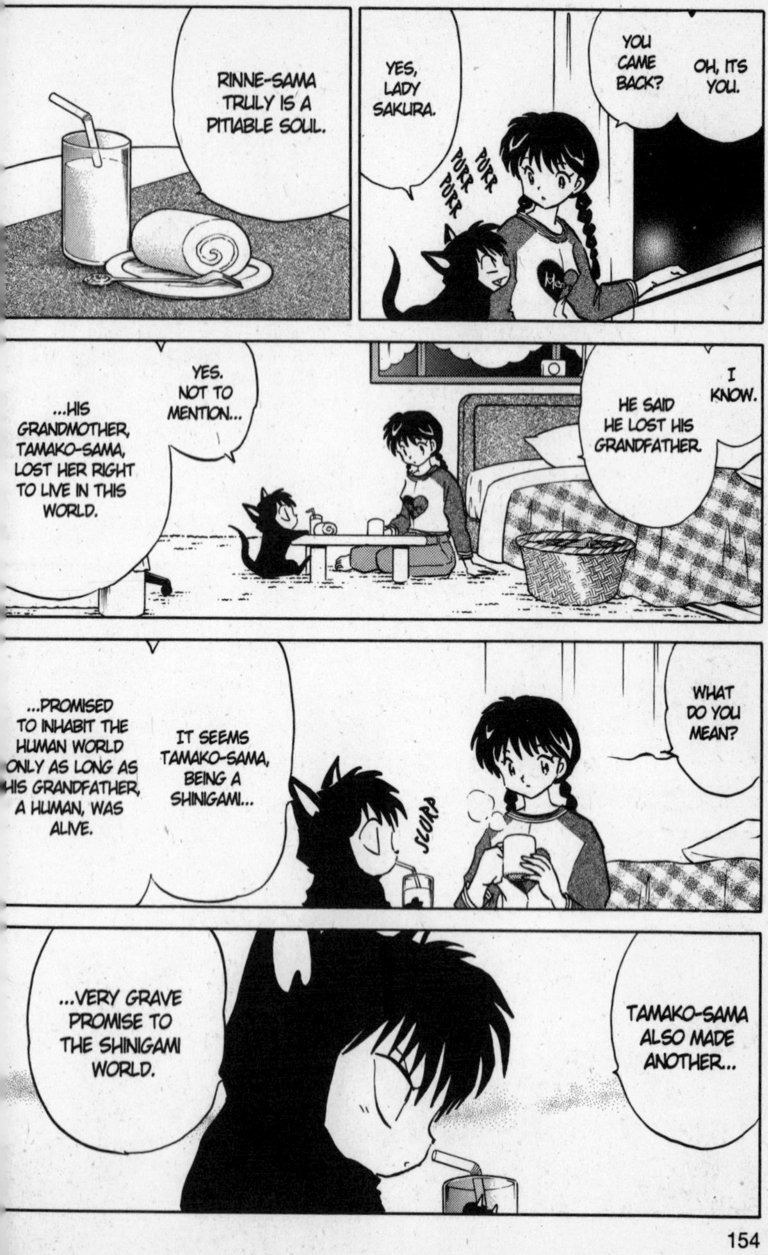
OH, ITS YOU.
YOU CAME BACK?
YES, LADY SAKURA.
PURR PURR PURR
RINNE-SAMA TRULY IS A PITIABLE SOUL.
I KNOW.
HE SAID HE LOST HIS GRANDFATHER.
YES. NOT TO MENTION...
...HIS GRANDMOTHER, TAMAKO-SAMA, LOST HER RIGHT TO LIVE IN THIS WORLD.
WHAT DO YOU MEAN?
SLURP
IT SEEMS TAMAKO-SAMA, BEING A SHINIGAMI...
...PROMISED TO INHABIT THE HUMAN WORLD ONLY AS LONG AS HIS GRANDFATHER, A HUMAN, WAS ALIVE.
TAMAKO-SAMA ALSO MADE ANOTHER...
...VERY GRAVE PROMISE TO THE SHINIGAMI WORLD.

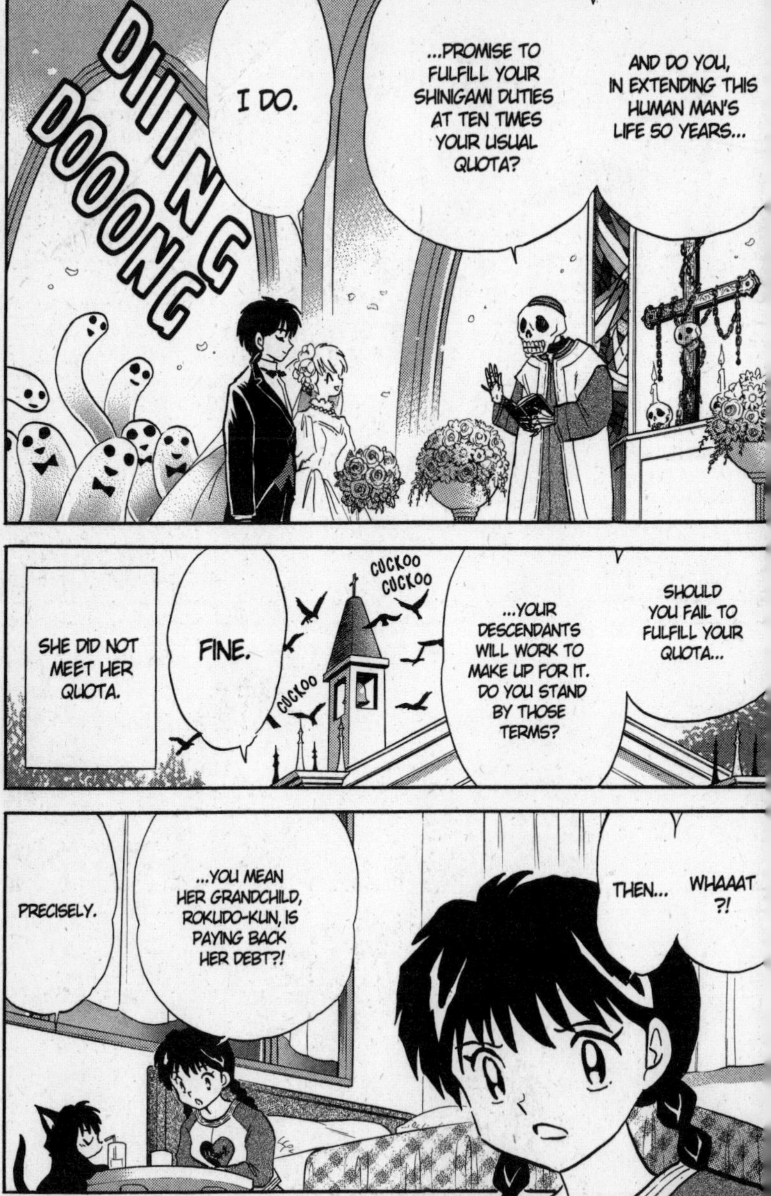
AND DO YOU, IN EXTENDING THIS HUMAN MAN'S LIFE 50 YEARS...
...PROMISE TO FULFILL YOUR SHINIGAMI DUTIES AT TEN TIMES YOUR USUAL QUOTA?
I DO.
DIIING DOOONG
SHOULD YOU FAIL TO FULFILL YOUR QUOTA...
...YOUR DESCENDANTS WILL WORK TO MAKE UP FOR IT. DO YOU STAND BY THOSE TERMS?
CUCKOO CUCKOO
FINE.
CUCKOO
SHE DID NOT MEET HER QUOTA.
WHAAAT ?!
THEN...
...YOU MEAN HER GRANDCHILD, ROKUDO-KUN, IS PAYING BACK HER DEBT?!
PRECISELY.

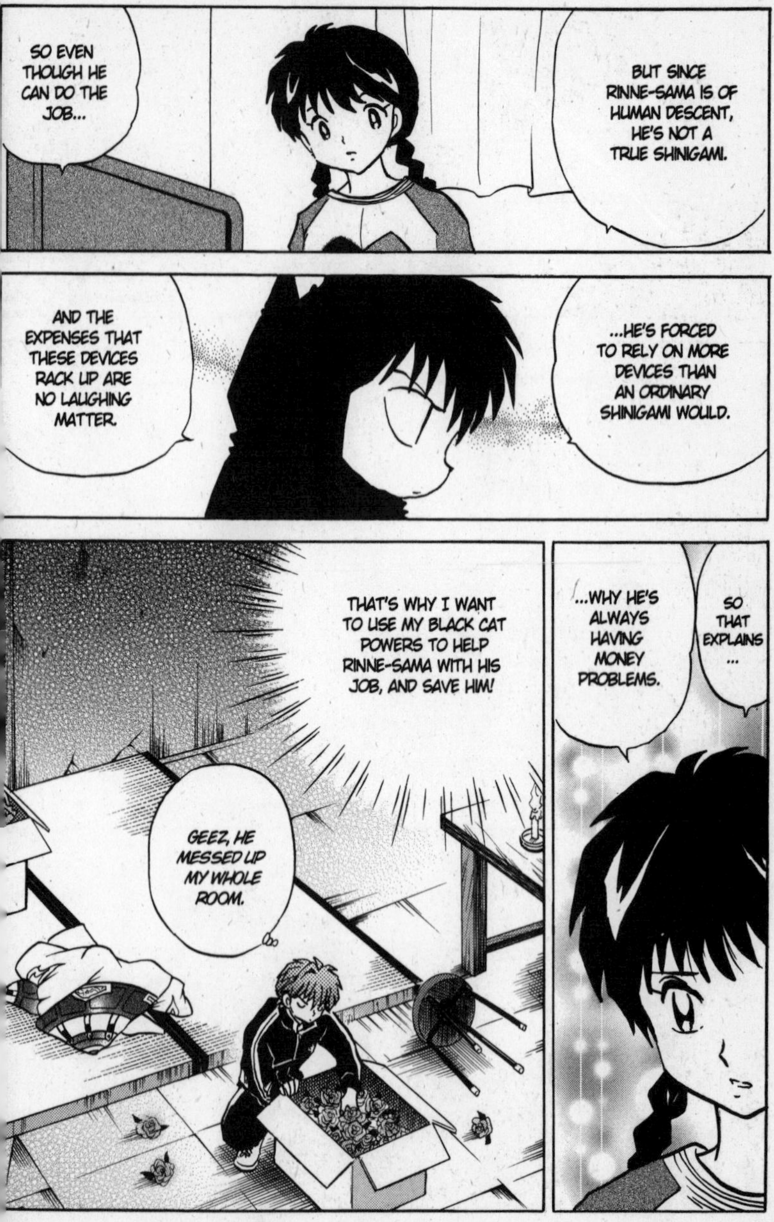
BUT SINCE RINNE-SAMA IS OF HUMAN DESCENT, HE'S NOT A TRUE SHINIGAMI.
SO EVEN THOUGH HE CAN DO THE JOB...
...HE'S FORCED TO RELY ON MORE DEVICES THAN AN ORDINARY SHINIGAMI WOULD.
AND THE EXPENSES THAT THESE DEVICES RACK UP ARE NO LAUGHING MATTER.
SO THAT EXPLAINS...
...WHY HE'S ALWAYS HAVING MONEY PROBLEMS.
THAT'S WHY I WANT TO USE MY BLACK CAT POWERS TO HELP RINNE-SAMA WITH HIS JOB, AND SAVE HIM!
GEEZ, HE MESSED UP MY WHOLE ROOM.

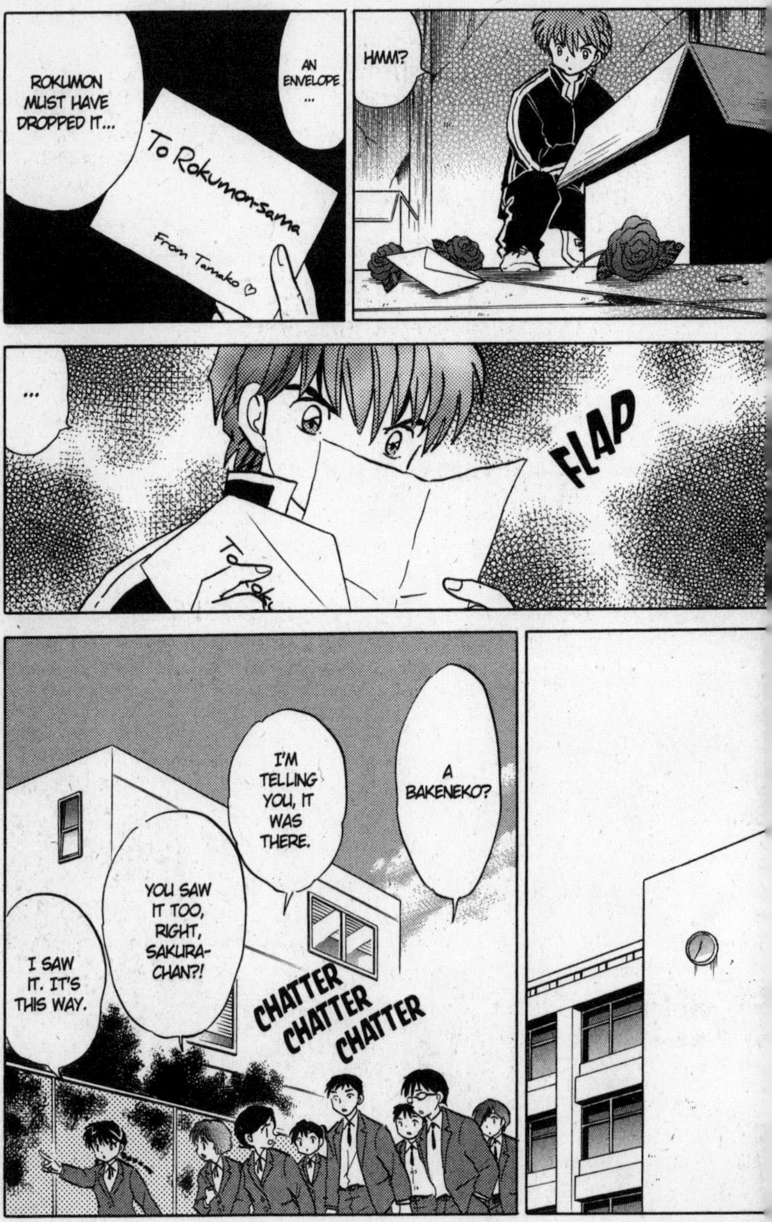
HMM?
AN ENVELOPE...
ROKUMON MUST HAVE DROPPED IT...
To Rokumon-sama
From Tamako ♡
...
FLAP
A BAKENEKO?
I'M TELLING YOU, IT WAS THERE.
YOU SAW IT TOO, RIGHT, SAKURA-CHAN?!
CHATTER CHATTER CHATTER
I SAW IT. IT'S THIS WAY.

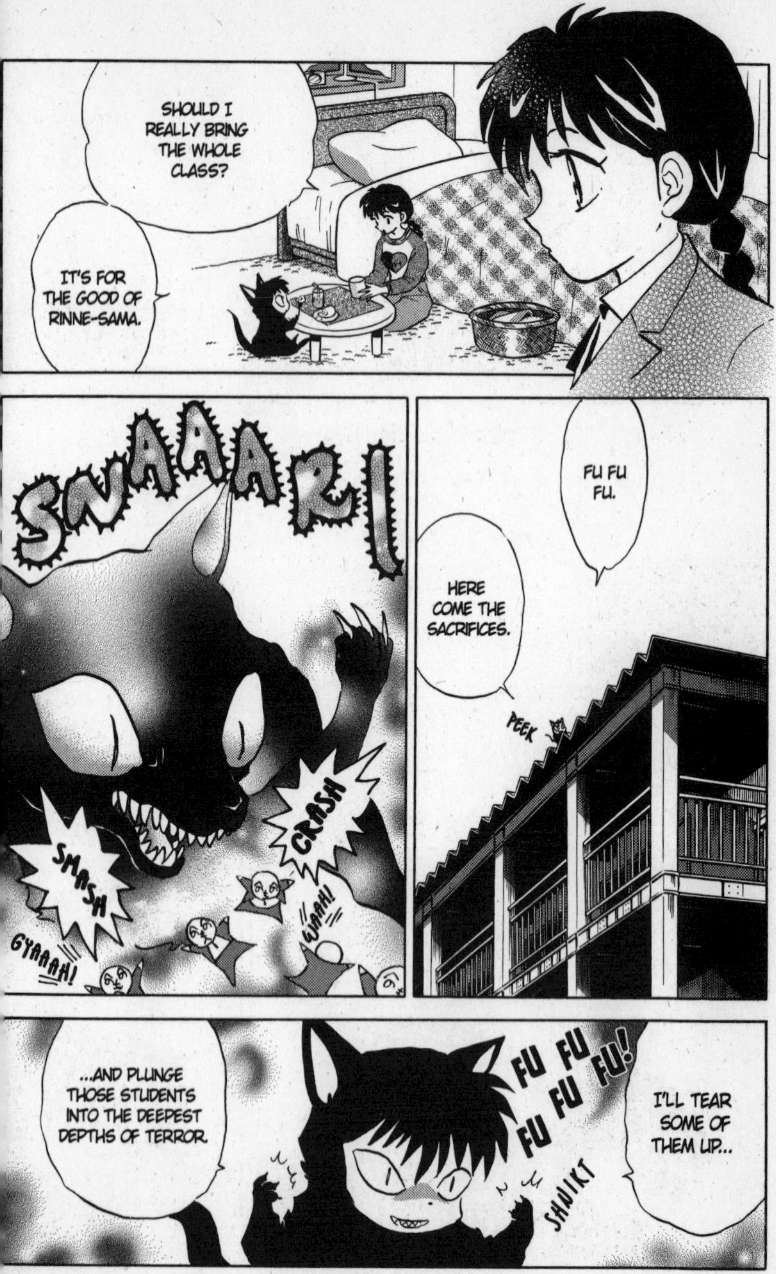
SHOULD I REALLY BRING THE WHOLE CLASS?
IT'S FOR THE GOOD OF RINNE-SAMA.
FU FU FU.
HERE COME THE SACRIFICES.
PEEK
SNAAARL
CRASH
SMASH
WAAH!
GYAAAH!
I'LL TEAR SOME OF THEM UP...
FU FU FU FU FU!
SHNIKT
...AND PLUNGE THOSE STUDENTS INTO THE DEEPEST DEPTHS OF TERROR.

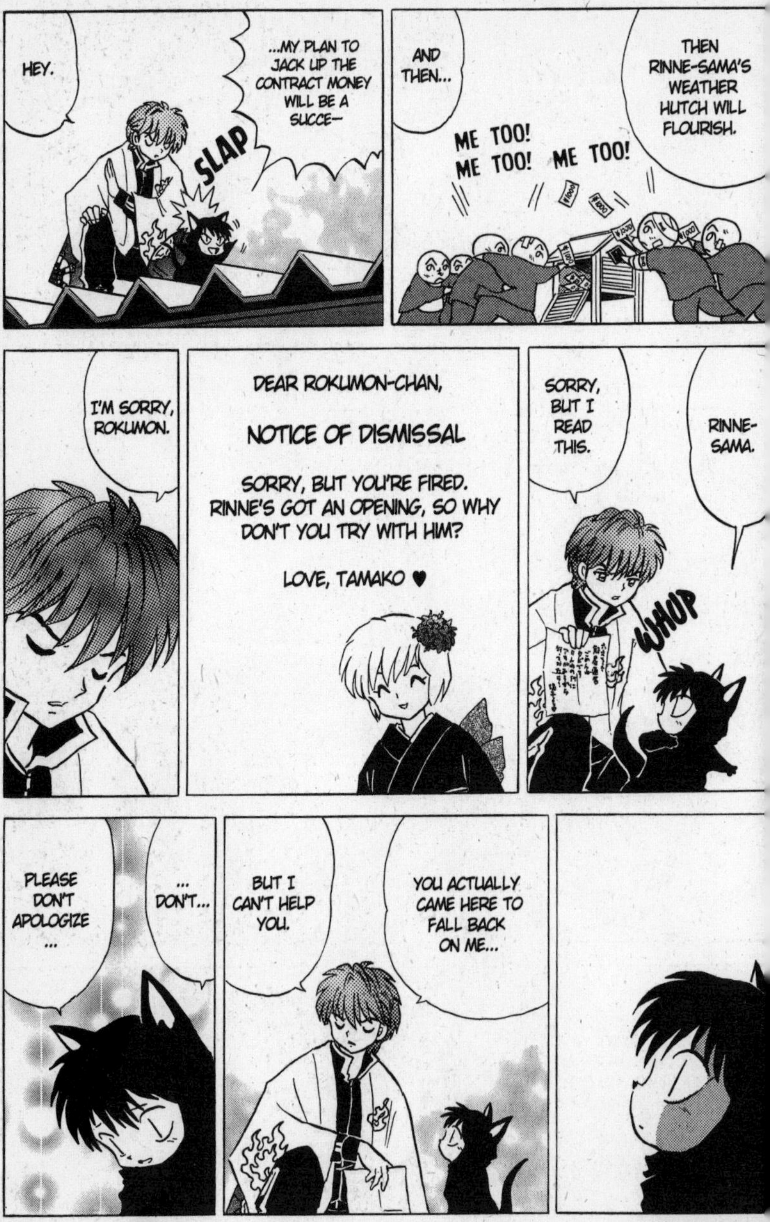
THEN RINNE-SAMA'S WEATHER HUTCH WILL FLOURISH.
ME TOO! ME TOO! ME TOO!
AND THEN...
...MY PLAN TO JACK UP THE CONTRACT MONEY WILL BE A SUCCE—
SLAP
HEY.
RINNE-SAMA.
SORRY, BUT I READ THIS.
WHOP
DEAR ROKUMON-CHAN,
NOTICE OF DISMISSAL
SORRY, BUT YOU'RE FIRED. RINNE'S GOT AN OPENING, SO WHY DON'T YOU TRY WITH HIM?
LOVE, TAMAKO ♥
I'M SORRY, ROKUMON.
YOU ACTUALLY CAME HERE TO FALL BACK ON ME...
BUT I CAN'T HELP YOU.
... DON'T...
PLEASE DON'T APOLOGIZE ...

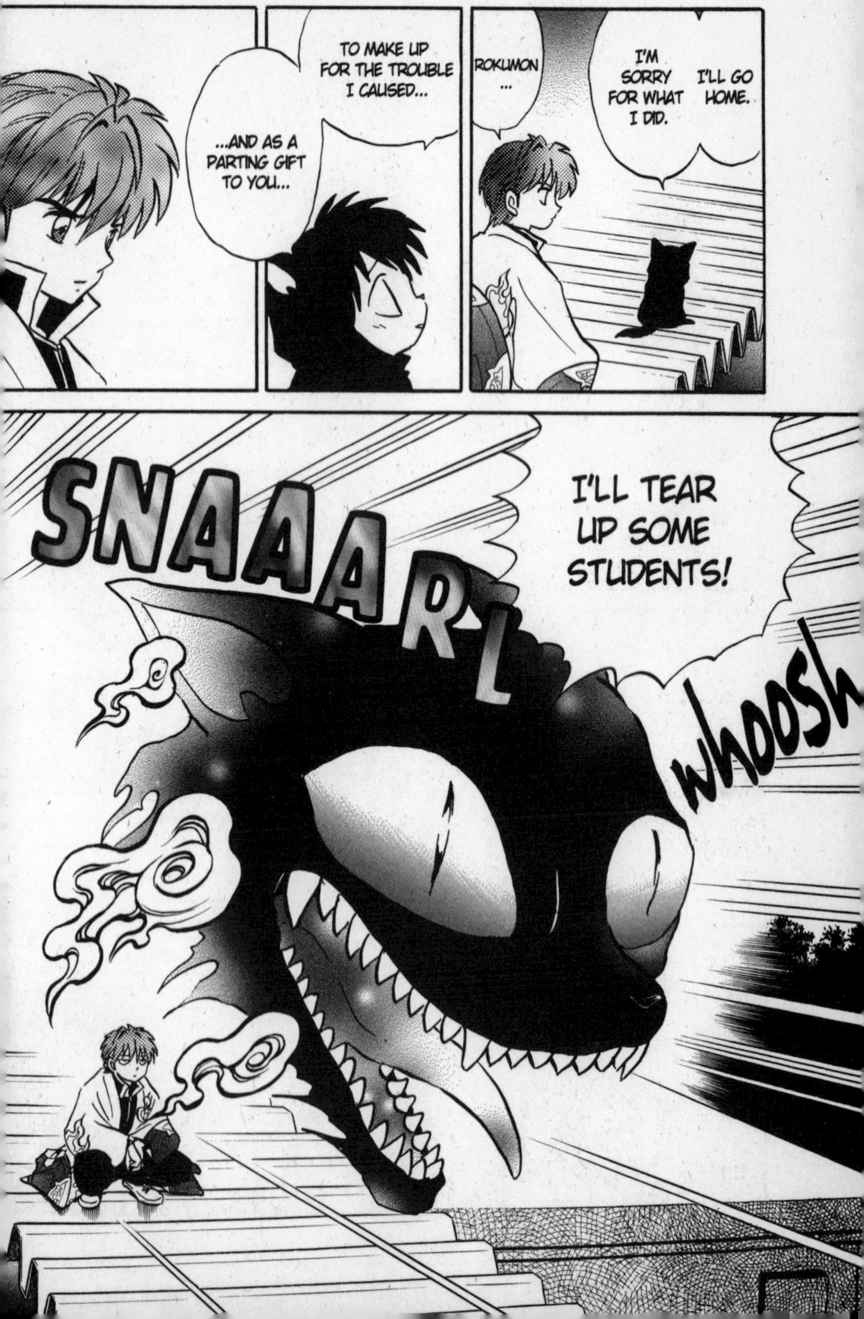
I'M SORRY FOR WHAT I DID. I'LL GO HOME.
ROKUMON ...
TO MAKE UP FOR THE TROUBLE I CAUSED...
...AND AS A PARTING GIFT TO YOU...
I'LL TEAR UP SOME STUDENTS!
SNAAARL
whoosh

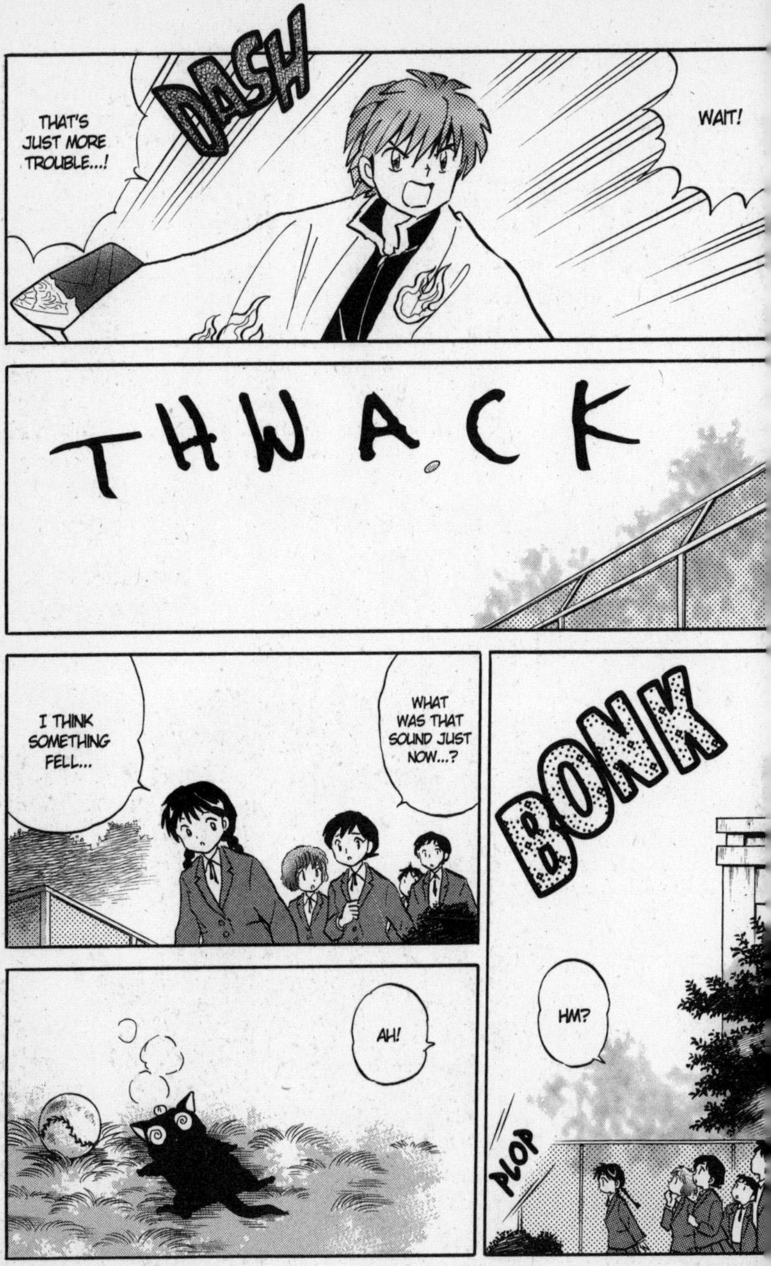
WAIT!
DASH
THAT'S JUST MORE TROUBLE...!
THWACK
BONK
HM?
PLOP
WHAT WAS THAT SOUND JUST NOW...?
I THINK SOMETHING FELL...
AH!

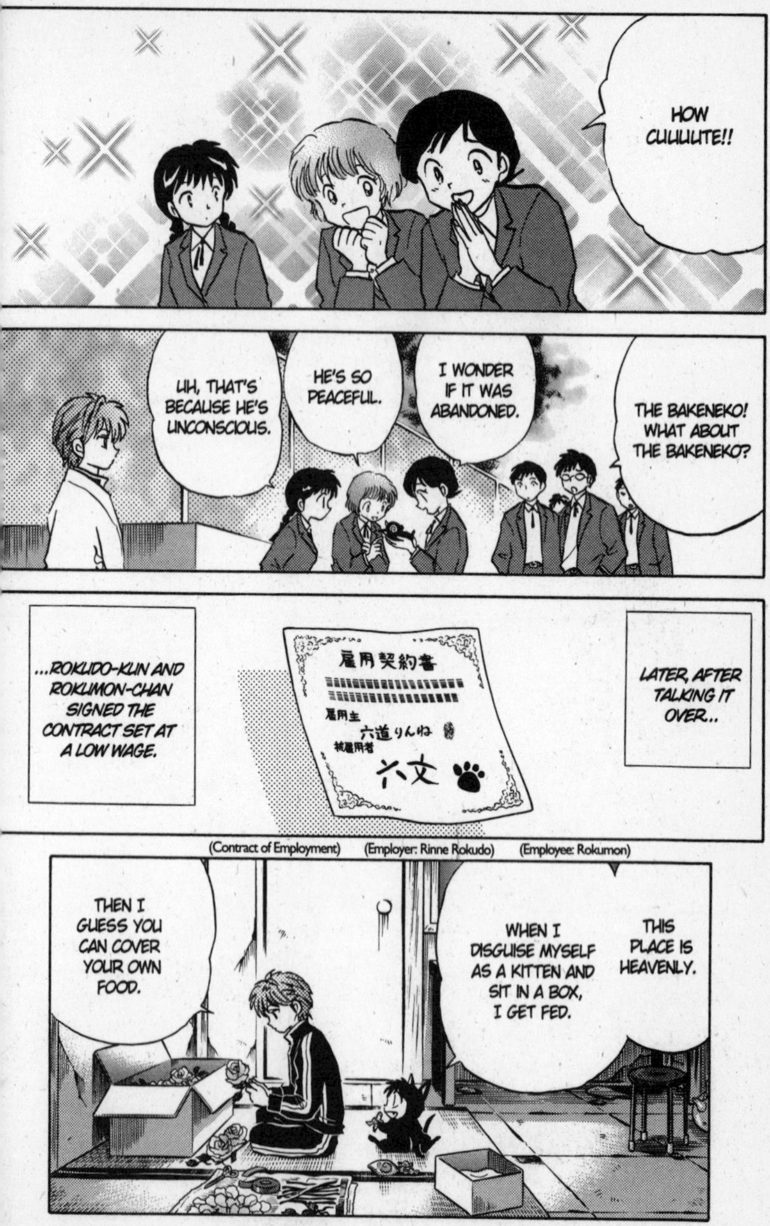
HOW CUUUUTE!!
THE BAKENEKO! WHAT ABOUT THE BAKENEKO?
I WONDER IF IT WAS ABANDONED.
HE'S SO PEACEFUL.
UH, THAT'S BECAUSE HE'S UNCONSCIOUS.
LATER, AFTER TALKING IT OVER...
雇用契約書
雇用主
六道りんね
被雇用者
六文
...ROKUDO-KUN AND ROKUMON-CHAN SIGNED THE CONTRACT SET AT A LOW WAGE.
(Contract of Employment) (Employer: Rinne Rokudo) (Employee: Rokumon)
THIS PLACE IS HEAVENLY.
WHEN I DISGUISE MYSELF AS A KITTEN AND SIT IN A BOX, I GET FED.
THEN I GUESS YOU CAN COVER YOUR OWN FOOD.

CHAPTER 8:
AFRAID TO FALL ASLEEP

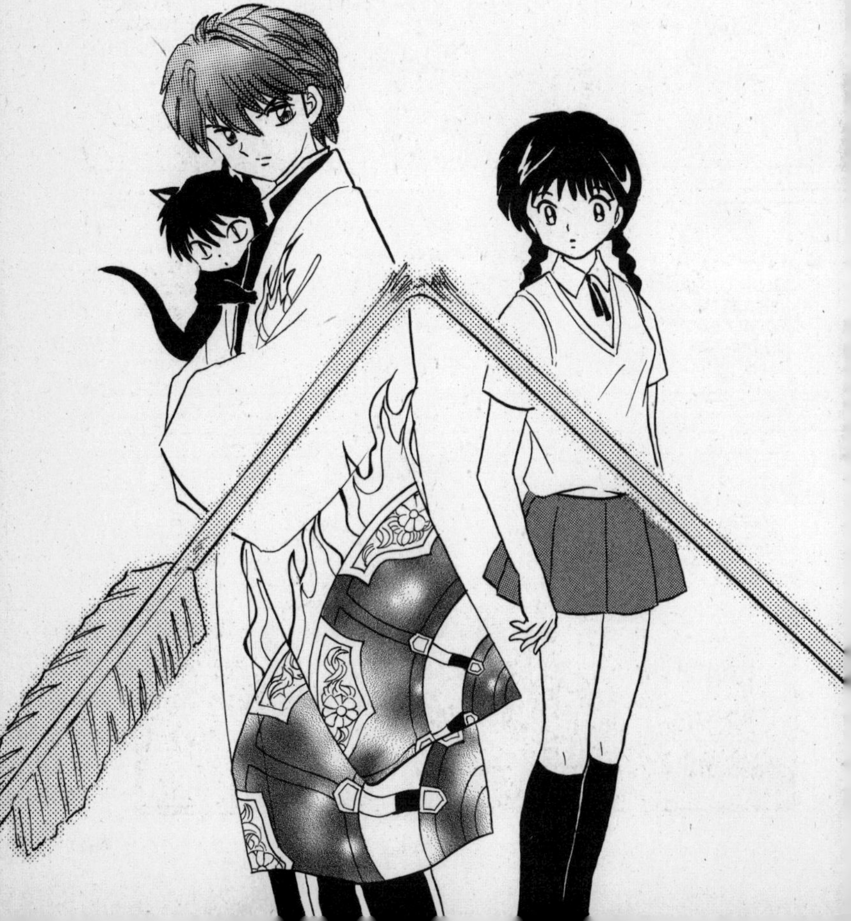

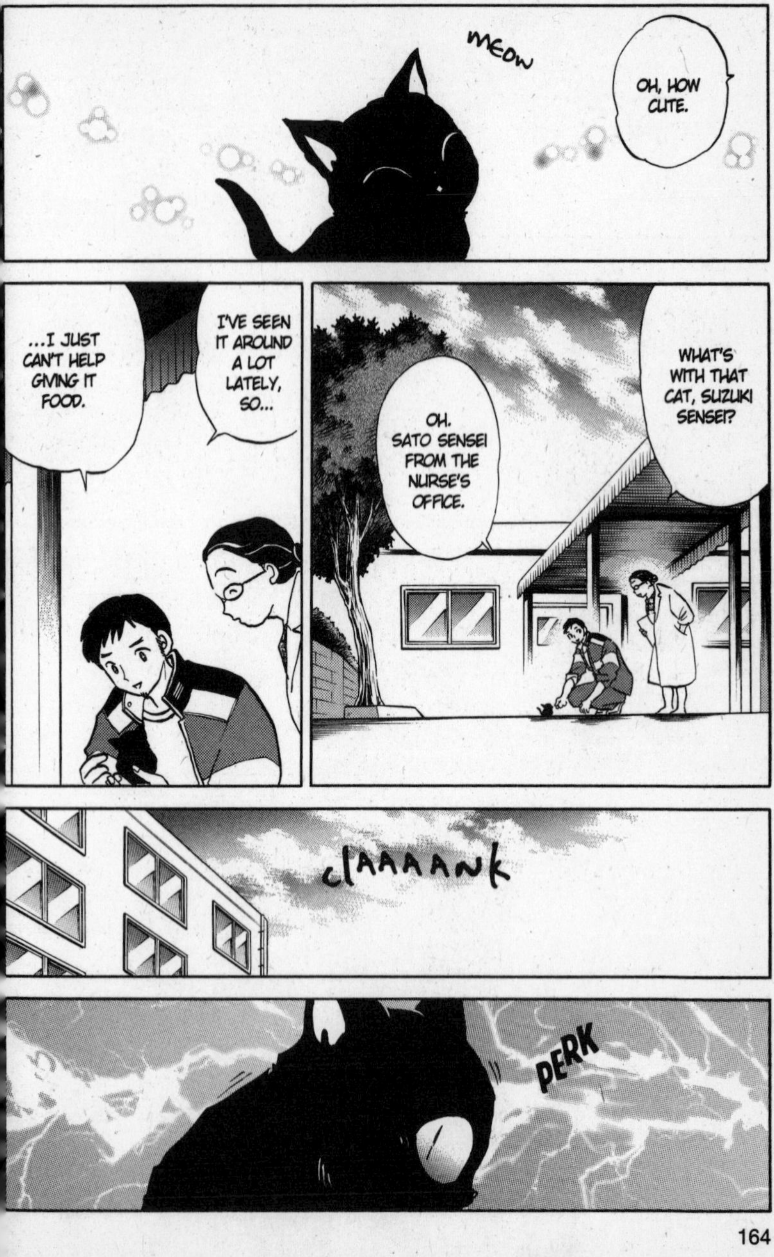
OH, HOW CUTE.
MEOW
WHAT'S WITH THAT CAT, SUZUKI SENSEI?
OH. SATO SENSEI FROM THE NURSE'S OFFICE.
I'VE SEEN IT AROUND A LOT LATELY, SO...
...I JUST CAN'T HELP GIVING IT FOOD.
CLAAAANK
PERK

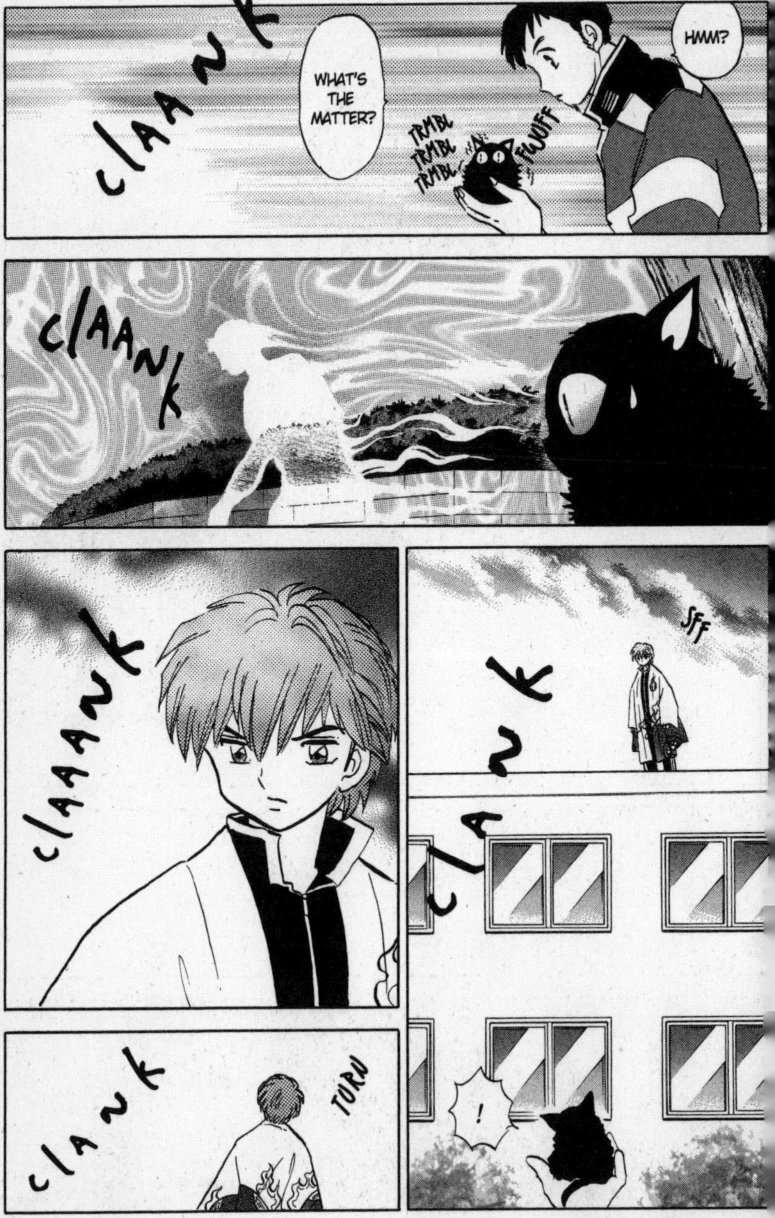
HMM?
FWUFF
TRMBL TRMBL TRMBL
WHAT'S THE MATTER?
CLAANK
CLAANK
SFF
CLANK
!
CLAAANK
TORU
CLANK

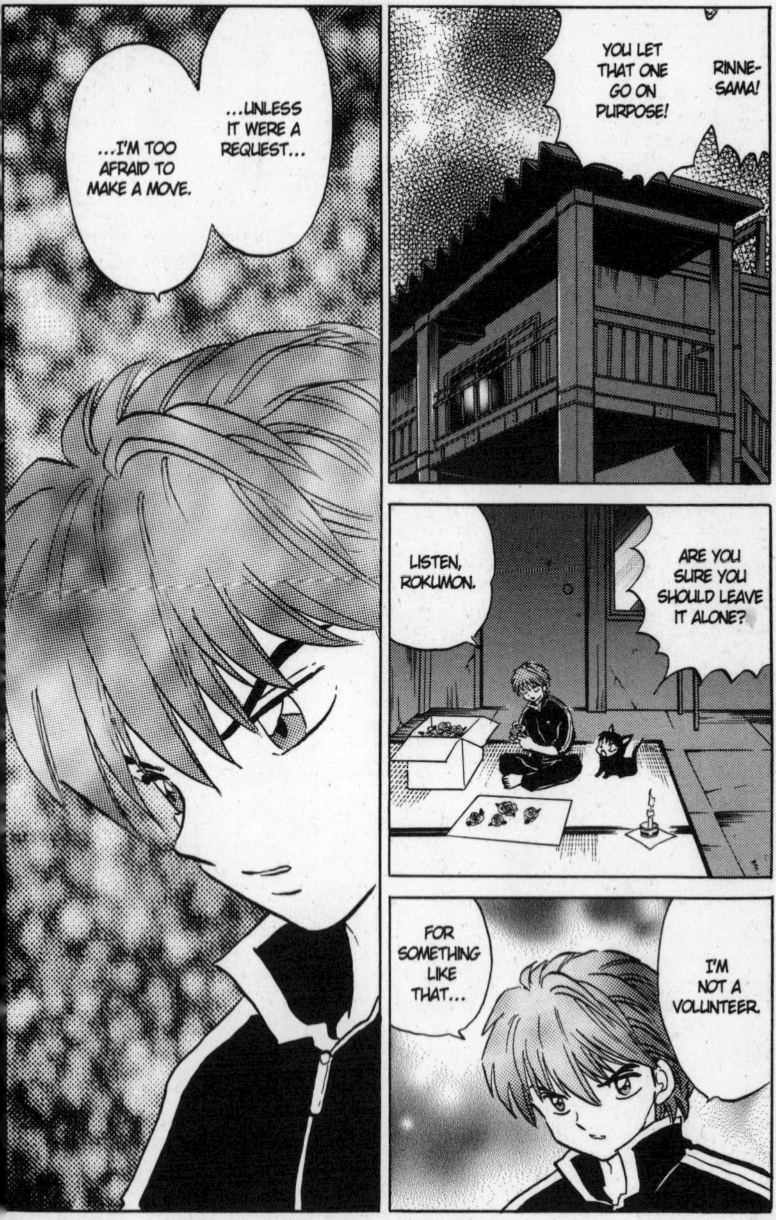
RINNE-SAMA!
YOU LET THAT ONE GO ON PURPOSE!
ARE YOU SURE YOU SHOULD LEAVE IT ALONE?
LISTEN, ROKUMON.
I'M NOT A VOLUNTEER.
FOR SOMETHING LIKE THAT...
...UNLESS IT WERE A REQUEST...
...I'M TOO AFRAID TO MAKE A MOVE.

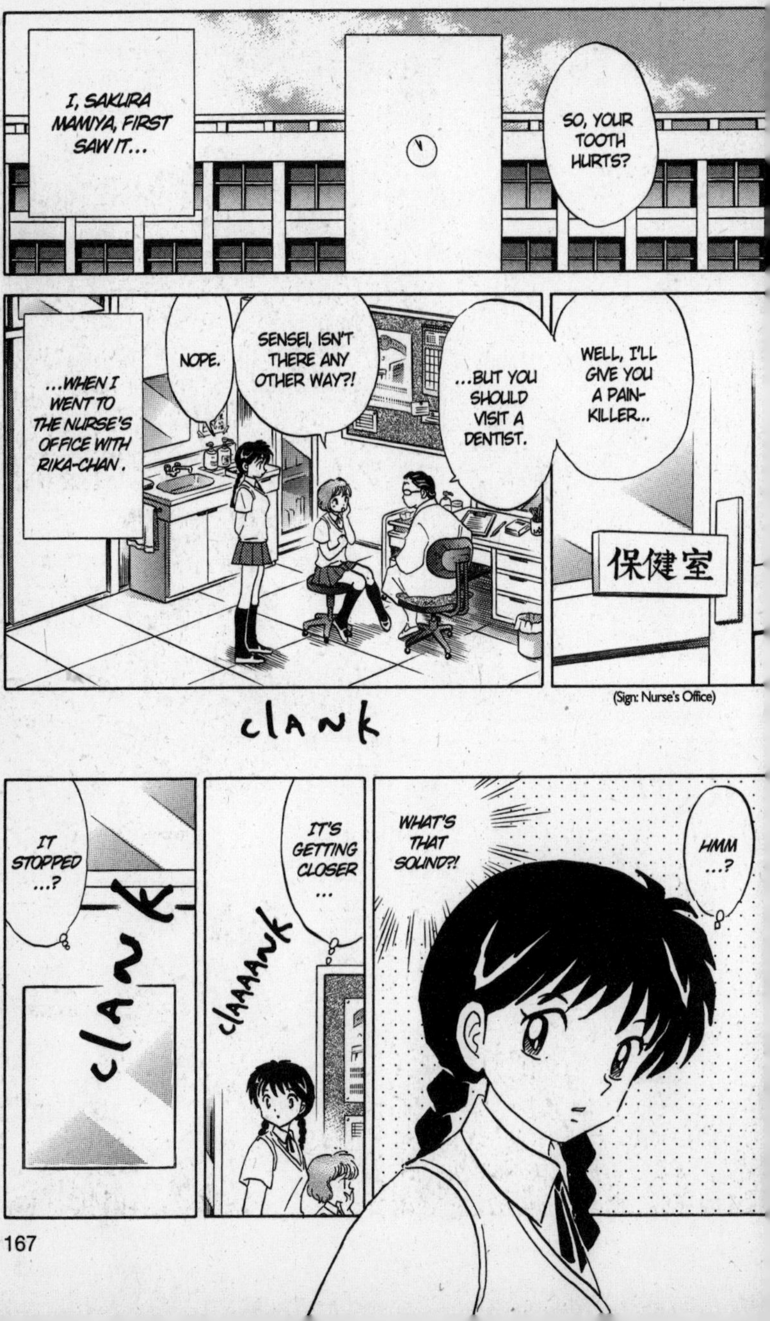
SO, YOUR TOOTH HURTS?
I, SAKURA MAMIYA, FIRST SAW IT...
WELL, I'LL GIVE YOU A PAIN-KILLER...
保健室
...BUT YOU SHOULD VISIT A DENTIST.
SENSEI, ISN'T THERE ANY OTHER WAY?!
NOPE.
...WHEN I WENT TO THE NURSE'S OFFICE WITH RIKA-CHAN.
(Sign: Nurse's Office)
clank
HMM ...?
WHAT'S THAT SOUND?!
IT'S GETTING CLOSER ...
claaaank
IT STOPPED ...?
clank

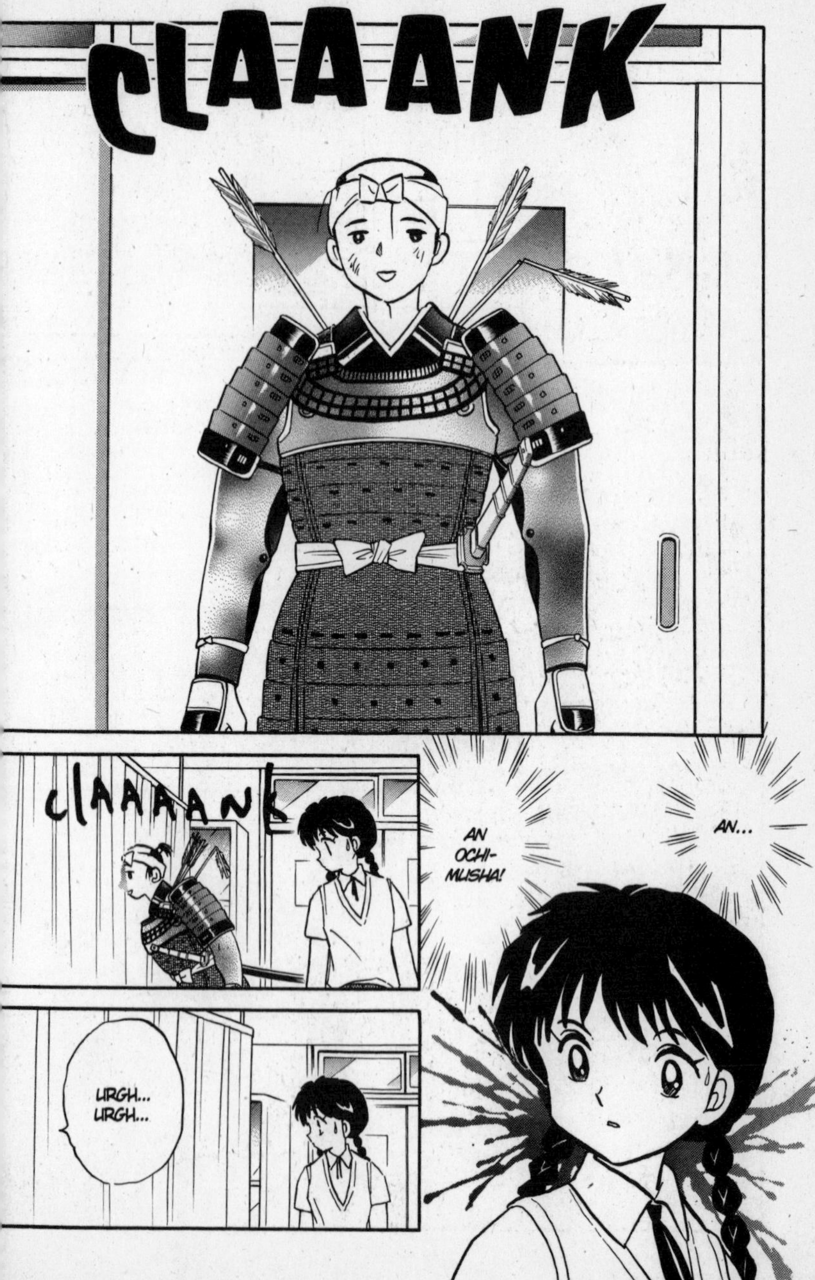
CLAAANK
AN...
AN OCHI-MUSHA!
CLAAAANK
URGH... URGH...

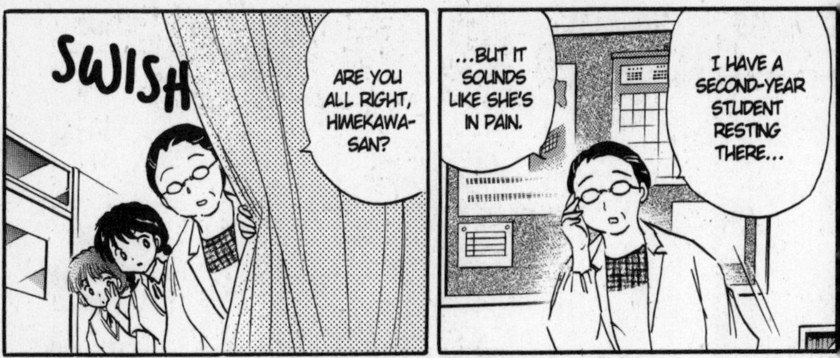
I HAVE A SECOND-YEAR STUDENT RESTING THERE...
...BUT IT SOUNDS LIKE SHE'S IN PAIN.
SWISH
ARE YOU ALL RIGHT, HIMEKAWA-SAN?

Note: *Hime* means "princess" in Japanese.

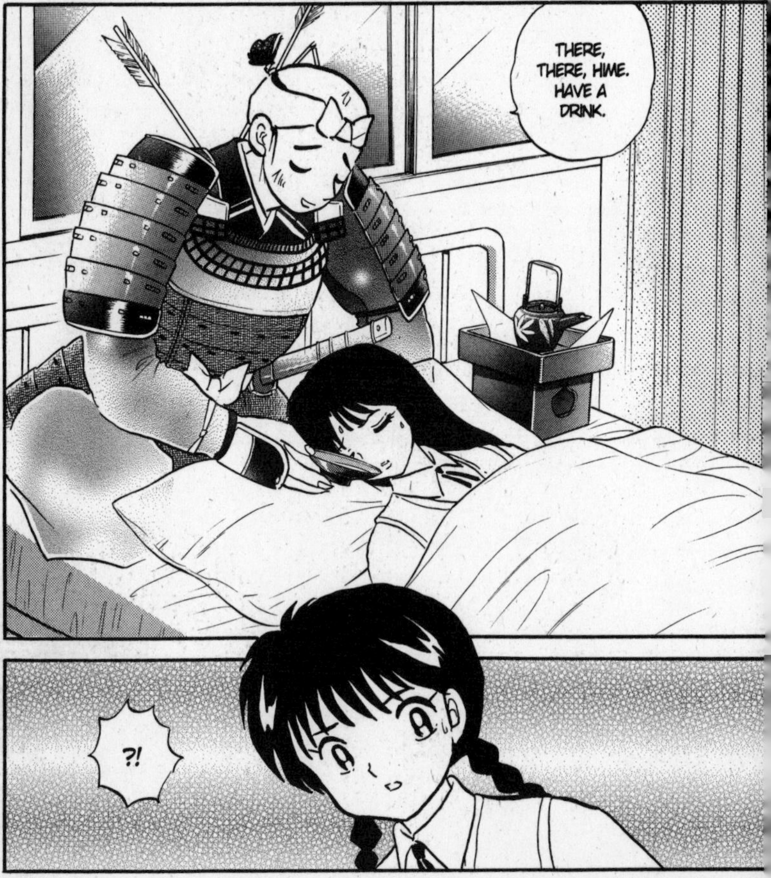
THERE, THERE, HIME. HAVE A DRINK.
?!

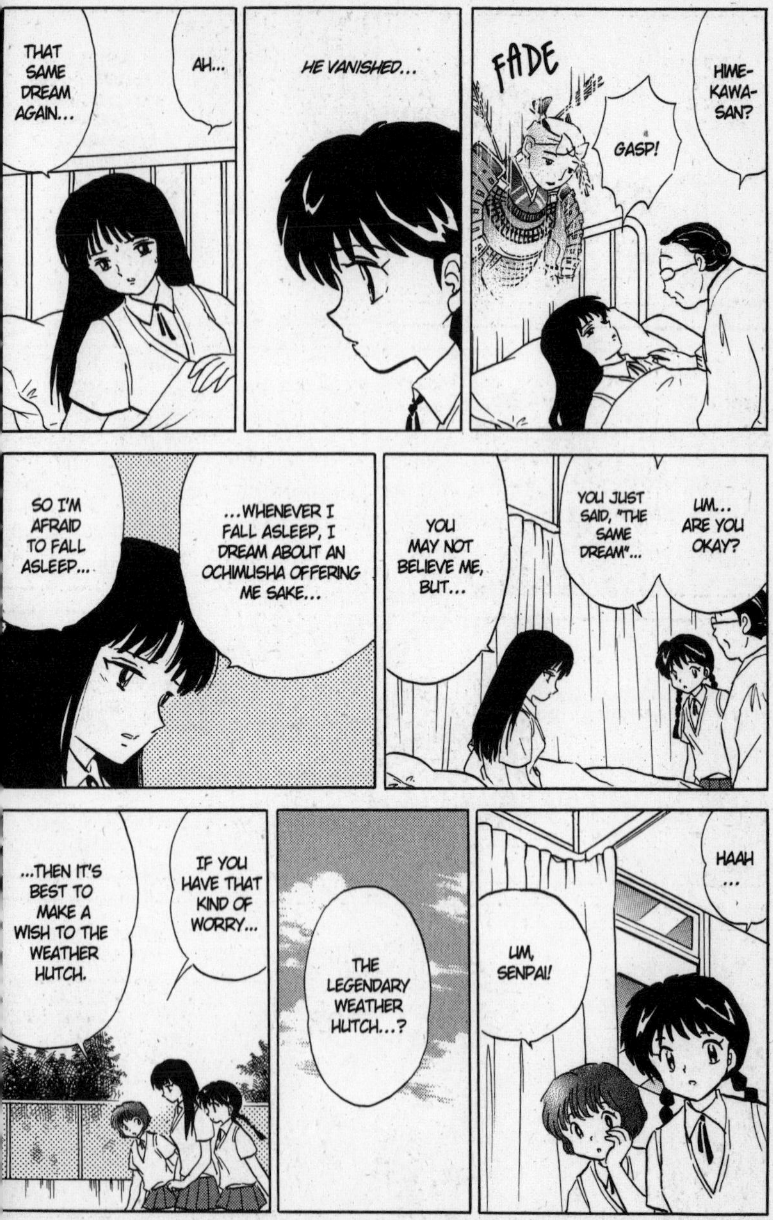
HIME-KAWA-SAN?
FADE
GASP!
HE VANISHED...
AH...
THAT SAME DREAM AGAIN...
UM... ARE YOU OKAY?
YOU JUST SAID, "THE SAME DREAM"...
YOU MAY NOT BELIEVE ME, BUT...
...WHENEVER I FALL ASLEEP, I DREAM ABOUT AN OCHIMUSHA OFFERING ME SAKE...
SO I'M AFRAID TO FALL ASLEEP...
HAAH ...
UM, SENPAI!
THE LEGENDARY WEATHER HUTCH...?
IF YOU HAVE THAT KIND OF WORRY...
...THEN IT'S BEST TO MAKE A WISH TO THE WEATHER HUTCH.

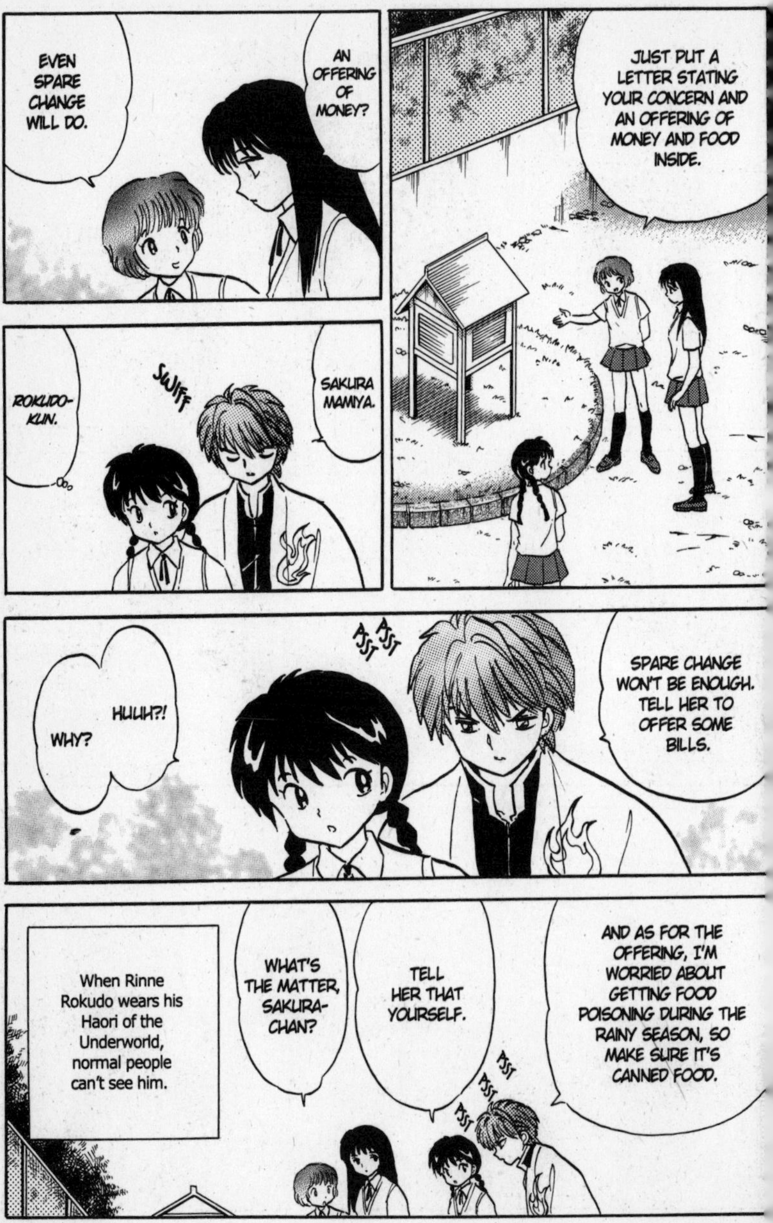
JUST PUT A LETTER STATING YOUR CONCERN AND AN OFFERING OF MONEY AND FOOD INSIDE.
AN OFFERING OF MONEY?
EVEN SPARE CHANGE WILL DO.
SAKURA MAMIYA.
SWIFF
ROKUDO-KUN.
SPARE CHANGE WON'T BE ENOUGH. TELL HER TO OFFER SOME BILLS.
PSST PSST
HUUH?!
WHY?
AND AS FOR THE OFFERING, I'M WORRIED ABOUT GETTING FOOD POISONING DURING THE RAINY SEASON, SO MAKE SURE IT'S CANNED FOOD.
PSST PSST PSST
TELL HER THAT YOURSELF.
WHAT'S THE MATTER, SAKURA-CHAN?
When Rinne Rokudo wears his Haori of the Underworld, normal people can't see him.

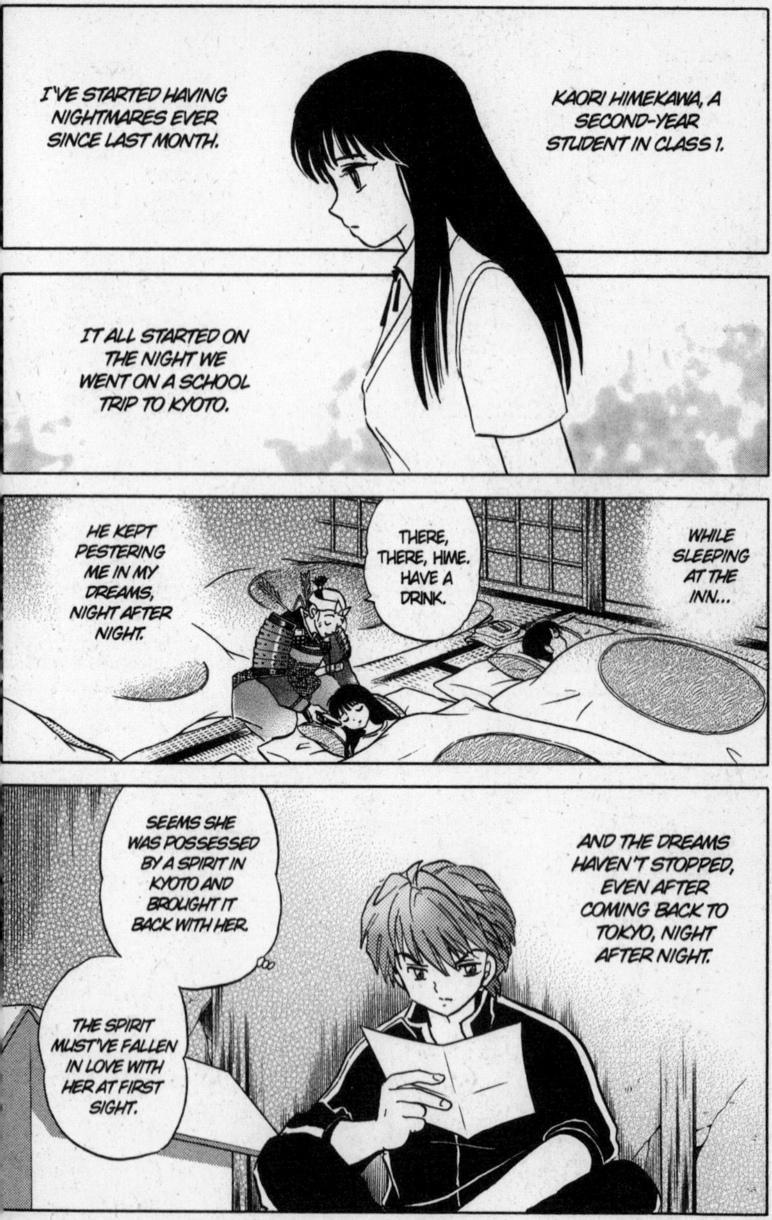

KAORI HIMEKAWA, A SECOND-YEAR STUDENT IN CLASS 1.
I'VE STARTED HAVING NIGHTMARES EVER SINCE LAST MONTH.
IT ALL STARTED ON THE NIGHT WE WENT ON A SCHOOL TRIP TO KYOTO.
WHILE SLEEPING AT THE INN...
THERE, THERE, HIME. HAVE A DRINK.
HE KEPT PESTERING ME IN MY DREAMS, NIGHT AFTER NIGHT.
AND THE DREAMS HAVEN'T STOPPED, EVEN AFTER COMING BACK TO TOKYO, NIGHT AFTER NIGHT.
SEEMS SHE WAS POSSESSED BY A SPIRIT IN KYOTO AND BROUGHT IT BACK WITH HER.
THE SPIRIT MUST'VE FALLEN IN LOVE WITH HER AT FIRST SIGHT.

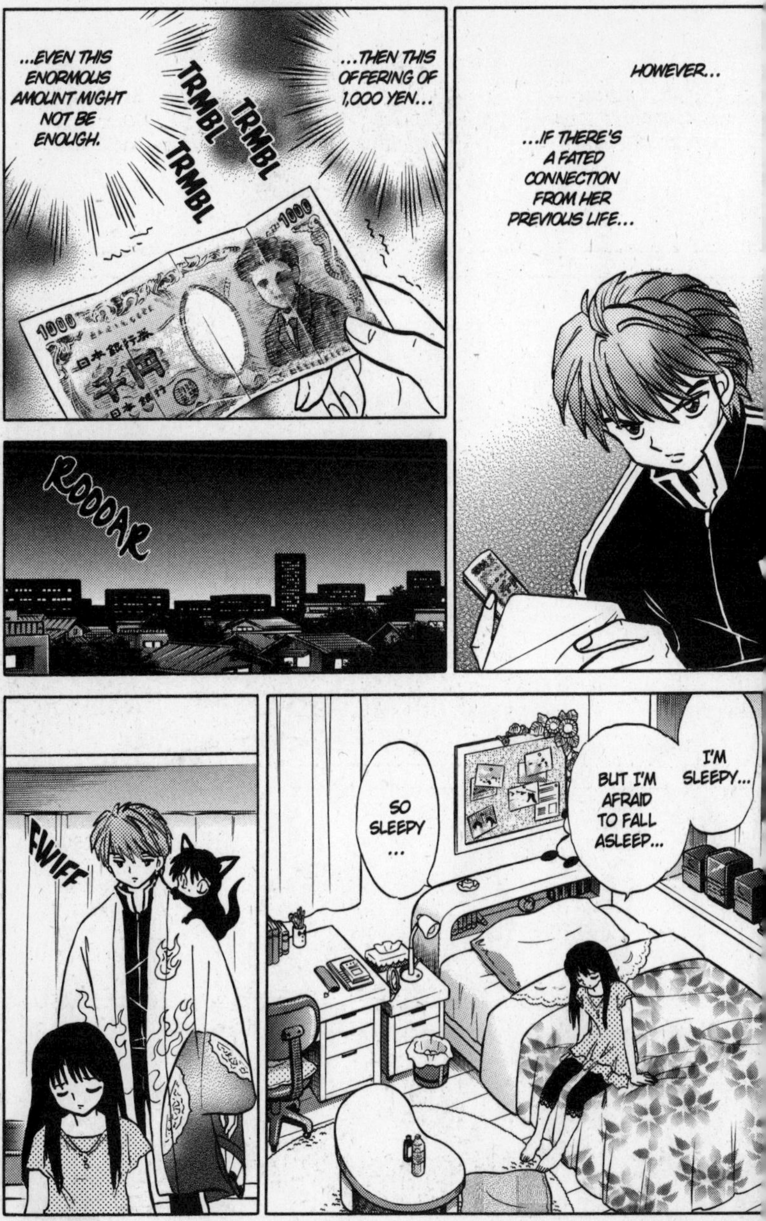
HOWEVER...
...IF THERE'S A FATED CONNECTION FROM HER PREVIOUS LIFE...
...THEN THIS OFFERING OF 1,000 YEN...
TRMBL
TRMBL
TRMBL
...EVEN THIS ENORMOUS AMOUNT MIGHT NOT BE ENOUGH.
ROOOAR
I'M SLEEPY...
BUT I'M AFRAID TO FALL ASLEEP...
SO SLEEPY ...
FWIFF

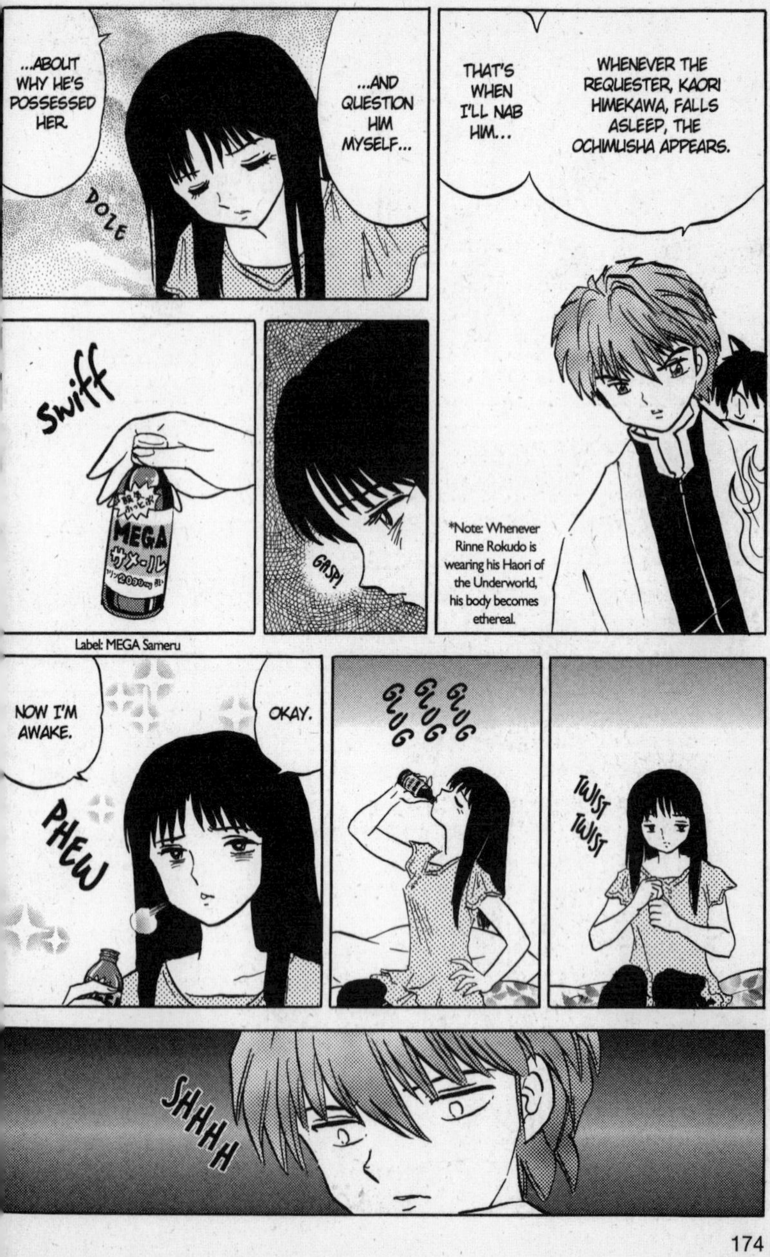
WHENEVER THE REQUESTER, KAORI HIMEKAWA, FALLS ASLEEP, THE OCHIMUSHA APPEARS.
THAT'S WHEN I'LL NAB HIM...
*Note: Whenever Rinne Rokudo is wearing his Haori of the Underworld, his body becomes ethereal.
...AND QUESTION HIM MYSELF...
...ABOUT WHY HE'S POSSESSED HER.
DOZE
GASP!
SWIFF
MEGA
TWIST TWIST
GLUG GLUG GLUG
OKAY.
NOW I'M AWAKE.
PHEW
SHHHH

Label: MEGA Sameru

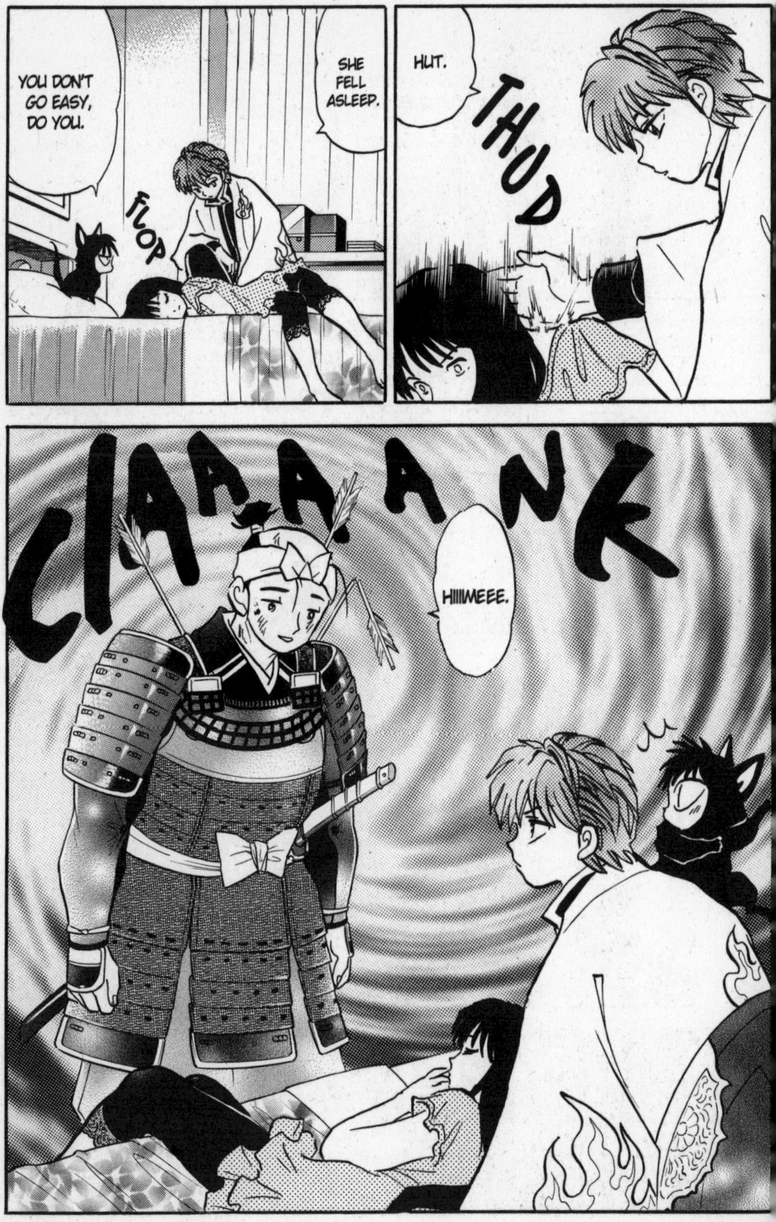

HUT.
THUD
SHE FELL ASLEEP.
YOU DON'T GO EASY, DO YOU.
FLOP
CLAAAANK
HIIIMEEE.

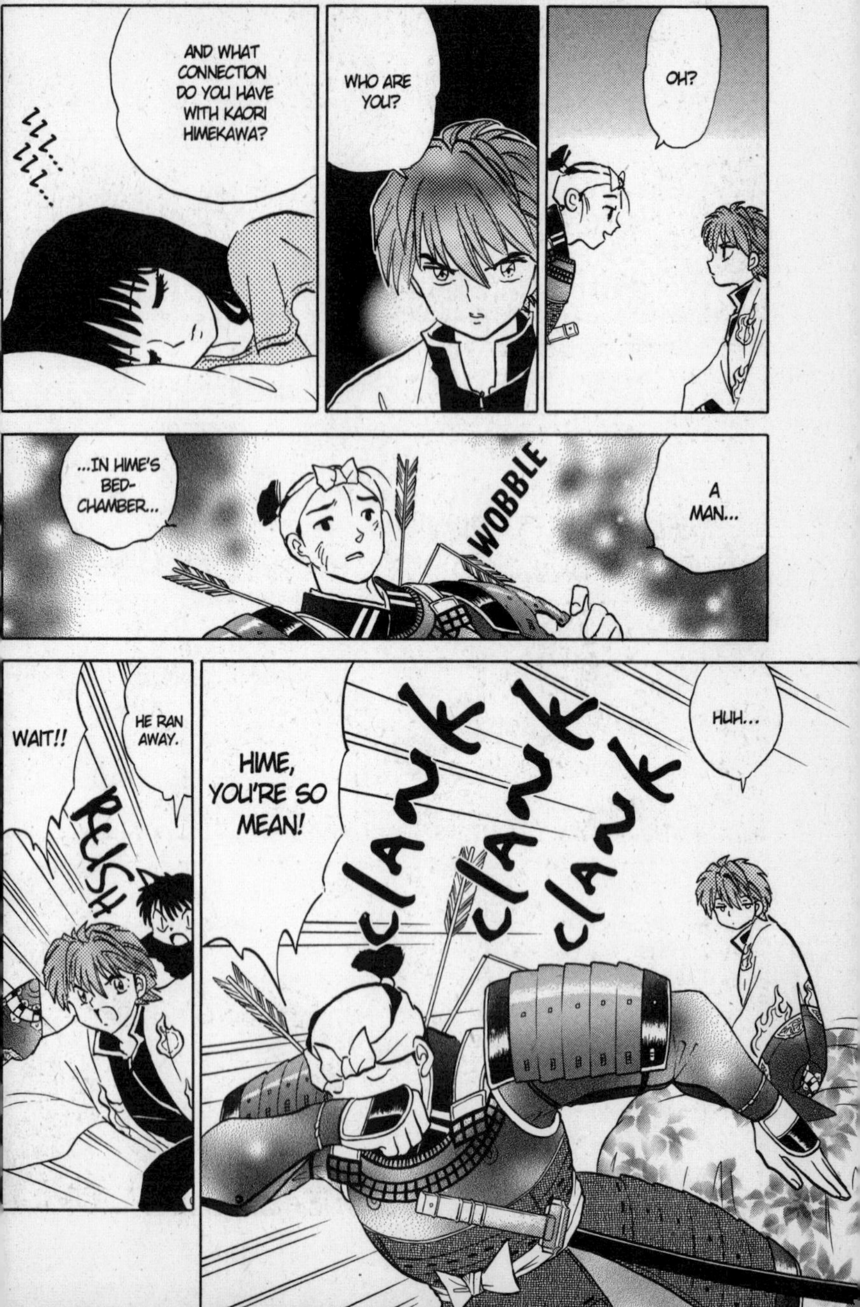
OH?
WHO ARE YOU?
AND WHAT CONNECTION DO YOU HAVE WITH KAORI HIMEKAWA?
ZZZ.....
ZZZ....
A MAN...
WOBBLE
...IN HIME'S BED-CHAMBER...
HUH...
HIME, YOU'RE SO MEAN!
CLANK CLANK CLANK
HE RAN AWAY.
WAIT!!
RUSH

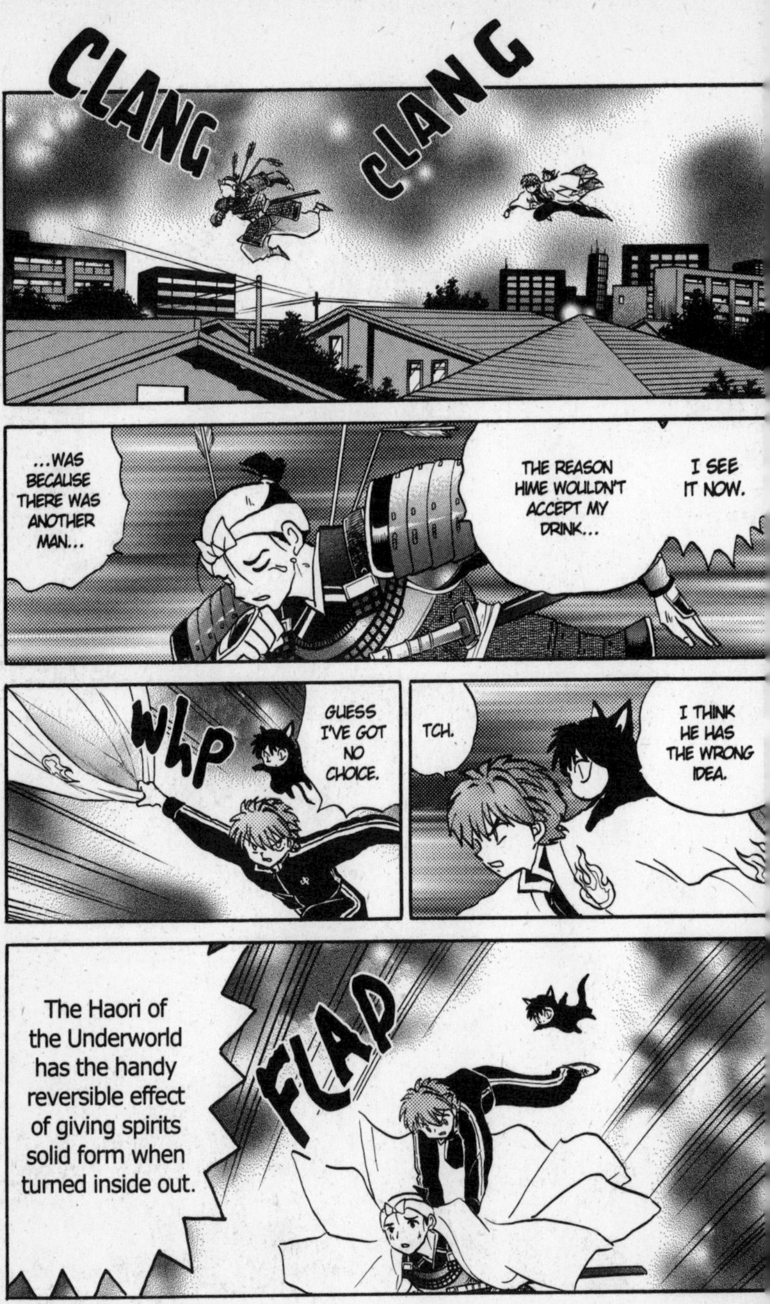

CLANG
CLANG
I SEE IT NOW.
THE REASON HIME WOULDN'T ACCEPT MY DRINK...
...WAS BECAUSE THERE WAS ANOTHER MAN...
I THINK HE HAS THE WRONG IDEA.
TCH.
GUESS I'VE GOT NO CHOICE.
WHP
FLAP
The Haori of the Underworld has the handy reversible effect of giving spirits solid form when turned inside out.

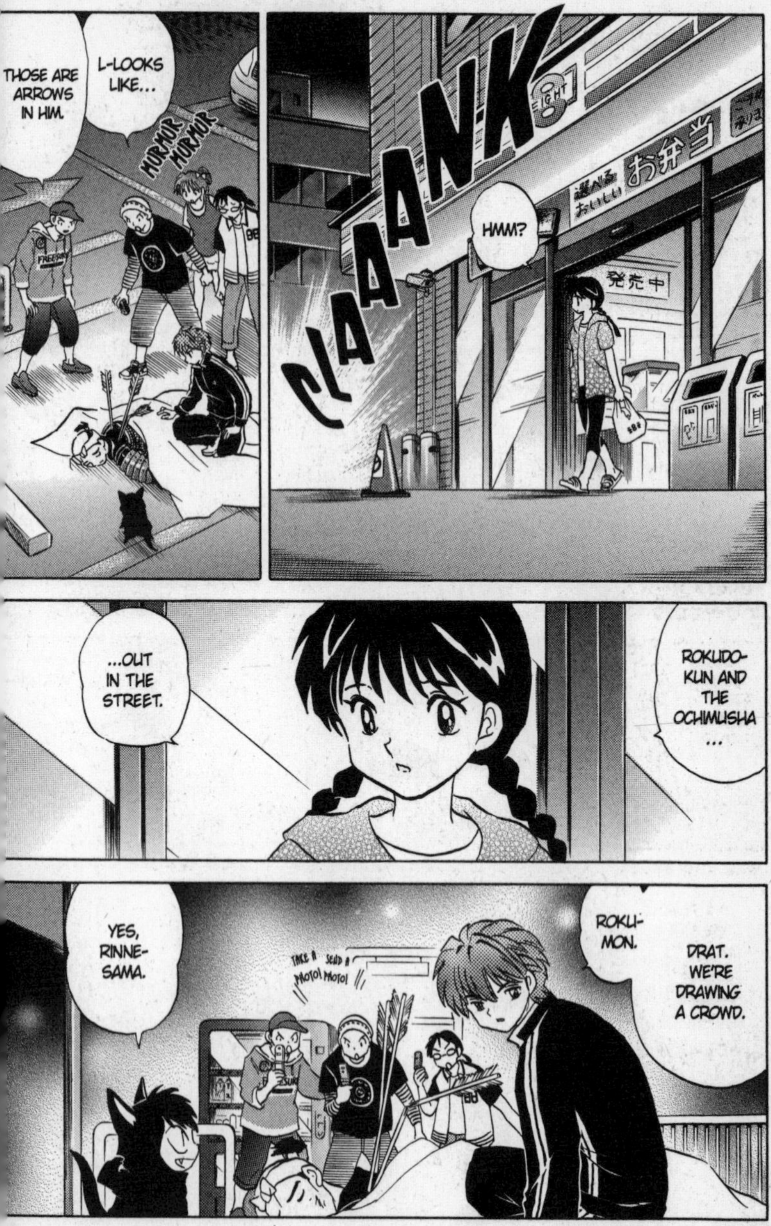
CLAAANK
お弁当
発売中
HMM?
L-LOOKS LIKE...
THOSE ARE ARROWS IN HIM.
MURMUR MURMUR
ROKUDO-KUN AND THE OCHIMUSHA ...
...OUT IN THE STREET.
ROKU-MON.
DRAT. WE'RE DRAWING A CROWD.
SEND A PHOTO!
TAKE A PHOTO!
YES, RINNE-SAMA.

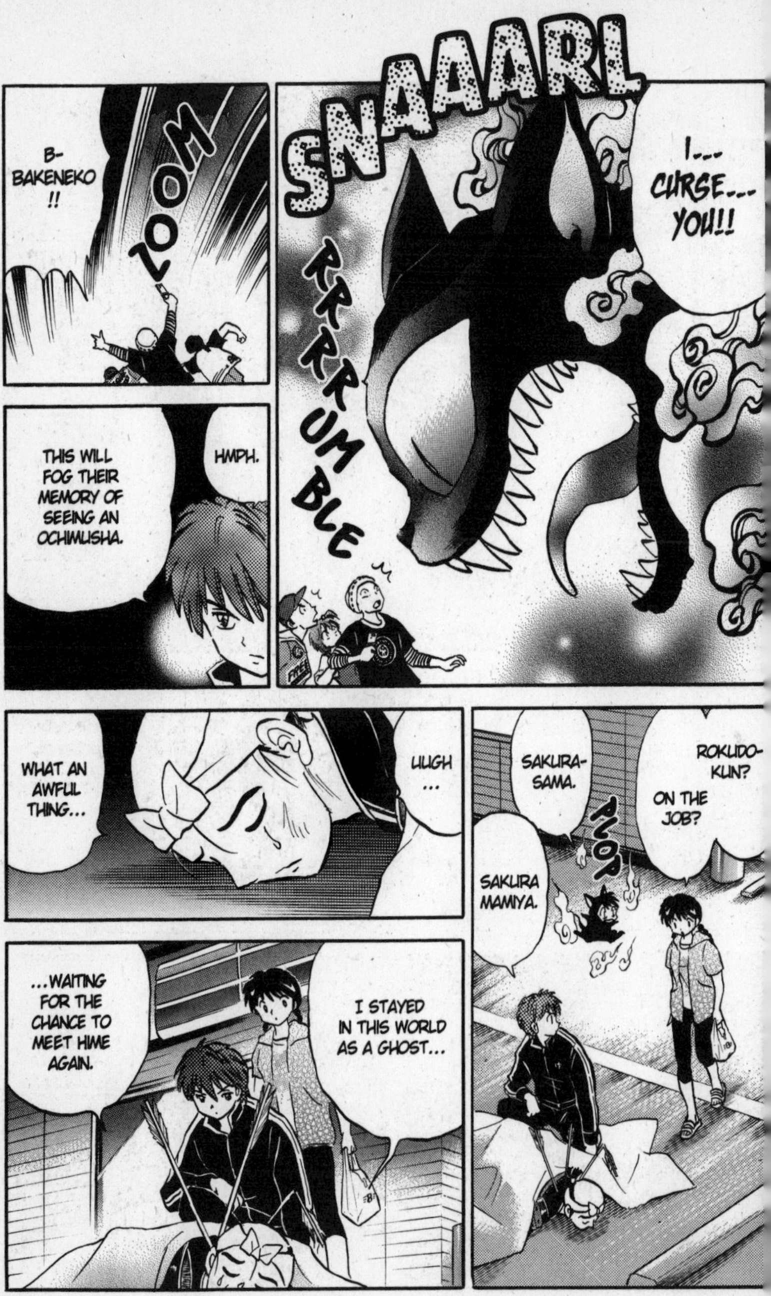
SNAAARL
I... CURSE... YOU!!
RRRRRUMBLE
B-BAKENEKO!!
ZOOM
HMPH.
THIS WILL FOG THEIR MEMORY OF SEEING AN OCHIMUSHA.
ROKUDO-KUN?
ON THE JOB?
SAKURA-SAMA.
PLOP
SAKURA MAMIYA.
UUGH...
WHAT AN AWFUL THING...
I STAYED IN THIS WORLD AS A GHOST...
...WAITING FOR THE CHANCE TO MEET HIME AGAIN.

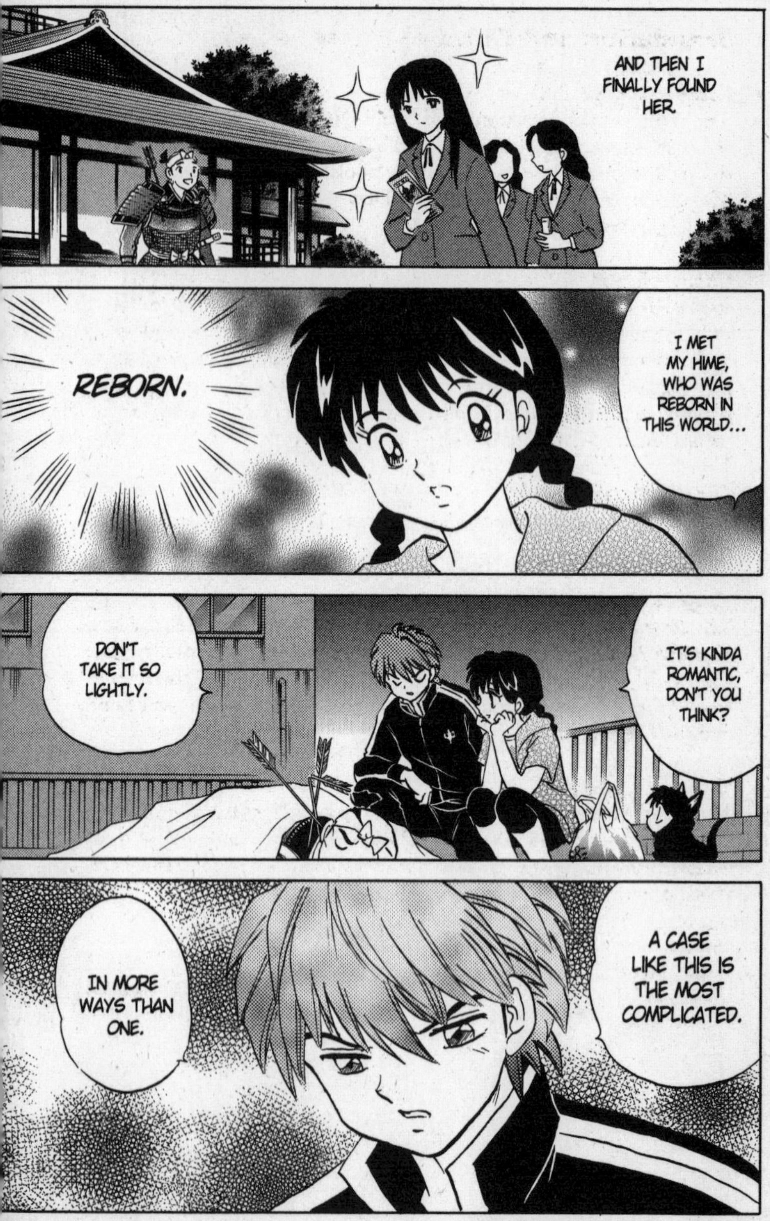
AND THEN I FINALLY FOUND HER.
I MET MY HIME, WHO WAS REBORN IN THIS WORLD...
REBORN.
IT'S KINDA ROMANTIC, DON'T YOU THINK?
DON'T TAKE IT SO LIGHTLY.
A CASE LIKE THIS IS THE MOST COMPLICATED.
IN MORE WAYS THAN ONE.

RIN-NE VOLUME 1 - END -

Translation and Cultural Notes

Chapter 5, page 111
The phonetic pronunciation of the kanji symbols on the rabbit's T-shirt is yo-ro-shi-ku, *yoroshiku* meaning "Hello!" or "Best regards!" (among other things). Taken individually, the kanji symbols have different meanings. They are, from left to right, "Night – Dew – Death – Pain." Equivalent translations would be like, "Hell Oh!"

Chapter 5, page 121
In panel 6 in the original Japanese, the *damashi* part of *damashigami* is written using hiragana syllabary, so it might look to Japanese readers like it means something like "trickster god." But then in the last panel on the page, Granny shows the kanji characters used to write it, which mean, in order from top to bottom, "Degenerate – Evil – Death – God." Sort of like saying, "Rotten Evil God of Death."

Chapter 8, page 168
An *ochimusha* is a soldier or warrior who has been defeated and has fled from battle.

Chapter 8, page 169
The *ochimusha* calls Kaori *hime*, which means "princess." Here's the kanji character for *hime*「姫」. Kaori's family name is Himekawa, written like this「姫川」. The Japanese word for "princess" and the first character in Kaori's family name are the same. The second character in Kaori's family name is *kawa*, "river."

Chapter 8, page 174
Kaori Himekawa drinks something to keep herself awake. The label reads "MEGA Sameru." But read another way, it's *me ga sameru*「目が覚める」, which means "wake up." Japanese wake-up drinks often contain several times as much caffeine as a cup of coffee.

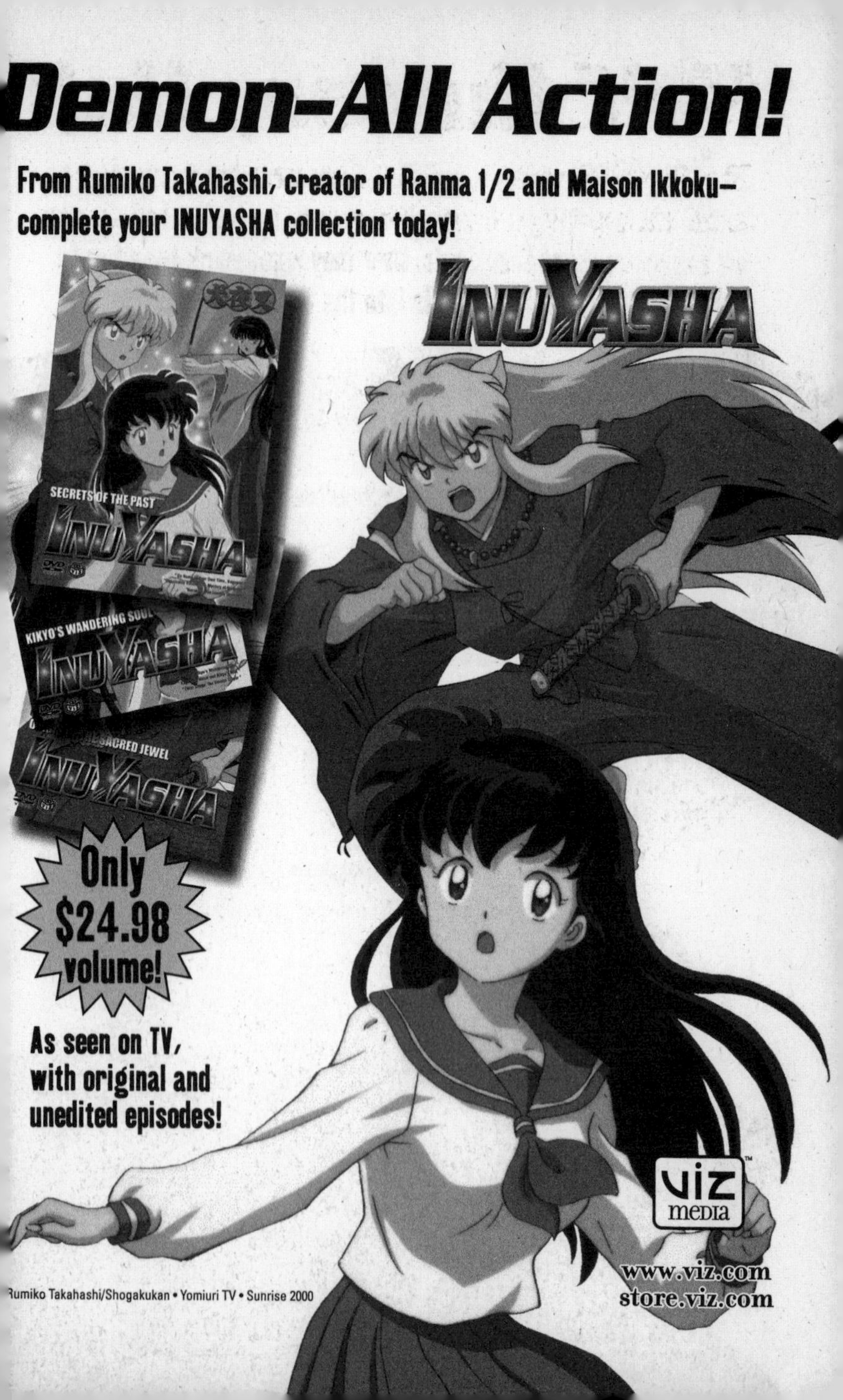
Demon-All Action!
From Rumiko Takahashi, creator of Ranma 1/2 and Maison Ikkoku–
complete your INUYASHA collection today!
INUYASHA
SECRETS OF THE PAST
INUYASHA
KIKYO'S WANDERING SOUL
INUYASHA
INUYASHA
Only $24.98 volume!
As seen on TV, with original and unedited episodes!
viz media
www.viz.com
store.viz.com
Rumiko Takahashi/Shogakukan • Yomiuri TV • Sunrise 2000